The Tourism Area Life Cycle

ASPECTS OF TOURISM

Series Editors: **Chris Cooper** *(Leeds Beckett University, UK)*, **C. Michael Hall** *(University of Canterbury, New Zealand)* and **Dallen J. Timothy** *(Arizona State University, USA)*

Aspects of Tourism is an innovative, multifaceted series, which comprises authoritative reference handbooks on global tourism regions, research volumes, texts and monographs. It is designed to provide readers with the latest thinking on tourism worldwide and in so doing will push back the frontiers of tourism knowledge. The series also introduces a new generation of international tourism authors writing on leading-edge topics.

The volumes are authoritative, readable and user-friendly, providing accessible sources for further research. Books in the series are commissioned to probe the relationship between tourism and cognate subject areas such as strategy, development, retailing, sport and environmental studies. The publisher and series editors welcome proposals from writers with projects on the above topics.

All books in this series are externally peer-reviewed.

Full details of all the books in this series and of all our other publications can be found on https://www.channelviewpublications.com, or by writing to Multilingual Matters, St Nicholas House, 31–34 High Street, Bristol BS1 2AW, UK.

ASPECTS OF TOURISM: 100

The Tourism Area Life Cycle

Review, Relevance and Revision

Edited by
Richard Butler

CHANNEL VIEW PUBLICATIONS
Bristol • Jackson

DOI https://doi.org/10.21832/BUTLER9134
Library of Congress Cataloging in Publication Data
A catalog record for this book is available from the Library of Congress.
   Names: Butler, Richard, editor.
   Title: The Tourism Area Life Cycle: Review, Relevance and Revision/
      Edited by Richard W. Butler.
   Description: Bristol; Jackson: Channel View Publications, [2024] |
      Series: Aspects of Tourism: 100 | Includes bibliographical references and index.
      | Summary: "The Tourism Area Life Cycle model has been cited and used by
      academics and those in the industry for over 40 years. This book provides
      an overview of the contribution of the model, its strengths and weaknesses,
      and particularly its relevance in the 21st century. The final section considers
      revisions and concludes with a new version of the model" – Provided by
      publisher.
   Identifiers: LCCN 2024004842 (print) | LCCN 2024004843 (ebook) |
      ISBN 9781845419134 (hardback) | ISBN 9781845419127 (paperback) |
      ISBN 9781845419158 (epub) | ISBN 9781845419141 (pdf)
   Subjects: LCSH: Tourism. | Economic development. | Tourism–Research–
      Methodology. | Tourism–Environmental aspects.
   Classification: LCC G155.A1 T5898283 2024 (print) | LCC G155.A1 (ebook) |
      DDC 338.4/791–dc23/eng/20240328
   LC record available at https://lccn.loc.gov/2024004842
   LC ebook record available at https://lccn.loc.gov/2024004843

British Library Cataloguing in Publication Data
A catalogue entry for this book is available from the British Library.

ISBN-13: 978-1-84541-913-4 (hbk)
ISBN-13: 978-1-84541-912-7 (pbk)

Channel View Publications
UK: St Nicholas House, 31-34 High Street, Bristol, BS1 2AW, UK.
USA: Ingram, Jackson, TN, USA.

Website: https://www.channelviewpublications.com
X: Channel_View
Facebook: https://www.facebook.com/channelviewpublications
Blog: https://www.channelviewpublications.wordpress.com

The policy of Multilingual Matters/Channel View Publications is to use papers that
are natural, renewable and recyclable products, made from wood grown in sustainable forests. In the manufacturing process of our books, and to further support our
policy, preference is given to printers that have FSC and PEFC Chain of Custody
certification. The FSC and/or PEFC logos will appear on those books where full
certification has been granted to the printer concerned.

Typeset in Sabon and Frutiger by R. J. Footring Ltd, Derby, UK.

Contents

Figures and Tables

Figures

Tables

Contributors

Peter Bolan, Ulster University, Northern Ireland, UK

Nilesh Borde, Goa University, India

Stephen Boyd, Ulster University, Northern Ireland, UK

Júlio Coelho, CiTUR–Politécnico de Leiria, Portugal

Rachel Dodds, Toronto Metropolitan University, Canada

Florian Eggli, Lucerne University of Applied Sciences and Arts, Switzerland

Tim Gale, Bournemouth University, UK

Surabhi Gore, Rosary College of Commerce and Arts, India

K. Michael Haywood, University of Guelph, Canada/The Haywood Group, Canada

Purva Hegde Desai, Goa University, India

David Jarratt, University of Central Lancashire, UK

C. Peter Keller, Simon Fraser University, Canada

Maximiliano E. Korstanje, University of Palermo, Argentina

Laura Lawton, Gold Coast, Australia

Beatriz Adriana López-Chávez, Universidad Autonoma de Sinaloa, Mexico

César Maldonado-Alcudia, Universidad Autonoma Occidente, Mexico

Shem Wambugu Maingi, Kenyatta University, Kenya

Bob McKercher, University of Queensland, Australia

Mike Peters, University of Innsbruck, Austria

João Romão ,Yasuda Women's University, Japan

Sarah Schönherr, University of Innsbruck, Austria

Hugues Séraphin, Oxford Brookes University, UK

Wantanee Suntikul, University of Cincinnati, USA

Ngoc Trang Vu, Laxsik Ecolodge, Sapa, Vietnam

David Weaver, Queensland University of Technology, Australia

IpKin Anthony Wong, University of Macau, Macau

Acknowledgements

I have to thank first the contributors to this volume for their efforts and support. All of them responded so positively to requests for chapters that I fear at times I drew too heavily on their good natures. Above all, I appreciate their patience as they cooperated with all of my often-unreasonable requests for editorial changes, deletions and even additions, sometimes at very short notice. Without their efforts there would, of course, have been no book. I hope my interpretations and comments on their chapters at various points in the volume meet with their approval, or at least acceptance, because they have added a great deal to the discussions on the old Tourism Area Life Cycle (TALC) model and attempts to bring it somewhat up to date.

Second, my thanks go to Sarah Williams and the team at Channel View who have put up with my editorial works over the past quarter century and still had the patience to work with me again. I felt sorry for Sarah in that her main work on this volume began as England failed to regain the Ashes but despite that disappointment, she remained a positive driving force in completing the book, and I very much appreciate her support from the onset of the project.

I would like personally to thank my daughter Antonia for her long-distance assistance with redrawing the TALC model and other graphics. She will, I am sure, be as glad to see the end of TALC books as I am but will probably have to suffer further calls on her skills to assist an ageing parent.

Finally, my thanks to those fellow academics, from undergraduates to emeritus professors, who have been interested enough to engage with the TALC and its implications over the past four decades, and particularly to the many who have made useful suggestions, criticisms and modifications to the model. I hope this book has addressed appropriately at least some of the concerns and ideas that have emerged over the years.

Richard Butler

1 Introduction and Context

Richard Butler

This book could, perhaps, be viewed as the third in a series, of which *Volumes 1* and *2* were published in 2006. These earlier volumes covered *Applications and Modifications* (Butler, 2006a) and *Conceptual and Theoretical Issues* (Butler, 2006b), and this volume, in Part 1, brings the literature on the Tourism Area Life Cycle model (TALC; Butler, 1980) up to date. The first two volumes were published almost two decades ago, which serves to emphasise how 'mature' (old?) the TALC model actually is and which justifies the case for a further review, not just of the original model itself, but also of its current relevance and possibilities for modification and refinement, if not replacement or rejection. As noted when discussing the evolution of the TALC (Butler, 2006c), the thought process involved and the examples examined were very much those of the 1960s and 1970s. Thus, if for no other reason than that, it would be appropriate to consider whether the bases of the model are still relevant two and a half decades into the next century, particularly after several major shocks to the tourism system, including of course, international conflicts and the COVID-19 pandemic, which had not been entirely played out at the time of writing (early 2023).

In making the case for a third volume on this model, I was motivated by both curiosity as to what might be produced by the contributors to this volume and by the nature of such material, as well as desiring the opportunity to personally address some of the material which has been published with respect to the validity, accuracy, limitations and criticisms of the model while I still had the chance to do that. In contemplating this volume, it was hoped contributors would consider a number of issues, including: the possible need to elaborate and clarify aspects of the model; and whether to add new elements and features to its assumptions about destination development. I was also keen to rationalise and perhaps defend the model against some of the criticisms of incorrect assumptions, missing details and inappropriate conclusions. To go back to one's earlier work is not always a successful or positive venture (Butler, 2024), as one's views at the initial time of writing, while appearing innovative and exciting (at least to the author), may later be regarded as mundane, predictive, irrelevant or wrong (even by the author some years later). If such appears to be the case, an author sometimes may be able to plead youthfulness, misplaced enthusiasm and lack of alternative viewpoints in the literature at the time of writing. All of these are possible options when looking back to the time, over 50 years ago, when the model first came into existence (Brougham & Butler, 1972).

Original Context

At least some of the then contemporary and recent papers that had provided support and examples for the development of the TALC model are still cited in the literature today (in particular, Cohen, 1972; Doxey, 1975; Plog, 1973), although with decreasing frequency as alternative ideas and concepts have emerged and as increasing attention is paid to recent publications at the expense of earlier efforts, even where some of those previous works are still highly relevant. A modern trend for bibliometric reviews of concepts, theories and models is partly to blame for this, as many such papers search the literature only over a relatively short period and tend to use citation lists from a limited number of specific subject-focused journals. In the context of the TALC model itself, such an approach would, ironically, almost certainly result in the original paper failing to appear in such a search on the topic of resort development for example, if based on tourism journals alone.

To cite history in explaining any development is fraught with danger, for, as Voltaire wrote, 'history is no more than accepted fiction' (Voltaire, 1829: 69), or as Napoleon is supposed to have remarked, 'History is simply a set of lies which everyone agrees on'. Increasingly in the modern era such a statement is less true, since many previously established views are regularly and frequently demolished or at least denied or cancelled. Thus, in reviewing the historical development of tourism we are, perhaps, a little too fond of seeing 'key moments' or 'agents of change', proposing patterns and causes that appear only with hindsight and, even then, may disappear with a new view or reinterpretation of events. Undoubtedly, tourism underwent major changes after the Second World War, partly due to a number of factors including but not limited to the widespread development of air travel, greater affluence in general, changing mores and attitudes, relative peace and stability, at least at the global level, and technological innovations and improvements, but many other factors, often underplayed and relatively unnoticed may have had great significance in tourism development, particularly at a local, regional and personal level (see Gale and Jarratt in this volume, Chapters 11 and 12; and Wheeller, 2006). Thus, a shift in numbers of visitors from northern to southern European resorts clearly occurred but the reasons may be both far more varied but spatially specific than broadly imagined, and while overarching theories like the TALC may have validity in some situations, it is as necessary as it is desirous to reassess the arguments underlying the model, to test their current relevance, and to suggest modifications where these are shown to be necessary or appropriate.

Such, then, are the purposes of this volume, namely, to review and to assess the relevance of, and to consider possible revisions to, the original TALC model, along with clarifying and elaborating on the basic elements of the model and expanding on the overall arguments made therein. The chapters which follow, apart from those by this writer, are all invited contributions by researchers who were chosen for a number of reasons. Some are researchers who have used the model themselves, some are researchers who have written about the model from a variety of viewpoints, while others have proposed alternative models or significant modification of the original model. I am grateful to them all for their contributions, criticisms and suggestions, and many of these are revisited in the final chapter, when the opportunity is taken to attempt to pull together their ideas and make a final comment or two on the original model.

Contemporary Context

The tourism scene in the mid-2020s is, not surprisingly, very different to that of the 1970s. While the basic pattern of tourism has not changed dramatically, in that many tourists are drawn to coastal locations (both fresh and marine water coasts) and to sites of cultural and natural heritage, as they have been for centuries, there are a vastly greater number of tourism destinations as well as new forms of tourism, greatly increasing competition for visitors and offering a much larger range of opportunities for them to experience. Forms of tourism come into and go out of favour over time and thus have 'life cycles' of their own, as Zimmermann (1997) illustrated (see Figure 1.1), reflecting changes in the appeal and viability of destinations catering to their enthusiasts. Changes in modes of travel, particularly the development of services by low-cost airlines, have seen new destinations emerge and others grow rapidly; relatively small urban centres can become major tourist destinations because of such services, combined with historical cultural features and often relatively low prices for other tourist services. Destinations once visited for a few days or longer have in some cases become weekend destinations (that is, for stays of one or two nights only), the changes driven greatly by the fact that the costs of travel to and accommodation in such places are less than a comparable stay in the tourist's own country. Some such locations have become the setting for celebratory visits such as 'stag' and 'hen' parties and anniversary celebrations, although such developments have not been viewed as positive in some destinations. They are evidence of the growing demand for international visits and breaks, in which the specific destination may be less important than travel convenience and overall cost, a phenomenon seen frequently during the COVID-19 pandemic (Butler, 2021b) The rise in significance and scale of sporting events and opportunities are noted by

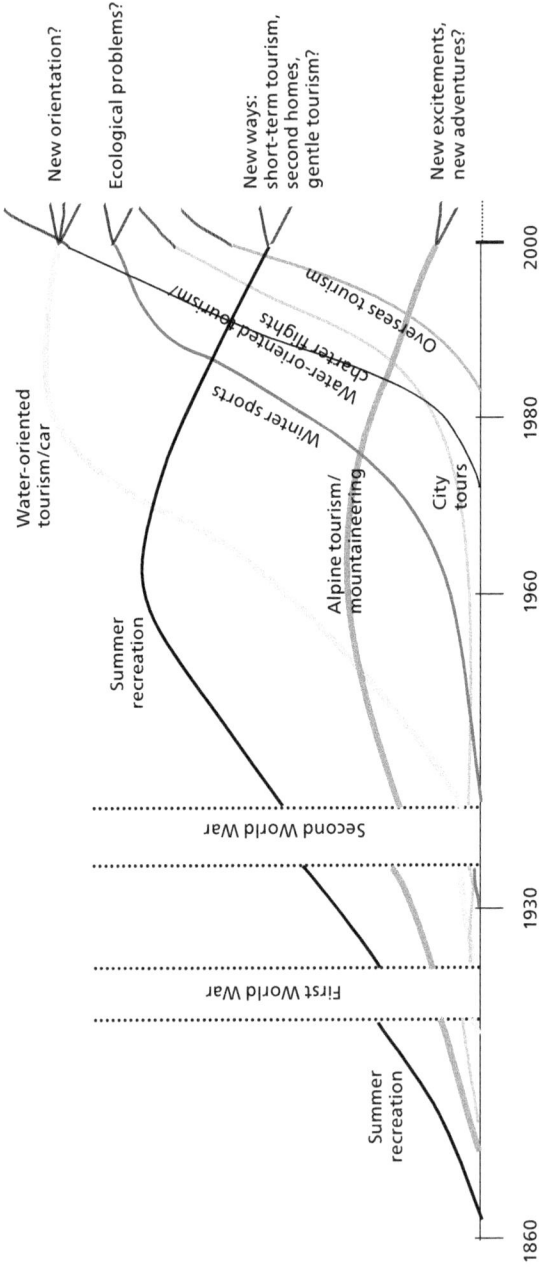

Figure 1.1 European tourism products – a product-cycle approach. Source: Zimmermann (1997)

Bolan and Boyd in this volume (Chapter 15), who demonstrate the possible stimulus effect of hosting a major sporting event, although the recent rejection of hosting the Commonwealth Games in Melbourne in 2026 by the state of Victoria is evidence also of the grotesque costs required to host what are now more than simply sporting events. While such events can put cities 'on the map', as Barcelona's hosting of the Olympic games did in 1992, the overall legacy of such events, in terms improving participation in sports, providing housing and other facilities, and increasing future tourist numbers does not always materialise and, in the case of Barcelona, may also lead to the apparent current problem of overtourism.

Of more relevance to the growth and changes in tourism over the last 40 years have been the massive developments in communications and related technology, in particular the internet and the emergence of search engines, influencers, promotion methods, and the ability to make personal reservations rather than being required to use travel agents to book vacation travel, accommodation and other services. Changes in marketing and promotion, with the ability to identify and focus on specific groups based on sociodemographic data, participation patterns and a host of other variables have altered the way destinations can promote their offerings and modify their appeal to meet the perceived needs of more closely defined groups of potential visitors than ever before. Examples of the sudden growth in appeal of specific destinations because of their appearance or reference in all forms of media (but particularly television and film) are widespread, from Dubrovnik and Northern Ireland in *Game of Thrones* (Boyd & Bolan, this volume, Chapter 21) to Rosslyn Chapel in Scotland in *The Da Vinci Code* and to Sicily in *White Lotus*. While tourists have been attracted to sites referenced in literature and art (Sir Walter Scott's books of the 19th century, which created the modern tourist image of Scotland, featured illustrations by J.M.W. Turner, and Sherlock Holmes' residence at 221b Baker Street, fictional at the time of writing, before the street was extended, continues to draw visitors), the scale and rate at which tourist numbers are growing at some new sites is overwhelming, particularly those featuring in the visual media, as forecast some decades ago (Butler, 1990).

As discussed in more detail later, the dynamics of tourist destinations are constantly changing. Whereas evolutionary change was at the heart of the TALC, proposing that tourist destinations grew in a generally predictable and consistent manner in terms of development, in recent decades the change has become increasingly revolutionary. In the traditional life cycle pattern, revolutionary growth, if experienced, was mostly in the first stages of development, when tourism began to appear and was stimulated by local entrepreneurs (see Peters & Schönherr, this volume, Chapter 20). Over the cycle, new developments would be both endogenous and exogenous, with inputs of capital and associated services and facilities coming from both within communities and from outside, with varying effects (see Keller, this volume, Chapter 10). It was suggested in the original article (Butler,

1980) that exogenous input would increase as destinations grew, with the implication that, for the most part, such new development would follow the established pattern and nature of tourism development in the specific destination. That is clearly not the case in many locations at the present, as large-scale, externally driven and funded developments change the face and nature of destinations. The growth of gambling in Macao far beyond its original scale is one example (Suntikul and McKercher & Wong, this volume, Chapters 16 and 22), while a failure to compete with new development and therefore a relative drop in competitiveness was typical of northern European resorts (Gale, this volume, Chapter 11) from the 1960s onwards, also marked by a decline in status in image and perceived 'class' (Jarratt, this volume, Chapter 12).

While entrepreneurs, both individually (Butler & Russell, 2010) and in the form of corporations, have been responsible for much of this development, public departments and agencies have also been involved, dating back to at least the establishment of Cancun in Mexico, as noted in the original TALC article. Revolutionary change, with rapid growth and marked differences in the nature of tourism, is not always appreciated by all local residents of destinations so affected (Doxey, 1975) and sometimes not by tourists, particularly those who had been attracted by the small scale and individual appeal of destinations in their earlier stages of growth, as suggested by Plog (1973). One result has been residents' negative reaction not only to the proposed physical changes in destinations but also to the growth and rate of increase in tourist numbers, as evidenced by the appearance of the phenomenon of overtourism. Whether overtourism really exists and, if so, at what point it occurs are sources of disagreement, with some tourist organisations arguing that it is not numbers but lack of management of numbers which is the problem (United Nations World Tourism Organization, 2018) while resident opposition is clearly against what it perceives as excessive numbers of visitors (Dodds & Butler, 2019; Milano et al., 2019).Whether there should limits to numbers of visitors to destinations and how these might be identified is related to the thorny issue of carrying capacity and its relevance to tourist destinations, and is discussed at some length in the present volume (for example Eggli, Chapter 18).

What is clear, however, is that the pattern of development modelled in the original TALC article has been and is under pressure from a variety of forces, both internal and external to destinations. Some of those forces are specifically aimed at tourism, to encourage or to restrict growth, while some are not directly related to tourism at all; some originate in the specific destinations, while others are introduced from outside. The simple matrix developed by Weaver and Oppermann (2000) is highly appropriate in this regard, encompassing these key elements of the forces of change acting on destinations, intentional and unintentional, and internal and external, and is utilised in Chapter 17 of this volume. Whereas after the Second

World War the world experienced mostly global peace and stability for several decades, allowing and encouraging the growth and spatial expansion of tourism. While important exceptions such as the conflicts in Korea, Vietnam, Afghanistan, revolutions in Cuba and Afghanistan, the partition of India, the end of apartheid in South Africa and the fall of the Soviet Union all affected tourism, they did so mostly in a minor and spatially specific way. Significant though these events were to the areas in which they took place, their impacts on global tourism were limited. In part, this was because most of the affected areas were not major tourist destinations at the time, and also because, in some cases, global media coverage was much narrower than now. Some of those locations have since become important tourist destinations, Vietnam, South Africa and Cuba in particular, and many of the remnants of conflict themselves have become tourist attractions (Butler & Suntikul, 2013).

Recently, however, several developments have changed the way such events impact tourist destination development. Media coverage is truly global and immediate; thus, conflict, whether war, terrorism or criminal, can and does receive massive publicity, even promotion, with major effects on tourism to the affected areas. Terrorist bombs (Bali), attacks on tourists (Egypt, Tunisia), border clashes (Kashmir), internal unrest (Myanmar, Peru) and civil war (former Yugoslavia) have all led to declines, often sudden and large scale, in tourist numbers to those regions and further afield. More recently, of course, conflict in Ukraine, while obviously impacting tourism to and from that country, has also seen impacts on the aggressor, Russia, through sanctions being applied to that state and some of its citizens, with spill-over effects on airline routes (following the downing of civilian aircraft), the closure of the Black Sea and its resorts to international tourism, and rises in the cost of energy and food worldwide.

At the global scale, however, nothing before has affected tourism on the scale of the COVID-19 pandemic, which effectively closed tourism activity in most of the world, both domestic and international, because of restrictions on travel and fear of contagion by potential tourists (Williams *et al.*, 2022). It is ironic and tragic that the infrastructure which has done so much to develop and enable tourism growth was a major factor in the spread of the virus. While Spanish flu could have had a similar or worse effect a century earlier, being far more fatal than COVID-19, its global spread was much more restricted by the lack of airline services and the rapid death of those infected. Earlier outbreaks of viruses such as SARS had much more limited impacts on global tourism and affected destinations do not appear to have been permanently affected. The full impact of COVID-19 on destinations and their life cycle is still unknown and likely to remain so for some years to come. While there has been rapid recovery in many areas to pre-COVID levels of visitation, many operations are not as they were (Cakmak *et al.*, 2023). Some facilities and services have disappeared, some have been replaced by alternatives or different forms, and some have been permanently lost, staff shortages are worldwide, and transport services have not returned to pre-COVID-19 levels in terms of frequency and coverage. COVID-19 represented a phenomenon not seen globally in tourism before, namely, a virtual complete break in visitation to destinations. This had occurred in specific destinations before, mostly as a result of conflict in or affecting specific regions, but there had been few studies of the effect of such events or, in particular, of what effect it might have on the life cycle of affected destinations, for example at different stages of development (Butler, 2021a). The major unknowns in such a situation are the impact of loss of investment and if and how quickly and completely destinations recover and resume their operations, the latter being difficult to predict (Fotiadis *et al.*, 2021). A break in the cycle had not been included or considered in the original article and had barely been discussed in the literature until the COID-19 pandemic, although Zimmerman (1997) included such a scenario. As well as the potential instability suggested by Keller (1987; and this volume, Chapter 10) that might coincide with a change in stage of development of a destination, one needs to consider other trends which might appear as a result of such a break in tourism in destinations heavily dependent on visitor flows.

Added to the above issues should be that of political change (Butler & Suntikul, 2007, 2017) in its many forms and the impacts of such changes on tourism and related development. Suntikul (this volume, Chapter 16) discusses this topic with three specific examples, but there are many more. Political factors intervened in the COVID-19 pandemic, related to the initial cause of the appearance of the virus, in terms of controls and restrictions imposed by multiple levels of government, from national to local, rises in xenophobia, and a reluctance to travel to specific countries for fear of contagion or quarantine controls. Generally, political restrictions on tourism have diminished in recent decades as visa requirements have been reduced, both in numbers and, in many cases, in costs in money and time, as states have realised and wanted to obtain the economic gains to be had from international tourism. The opening up of China, as both a destination and an origin of outgoing tourists, has perhaps been the most significant change in global tourism in this regard, although recent restrictions on various populations in China and Hong Kong may have had negative effects on the overall appeal to some tourists, particularly those from Western countries. Despite calls dating back to Richter (1989) for researchers to place more focus on the political aspects of tourism, there is still a dearth of studies on the inter-relationship between tourism and politics. The appearance and reappearance of tourism in countries like Vietnam and Cuba following political change and conflict have made clear how dependent tourism is on good political relations between origin and destination countries. This is not because tourism is a force for peace (somewhat contradicted by the fact that most conflicts are between states which have had a high degree of tourism and personal interaction before such conflict) but because tourists are understandably concerned about safety and security when they consider potential holiday destinations.

Conclusion

The current global situation demonstrates that the forces affecting tourism generally and destinations in particular are highly dynamic and perhaps more varied and faster in their effects than ever before. The validity of the TALC model and others like it are inevitably affected by such developments, and assessing that validity, as well as their relevance, is a major focus of this volume. It does that in Part 1 by reviewing the way in which the model has been used and interpreted, focusing particularly on the literature on the model which was published during the period (2006–2022) since the previous volumes appeared. In Part 2, previous examples are revisited and the exploration of new influences and approaches to development and redevelopment are examined in the context of the continued relevance of the model. Finally, in Part 3, suggested modifications to the existing model, new elements to be included and alternative approaches to depicting destination development pathways are considered.

References

Brougham, J.E. and Butler, R. (1972) The applicability of the asymptotic curve to the forecasting of tourism development. Paper presented to the Research Workshop, Travel Research Association 4th Annual Conference, Quebec, July.

Butler, R. (1980) The concept of a tourist area cycle of evolution and implications for management of resources. *Canadian Geographer* 24 (1), 5–12.

Butler, R. (1990) The role of the media in influencing the choice of vacation destinations. *Tourism Recreation Research* 15 (2), 46–53.

Butler, R. (ed.) (2006a) *The Tourism Area Life Cycle, Volume 1: Applications and Modifications.* Clevedon: Channel View Publications.

Butler, R. (ed.) (2006b) *The Tourism Area Life Cycle, Volume 2: Conceptual and Theoretical Issues.* Clevedon: Channel View Publications.

Butler, R. (2006c) The origins of the tourism area life cycle. In R. Butler (ed.) *The Tourism Area Life Cycle, Volume 1: Applications and Modifications* (pp. 13–26). Clevedon: Channel View Publications.

Butler, R. (2021a) COVID 19 and its potential impact on stages of tourist destination development. *Current Issues in Tourism* 77 (1), 35–53. https://doi.org/10.1108/TR-04-2021-0215.

Butler, R. (2021b) COVID-19: Impacts on the changed and changing nature of the tourism journey. In S. Elias-Varotsis, C. Petr and P. Callot (eds) *Tourism Post COVID-19: Coping, Negotiating, Leading Change* (pp. 3–16). Vienna: TRC.

Butler, R. (2024) Never look back? Revisiting the past. *Annals of Tourism Research.* https://doi.org/10.1016/j.annals.2023.103690.

Butler, R. and Russell, R. (2010) *Giants of Tourism: Key Individuals in the Development of Tourism.* Wallingford: CABI.

Butler, R. and Suntikul, W. (2010) *Tourism and Political Change.* Oxford: Goodfellow.

Butler, R. and Suntikul, W. (2013) *Tourism and War: A Complex Relationship*. London: Routledge.

Butler, R. and Suntikul, W. (2017) *Tourism and Political Change* (2nd edn). Oxford: Goodfellow.

Çakmak, E., Isaac, R.K. and Butler, R. (2023) *Changing Practices of Tourism Stakeholders in Covid-19 Affected Destinations*. Bristol: Channel View Publications.

Cohen, E. (1972) Toward a sociology of international tourism. *Social Research* 39 (1), 164–182.

Darwin, C. (1859) *On the Origin of Species by the Means of Natural Selection*. London: John Murray.

Dodds, R. and Butler, R. (2019) *Overtourism Issues: Realities and Solutions*. Berlin: De Gruyter.

Doxey, G.V. (1975) A causation theory of visitor–resident irritants: Methodology and research inferences. In *Proceedings of the Travel Research Association 6th Annual Conference* (pp. 195–198). San Diego: Travel Research Association.

Fotiadis, A., Polyzos, S. and Huan, T.C. (2021) The good, the bad, and the ugly on COVID-19 tourism recovery. *Annals of Tourism Research*. https://doi.org/10.1016/j.annals.2020.103117.

Keller, C.P. (1987) Stages of peripheral tourism development – Canada's Northwest Territories. *Tourism Management* 8, 20–32.

Milano, C., Cheer, J.M. and Novelli, M. (2019) *Overtourism Excesses, Discontents, and Measures in Travel and Tourism*. Wallingford: CABI.

Plog, S.C. (1973) Why destination areas rise and fall in popularity. *Cornell Hotel and Restaurant Association Quarterly* 13, 55–58.

Richter, L. (1989) *The Politics of Tourism in Asia*. Honolulu: University of Hawaii Press.

United Nations World Tourism Organization (2018) *'Overtourism'? Understanding and Managing Urban Tourism Growth Beyond Perceptions*. Madrid: UNWTO.

Voltaire, F. (1829) *Jeannot et Colin*. At www.gutenberg.org, downloaded 10 May 2023.

Weaver, D.A. and Oppermann, M. (2000) *Tourism Management*. Brisbane: John Wiley.

Wheeller, B. (2006) The king is dead. Long live the product: Elvis, authenticity, sustainability and the product life cycle. In R. Butler (ed.) *The Tourism Area Life Cycle, Volume 1: Applications and Modifications* (pp. 339–347). Clevedon: Channel View Publications.

Williams, A.M., Chen, J., Li, G. and Baláž, V. (2022) Risk, uncertainty and ambiguity amid Covid-19: A multinational analysis of international travel intentions. *Annals of Tourism Research*. https://doi.org/10.1016/j.annals.2021.103346.

Zimmermann, F. (1997) Future perspectives of tourism: Traditional versus new destinations. In M. Oppermann (ed.) *Pacific Rim Tourism* (pp. 231–239). Wallingford: CABI.

Part 1

Review

The first three chapters of this section describe and discuss citations and uses of the TALC model in a variety of ways. Gore *et al.* in Chapter 3 review the literature citing and using the model over the past two decades, and present a number of key linkages between segments of the literature. It is important to acknowledge that the vast bulk of the literature discussed in that chapter and the others in Part 1 is in English, which reflects reality, but does run the risk of missing important case studies, comments and criticisms made in other languages, particularly Spanish. I am most grateful, therefore, to Abel Capote-Barreras for sending me a bibliography from a paper he presented (with Martinez, in 2022) which contains a considerable number of papers by authors writing about the TALC in Spanish, and it has been appended below, as readers may wish to follow up this literature. Following Gore *et al.*, Dodds in Chapter 4 reviews the initial uses and criticisms of the model, and goes on to consider a new version of the model focused on the concept of sustainability. Weaver and Lawton in Chapter 5 continue the review of the model by examining the literature that has cited the TALC in discussions of the impacts of COVID-19 on tourism and its related developments, and present a figure relating that literature to the model itself.

Chapters 6 and 7, by Trang Vu and Coelho, review the model in the light of quantitative analyses and assess its application in those contexts. Haywood's Chapter 8 provides a critical overview of the model, particularly in relation to the tourist industry, and builds on a number of his papers which have examined the TALC over the last four decades. Chapter 9, the last in Part 1, provides a conclusion by responding in more detail to some of the concerns expressed about the model and discussing briefly other aspects it was felt deserved attention. It also takes advantage of the opportunity to address some of the misattributions, incorrect comments made about and misinterpretations of the model.

Bibliography of chiefly Spanish-language papers

Álvarez Alonso, A. (2004) El ciclo de vida de los destinos turísticos litorales. En Turismo y territorio en la sociedad globalizada (pp. 123–155).
Cacciutto, M., Castellucci, D., Roldán, N., Cruz, G., Corbo, Y. and Barbini, B. (2020)

Reflexiones a propósito del turismo masivo y alternativo. *Aportes para el abordaje local* 18 (1), 103–119.

Cáceres, E. and Rodríguez, J. (2002) Génesis y desarrollo del espacio turístico en Canarias: Una hipótesis de trabajo. Universidad de Las Palmas de Gran Canaria. Gobierno de Canarias.

Callizo Soneiro, J. (1989) El Espacio turístico de Chadefaud. Un entretevero teórico: Del historicismo al materialismo dialéctico y el sistemismo behaviourista.

Cánoves, G. and Prat, J.M. (2011) La Costa Brava de Catalunya: Del tradicional modelo de sol y playa a las nuevas opciones de turismo cultural. Seminario Internacional Renovación y Reestructuración de destinos turísticos consolidados del Litoral, Universidad de Alicante.

Cardona, J.R. and Serra Cantallops, A. (2012) Inicios de un destino turístico. El caso de Ibiza. En Gestión de destinos turísticos (pp. 93–100). AECIT.

Casero Marín, B., Escandell Sievert, M., Espada Bellido, R., Ferrer Juan, A., Redzhebova Mustafova, S., Martínez Hernández, A. and Cardona, J.R. (2021) Ibiza: Ciclo de vida y evolución como destino turístico 4(1), 124–147.

Chadefaud, M. (1987) Aux origines du tourisme dans les pays de l'Adour, du mythe à l'espace: Un essai de géographie historique. Dép. de géographie et d'aménagement de l'Université de Pau et des pays de l'Adour, Centre de recherche sur l'impact socio-spatial de l'aménagement, UA 911, CNRS.

Díez Santo, D. and Gandia Álvarez, E. (2011) La diversificación turística como estrategia clave para la reactivación de destinos consolidados del litoral; la reinvención de Cullera (España). Seminario Internacional Renovación y Reestructuración de destinos turísticos consolidados del Litoral, Universidad de Alicante.

Diez, V.A. (2019) El Modelo de Ciclo de Vida de los Destinos Turísticos. Vigencia, crpiticas y adaptaciones al Modelo Butler. *Revista Realidad, Tendencias y Desafíos en Turismo* 17 (1), 19–34.

Garay Tamajon, L. and Cánoves Valiente, G. (2010) Un análisis del desarrollo turístico en Cataluña a través del ciclo de evolución del destino turístico. *Boletín de la Asociación de Geógrafos Españoles* 52, 43–58.

García Henche, B., Reinares Lara, E. and Armelini, G. (2013) Ciclo de vida de los destinos turísticos y estrategias de comunicación: Los casos de España y Chile. *Revista Internacional de Investigación en Comunicación* 7 (7), 76–93. http://dx.doi.org/10.7263/adresic-007-05

González Reverté, F. (2012). Destinos turísticos. Concepto y estructura. Universitat Oberta de Catalunya.

López Guevara, V.M. (2011) La reorientación del ciclo de vida del área turística. *Investigaciones Turísticas* 1, 107–121. http://dx.doi.org/10.14198/INTURI2011.1.07

López Guevara, V.M.L. (2011) ¿El mismo modelo para siempre? Comentarios sobre el Ciclo de Vida del Área Turística a partir de la experiencia de Bahías de Huatulco (México). Seminario Internacional Renovación y Reestructuración de destinos turísticos consolidados del Litoral, Universidad de Alicante.

López Guevara, V.M. and Pérez Serrano, A.M. (2021) Bases para el fortalecimiento de la experiencia en los servicios turísticos (recorridos, alojamiento, así como alimentos y bebidas) ofrecidos en Tlaxcala, para diferenciar y posicionar la oferta del estado (Primeros 100 días de gobierno). Secretaría de Turismo.

Marín Moyano, J.A. and Navarro Jurado, E. (2011) Destinos turísticos consolidados ante el cambio del modelo turístico: Costa del Sol Occidental. Seminario Internacional Renovación y Reestructuración de destinos turísticos consolidados del Litoral, Universidad de Alicante.

Martínez González, J.A. (2014) El modelo del ciclo de vida del destino turístico y sus implicaciones para la dirección de las empresas turísticas. I Congreso online sobre Los Modelos Latinoamericanos de Desarrollo, Tenerife.

Miossec, J.M. (1977) Un model de l'espace touristique. *L'Espace géographique* 6 (1), 41–48. https://doi.org/10.3406/spgeo.1977.1690.

Oliveros Ocampo, C.A., Virgen Aguilar, C.R. and Chávez Dagostino, R.M. (2018) Enfoques de las investigaciones acerca del ciclo de vida del área turística (TALC). *Turismo y Sociedad* 24, 51–75. https://doi.org/10.18601/01207555.n24.03.

Osorio García, M. (2010) Turismo masivo y alternativo. Distinciones de la sociedad moderna/posmoderna. *Revista de Ciencias Sociales*, 17 (52), 235–260.

Osorio García, M., Deverdum Reyna, M.E., Mendoza Ontiveros, M.M. and Benítez López, J. (2019) La evolución de Ixtapa-Zihuatanejo, México, desde el modelo del ciclo de vida del destino turístico.

Ramos Calderón, J.A. (2011) Caso Cartagena de Indias: La transición de sol y playa a destino cultural como estrategia de innovación, renovación y reestructuración del destino turístico en su ciclo de vida. Seminario Internacional Renovación y Reestructuración de destinos turísticos consolidados del Litoral, Universidad de Alicante.

Rodríguez Jiménez, G., Martínez Martínez, C.C. and Martín Fernández, R.A. (2018) Identificación de los factores influyentes en la estrategia de crecimiento de Villa Clara, Cuba a partir del análisis del ciclo de vida del destino turístico. *Transitare* 4(2), 27–47.

Sánchez, A., Vargas, E.E., Castillo, M., Rodríguez, F., Nava, R.M. and Guadarrama, E. (2018) Análisis sustentable a partir del Modelo del Ciclo de Vida. Situación y perspectivas de Ixtapan de la Sal, México. *Revista Ibero-Americana De Estratégia* 17 (2), 124–136. https://doi.org/10.5585/riae.v17i2.2516.

Sánchez Martínez, L.F. (2019) Nuevas formas y tendencias de hacer turismo. *RaRío* 2 (5), 7–12.

Sánchez Valdés, A., Vargas Martínez, E.E. and Castillo Nechar, M. (2017) Origen, concepción y tratamiento del Ciclo de Vida de los Destinos Turísticos: Una reflexión entorno al modelo de Butler. *Compendium* 20 (38).

SECTUR (2004) Turismo alternativo: Una nueva forma de hacer turismo. http://190.57.147.202:90/jspui/bitstream/123456789/340/1/Turismo-Alternativo-una-nueva-forma-de-hacer-turismo.pdf.

SECTUR, CONACYT and CESTUR (2012) Evaluación de desempeño de los destinos turísticos en el marco de los Convenios de Coordinación en materia de Reasignación de Recursos (CCRR).

Soares, J.C., Ivars Baidal, J.A. and Gándara, J.M. (2015) La evolución de destinos turísticos litorales consolidados. Análisis comparado de Balneario Camboriú (Brasil) y Benidorm (España). *Anales de Geografía de la Universidad Complutense* 35 (2), 143–166.

Sonda de la Rosa, R., Ruiz Lanuza, A. and Alcudia Rocha, J. (2021) Tourist area life cycle analysis in San Miguel de Allende Guanajuato. *ECORFAN Journal Republic of Peru* 7 (12), 7–21. http://dx.doi.org/10.35429/EJRP.2021.12.7.7.21.

Torres Valdez, J.C. and Martínez Díaz, A.J. (2018) Etapas del ciclo de vida de los destinos turísticos en México.

Virgen Aguilar, C.R. (2009) El ciclo de vida de un destino turístico: Puerto Vallarta, Jalisco, México. *Revista de Cultura e Turismo* 3 (1).

2 Revisiting the TALC Model

Richard Butler

There have been many examples of the application of the TALC model, as noted by Gore *et al.* (this volume, Chapter 3); inevitably, there have been a large number of criticisms and suggested modifications of the model, some of which are addressed in subsequent chapters. Of particular relevance is the article by Wang *et al.* (2016). That paper is a salutary warning to all academic researchers about the potential dangers of taking highly cited articles for granted, giving them an importance that may or may not be deserved – sometimes even granting them mythological status, as noted by McKercher and Prideaux (2014), and sometimes failing to accurately represent the views expressed by the original author. McKercher and Prideaux (2014, 20) note:

> Simkin and Roychowdhury (2003) conclude about 80% of authors who cite highly regarded works have never read the original document, while both Kompier (2006) and Todd, Yeo, Li, and Ladle (2007) found a high level of inaccurate interpretation and the selective omission of facts that do not support the author's thesis, even among those who have ostensibly read the works.

In the context of the TALC, McKercher and Prideaux (2014) went on to comment on a misinterpretation – that the TALC implies an ultimate decline of all destinations:

> The myth became entrenched by the inaccurate interpretation of Butler's (1980) destination lifecycle model, where decline was identified as one of five possible outcomes. Interestingly, few people discuss the other potential post-maturity phases which include ongoing stability, recovery or rejuvenation.

Those comments apply to the TALC model and emphasise the necessity of reviewing its development, refinement, use and criticism over the past four decades. As well, interest has grown in related concepts, such as path dependency, and evolutionary economic geography (Brouder, 2017; Brouder *et al.*, 2017; Saarinen *et al.*, 2017), which are discussed in more detail by Romão and Butler in this volume (Chapters 13 and 17). This suggests that such a review is probably overdue.

Revisiting the Basic Elements of the TALC Model

There were six key elements or features involved in the conception of the TALC model, namely: dynamism, process, carrying capacity, management, spatiality and triggers. Each of these is discussed briefly below to serve as a reminder of the content of the model, as these elements were essentially underlying and implicit in its formulation. They were not discussed in any great detail in the original article (Butler, 1980), which perhaps explains some of the misconceptions and concerns expressed about the original model.

The starting point for the model was that 'tourist areas' (the term is described in more detail in Chapter 9) are clearly dynamic and change, or are changed, over time. Such changes may be positive or negative, or both, depending on the viewpoint taken and position held, in terms of overall impacts on the destination being considered. It was argued that all destinations are dynamic, albeit at different rates and in differing ways, and that the change experienced could result from any or all of overuse, obsolescence, removal, replacement, renovation and addition of elements, by investment and by disasters. At the time of the model's original conception (late 1960s to early 1970s), tourism of all sorts was undergoing massive changes, many resulting from political, economic and technological developments brought about by the Second World War. The shift from northern (often domestic) destinations to southern (generally international) destinations (in both Europe and North America) had already begun to produce significant changes in holiday travel patterns, which led to growing interest both in how destinations began and grew, and how and why they declined. Many of the forces behind those changes were ignored or dealt with only briefly in the original paper.

The third feature, carrying capacity, was illustrated in the original figure in terms of suggested 'limits' (the use of the plural was important, to avoid the implication there was only one capacity limit) and was perhaps, along with dynamism, one of the two most fundamental characteristics of destination development. It was regarded as being of crucial importance, in that the model argued that if and when the carrying capacity of a tourist area was exceeded, there would be a resulting loss of quality of experience and attractiveness of the destination, which might set in motion a series of potentially negative consequences (Russo, 2002). These could include a loss of competitiveness and market share, a failure to gain investment funding and, possibly, the beginning of a spiral of decline in terms of business. The concept of carrying capacity, particularly in the context of tourism and tourism destinations, has been discussed and often rejected in the literature over the past half century (McCool & Lime, 2001). The seminal work of researchers in the US Forest Service (see, for example, Lucas, 1964; Wagar, 1964) had demonstrated that identifying limits to the levels of use could be calculated for wilderness areas, but the application of that research to tourist destinations proved difficult, if not wholly impractical. This was partly because the tourism population at a destination is far more heterogeneous than is the case in wilderness areas, where visitors share many demographic, economic, sociological and activity participation characteristics. As well, tolerance of crowding and levels of use in tourist destinations seemed to be at much higher levels than in wilderness areas, with the presence of other visitors desired rather than unwelcomed. Thus, while there is still frequent reference in the academic and non-academic literature to limits and carrying capacity of destinations, particularly related to the appearance of 'overtourism' (Dodds & Butler, 2019a, 2019b), ways of measuring and identifying such levels have remained next to impossible to find. Perhaps of even more significance is the fact that it is clear that there is not a single and unchanging capacity figure for any location: there are different levels of capacity for many elements, including beaches, natural areas, accommodation, water supply, sewage treatment, car parking, transportation capacity, as well as of residents' perceptions. There is also a further factor to consider in the context of the TALC, as it suggested exceeding a destination's capacity could bring about a decline in visitation, perhaps leading to the exit from tourism noted by Baum (2006). In hindsight, it is difficult to document categorically that operating at overcapacity levels has ever caused a destination to go into decline, temporarily or permanently, although a few destinations have closed temporarily (see Dodds & Butler, 2019b) to enable recovery and adoption of new management approaches. This is discussed later in the volume.

Closely related to carrying capacity was management, as appropriate management was envisaged to be essential to avoiding exceeding carrying capacity and ensuring the destination followed a suitable development path. Management was seen as critical to avoiding or delaying possible decline, hence the term featuring in the title of the original article. In subsequent academic discussions and in the real world, management is an oft-cited but equally oft-unimplemented feature (Dodds & Butler, 2010) of destinations as entities, which makes decline from neglect, oversight, and ignorance possible, if not likely, over time. Other authors (Dredge, 2016; Haywood in this volume, Chapter 8) have noted that destination management organisations are rarely what their name implies, and that they are most often destination promotion and development organisations, at least with regard to their terms of reference and general expectations, generally measuring 'success' in terms of increased visitor numbers. That is not what was meant by 'management' in terms of the title of the TALC article, where 'management' was taken to involve directing and controlling tourism, in terms of both numbers and types of tourists, such that the 'right' numbers and 'right' types of tourists (in terms of desired facilities, experiences and services, as well as levels of visitation) came to specific destinations. In recent years, such a then apparently fanciful concept appears to have been taken up in destinations such as Amsterdam (Gerritsma, 2019).

The TALC model is essentially a geographical model, in that it deals with the 'why what is where' (the essence of geography as portrayed on a sweatshirt presented to the author by the High School Teachers of Ontario) and also 'what effect that has had on the location', which reflects the core elements of the subject, the spatial context and the integration of the human and physical worlds. The spatial aspect of the model was, therefore, important in its formulation but much underplayed in the 1980 paper. It was argued that decline in one destination area would result in development in one or more similar spatially close settings and that this process would be repeated as long as new development sites were available in an area. Such a process could be seen in the Mediterranean and the Caribbean in particular in the years preceding the initial appearance of the model (Brougham & Butler, 1972). Implicit in any discussion of spatial characteristics should have been the question of scale, that is, what constituted a 'tourist area'. This was, perhaps regrettably, ignored in the original paper and almost inevitably allowed readers and critics to note that the model did not work effectively in a variety of situations and scales, including as wide a region as the South Pacific (Choy, 1992). Clearly, the model was conceived in the context of communities, villages and towns, rather than amorphous regions, and the example of the development of Cancun in Mexico, in a previously undeveloped region, illustrated the intended but unstated focus on settlements, existing or planned. The absence of such definition also complicated any discussion of carrying capacity, which needs defined boundaries for the calculation of any levels of use within a specific area, and the collection of usable statistics, which also requires a formal, defined catchment area. It is recognised that even using the term 'community' or 'settlement' would hardly have been sufficient, as those terms could include a range of places, from a small village at the time of its initiation into tourism, like St Tropez in the 1960s, to Las Vegas at the present time.

The final element, triggers, was not discussed directly in the paper, which was certainly a major omission, as development and redevelopment require forces of some form, including chance, to bring about change. Christaller (1963) implied the resort development process was organic, and this assumption was to some degree implicit in the TALC, as evidenced in the use of the term 'evolution' in the title of the 1980 paper. Whether evolution was an appropriate term has been challenged (see for example Ravenscroft & Hadjihambi, 2006) and it is perhaps appropriate to criticise its use. It was applied in order to suggest that the process of growth and development of a tourist area was somewhat akin to the way a life form develops, and also that, as Darwin (1859) noted, the species with the most suitable adaptations are the fittest and so survive the longest. Suggesting an evolutionary pathway was not meant to deny the influence of internal or external forces, but to imply an ongoing changing pattern of development adjusting to, and also changing, conditions around it. In later papers, the author has used the simple matrix developed by Weaver and Opperman (2000) to illustrate the varying nature of triggers to development and change, ranging from intentional to unintentional and from internal (to the destination) to external. Major triggers like conflict and pandemics fit well within such a framework, as other contributors to this volume note.

Conclusion

The six elements discussed above illustrate the key factors in the skeleton or framework on which the TALC was based; at the time of the production of the 1980 paper, further elaboration of these points was not considered necessary. It should be remembered that that paper was first presented at an academic meeting (Canadian Association of Geographers, Victoria, Canada, in 1980) and submitted for review and consideration for publication in its original form in response to an invitation to do so by the editor of the special issue in which it finally appeared. Inevitably, therefore, it is relatively short, and had it originally been designed as a paper for submission to a journal, it would have been longer, with considerably more detail included on the above elements and others. Its brevity, compared with most current academic journal papers, in terms of overall length and works cited, is therefore, perhaps understandable, if surprising or even amazing to current academics.

Some of the criticisms of the model (Stock *et al.*, 2014) clearly stem in part from the lack of detail on a number of points in the original paper – such as explanations and elaborations of key suppositions, arguments supporting the generalised assumptions, an overall lack of empirical data – some of which are addressed in this volume. In subsequent years there has been no lack of case studies of applications of the model in destinations, which have provided empirical data that suggest that the model 'works' or is applicable in many cases. There has been much less work examining some of the major elements of the model, particularly spatial aspects, carrying capacity and triggers and, in a more general sense, the whole idea of managing tourism in destinations or elsewhere. The chapters which follow expand on some of these issues, noting issues and problems, as well as potential revisions and solutions to what have been seen to be problematic areas of the model.

References

Baum, T. (2006) Revisiting the TALC: Is there an off ramp? In R. Butler (ed.) *The Tourism Area Life Cycle, Volume 2: Conceptual and Theoretical Issues* (pp. 219–230). Clevedon: Channel View Publications.

Brouder, P. (2017) Evolutionary economic geography: Reflections from a sustainable tourism perspective. *Tourism Geographies* 19 (3), 438–447.

Brouder, P., Clavé, S.A., Gill, A.M. and Ioannides, D. (2017) *Tourism Destination Development*. London: Routledge.

Brougham, J.E. and Butler, R. (1972) The applicability of the asymptotic curve to the forecasting of tourism development, Paper presented to the Research Workshop, Travel Research Association 4th Annual Conference, Quebec, July.

Butler, R. (1980) The concept of a tourist area cycle of evolution and implications for management of resources. *Canadian Geographer* 24 (1), 5–12.

Capote-Barreras, A. and Martinez, M.A.E. (2022) The study of the tourist area life cycle: A review 42 years after Butler's model. Paper presented at the XVI Congreso Internacional de Investigación Turística de la Academia Mexicana de Investigación Turística, Tijuana, Mexico, 29 September.

Christaller, W. (1963) Some considerations of tourism location in Europe: The peripheral regions – underdeveloped countries – recreation areas. *Regional Science Association Papers* 12, 95–105.

Choy, D.J.L. (1992) Life cycle models for Pacific Island destinations. *Journal of Travel Research* 30, 26–38.

Darwin, C. (1859) *On the Origin of Species by the Means of Natural Selection*. London: John Murray.

Dodds, R. and Butler, R. (2010) Barriers to implementing sustainable tourism policy in mass tourism destinations. *Tourismos* 5 (1), 35–54.

Dodds, R. and Butler, R. (2019a) The phenomena of overtourism: A review. *International Journal of Tourism Cities* 5 (4), 519–528.

Dodds, R. and Butler, R. (2019b) *Overtourism: Issues, Realities and Solutions*. Berlin: De Gruyter.

Dredge, D. (2016) Are DMOs on the path to redundancy? *Tourism Recreation Research* 41 (3), 348–353.

Gerritsma, R. (2019) Overcrowded Amsterdam: Striving for a balance between trade, tolerance and tourism. In C. Milano, J.M. Cheer and M. Novelli (eds) *Overtourism: Excesses, Discontents and Measures in Travel and Tourism* (pp. 125–148). Wallingford: CABI.

Kompier, M. (2006) The 'Hawthorne' effect is a myth but what keeps the story going? *Scandinavian Journal of Work, Environment and Health* 32 (5), 402–412.

Lucas, R. (1964) *The Recreational Carrying Capacity of the Quetico-Superior Area*. Forest Service Research Paper LS-15. St Paul, MN: USDA.

McCool, S. and Lime, D. (2001) Tourism carrying capacity: Tempting fantasy or useful reality? *Journal of Sustainable Tourism* 9 (5), 372–388.

McKercher, B. and Prideaux, B. (2014) Academic myths of tourism. *Annals of Tourism Research* 46, 16–28. https://doi.org/10.1016/j.annals.2014.02.003.

Ravenscroft, N. and Hadjihambi, I. (2006) The implications of Lamarckian theory for the TALC model. In R. Butler (ed.) *The Tourism Area Life Cycle, Volume 2: Conceptual and Theoretical Issues* (pp. 150–163). Clevedon: Channel View Publications.

Russo, A.P. (2002) The vicious circle of tourism development in heritage cities. *Annals of Tourism Research* 29 (1), 165–182.

Saarinen, J., Rogerson, C.M. and Hall, C.M. (2017) Geographies of tourism development and planning. *Tourism Geographies* 19 (3), 307–317.

Simkin, M. and Roychowdhury, V. (2003) Read before you cite! *Complex Systems* 14, 269–274.

Stankey, G., Cole, D., Lucas, R., Peterson, M., Frissell, S. and Washbourne, R. (1985) *The Limits of Acceptable Change (LAC) System for Wilderness Planning*. Forest Service General Technical Report INT-176. Washington, DC: USDA.

Stock, M., Cliva, C., Crevoisier, O., Kebir, L. and Nahrath, S. (2014) *The Circulation of*

Wealth: Resort Development and Touristic Capital of Space. Neuchatel: University of Neuchatel, MAPS.

Todd, P., Leo, D., Li, D. and Ladle, R. (2007) Citing practices in ecology: Can we trust our own words? *Oikos* 1599–1601.

Wagar, J.A. (1964) *The Carrying Capacity of Wildlands for Recreation.* Forest Science Monograph No. 7. Washington, DC: Society of American Foresters.

Wang, X., Weaver, D.B., Xiang, L. and Zhang, Y. (2016) In Butler (1980) we trust? Typology of citer motivations. *Annals of Tourism Research* 21, 216–218.

Weaver, D.A. and Oppermann, M. (2000) *Tourism Management.* Brisbane: John Wiley.

3 Mapping Tourism Area Life Cycle Research: A Bibliometric Analysis

Surabhi Gore, Nilesh Borde and Purva Hegde Desai

Since its introduction, the TALC model has been under continued scrutiny from tourism scholars and has undergone extensive modifications by researchers using it. The early research began by investigating the development of coastal and island resorts, which included evaluating the model's applicability and identifying the stages of destination development. The model received critical reviews on the identification of the stages, applicability across destinations, the time frame of analysis, practical utility and evaluation of carrying capacity. Keeping these problems in mind, researchers progressed their study to evaluate the life cycle based on the impacts of tourism and individual stages, and suggested variations that would help solve some difficulties in TALC analysis. The availability of time series data and statistical software allowed scholars to validate the TALC and its stages statistically. Apart from geographical regions, researchers also explored the influence of stakeholders, different tourism products and disasters like bombings, tsunamis and the COVID-19 pandemic. The integration of the TALC model with other theories, such as evolutionary economic geography, resilience, product life cycle, social exchange and strategy analysis extended its use. New perspectives on the shape of the TALC curve have also come to the fore. Multiple cycles (cycle–recycle pattern), non-linear cyclical patterns and U-shaped and N-shaped curves have also been discussed. Authors have also discussed 'maturity' as a combination or overlapping of the development, consolidation and stagnation stages.

This chapter presents a mixed literature review involving bibliometric and content analysis. It tracks the distribution of publications and citations, the evolution of the theme, the level of co-authorship and bibliometric coupling within documents. Bibliometric analysis is a rigorous method of analysing scientific data. It helps to identify the impact of publications and authors. It also allows one to find research gaps and visualise research topics (Donthu *et al.*, 2021). The analysis consists of evaluative and relational techniques. The evaluative technique assesses the distribution of studies, journals, most contributing authors, largest numbers of citations and keywords. The relational techniques include analysis of co-authorship, co-citation and bibliometric coupling (Ülker *et al.*, 2023). Content analysis helps evaluate themes, keywords and concepts within the quantitative data and helps organise the text into predefined groups linking its components (Shelley & Krippendorff, 1984).

Methodology

The initial data on TALC publications was obtained from the Scopus and Web of Science databases (Ülker *et al.*, 2023). Table 3.1 provides the search parameters. The search returns were downloaded and thoroughly scanned to check for relevance and duplicate entries. Articles that used the TALC model were selected for the review. Both datasets were combined and saved as Microsoft Excel files (.csv and .xlsx). In total, 228 articles were found to be relevant to the study. The VOS Viewer, which is a software tool for constructing and visualising bibliometric networks (Ülker *et al.*, 2023), was used for analysing co-authorship, citation, co-citation and bibliometric coupling.

Distribution of publications

The data on publications, citations and journals were obtained. The graph showing the evolution of publications and citations was drawn using MS Excel. The citation links of journals were evaluated by performing a co-citation analysis using VOS Viewer. Co-citation refers to the citation of two studies in a subsequent study; it helps to evaluate the association between publications and clusters (Eaton *et al.*, 1999; Ülker *et al.*, 2023). Frequent co-citation makes the links stronger (Small, 1973).

Table 3.1 Search parameters

Keywords	Tourism Area Life Cycle	OR
	Tourism Cycle	OR
	Destination Life Cycle	OR
	Resort Cycle	OR
	TALC	OR
Time frame	1980–2022	
Subject area	Social sciences, Management, Accounting, Arts and humanities, Multidisciplinary, Economics, Hospitality, Leisure and sports management	
Document type	Articles, Conference papers	
Source type	Journal, Conference proceedings	
Language	English	
Search date	15 December 2022	

Changes in the themes

Content and co-word analysis were used to evaluate the changes in the themes. Co-word analysis reveals the words commonly used by authors in the titles, abstracts and keywords of their publications. The analysis helps to analyse the evolution of the topic and identify trends (Ülker *et al.*, 2023).

Content analysis was performed on the abstracts of the papers, and the data were tabulated in Microsoft Excel. The papers were analysed based on the unit of analysis, methodology, variables, themes and results.

Level of co-authorship and citations

Co-author analysis is concerned with evaluating research collaborations (Mavric *et al.*, 2021; Ülker *et al.*, 2023). It identifies research groups and institutions and clarifies the structure of scientific communication. The citation analysis presumes that authors cite papers relevant to their studies and have influence in the field (Benckendorff, 2009; Ülker *et al.*, 2023; Uysal, 2010). It identifies a given field's most cited authors, studies and journals, which are then considered to be the most helpful studies (Uysal, 2010).

Bibliometric coupling

If two studies cite the same third study, the documents are said to be bibliometrically coupled (Kessler, 1963). The number of times two documents cite the same third document determines the strength of their association. A higher strength indicates that the documents are similar (Ülker *et al.*, 2023).

Results

Distribution of the publications

The analysis of the 228 articles, published in 79 journals from 1980 to 2022, revealed that 430 authors had published papers on TALC individually and in collaboration. A graph showing the number of publications and citations over time is presented in Figure 3.1. It shows a consistent increase in publication, with an average of five papers published in Scopus and Web of Science journals each year. Table 3.2 lists the top 15 journals and gives the numbers of co-authorship links.

The journals publishing TALC research belong to the tourism and multidisciplinary fields. Table 3.2 shows that *Annals of Tourism Research, Tourism Management* and *Journal of Travel Research* are the major journals based on average citations. In addition, *Annals of Tourism Research* is also the most co-cited journal.

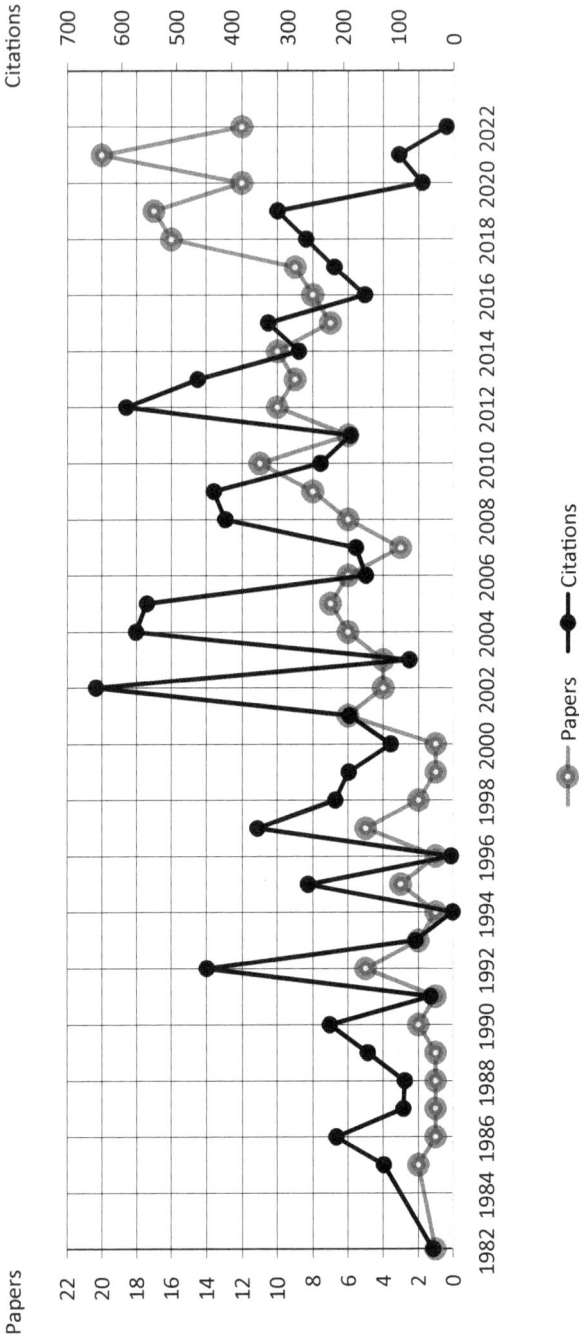

Figure 3.1 Year-wise numbers of publications and citations

Table 3.2 Top 15 journals

Journals	Number of articles	Total number of citations	Average number of citations	Number of co-citation links
Annals of Tourism Research	35	3,273	94	22,602
Tourism Management	23	2,286	99	22,395
Tourism Geographies	12	316	26	2,357
Tourism Economics	11	156	14	2,982
Sustainability (Switzerland)	10	161	16	1,430
Journal of Sustainable Tourism	7	444	63	5,684
Journal of Travel Research	7	644	92	9,851
Tourism Recreation Research	7	190	27	1,818
Current Issues in Tourism	6	133	22	2,956
Tourism Review	5	48	10	1,156
International Journal of Tourism Research	4	152	38	2,343
Tourism Analysis	4	35	9	786
Journal of Travel and Tourism Marketing	3	34	11	1,843
Asia Pacific Journal of Tourism Research	3	42	14	1,003
Scandinavian Journal of Hospitality and Tourism	3	64	21	663

Evolution of research themes

Co-occurrence of keywords (co-word) analysis and content analysis were performed on the abstracts of the papers to assess the change in the unit of analysis, variables, themes and methodologies from 1980 to 2022. Figure 3.2 presents the overlay of keywords used by authors in publications. It shows the evolution of the research themes from 1980 to 2022.

An evolutionary summary of the studies is discussed below.

1980–1990

Early research on TALC was based on evaluating the model's applicability using case study methodology (Butler, 1985; Debbage, 1990; Hovinen, 1982; Meyer-Arendt, 1985; Wilkinson, 1987). The authors evaluated the carrying capacity and the pattern of changes at the destination based on tourist arrivals and management actions. Haywood (1986) operationalised the TALC and suggested focusing on the unit of analysis, time frame and life cycle stages for TALC research. Martin and Usyal (1990) suggested management strategies for each stage of TALC. Carrying capacity, transport and diversification of tourism products were suggested as crucial factors in managing tourism. The authors highlighted managers' varying roles and skills for different TALC stages; for example,

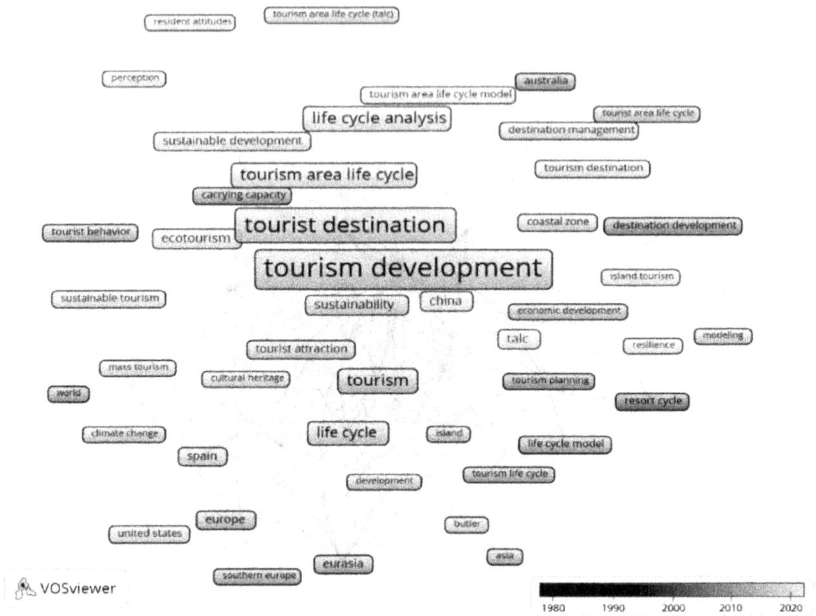

Figure 3.2 Overlay of keywords

it was argued that the exploration stage requires dynamic managers, whereas the maturity stage requires stable, mature managerial decisions (Cooper & Jackson, 1989).

1991–2000

The research explored different regions/tourist areas. Cooper (1992) suggested using TALC for strategic planning, while Douglas (1997) and Agarwal (1997) raised operational issues with the applicability of the TALC, concerning its stages and carrying capacity. The methodologies for research included case studies (Choy, 1992; Foster & Murphy, 1991), surveys (Opperman, 1995), mixed methods (Getz, 1992) and quantitative analysis (Di Benedetto & Bojanic, 1993). The role of government in developing policies was emphasised (Getz, 1992; Ioannides, 1992). Tooman (1997) suggested the involvement stage was the most critical for sustainable development. TALC's scope was expanded by integrating it with sigmoid curve theory (Baum, 1998) and product life cycle theory (Da Conceição Gonçalves & Aguas, 1997). Authors also suggested extended TALC models (Baum, 1998; Prideaux, 2000; Priestley & Mundet, 1998).

2001–2010

Tourism-related phenomena like spas (Kapczyński & Szromek, 2008), conference centres (Whitfield, 2009), canal systems (Tang & Jang, 2009) and disasters (Cohen, 2008) were evaluated through TALC. Alongside comparative case studies (Cochrane, 2010; Henderson, 2007; McElroy & Hamma, 2010), quantitative studies gained prominence (Gouveia & Rodrigues, 2005; Moore & Whitehall, 2005; Papatheodorou, 2004). Surveys of entrepreneurs, tourists and locals were done to measure the trends and impact of tourism (Hovinen, 2002; Pásková, 2002). In addition, various theories were integrated with TALC, including ontological and epistemological analysis (Gale & Botterill, 2005; Johnston, 2001), comparative advantage theory (O'Hare & O'Hare, 2001), evolutionary economic geography (Papatheodorou, 2004), restructuring theory (Agarwal, 2002), chaos and complexity theory (Russell & Faulkner, 2004) and force field analysis (Butler, 2009).

Authors proposed real estate development (second homes) as a decline avoidance strategy (Cohen-Hattab & Shoval, 2004). Incorporation of place distinctiveness (Agarwal, 2002), shoreline and hydrological cycle management (Essex et al., 2004; Jennings, 2004), computing the investor index during the early stages of the life cycle (Gołembski et al., 2010), environmental concerns (Cochrane, 2010; Weiermair et al., 2007), cultural changes (Gale, 2005) and developing quality tourism services (Lozano et al., 2008) were also studied. Cyclical life cycle patterns showing multiple simultaneous stages were revealed (Cohen, 2008; Hovinen, 2002). Pásková (2002) critiqued the model's validity. Toh et al. (2001) proposed a Travel Balanced Approach (TBA), while Moss et al. (2003) proposed scalable and fad life cycles to assess destination growth.

2011–2022

Authors assessed specific tourism offerings such as world heritage sites (Lee & Rii, 2016), pilgrimage research (Collins-Kreiner, 2016), amusement parks (Chapman & Light, 2016), municipalities (Albaladejo et al., 2016), events and festivals (Holmes & Ali-Knight, 2017), trails (Lemky, 2017), wine, disaster and sports tourism (Ferreira & Hunter, 2017; Heuwinkel & Venter, 2018; Rindrasih, 2019), homestays, caravans and peer-to-peer accommodation (Long et al., 2018; Promnil, 2019), economic corridors (Nazneen et al., 2019), communities (Lee & Jan, 2019), whale and dolphin watching (Tischer et al., 2018), family businesses (Chauhan & Madden, 2020; López-Chávez & Maldonado-Alcudia, 2022) and floating and community markets (Fakfare et al., 2021).

Additional models and theories continued to be integrated with TALC. The evaluation of resident and tourist perceptions dominated TALC research (de Jager & Nicolau, 2020; Donaldson & Forssman, 2020; Ferreira & Hunter, 2017; Lee et al., 2018). Other variables investigated included ecological and carbon emissions (Kruczek *et al.*, 2018; Lee *et al.*, 2018), community-based tourism (Giampiccoli & Saayman, 2018), innovations/developments (Alexandrova *et al.*, 2019; Kranjčević, 2019; Setiawan & Wiweka, 2018), partnerships or collaborations (Lemky, 2017; Pilving *et al.*, 2019), entrepreneur roles (Butler & Weidenfeld, 2012), GIS for mapping structural changes (Garcia-Ayllon, 2016), synergy and congestion analysis (Albaladejo *et al.*, 2016; Cole, 2012; Lee & Rii, 2016) and assessment of human capital (Promnil, 2019).

Chai (2012) discussed how the cognitive learning patterns of consumers help them choose a destination, thus impacting the TALC. Weaver (2012) proposed three evolution paths for destinations (organic, regulated/deliberate alternative and hybrid). Philander and Roe (2013) proposed that labour costs impact tourism growth. Butler (2014) reviewed the literature and suggested investigating instant resorts, triggers, non-linear cycles, stages, politics, vulnerability, climate, investments and interruptions. Haraldsson and Ólafsdóttir (2018) developed a 'purism' scale using a casual loop diagram approach to analyse feedback and impacts over time.

Most authors support a non-linear cyclical development of the destination rather than an S-shaped curve. Singh (2011) critiqued the model (highlighting issues with carrying capacity) and proposed marketing as the primary determinant of demand, explaining why the destination's popularity rises and falls.

Level of co-authorship, citations and co-citation analysis

Co-authorship refers to scientific collaborations. The analysis of co-authorship (Figure 3.3) revealed that out of 430 authors, 61 have more than one relevant publication. However, only five distinct co-authorship clusters, involving 24 authors, emerged. Very few authors formed collaborations, and most collaborations are intra-cluster.

Table 3.3 shows the results of the co-authorship analysis of the top-ranked countries, as well as the numbers of citations based on each country and the links. The US and the UK top the list of countries publishing TALC research during the period examined. In recent years, Spain and China have published more papers. The most cited authors and documents based on citation analysis are listed in Table 3.4.

The citation links of authors over 2000–2020 are presented in Figure 3.4. Fourteen clusters with 211 items were observed. The largest cluster has 25 authors. The analysis reveals a strong link among the cited authors.

Co-citation reveals the association between publications (Eaton *et al.*, 1999). The co-citation link of authors (Figure 3.5) shows five clusters, with a total of 219 authors, with the largest cluster having 60 co-cited authors. The co-citation links between the documents (Figure 3.6) show clusters with 19 themes, whereas the co-citation analysis between journals (Figure 3.7) shows six clusters with a total of 41 items. The two most significant

Figure 3.3 Co-authorship analysis of authors

Table 3.3 Co-authorship analysis of the top-ranked countries

S. no	Country	Documents	Citations	Links
1	China	22	558	17
2	UK	32	1792	15
3	USA	43	2260	15
4	Australia	18	1028	9
5	Portugal	9	366	8
5	Spain	23	1216	8

Table 3.4 Top 10 cited authors (other than Butler, 1980)

Authors	Source title	Cited by	Links
Getz (1992)	*Annals of Tourism Research*	182	42
Haywood (1986)	*Tourism Management*	212	40
Agarwal (2002)	*Annals of Tourism Research*	268	39
Zhong et al. (2008)	*Tourism Management*	106	36
Ma and Hassink (2013)	*Annals of Tourism Research*	158	36
Cooper and Jackson (1989)	*Annals of Tourism Research*	155	35
Priestley and Mundet (1998)	*Annals of Tourism Research*	129	28
Hovinen (2002)	*Annals of Tourism Research*	129	28
Prideaux (2000)	*Tourism Management*	114	25
Debbage (1990)	*Annals of Tourism Research*	89	24

clusters have nine sources each. The analysis reveals strong co-citation links (see Table 3.2).

Bibliometric coupling

Bibliographic coupling is a method of grouping documents. It shows if two separate articles cite the same third article (Kessler, 1963). The citing documents are said to be bibliographically coupled (Ferreira, 2018). If the strength of the coupling is high, it indicates similarities between the

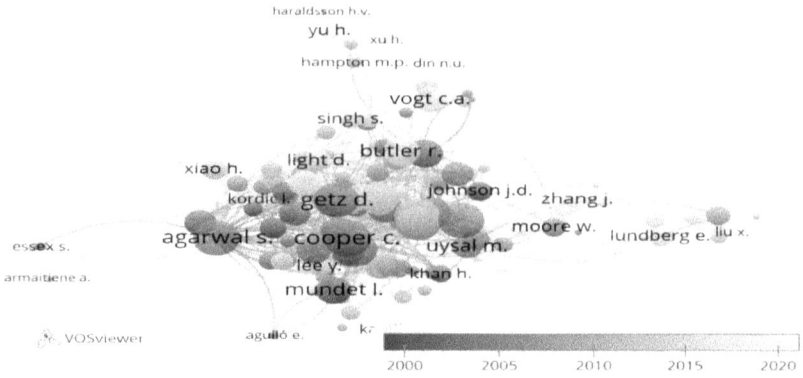

Figure 3.4 Citation links of authors

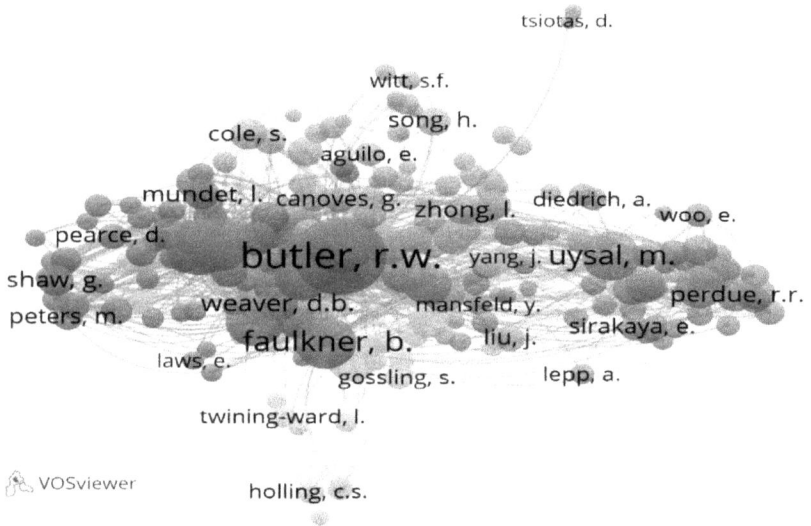

Figure 3.5 Co-citation links among authors

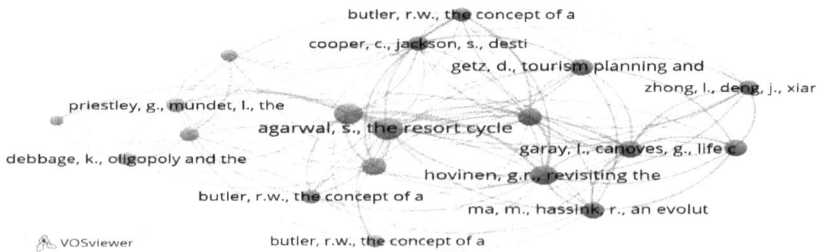

Figure 3.6 Co-citations links between documents

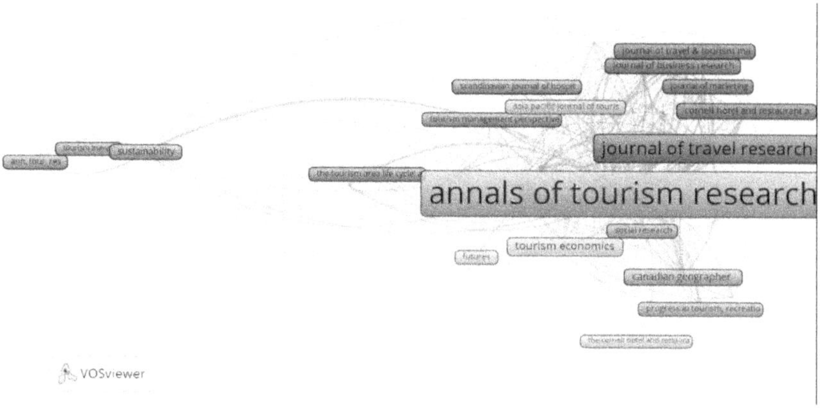

Figure 3.7 Co-citation link with journals

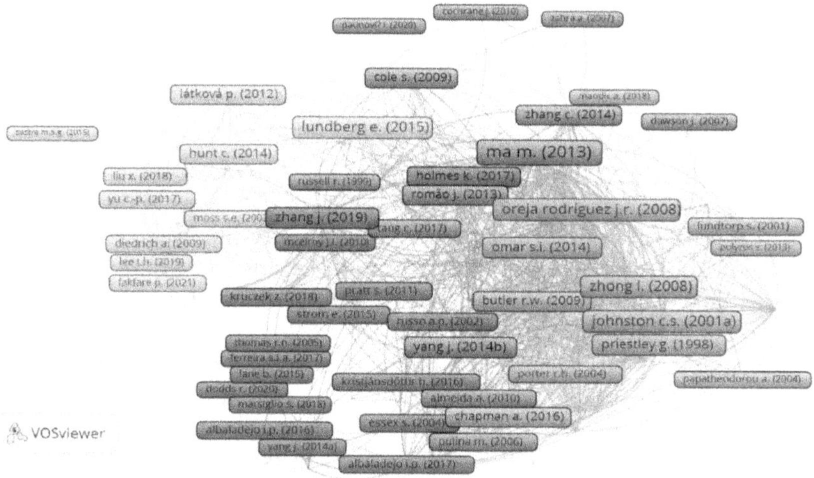

Figure 3.8 Bibliographic coupling

articles (Ülker *et al.*, 2023). The analysis revealed four prominent clusters (Figure 3.8) with 5883 links and a strength of 12,271. The largest cluster comprises 42 documents.

Future Research Areas

This section identifies areas proposed by authors during the period investigated for future research using the TALC (Figure 3.9). Several authors suggest studies on tourist-generating markets and segments and their impacts on the destination (Garcia-Ayllon, 2016; Giampiccoli &

Tourist	Destination	Concepts	Variables	Stakeholders
Generating markets	Absorbtion capacity	Resilience theory	Environment	Entrepreneurs
Segments	Congestion	Tourism planning	Carrying capacity	Government
Behaviour	Saturation	Strategic and marketing plans	Technology	Family businesses
Loyalty	Disasters		Economic demand/ supply	DMOs
Perceptions/ attitudes	Quality/ standards	Infrastructure development	Tourism products/ attractions	Local perceptions/ attitudes

Figure 3.9 Future research areas

Saayman, 2018; Kozak & Martin, 2012). Scholars have also suggested further research on tourist behaviour (Cruz-Milán, 2019) and loyalty (Weaver et al., 2019). Dodds (2019) recommended assessing the life cycle of a loyal tourist through the tourism experience life cycle. Congestion (Albaladejo et al., 2016), tourist saturation (Amoiradis et al., 2022) and tourist absorption capacity (Szromek, 2019) at the destination are other variables to be considered.

Resilience analysis also is gaining importance in TALC literature. Authors have suggested considering resilience to assess the TALC. Resilience focuses on variables that interfere with developmental trajectories, such as human or natural disasters or health risks (Holladay, 2018; Horne et al., 2022; Rindrasih, 2019). Kranjčević (2019) suggests measuring the effect of world events on tourism at the destination.

Xu et al. (2022) suggest exploring sustainability concerns by exploring the potential for destinations to reverse the decline stage of their life cycle. Environmental changes, coastal zone regulation, the impact of climate change and identifying tourist limits are proposed research areas (Kristjánsdóttir, 2016). Carrying capacity is still contentious and requires further investigation (Haraldsson & Olafsdóttir, 2018; Singh, 2021).

Other authors suggest using panel data (supply and demand variables) for TALC analysis (Kristjánsdóttir, 2021; Kosova & Sinaj, 2021). Examining the impact of technology, such as the proliferation of online review sites, social media, technology roadmaps (Gore et al., 2021a) and peer-to-peer accommodation on a destination's life cycle also need further assessment (Avdimiotis & Poulaki, 2019; Gore et al., 2021b).

Authors have reported different results from their evaluation of tourism and economic growth factors. For example, some destinations support tourism-led economic growth (Tai *et al.*, 2022; Zuo & Huang, 2018), while others support bidirectional (Yazdi *et al.*, 2017), conservational (Lee, 2012) and neutral growth (Tang & Jang, 2009). Hence, studies on similar parameters across destinations can be done. Examining the impact of economic downturns also needs further investigation, as do the social, cultural and political factors (Fan *et al.*, 2019; Javed & Tučková, 2020; Maralbayeva *et al.*, 2021; Marsiglio & Tolotti, 2022; Rindrasih, 2019).

The literature highlights the need for planning and stage-based development of the destination. Authors suggest research on strategic and marketing plans (Albaladejo & Martínez-García, 2017; Gore *et al.*, 2022; Whitfield, 2009). Few papers, however, assess tourism plans to analyse destination development (Cohen-Hattab & Shoval, 2010; Gore *et al.*, 2022). Researchers suggest study of the quality of the destination (Báez-García *et al.*, 2018), developing green tourism policy, marketing to manage demand, measuring residents and other stakeholders' perceptions for quality assessment based on sensory receptors and identifying the development thresholds (Fakfare *et al.*, 2021; Koens *et al.*, 2021; Su *et al.*, 2022). Research on benchmarking and establishing quality standards to increase competitive advantage could be pursued (Assaf & Dwyer, 2013; Gore *et al.*, 2022; Kozak, 2002).

The authors reinforced looking at entrepreneurs, stakeholders and their networks for managing the destination. A study on the role of destination management organisations in shaping a destination's life cycle (Javed & Tučková, 2020) could be undertaken and stakeholder collaborations assessed for each life cycle stage (Clark & Nyaupane, 2022; Gore *et al.*, 2021b; Nazneen *et al.*, 2019). The impact of family businesses and other entrepreneurs (Chauhan & Madden, 2020; López-Chávez & Maldonado-Alcudia, 2022; Szromek, 2019) on destination development is an emerging area of TALC research.

As a predictive tool, TALC can help assess how the destination may experience future growth cycles. Evaluation of local and tourist perceptions and attitudes is suggested. The authors recommend using road maps, destination designs and systems theory to predict growth paths (Clark & Nyaupane, 2022; Hell & Petrić, 2021; Klein-Hewett, 2021; Koens *et al.*, 2021; Xu *et al.*, 2022). Economic growth models to predict growth cycles are also put forward (Correani & Garofalo, 2010; Gouveia & Rodrigues, 2005; Papatherodou, 2004).

Marketing and strategic management concepts like PLC (Collins-Kreiner, 2016), SWOT (Tang & Jang, 2009), Mintzberg strategies (Gore *et al.*, 2021b) and the McKinsey model (Maralbayeva *et al.*, 2021) have been used to evaluate TALC. Competitive strategies like cost leadership, differentiation or focus at different life cycle stages can be evaluated (Chauhan & Madden, 2020). Constituents of the tourism system, including the restaurant/food sector and green transport (Gore *et al.*, 2022; Henderson, 2007; Lee *et al.*, 2018), can also be assessed, along with tourism products using BCG matrix analysis (Gore *et al.*, 2022; McKercher, 2005). The impact of tourist attractions and infrastructure development on the destination life cycle requires further assessment (Albaladejo & Martínez-García, 2017; Setiawan & Wiweka, 2018; Szromek, 2019).

Authors also recommend evaluating triggers and transitions (Butler, 2014; Liu *et al.*, 2016). Many scholars have reported multiple life cycles (Butler, 2022; McKercher & Wong, 2021), U-shaped and N-shaped cycles (Zuo & Huang, 2018), cyclical and non-linear patterns (Butler, 2014; Nugroho & Numata, 2021; Pavlovich, 2014) and the presence of sub-cycles and super-cycles (Singh, 2021). Hence, uniform parameters or models for assessing the evolution or predicting the trajectory need to be developed. The vicious cycle model suggested by Russo (2002) needs further investigation, especially for developing countries.

Co-authorship analysis reveals that TALC scholars might usefully form inter-group collaborations as the publications show that authors are collaborating within the same groups. Senior scholars and professors need to take the initiative to collaborate with junior professors and researchers in the field. Authors from the countries that contribute most to this literature (the US, UK and Spain) could form collaborations with developing countries where TALC research is not very common. Such collaborations would help researchers in other countries participate in professional research groups. It would also help to broaden the scope of TALC and might offer new perspectives on how tourist destinations develop. Gore *et al.* (2022) reported a lack of TALC research on developing countries and emerging economies, hence, research on developing and emerging economies could be done through collaborative studies. Co-authorship analysis of organisations shows evidence of just one cluster. Hence, funding institutions, tourism organisations, universities and colleges should form collaborations and take up TALC studies. In addition, destination management organisations should collaborate with local colleges and universities to promote TALC research to ensure sustainable destination planning and management.

Lastly, comparative case analysis or mixed methodologies can be used to evaluate destination development, and the correlation between the quantitative and qualitative data variables would strengthen the impact of studies (Alexandrova *et al.*, 2019; de Jager & Nicolau, 2020; Gore *et al.*, 2022).

Conclusion

During the last 40 years, the TALC literature has witnessed many different perspectives. The authors agree that the model has become indispensable and adds valuable insights into the development process.

TALC research helps to bring about a macro-level understanding of the past so that future strategies can be developed. There is still much scope for TALC research, especially in developing and emerging economies. Multidisciplinary research with collaborations between academicians and industry professionals is required. Scholarly cooperation is required to develop an integrative model for the assessment of tourism destination transformation.

The authors have concisely analysed the TALC literature in this chapter, but this research nevertheless has some limitations. The results and analysis are restricted to the journal articles downloaded based on search criteria and, thus, the review cannot be generalised to the entire volume of TALC research.

References

Agarwal, S. (1997) The resort cycle and seaside tourism: An assessment of its applicability and validity. *Tourism Management* 18 (2), 65–73.

Agarwal, S. (2002) Restructuring seaside tourism: The resort life-cycle. *Annals of Tourism Research* 29 (1), 25–55.

Albaladejo, I.P. and Martínez-García, M.P. (2017) The post stagnation stage for mature tourism areas: A mathematical modelling process. *Tourism Economics* 23 (2), 387–402.

Albaladejo, I.P., González-Martínez, M.I. and Martínez-García, M.P. (2016) Nonconstant reputation effect in a dynamic tourism demand model for Spain. *Tourism Management* 53, 132–139.

Alexandrova, A.Y., Aigina, E.V. and Minenkova, V.V. (2019) The impact of 2014 Olympic Games on Sochi tourism life cycle. *Journal of Environmental Management and Tourism* 10 (6), 1224–1234.

Amoiradis, C., Velissariou, E., Stankova, M. and Poulios, T. (2022) Spatial analysis of cultural resources and their contribution to the sustainable tourism development of Greece. In V. Katsoni and A.C. Şerban (eds) *Transcending Borders in Tourism Through Innovation and Cultural Heritage* (pp. 3–31). Cham: Springer.

Assaf, A.G. and Dwyer, L. (2013) Benchmarking international tourism destinations. *Tourism Economics* 19 (6), 1233–1247. https://doi.org/10.5367/te.2013.0354.

Avdimiotis, S. and Poulaki, I. (2019) Airbnb impact and regulation issues through destination life cycle concept. *International Journal of Culture, Tourism and Hospitality Research* 13 (4), 458–472.

Báez-García, A.J., Flores-Muñoz, F. and Gutiérrez-Barroso, J. (2018) Maturity in competing tourism destinations: The case of Tenerife. *Tourism Review* 73 (3), 359–373.

Baum, T. (1998) Taking the exit route: Extending the tourism area life cycle model. *Current Issues in Tourism* 1 (2), 167–175.

Benckendorff, P. (2009) Themes and trends in Australian and New Zealand tourism research: A social network analysis of citations in two leading journals (1994–2007). *Journal of Hospitality and Tourism Management* 16, 1–15.

Benckendorff, P. and Zehrer, A. (2013) A network analysis of tourism research. *Annals of Tourism Research* 43, 121–149.

Butler, R. (2014) Coastal tourist resorts: History, development and models. *ACE: Architecture, City and Environment* 9 (25), 203–228.

Butler, R. (2022) Managing tourism – A missing element? *PASOS Revista de Turismo y Patrimonio Cultural* 20 (2), 255–263.

Butler, R. and Weidenfeld, A. (2012) Cooperation and competition during the resort life-cycle. *Tourism Recreation Research* 37 (1), 15–26.

Butler, R. (1985) Evolution of tourism in the Scottish Highlands. *Annals of Tourism Research* 12 (3), 371–391.

Butler, R. (2009) Tourism destination development: Cycles and forces, myths and realities. *Tourism Recreation Research* 34 (3), 247–254.

Chai, A. (2012) Consumer specialisation and the demand for novelty: A reconsideration of the links and implications for studying fashion cycles in tourism. *Jahrbücher für Nationalökonomie und Statistik* 232 (6), 678–701.

Chapman, A. and Light, D. (2016) Exploring the tourist destination as a mosaic: The alternative life-cycles of the seaside amusement arcade sector in Britain. *Tourism Management* 52, 254–263.

Chauhan, A.A. and Madden, K. (2020) Tourism development using family business entrepreneurs: A new paradigm. *International Journal of Public Sector Performance Management* 6 (4), 508–525.

Choy, D.J. (1992) Life cycle models for Pacific Island destinations. *Journal of Travel Research* 30 (3), 26–31.

Clark, C. and Nyaupane, G.P. (2022) Connecting landscape-scale ecological restoration and tourism: Stakeholder perspectives in the great plains of North America. *Journal of Sustainable Tourism* 30 (11), 2595–2613.

Cochrane, J. (2010) The sphere of tourism resilience. *Tourism Recreation Research* 35 (2), 173–185.

Cohen, E. (2008) The tsunami waves and the paradisiac cycle: The changing image of the Andaman coastal region of Thailand. *Tourism Analysis* 13 (3), 221–232.

Cohen-Hattab, K. and Shoval, N. (2004) The decline of Israel's Mediterranean resorts: Life cycle change versus national tourism master planning. *Tourism Geographies* 6 (1), 59–78.

Cole, S. (2012) Synergy and congestion in the tourist destination life cycle. *Tourism Management* 33 (5), 1128–1140.

Collins-Kreiner, N. (2016) The life-cycle of concepts: The case of 'pilgrimage tourism'. *Tourism Geographies* 18 (3), 322–334.

Cooper, C. (1992) The life cycle concept and strategic planning for coastal resorts. *Built Environment* 18 (1), 57–66.

Cooper, C. and Jackson, S. (1989) Destination life cycle: The Isle of Man case study. *Annals of Tourism Research* 16 (3), 377–398.

Correani, L. and Garofalo, G. (2010) Chaotic paths in the tourism industry. *Economia Politica* 27 (1), 103–146.

Cruz-Milán, O. (2019) Integrating venturesomeness and consumption needs: Effects on destination choice along the TALC. *Journal of Travel and Tourism Marketing* 36 (6), 747–767.

Da Conceição Gonçalves, V.F. and Aguas, P.M.R. (1997) The concept of life cycle: An application to the tourist product. *Journal of Travel Research* 36 (2), 12–22.

de Jager, A.E. and Nicolau, M.D. (2020) Opening the door for wider application of the tourism area life cycle model with application to the Rietvlei Nature Reserve, Tshwane, South Africa. *African Journal of Hospitality, Tourism and Leisure* 9 (6), 912–929.

Debbage, K.G. (1990) Oligopoly and the resort cycle in the Bahamas. *Annals of Tourism Research* 17 (4), 513–527.

Di Benedetto, C.A. and Bojanic, D.C. (1993) Tourism area life cycle extensions. *Annals of Tourism Research* 20(3), 557–570.

Dodds, R. (2019) The tourist experience life cycle: A perspective article. *Tourism Review* 75 (1), 216–220.

Donaldson, R. and Forssman, A. (2020) Opening up to the world: An exploration of residents' opinions on and perceptions of St Helena Island's tourism development. *African Journal of Hospitality, Tourism and Leisure* 9 (6), 944–958.

Donthu, N., Kumar, S., Mukherjee, D., Pandey, N., and Lim, W.M. (2021) How to conduct a bibliometric analysis: An overview and guidelines. *Journal of Business Research* 133, 285–296.

Douglas, N. (1997) Applying the life cycle model to Melanesia. *Annals of Tourism Research* 24 (1), 1–22.

Eaton, J.P., Ward, J.C., Kumar, A. and Reingen, P.H. (1999) Structural analysis of co-author relationships and author productivity in selected outlets for consumer behaviour research. *Journal of Consumer Psychology* 8 (1), 39–59.

Essex, S., Kent, M. and Newnham, R. (2004) Tourism development in Mallorca: Is water supply a constraint? *Journal of Sustainable Tourism* 12 (1), 4–28.

Fakfare, P., Cho, G., Hwang, H. and Manosuthi, N. (2021) Examining the sensory impressions, value perception, and behavioural responses of tourists: The case of floating markets in Thailand. *Journal of Travel and Tourism Marketing* 38 (7), 666–681.

Fan, D.X., Liu, A. and Qiu, R.T. (2019) Revisiting the relationship between host attitudes and tourism development: A utility maximisation approach. *Tourism Economics* 25 (2), 171–188.

Ferreira, F.A. (2018) Mapping the field of arts-based management: Bibliographic coupling and co-citation analyses. *Journal of Business Research* 85, 348–357.

Ferreira, S.L. and Hunter, C.A. (2017) Wine tourism development in South Africa: A geographical analysis. *Tourism Geographies* 19 (5), 676–698.

Foster, D.M. and Murphy, P. (1991) Resort cycle revisited: The retirement connection. *Annals of Tourism Research* 18 (4), 553–567.

Gale, T. (2005) Modernism, post-modernism and the decline of British seaside resorts as long holiday destinations: A case study of Rhyl, North Wales. *Tourism Geographies* 7 (1), 86–112.

Gale, T. and Botterill, D. (2005) A realist agenda for tourist studies, or why destination areas really rise and fall in popularity. *Tourist Studies* 5 (2), 151–174.

Garcia-Ayllon, S. (2016) Geographic information system (GIS) analysis of impacts in the tourism area life cycle (TALC) of a Mediterranean resort. *International Journal of Tourism Research* 18 (2), 186–196.

Getz, D. (1992) Tourism planning and destination life cycle. *Annals of Tourism Research* 19 (4), 752–770.

Giampiccoli, A. and Saayman, M. (2018) Community-based tourism development model and community participation. *African Journal of Hospitality, Tourism and Leisure* 7 (4), 1–27.

Gołembski, G., Nawrot, Ł., Olszewski, M. and Zmyślony, P. (2010) Investment decisions in the early stages of the Tourism Area Life Cycle. *Tourism: An International Interdisciplinary Journal* 58 (4), 361–377.

Gore, S., Borde, N. and Hegde Desai, P. (2021a) Assessment of technology strategies for sustainable tourism planning. *Foresight* 23 (2), 172–187.

Gore, S., Borde, N., Hegde Desai, P. and George, B. (2021b) Empirically mapping the evolutionary phases of Tourism Area Life Cycle (TALC): The case of Goa, India. *Tourism: An International Interdisciplinary Journal* 69 (3), 346–366.

Gore, S., Borde, N., Desai, P.H. and George, B. (2022) A structured literature review of the tourism area life cycle concept. *Journal of Tourism, Sustainability and Well-being* 10 (1), 1–20.

Gouveia, P.M. and Rodrigues, P.M. (2005) Dating and synchronising tourism growth cycles. *Tourism Economics* 11 (4), 501–515.

Haraldsson, H.V. and Ólafsdóttir, R. (2018) Evolution of tourism in natural destinations and dynamic, sustainable thresholds over time. *Sustainability* 10 (12), 4788.

Haywood, K.M. (1986) Can the tourist-area life cycle be made operational? *Tourism Management* 7 (3), 154–167.

Hell, M. and Petrić, L. (2021) System dynamics approach to TALC modelling. *Sustainability* 13 (9), 4803.

Henderson, J.C. (2007) Destination development: Singapore and Dubai compared. *Journal of Travel and Tourism Marketing* 20(3–4), 33–45.

Heuwinkel, K. and Venter, G. (2018) Applying the tourist area life cycle within sports tourism: The case of Stellenbosch and German athletes. *Journal of Sport and Tourism* 22 (3), 247–263.

Holladay, P.J. (2018) Destination resilience and sustainable tourism development. *Tourism Review International* 22(3–4), 251–261.

Holmes, K. and Ali-Knight, J. (2017) The event and festival life cycle – Developing a new model for a new context. *International Journal of Contemporary Hospitality Management* 29 (3), 986–1004.

Horne, L., De Urioste-Stone, S., Rahimzadeh Bajgiran, P. and Seekamp, E. (2022) Understanding tourism suppliers' resilience to climate change in a rural destination in Maine. *Tourism Planning and Development*. https://doi.org/10.1080/21568316.2022.2083222.

Hovinen, G.R. (1982) Visitor cycles: Outlook for tourism in Lancaster County. *Annals of Tourism Research* 9 (4), 565–583.

Hovinen, G.R. (2002) Revisiting the destination life-cycle model. *Annals of Tourism Research* 29 (1), 209–230.

Ioannides, D. (1992) Tourism development agents: The Cypriot resort cycle. *Annals of Tourism Research* 19 (4), 711–731.

Javed, M. and Tučková, Z. (2020) The role of government in tourism competitiveness and tourism area life cycle model. *Asia Pacific Journal of Tourism Research* 25 (9), 997–1011.

Jennings, S. (2004) Coastal tourism and shoreline management. *Annals of Tourism Research* 31 (4), 899–922.

Johnston, C.S. (2001) Shoring the foundations of the destination life cycle model, part 1: Ontological and epistemological considerations. *Tourism Geographies* 3 (1), 2–28.

Kessler, M.M. (1963) Bibliographic coupling between scientific papers. *American Documentation* 14 (1), 10–25.

Klein-Hewett, H. (2021) Design as an indicator of tourist destination change: The concept renewal cycle at Watkins Glen State Park. *Land* 10 (4), 367.

Koens, K., Smit, B. and Melissen, F. (2021) Designing destinations for good: Using design road mapping to support pro-active destination development. *Annals of Tourism Research* 89, 103233.

Kosova, R. and Sinaj, V. (2021) Mathematical modeling of tourism development. An application to Albanian tourism. *Journal of Environmental Management and Tourism* 12 (6), 1707–1715.

Kozak, M. (2002) Destination benchmarking. *Annals of Tourism Research* 29 (2), 497–519.

Kozak, M. and Martin, D. (2012) Tourism life cycle and sustainability analysis: Profit-focused strategies for mature destinations. *Tourism Management* 33 (1), 188–194.

Kranjčević, J. (2019) Tourism on the Croatian Adriatic Coast and World War I. *Academica Turistica – Tourism and Innovation Journal* 12 (1), 41–53.

Kristjánsdóttir, H. (2016) Can the Butler's tourist area cycle of evolution be applied to find the maximum tourism level? A comparison of Norway and Iceland to other OECD countries. *Scandinavian Journal of Hospitality and Tourism* 16 (1), 61–75.

Kristjánsdóttir, H. (2021) Tax on tourism in Europe: Does higher value-added tax (VAT) impact tourism demand in Europe? *Current Issues in Tourism* 24 (6), 738–741.

Kruczek, Z., Kruczek, M. and Szromek, A.R. (2018) Possibilities of using the tourism area life cycle model to understand and provide sustainable solutions for tourism development in the Antarctic Region. *Sustainability* 10 (1), 89.

Lee, C.G. (2012) Tourism, trade, and income: Evidence from Singapore. *Anatolia* 23 (3), 348–358.

Lee, M.Y. and Rii, H.U. (2016) An application of the vicious circle schema to the World Heritage Site of Macau. *Journal of Heritage Tourism* 11 (2), 126–142.

Lee, S.H., Wu, S.C. and Li, A. (2018) Low-carbon tourism of small islands responding to climate change. *World Leisure Journal* 60 (3), 235–245.

Lee, T.H. and Jan, F.H. (2019) Can community-based tourism contribute to sustainable development? Evidence from residents' perceptions of sustainability. *Tourism Management* 70, 368–380.

Lemky, K. (2017) The revitalisation of a heritage travel route: Canada's Cabot Trail. *Journal of Heritage Tourism* 12 (5), 526–535.

Liu, W., Vogt, C.A., Lupi, F., He, G., Ouyang, Z. and Liu, J. (2016) Evolution of tourism in a flagship protected area of China. *Journal of Sustainable Tourism* 24 (2), 203–226.

Long, F., Liu, J., Zhang, S., Yu, H. and Jiang, H. (2018) Development characteristics and evolution mechanism of homestay agglomeration in Mogan Mountain, China. *Sustainability* 10 (9), 2964.

López-Chávez, B.A. and Maldonado-Alcudia, C. (2022) Exploring the life cycle of family-owned tourism businesses in maturity. *Journal of Family Business Management* 12 (3), 494–512.

Lozano, J., Gomez, C.M. and Rey-Maquieira, J. (2008) The TALC hypothesis and economic growth theory. *Tourism Economics* 14 (4), 727–749.

Ma, M. and Hassink, R. (2013) An evolutionary perspective on tourism area development. *Annals of Tourism Research* 41, 89–109.

Maralbayeva, S.M., Nikiforova, N.V. and Smykova, M.R. (2021) The destination life cycle concept in developing a tourist Brand. Case of Mangystau of Kazakhstan. *Journal of Environmental Management and Tourism* 12 (6), 1472–1494.

Marsiglio, S. and Tolotti, M. (2022) The tourism area life cycle hypothesis: A micro-foundation. *Tourism Economics* 30 (2). https://doi.org/10.1177/13548166221138645.

Martin, B.S. and Uysal, M. (1990) An examination of the relationship between carrying capacity and the tourism life-cycle: Management and policy implications. *Journal of Environmental Management* 31 (4), 327–333.

Mavric, B., Öğretmenoğlu, M. and Akova, O. (2021) Bibliometric analysis of slow tourism. *Advances in Hospitality and Tourism Research* 9 (1), 157–178.

McElroy, J.L. and Hamma, P.E. (2010) SITEs revisited: Socioeconomic and demographic contours of small island tourist economies. *Asia Pacific Viewpoint* 51 (1), 36–46.

McKercher, B. (2005) Destinations as products? A reflection on Butler's life cycle. *Tourism Recreation Research* 30 (3), 97–102.

McKercher, B. and Wong, I.A. (2021) Do destinations have multiple life cycles? *Tourism Management* 83, 104232.

Meyer-Arendt, K.J. (1985) The Grand Isle, Louisiana resort cycle. *Annals of Tourism Research* 12 (3), 449–465.

Moore, W. and Whitehall, P. (2005) The tourism area life-cycle and regime-switching models. *Annals of Tourism Research* 32 (1), 112–126.

Moss, S.E., Ryan, C., and Wagoner, C.B. (2003) An empirical test of Butler's resort product life cycle: Forecasting casino winnings. *Journal of Travel Research* 41 (4), 393–399.

Nazneen, S., Xu, H., and Din, N.U. (2019) Cross-border infrastructural development and residents' perceived tourism impacts: A case of China–Pakistan economic corridor. *International Journal of Tourism Research* 21 (3), 334–343.

Nugroho, P. and Numata, S. (2021) Changes in residents' attitudes toward community-based tourism through destination development in Gunung Ciremai national park, Indonesia. *Tourism Recreation Research* 46 (3), 403–421.

O'Hare, A. and O'Hare, G. (2001) Tourism in Cuba Part 1. *Geography Review* 14 (4), 20–25.

Oppermann, M. (1995) Travel life cycle. *Annals of Tourism Research* 22 (3), 535–552.

Papatheodorou, A. (2004) Exploring the evolution of tourism resorts. *Annals of Tourism Research* 31 (1), 219–237.

Pásková, M. (2002) Destination life cycle of the historic town Ceský Krumlov. *Tourism (Zagreb)* 50 (3), 249–264.

Pavlovich, K. (2014) A rhizomic approach to tourism destination evolution and transformation. *Tourism Management* 41, 1–8.

Philander, K. and Roe, S.J. (2013) The impact of wage rate growth on tourism competitiveness. *Tourism Economics* 19 (4), 823–834.

Pilving, T., Kull, T., Suškevics, M. and Viira, A.H. (2019) The tourism partnership life cycle in Estonia: Striving towards sustainable multisectoral rural tourism collaboration. *Tourism Management Perspectives* 31, 219–230.

Prideaux, B. (2000) The resort development spectrum – a new approach to modeling resort development. *Tourism Management* 21 (3), 225–240.

Priestley, G. and Mundet, L. (1998) The post-stagnation phase of the resort cycle. *Annals of Tourism Research* 2 5(1), 85–111.

Promnil, N. (2019) Human capital in the exploration stage of community-based homestay Nawatwithi. *International Journal of Innovation, Creativity and Change* 7 (1), 71–86.

Rindrasih, E. (2019) Life after tsunami: The transformation of a post-tsunami and post-conflict tourist destination; the case of halal tourism, Aceh, Indonesia. *International Development Planning Review* 41 (4), 517–541.

Russell, R. and Faulkner, B. (2004) Entrepreneurship, chaos and the tourism area life-cycle. *Annals of Tourism Research* 31 (3), 556–579.

Russo, A.P. (2002) The 'vicious circle' of tourism development in heritage cities. *Annals of Tourism Research* 29 (1), 165–182.

Setiawan, B. and Wiweka, K. (2018) A study of the tourism area life cycle in Dieng Kulon village. *Pertanika Journal of Social Sciences and Humanities* 26, 271–278.

Shelley, M. and Krippendorff, K. (1984) Content analysis: An introduction to its methodology. *Journal of the American Statistical Association* 79 (385), 240.

Singh, S. (2011) The tourism area 'life cycle': A clarification. *Annals of Tourism Research* 38 (3), 1185–1187.

Singh, S. (2021) Time, tourism area 'life-cycle' evolution and heritage. *Journal of Heritage Tourism* 16 (2), 218–229.

Small, H. (1973) Co-citation in the scientific literature: A new measure of the relationship between two documents. *Journal of the American Society for Information Science* 24 (4), 265–269.

Su, L., Yang, X. and Swanson, S.R. (2022) The impact of spatial-temporal variation on tourist destination resident quality of life. *Tourism Management* 93, 104572.

Szromek, A.R. (2019) An analytical model of tourist destination development and characteristics of the development stages: Example of the Island of Bornholm. *Sustainability* 11 (24), 6989.

Tai, A.C., Wong, D.W., Lee, H.F. and Qiang, W. (2022) Tourism's long-and short-term influence on global cities' economic growth: The case of Hong Kong. *Plos One* 17 (9), e0275152.

Tang, C.H. and Jang, S.S. (2009) The tourism–economy causality in the United States: A sub-industry level examination. *Tourism Management* 30 (4), 553–558.

Tischer, M.C., Schiavetti, A., de Lima Silva, F.J. and da Silva Jr, J.M. (2018) A historical perspective on the life cycle of a tourist activity: Dolphin watching in Brazil's Fernando de Noronha archipelago. *Ethnobiology and Conservation*, 7. http://orcid.org/0000-0001-8429-7646.

Toh, R.S., Khan, H., and Koh, A.J. (2001) A travel balance approach for examining tourism area life cycles: The case of Singapore. *Journal of Travel Research* 39 (4), 426–432.

Tooman, L.A. (1997) Applications of the life-cycle model in tourism. *Annals of Tourism Research* 24 (1), 214–234.

Ülker, P., Ülker, M. and Karamustafa, K. (2023) Bibliometric analysis of bibliometric studies in the field of tourism and hospitality. *Journal of Hospitality and Tourism Insights* 6 (2), 797–818. https://doi.org/10.1108/JHTI-10-2021-0291.

Uysal, O.O. (2010) Business ethics research with an accounting focus: A bibliometric analysis from 1988 to 2007. *Journal of Business Ethics* 93 (1), 137–160.

Weaver, D., Tang, C., Lawton, L. and Liu, Y. (2019) Cultivating the Chinese market through destination loyalty: Enhancing resilience in the Maldives. *Tourism Geographies* 23 (3), 552–572.

Weaver, D.B. (2012) Organic, incremental and induced paths to sustainable mass tourism convergence. *Tourism Management* 33 (5), 1030–1037.

Weiermair, K., Peters, M. and Schuckert, M. (2007) Destination development and the tourist life-cycle: Implications for entrepreneurship in Alpine tourism. *Tourism Recreation Research* 32 (1), 83–93.

Whitfield, J. (2009) The cyclical representation of the UK conference sector's life cycle: The use of refurbishments as rejuvenation triggers. *Tourism Analysis* 14 (5), 559–572.

Wilkinson, P.F. (1987) Tourism in small island nations: A fragile dependence. *Leisure Studies* 6 (2), 127–146.

Xu, L., Yu, H. and Zhou, B. (2022) Decline or rejuvenation? Efficiency development of China's national scenic areas. *Forests* 13 (7), 995.

Yazdi, S.K., Salehi, K.H. and Soheilzad, M. (2017) The relationship between tourism, foreign direct investment, and economic growth: Evidence from Iran. *Current Issues in Tourism* 20 (1), 15–26.

Zhong, L., Deng, J. and Xiang, B. (2008) Tourism development and the tourism area life-cycle model: A case study of Zhangjiajie National Forest Park, China. *Tourism Management* 29 (5), 841–856.

Zuo, B. and Huang, S. (2018) Revisiting the tourism-led economic growth hypothesis: The case of China. *Journal of Travel Research* 57 (2), 151–163.

4 An Evaluation of the Tourism Resort Life Cycle and the Need for Sustainability Planning

Rachel Dodds

Much research has been done on the concept of the tourism resort life cycle and its applicability, yet few researchers have attempted to chronicle its evolution by retrospectively examining and comparing the various models and their assessments. This chapter analyses the literature relating to the resort life cycle historically, with two specific goals: to examine these models collectively, and to determine historical themes and relationships to sustainability. It then evaluates and synthesises, more systematically, the trends that emerge from the historical chronicle of the TALC. The analysis culminates in the presentation of the author's own resort cycle model, which is proffered in order to rectify the shortcomings of the TALC recognised in the literature. Salient characteristics of models selected for discussion purposes are also summarised.

Early writers (such as Gilbert, 1949) outlined, in a highly descriptive manner, fundamental patterns and spatial processes and implied that these interactions are present in all forms of tourism. Coherent spatial structures emerged in the late 1960s and 1970s, often with the adoption of a more critical and theoretical approach towards tourism. Butler's 1980 model is the resort cycle benchmark, and much of the relevant research since then has employed the TALC model as their primary frame of reference, with varying degrees of originality and research integration. Models play crucial roles in describing and interpreting information and their interlinking relationships. The literature shows that there was relatively little research on such models in tourism in the early 1950s and 1960s but a steady increase has occurred since. Researchers have consistently built upon prior research and the volume of literature has increased exponentially. The modelling of the dynamic element of destinations now constitutes a major theme of research in the tourism literature. This emphasis is commonly referred to as the *resort cycle concept* as outlined by Butler (1980). The cycle implies growth, often excessive, and this illuminates the problems of unstructured tourism growth, while highlighting the need for sustainable tourism. Such models have evolved in response to the frequent criticisms and refinements of Butler's 1980 model. This chapter first outlines the applicability of the life cycle and more specifically Butler's life cycle; patterns within the literature are then discussed before a proposed new model is presented.

Applicability of the TALC

There has been much discussion of the operationalisation of the life cycle model in relation to broad evolutionary patterns (Agarwal, 1997). Controversy over the exact shape and pattern of the life cycle curve and detailed specification of its parameters has characterised this literature. The cycle could be applied at a micro level (i.e. to a specific resort) or at a macro level or on a regional scale. There are three evaluative views regarding the applicability of Butler's model: corroboration, refinement or disagreement, although some authors do not cite Butler at all, due to the nature of research or time of publishing.

Corroboration of the Butler model

Meyer-Arendt (1985) was the first to corroborate the concept of the resort cycle and maintained this stance in a second article (1993). The resorts of these studies fit with Butler's depiction of each stage of the resort cycle and the usefulness of the Butler model was validated. Benedetto and Bojanic (1993) declared that resorts are able to revitalise themselves during the stagnation stage, the model therefore providing accurate forecasting of tourist numbers for the time period.

Refinement of the Butler model

Many authors found differences in the nature of the life cycle specific to the product or destination, and therefore recommended modifications to Butler's idealised model (Choy, 1992; Cooper & Jackson, 1989; Douglas, 1997; Getz, 1992; Haywood, 1986; Strapp, 1988). Lundgren (1983) emphasised that only a major overhaul of older attractions and facilities, often together with revitalisation combinations, can bring an area back to a new cycle of growth. One of the first conceptual and measurement criticisms regarding the life cycle was raised by Haywood (1996), who thought the applicability of the model was limited and that it was too general. The model should show life extension ideas, assuming that all areas follow the general life cycle. Haywood concluded that there were a range of intervening variables beyond the control of a destination's planner and infinite variables exist in various destinations, such as social, geographic, political and economic factors. Haywood (1986) questioned whether tourism, expenditures and profits could be used instead of tourist numbers to indicate carrying capacity and emphasised that it is difficult to predict what units of analysis are best used and how to define stages of movement clearly. Douglas (1997) concurred with Haywood, declaring that although the model can be used as a conceptual framework, various factors exist in different destinations. Strapp's (1988) study argued that the application of the resort cycle differs across geographical scales and that study areas must examine all aspects that affect a community rather than just tourism, as Butler's model does not differentiate between a decline in tourism and an overall decline in a community.

Agarwal (1994) contended that more emphasis needed to be placed on the rejuvenation stage of Butler's model rather than the decline stage. A positive contribution to the development cycle is that the rejuvenation and decline stages allow for alternative untapped resources to be used or adjustments to be made. Weaver (1988, 1990) refined the model to accommodate plantation-economy destinations and questioned the validity in this context of 'local control' in the early stages of the cycle.

Disagreement with Butler

A negative interpretation of the life cycle is that attractiveness is often determined by cost and accessibility rather than specific preferences and amount of facilities. Butler, however, had stated that some resort developments do not experience all stages of the model; for example, 'instant resorts' such as Cancun missed the exploration and involvement stage but instead headed immediately into the development stage (Butler, 1980). Another critique is that the life span or life cycle of a tourist destination is not measured in the model and the area may lose attractiveness before capacity levels are reached. Hovinen (1981) found that, overall, the cycle did not describe the evolution of the industry in a rural region of Pennsylvania, and Cooper and Jackson (1989) note that the shape of the curve of their destination (the Isle of Man) did not correspond to the suggested path of the resort cycle. The authors did, however, note that the model provided an enlightening descriptive tool for how destinations and their markets evolve. The model's simplicity is both a virtue and a weak point; it could be termed a descriptive rather than a predictive tool (Cooper & Jackson, 1989).

Choy (1992) disagreed with the efficiency of Butler's cycle and said that it is not applicable to all destinations, and can be misleading in the case of Pacific Island destinations. Choy argued that it is better to treat each destination individually, as a unique entity rather than describe the evolution of the region involved, and that the model was at best a diagnostic tool, to be utilised after the fact. Getz (1992) emphasised that the life cycle model describes stages of tourism development, but tourism planners needed to be more aware of monitoring. For the forecasting of the performance of a number of important products, market- and impact-related indicators would reveal the health of the industry from the point of the view both of the private sector and of public goods. Getz (1992) discussed the problems associated with differentiating the hypothetical life cycle stages of the model in regard to 'capacity' as a management context and 'rejuvenation' as a planning initiative. Much of the criticism of the model concerns its inherent theoretical weaknesses, including vague geographical scale, the notion of carrying capacity, and the assumption that all tourist centres are destined for some form of decline (Agarwal, 1997).

Pre- and post-Butler

The pre-Butler and post-Butler eras show interesting trends with regard to applicability and disagreement with Butler. In the pre-Butler years, only Miossec (1977) refers to other authors in his study, and he uses Christaller (1963) in his framework. Cohen (1972) and Plog (1974) are seen as highly influential to later research, as their typologies characterise various stages of development and are widely applicable in theory. Christaller (1963) is also widely referenced as he was the first to conceptualise the idea of destination cyclicity.

Butler synthesised the majority of the literature that had appeared before his work, with the exception of three studies (Fussell, 1965; Miossec, 1977; Smith, 1978), to formulate the hypothetical evolution of a resort cycle. Butler's model was the first to use a diagram to conceptualise the idea and is the reference point for much of the subsequent literature, though this excludes Gormsen (1981), a 'one off' who does not refer to Butler. The TALC model has become the benchmark for sequential research due to the simplicity and apparent universality of its adoption of the product cycle curve. Perhaps it is these qualities which have set up this model for both praise and criticism.

In post-Butler cases, Hovinen (1981) and Meyer-Arendt (1985) empirically test Butler's cycle and are highly influential as they provide two different stances with regard to the applicability of Butlers' theory: to disagree or corroborate. Haywood (1986) is also highly influential as he was the first to refine and adjust Butler's model. Less influential in terms of impact are Lundgren (1983), Getz (1983) and Foster and Murphy (1991), while Choy (1992) and Wall (1993) are not cited at all by other researchers and therefore the usefulness of their studies may be in question. Later authors had little influence at this stage, but their research sources are extensive, reflecting the growing maturity of the field.

The Life Cycle and Patterns of the Literature

The literature cited relates well to Butler's cycle itself. For example, there are few initial 'discoveries' in the 1950s and 1960s, representing irregular research topics, and these characterise the *exploration* stage. As the literature increased and assumed some regularity, the basic *involvement* stage was entered in the 1970s, with tourism becoming a better-known subject. Like Butler's cycle, the literature began to include research specifically on tourism and adjustments in social typologies, and resort cycle references emerged. The 1980s typified the beginning of the *development* (growth) stage as more research appeared. Butler, critically, provided the catalyst for the emergence of this stage, with his own model. Butler did not work in isolation but exploited the ground broken by earlier researchers (explorers). Accessibility by researchers to other studies increased as global tourism development alongside other growth issues became more prominent. The literature continued to increase in the 1990s, thus characterising the *development* stage of the life cycle. These researchers, travelling well-trodden ground, may be seen as the equivalent of the mid-centric or even psychocentric tourist. As well, studies on specific destinations and regions developed and changes in the operalisation and validity of the resort cycle concept evolved. Although a consistent evolution of resort cycle literature can be conceptualised, it must be emphasised that not all areas experience the stages of the cycle as clearly as others (Butler, 1980). The time period of the growth stage is not evident at this point; however, an interesting question will be determining the stage when the literature will taper off to a *consolidation* stage and whether new models will rejuvenate the cycle or if it will *decline* in citation and application.

A vast array of tourism elements constitute a destination resort. Two general themes of particular importance have emerged in the literature.

Spatial elements

Miossec (1977) established a pattern of tourist space early in the literature, with Gormsen (1981) and Lundgren (1983) following suit, though the latter two are rarely cross-referenced by other authors. The studies by Smith (1978), Weaver (1988), Opperman (1995) and Tooman (1997), among others, relate to the concept of geographical space. Weaver (1988) makes a major contribution, as he ties this explicitly to the life cycle, and in his model a modified resort cycle is recognised and interpreted, placing tourism as a consequence of changing relationships between core and periphery. A dominance of geographers, as might be expected, is evident throughout this literature and reflected in abstract models. Miossec (1977), Lundgren (1983), Weaver (1988) and Opperman (1995) all provide general models to define tourism space, whereas other approaches were idiosyncratic, that is, destination specific.

Miossec (1977) provided the introduction to (geographical) and development characteristics. The large-scale model of interaction between source and destination provided by Miossec displays one of the more articulate attempts to examine the concept of tourism space at any scale of analysis but does not consider the spatial characteristics of the destinations themselves (Weaver, 1988). The model associates changing perceptions of resorts and changing sources of investment, but Pearce (1989) declared that Miossec failed to elaborate either on the context of development or on the agents that precipitate and sustain it. Miossec (1977) was one of the first to suggest that it is eventually tourism itself, rather than the original features of a destination, that attracts further tourists. Gormsen (1981) followed the pattern of spatial dynamics through the illustration of externally orientated growth patterns in peripheral destination areas. However, he ignored the impact of development upon the destination and its unilinear analysis and simplification (Bianchi, 1994).

Lundgren (1983) discussed a spatial hierarchy of tourist flows and related his model to the TALC and also general tourist typologies; however, he failed to provide detail on some of the categories and it is also unclear where his metropolitan flows originate from. Pearce (1995) noted that the model was useful to identify the functions of a particular place and its associated tourist flow.

Meyer-Arendt (1993) analysed physical degradation and decrease in attractions of a resort in relation to Butler's cycle and revealed that cultural processes are largely responsible for these developments. The resort area he examined fits into Butler's cycle, as each stage of that resort area followed a distinct settlement pattern that reflected changing environmental patterns, perceptions and expansion; thus, Meyer-Arendt depicted a correlation between the interaction of recreationalists and their physical environment. Smith (1978) examined the spatial development of a resort in a purely geographical sense, as did Opperman (1995), with the latter building upon Miossec (1977) but focusing more on developing countries.

In sum, many resort cycle researchers contribute an explicitly spatial component to the literature, ranging from the highly abstract and nomothetic, to the highly realistic and idiosyncratic.

Case study elements

The majority of the literature on the TALC has related to specific geographical case studies. Most of these relate to coastal development, although some frequently cited articles concern non-coastal destinations (e.g. Hovinen, 2002). A relatively even distribution of mainland and island development occurs, with equal reference to the context of sustainability. The early literature tended to focus on the development of mainland destination, while island studies appeared in the mid-1980s and early 1990s, which possibly reflects the emergence at that time of the 'pleasure periphery' (Turner & Ash, 1972). Another trend is a focus on general regions in the early phase, followed by a shift toward specific destination studies, and then a return to regional assessment. Overall, the large majority of the studies concern specific destinations rather than large regions. It should be pointed out that some authors (Agarwal, 1994, 1997; Choy, 1992) discuss particular destinations within a region. Relatively few very large-scale case studies are reported, because significant variation (and hence concurrent differential stages) is likely at such a scale.

A final issue to note is the dearth of case studies in broad areas, including South America, through Africa, and into Asia. One possible reason for this poor coverage may be the relatively low level of tourism development in the 1980s, another the limited number of tourism researchers in these regions in earlier decades.

The Impact of Sustainability

The impact of sustainability issues on tourism has become increasingly important, yet there has been little research on the evolution of sustainable tourism development in relation to resort cycles. Sustainability did become a theme in resort cycle models and related literature, through Williams (1993), Wall (1993), Getz (1992) and Smith (1992) making implicit references to the concept. These authors took a resource-oriented approach and generally argued that the control of growth should result in greater protection of the original cultural, historical and environmental assets of the destination. As Tooman (1997: 228) declared:

> protection of the 'foundation assets' will aid in the prolonging or maintenance of stages or characteristics most desired. In this way, tourism can be utilized as a positive agent of change rather than one directed by outside interests.

Wall (1982) noted that there is a contradiction between resort cycle and carrying capacity: capacity implies a fixed limit, whereas resort cycles imply change. However, for resort tourism development to be sustainable, a route must be found between limits to use and change, in order that continuous changing, monitoring and planning of a destination ensure that carrying capacity is not exceeded. As Conlin and Baum (1994: 259) conclude:

> Sustainability, if it is to be effective, will need to consider the overall 'environment' in which tourism development takes place, not just the physical environment.

To prevent environmental or cultural damage, particularly that which could curtail tourism, hotel operators and planners need to cooperate with government authorities and managers to ensure that a destination's tourism does not exceed its limits. The goal of sustainable tourism can be achieved if the capacity of many attributes of a destination to support human activity can be assessed, and then not exceeded (Manning & Dougherty, 1995). Manning and Dougherty discuss several possibilities to ensure sustainable development for destinations through preservation of their cultural, environmental and historical attributes, and conclude that carrying capacity must be determined and abided by to counter negative effects.

Proposed New Model

Although numerous research models have been put forward and draw directly from other models, as discussed above, there is little evidence of a comprehensive effort to build a wider cohesive body of theory. Too many uncertainties relating to theoretical and empirical validity remain and independent factors have not been synthesised for future planning and development. Prior research on resort development is neither conclusive nor cohesive. Many models discuss one or a few issues of resort planning but none predicts or offers effective guidelines for sustainable development. Though there has been much research on the resort cycle, it has proved difficult to project trends and incorporate all issues in planning in areas of recreation and tourism. The consequences of abrupt change in development stages are at times difficult to plan and account for.

The following model is a preliminary attempt to synthesise the research into an alternative model for future tourism resort planning. The model draws and builds from Butler's (1980) model and from those researchers who have identified inefficiencies in life cycle relationships through an adaptation of the supply–demand relationship. The economic supply–demand curve, essentially, could be related to the resort life cycle. Supply can be defined as the quantity of a good consumed, depending also upon the supplies that are available to the market (Hocking, 1975). As Hocking declared, the supply curve shows the relationship between price and the quantity supplied per unit of time, *other things being equal*. 'Demand' exists for a product if consumers possess the desire to purchase it and the necessary financial ability to do so (Hocking, 1975). The quality of goods demanded by a customer will be adversely affected by the supply. Integrating the concept of demand and supply establishes a framework for understanding how these interact to determine market prices and quantities for all goods and services (Hirschey & Pappas, 1993). Jackson and McConnell (1975) state that the intersection of the down-sloping demand curve and the up-sloping supply curve indicates equilibrium (or, in tourism terms, the carrying capacity). This is illustrated in Figure 4.1.

It should be noted that economics assumes *other things being equal,* which is of crucial importance to this model. Other things are *not* always equal, and an external analysis of social, political, environmental factors and competition needs to be done for future strategic planning, especially the needs of the local community and limits of acceptable change. The demand and development of a resort will depend upon factors such as competition and trends in the immediate and external environment. Unlike economics, the *ceteris paribus (other things being equal)* cannot be considered equal in the resort model.

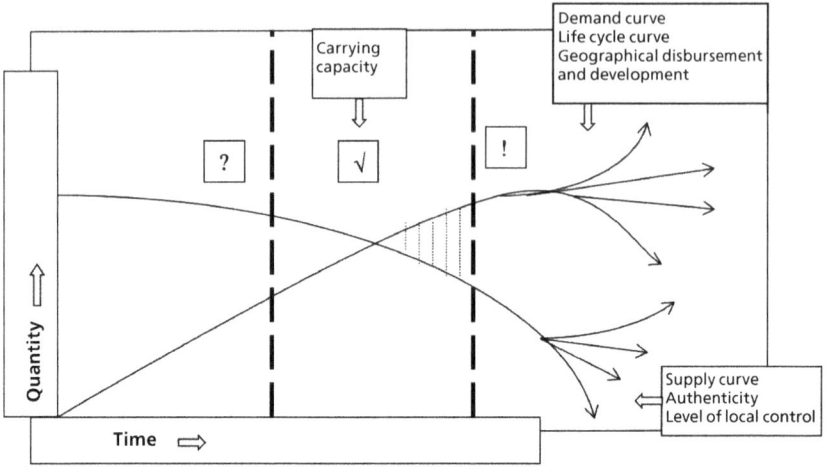

Figure 4.1 Critical capacity and sustainability cycles

Key

? *Under-utilisation*
   Area is not well developed, in exploration stage, no external activity or profits being made

√ *Optimum utilisation*
   Sustainable area, beneficial to developers, local community and tourists

! *Over-utilisation*
   Attention area, antagonism from host community develops, environment at risk, unsustainable

||| Area where sustainability and carrying capacity are lost

* All arrows coordinate – i.e. the top arrow for the demand curve corresponds with the top arrow from the supply curve, showing that one movement is likely to affect the other

The model curve can be related to the resort life cycle in a variety of ways. As destinations can lose their attractiveness before reaching carrying capacity, this also needs to be related to the surrounding environment. Once the curve has been established, the reward is that geo-development can be placed on the same curve, as 'demand'. As time passes or visitor numbers increase, so do the geographical dispersal and level of development, usually to accommodate increased interest. The demand curve can also be related directly to the TALC model although the *involvement*, *maturity* and *decline* stages are not visual. The general model of a resort's life cycle can be applied to this demand and supply curve, as one can alter the time and visitor numbers accordingly, which will alter the shape of the curve.

The supply curve can relate to measurements of government control, usually (although some exceptions occur) as local control tends to decrease with rising level of development and increasing visitor numbers, and authenticity is also often lost over time, as commercialisation increases (although time and development can be independent of each other). All factors can be mutually exclusive of one another, although such a scenario is rare, as for the majority of the time all interact with one another. The dotted lines show the centre section of the curve, which signifies loss of carrying capacity and sustainability, which should be the aim for both developers and tourism committees.

Units of measurement and time frames are concerns not clearly addressed in previous life cycle models, although these issues should be incorporated into stages of development. Specific time frames cannot be guaranteed, yet research on future market trends, analysis of the environment, the financial sector and government involvement can be predicted and should be considered. As geographical and political issues vary from region to region, the curves can be moved along the continuum.

Another issue that needs to be considered when looking at the resort cycle is that of tourist typologies. Cohen (1972) especially, argues that certain types of tourists visit certain types of destinations, with intensity of development being the critical point of differentiation. Although every destination cannot be mapped along one or even two continua, the allocentric visitor could be plotted at the beginning (left side) of both the upward and downward sloping curves as any sort of move along the continuum would affect typologies. This method of reflection could incorporate more than one ideology and model in an attempt to predict or decipher a destination. The incorporation of two continua within a model, each mutually independent yet correlated to some degree, might shed some light upon tourism issues. It is emphasised, however, that this model is preliminary and tentative, and will require additional clarification and empirical corroboration.

Finally, financial rewards are often thought to be reaped in relation to size; however, long-term planning and the sustainability of an area can not only reduce financial requirements but also preserve environmental and social agendas.

The model proposed by this author is an attempt to prescribe limits of sustainability and carrying capacity. It does not attempt to prescribe a conclusive model, but rather attempts to incorporate some of the implications of sustainability earlier discussed. The model has yet to be empirically tested for its applicability to sustainability and omits many issues that other authors pointed out with regard to Butler's 1980 model, such as the final processes of the *decline* and *rejuvenation* stages (Agarwal, 1994, 1997; Tooman, 1997). The model, although an academic generalisation, provides some practical application for managers and resort planners and developers. In addition, it is very simple, having advantage in its universality although it is difficult to disguise individual variation and the uniqueness of particular destinations. The model may be difficult to quantify and operationalise, and suggests that every destination would follow the same route in regard to the supply and demand variables. It is an idealistic approach for many destinations and could be applied for planning purposes primarily to new resorts, as established resorts would possibly already fit upon the continuum. It is an attempt to relate to the imperative issue of the need for sustainability and a measurement to some degree of what limitations and carrying capacities exist and how they will be inversely affected by different degrees of economic, sociocultural, geographical and political factors.

Discussion

There are four general observations regarding the life cycle literature. First is that the level of external or government control affects development stages and the authenticity of the destination. Many destinations have fallen for the vision of economic gain with little or no consideration to long-term negative effects. Gormsen (1981), Keller (1987), Weaver (1988), Butler (1993) and Williams (1993) all refer to the effects of external control and the need for the utilisation of local sector linkages and control. Tooman (1997) linked this notion to Butler's model by suggesting that tourism has become the dominant industry in many areas accompanied by a general decline of agriculture so that economic diversity of sources of primary income and control was lacking. Tourism is by nature characterised by growth, urbanisation, commercialisation and functional diversification and will always result in environmental change to some degree. The outcome of environmental damage, however, is not inevitable. Wilkinson (1989) claimed that government involvement in integrating tourism into national and regional planning is much needed, as multinational hotel chains, tours and airline companies often have their own agendas and are not sensitive to local issues, a point still very valid (Dodds & Butler, 2019; Butler & Dodds, 2022). Keller (1987) suggested that governments often encourage economic growth in tourism in order to increase overall welfare in a local jurisdiction. Russell and Faulkner (1999, 2004) outlined that development is influenced by the ongoing tension between entrepreneurs and regulators. Clearly, the measurement of capacity and the subsequent imposition of limits in tourism planning need to be incorporated into models for future predictions and analysis.

The second observation is that the bulk of the literature has focused upon coastal areas. Historically, tourist developers have found themselves to be attracted by the pleasure periphery and three-'S' tourism, most commonly found in coastal locations. Modern coastal resorts began to develop in France, England and other parts of Europe in the late 18th and 19th centuries. Domestic resorts proliferated along the coasts (peripheries) of developed countries throughout this period while international tourism, often on a large scale, became widespread in tropical and sub-tropical regions equating to the broader pleasure periphery. Resorts vary in the extent and length of development and variation occurs in ranges of accommodation and degree of involvement of local and external developers for different social classes (Pearce, 1995). Many studies have identified historical common features of coastal resorts and discussed their evolution; however, few models have taken into consideration resulting morphological and environmental changes (an exception is that of Stansfield, 1970) which could enable processes and development to be better understood and evolution more easily anticipated (Pearce, 1995).

The third observation is the discussion of coastal versus non-coastal and island versus mainland development, which is apparent in researchers' focus from the mid-1980s. Destinations' loss of local control in relation to the developmental stages of small islands was early discussed by Gormsen (1981) and further explored by Wilkinson (1989), Weaver (1988), Foster and Murphy (1991), Williams (1993) and Russell and Faulkner (1999, 2004). Many (less developed) island states earn the bulk of their foreign exchange through tourism (McLeod *et al.*, 2022) and related development is inevitable when international tourism continues to grow and the resulting economic, social and political problems relate to size and local control. Wilkinson (1989) suggested that the smaller the microstate, the greater the probability that tourism will dominate social and economic environments. It is imperative that the relative location of destinations (i.e. island or mainland) is incorporated into development and cycle models, as levels of control and stages of development are specifically affected by these characteristics.

A fourth observation is spatial design. Support for concentrated or dispersed development has gone back and forth in importance in patterns relating to time and location of destinations. There have been positive and negative arguments with respect to development patterns, with a preference of late for dispersed development, on the assumption that such a model reduces negative environmental effects. The majority of spatial design studies were done in the early 1990s, as environmental aspects of tourism development became recognised, such as May's (1993) discussion of geomorphology as a tourism resource, a tourism attraction and a management issue. Tourism–environmental relationships are often perceived as linear, with greater levels of tourism development correlated with greater negative environmental impacts (Meyer-Arendt, 1993). Prevailing adverse physical parameters can induce environmental degradation during the advanced stages of the life cycle and rejuvenation is usually costly and rarely successful. Few resorts have been planned specifically to avoid or withstand potential natural hazards and in an era of increasing climatic turbulence, more careful environmental planning is greatly needed in the extension of resorts and the development of new areas, in order to preserve not only the natural environment but also the social welfare of a destination.

Conclusion

The conclusions are fourfold. First, there has been an exponential growth in research on destination development, with the majority of studies largely descriptive, possibly a reflection of the 'state of the art' in early contemporary tourism research. Second, there has been no clear historical pattern in terms of corroboration, refinement or rejection of the TALC model. Perhaps it is because tourism is still in the 'mid-development' stage of its life cycle in terms of published literature, with Butler (1980) having provided the catalyst for the development stage. Third, research foci that have been identified from the literature analysis on resort development are those with regard to sustainability, government and local control, spatial development and geographical location (coastal versus non-coastal and island versus mainland). Those issues were then incorporated into a discussion of an alternative model that attempts to rectify shortcomings in the literature and that links the carrying capacity issue of the TALC to sustainability. Finally, the issue of sustainability in the resort cycle literature, in sum, has evolved from an implicit, vaguely articulated corollary of the models to a central focus point and organising principle of the more recent resort cycle literature.

References

Agarwal, S. (1994) The resort cycle revisited: Implications for resorts. In C.P. Cooper and A. Lockwood (eds) *Progress in Tourism Recreation and Hospitality Management* (vol. 5, pp. 194–208). New York: Wiley.

Agarwal, S. (1997) The resort cycle and seaside tourism: An assessment of its applicability and validity. *Tourism Management* 18 (2), 65–73.

Benedetto, C. and Bojanic, D. (1993) Tourism Area Life Cycle extensions. *Annals of Tourism Research* 20, 557–570.

Bianchi, R. (1994) Tourism development and resort dynamics: An alternative approach. In C.P. Cooper and A. Lockwood (eds) *Progress in Tourism Recreation and Hospitality Management* (vol. 5, pp. 181–193). New York: Wiley.

Butler, R. (1980) The concept of a tourist area cycle of evolution: Implications for management of resources. *Canadian Geographer* 24 (1), 5–12.

Butler, R. (1993) Tourism – An evolutionary perspective. In J. Nelson, R. Butler and G. Wall (eds) *Tourism and Sustainable Development: Monitoring, Planning, Managing* (pp. 27–41). Canada: University of Waterloo.

Butler, R. and Dodds, R. (2022) Overcoming overtourism: A review of failure. *Tourism Review* 77 (1), 35–53.

Choy, D.J. (1992) Life cycle models for Pacific Island destinations. *Journal of Travel Research* 30 (3), 26–31.

Christaller, W. (1963) Some considerations of tourism location in Europe: The peripheral regions – underdeveloped countries – recreation areas. *Regional Science Association Papers* 12, 95–105.

Cohen, E. (1972) Toward a sociology of international tourism. *Social Research* 39 (1), 164–182.

Colin, M.V. and Baum, T. (1994) Comprehensive human resource planning: An essential key to sustainable tourism in island settings. In C.P. Cooper and A. Lockwood (eds)

Progress in Tourism Recreation and Hospitality Management (vol. 5, pp. 259–270). New York: Wiley.

Cooper, C. and Jackson, S. (1989) Destination life cycle: The Isle of Man case study. *Annals of Tourism Research* 16 (3), 377–398.

Denzin, N.K. and Lincoln, Y.S. (eds) (1994) *Handbook of Qualitative Research*. Los Angeles, CA: Sage.

Dodds, R. and Butler, R. (2019) The phenomena of overtourism: A review. *International Journal of Tourism Cities* 5 (4), 519–528.

Douglas, N. (1997) Applying the life cycle model to Melanesia. *Annals of Tourism Research* 24 (1), 1–22.

Foster, D.M. and Murphy, P.E. (1991) Resort cycle revisited: The retirement connection. *Annals of Tourism Research* 18, 553–567.

Fussell, R. (1965) Recreation and the South Carolina coast. *Southeastern Geographer* 5, 48–56.

Getz, D. (1983) Capacity to absorb tourism: Concepts and implications for strategic planning. *Annals of Tourism Research* 10, 239–263.

Getz, D. (1992) Tourism planning and destination life cycle. *Annals of Tourism Research* 19 (4), 752–770.

Gilbert, E.W. (1949) The growth of Brighton. *Geographic Journal* 14 (1), 30–52.

Gormsen, E. (1981) The spatio-temporal development of international tourism, attempt at a centre-periphery model. In *La Consommation d'Espace par le Tourisme et sa Preservation*. Aix-en-Provence: Centre d'etudes touristiques.

Haywood, K.M. (1986) Can the tourist-area life cycle be made operational? *Tourism Management* 7 (3), 154–167.

Hirschey, M. and Pappas, J. (1993) *Managerial Economics*. New York: Dryden Press.

Hocking, A. (1975) *Investigating Economics*. Melbourne: Cheshire Publishing.

Hovinen, G. (1981) A tourist cycle in Lancaster Country, Pennsylvania. *Canadian Geographer* 25, 283–286.

Hovinen, G.R. (2002) Revisiting the destination life-cycle model. *Annals of Tourism Research* 29 (1), 209–230.

Jackson, J. and McConnell, C.R. (1975) *Economics*. Sydney: McGraw-Hill Book Co.

Keller, C.P. (1987) Stages of peripheral tourism development – Canada's Northwest Territories. *Tourism Management* 8, 20–32.

Lundgren, J. (1983) Development patterns and lessons in the Montreal Laurentians. In P.E. Murphy (ed.) *Tourism in Canada: Selected Issues and Options,* Western Geographical Series, Vol. 21 (pp. 183–209). Victoria: University of Victoria.

Manning, E. and Dougherty, D. (1995) Sustainable tourism: Preserving the golden goose. *Cornell Hotel and Restaurant Administration Quarterly* 36 (2), 29–42.

May, V. (1993) Coastal tourism, geomorphology and geological conservation: The example of south-central England. In P.P. Wong (ed.) *Tourism vs Environment: The Case for Coastal Areas* (pp. 3–10). Dordrecht: Kluwer Academic Publishers.

McLeod, M., Dodds, R. and Butler, R. (2022) *Island Tourism Sustainability and Resiliency*. London: Routledge.

Meyer-Arendt, K.J. (1985) The Grand Isle, Louisiana resort cycle. *Annals of Tourism Research* 12 (3), 449–465.

Meyer-Arendt, K.J. (1993) Geomorphic impacts of resort evolution along the Gulf of Mexico Coast: Applicability or resort cycle models. In P.P. Wong (ed.) *Tourism vs Environment: The Case for Coastal Areas* (pp. 125–138). Dordrecht: Kluwer Academic Publishers.

Miossec, J.M. (1977) Un modele de l'espace touristique. *L'espace Geographique* 6 (1), 41–48.

Oppermann, M. (1995) Travel life cycle. *Annals of Tourism Research* 22 (3), 535–552.

Pearce, D. (1989) *Tourism Today: A Geographical Analysis* (1st edn). Auckland: Longman Scientific and Technical.

Pearce, D. (1995) *Tourism Today: A Geographical Analysis* (2nd edn). Auckland: Longman Scientific and Technical.

Plog, S.C. (1974) Why destination areas rise and fall in popularity. *Cornell Hotel and Restaurant Association Quarterly* 14 (4), 55–58.

Russell, R. and Faulkner, B. (1999) Movers and shakers: Chaos makers in tourism development. *Tourism Management* 20 (4), 411–423.

Russell, R. and Faulkner, B. (2004) Entrepreneurship, chaos and the tourism area lifecycle. *Annals of Tourism Research* 31 (3), 556–579.

Smith, R. (1992) Beach resort evolution: Implications for planning. *Annals of Tourism Research* 19, 304–322.

Smith, V.L. (1978) Introduction. In V.L. Smith (ed.) *Hosts and Guests: The Anthropology of Tourism* (pp. 1–14). Philadelphia, PA: University of Pennsylvania Press.

Stansfield, C. (1978) Atlantic City and the resort cycle: Background to the legalization of gambling. *Annals of Tourism Research* 5(2), 238–251.

Strapp, J. (1988) The resort cycle and second homes. *Annals of Tourism Research* 15, 504–516.

Turner, L. and Ash, J. (1975) *The Golden Hordes: International Tourism and The Pleasure Periphery*. New York: St Martin's Press.

Tooman, L. (1997) Application of the life-cycle model in tourism. *Annals of Tourism Research* 24 (1), 214–234.

Wall, G. (1982) Cycles and capacity: Incipient theory or conceptual contradiction. *Tourism Management* 3, 189–193.

Wall, G. (1993) Towards a tourism typology. In G. Nelson, R. Butler and G. Wall (eds) *Tourism and Sustainable Development: Monitoring, Planning, Managing* (pp. 45–57). Waterloo: University of Waterloo.

Weaver, D. (1988) The evolution of a 'plantation' tourism landscape on the Caribbean island of Antigua. *Tijdschrift voor Economische en Sociale Geografie* 79, 319–31.

Weaver, D. (1990) Grand Cayman Island and the resort cycle concept. *Journal of Travel Research* 29 (2), 9–15.

Williams, M. (1993) An expansion of the tourist site cycle model: The case of Minorca (Spain). *Journal of Tourism Studies* 4 (2), 24–32.

Wilkinson, P. (1989) Strategies for tourism island microstates. *Annals of Tourism Research* 16, 153–177.

5 When Iconic Theory Meets Existential Threat: How the TALC Model Informed Engagement With COVID-19

David Weaver and Laura Lawton

Attracting 8844 Google Scholar citations as of 29 December 2022, the TALC's status as an iconic tourism model is incontestable. What appears to underpin its enduring popularity is that it captures the idealised local dynamics that have attended tourism's impressive worldwide growth in the modern era, which exemplifies the broader post-1950 'Great Acceleration' of human systems (Steffen *et al.*, 2015). In the 70-year period prior to 2020, declines in the number of international stayover arrivals, and relatively small ones at that, were reported in only four of those years. Such consistency, not surprisingly, reinforced the myth of tourism's inevitable global growth trajectory and gave rise to a widespread sense of complacency among tourism stakeholders. Yet, in 2020, this myth was shattered after the COVID-19 pandemic induced an 80% collapse in international stayover arrivals compared with 2019 (Sigala, 2020). Tourism, ironically, was not only a high-profile victim of the pandemic, but also a major perpetrator, given the infection-expediting effects of global travel (Nunkoo *et al.*, 2022). Prompted by sustained consumer demand, tourism was on track in 2022 to recover 65% of its pre-pandemic peak of 1.5 billion stayovers (UNWTO, 2022). Prospects for a full recovery, however, were blunted in late 2022 by the surge of COVID-19 infections in China, which compelled many countries to consider or enact new international travel restrictions (Al Jazeera, 2022).

We can say therefore that the COVID-19 pandemic triggered the first 'Great Collapse' (Steffen *et al.*, 2015) of a major human system in the modern era, with highly uncertain prospects for recovery and growth resumption persisting as of late 2022. But more fundamentally, the pandemic has exposed the tourism sector's lack of sustainability and resilience, even though these have been prominent aspirations and topics of attention for tourism practitioners and academics since the 1990s (Weaver, 2020). Unique pandemic-induced opportunities for new frameworks to reset tourism along a more sustainable and resilient path have been noted (Guia, 2021; Jamal & Higham, 2021), yet industry and government still appear far more interested in restoring the tourism status quo ante as quickly as possible (Zhang *et al.*, 2021).

The TALC, of course, is not a new framework, but this could be advantageous since new frameworks are unproven and risky. In the case of Guia (2021), Jamal and Higham (2021) and others, radical shifts in thinking are endorsed that are not likely to be well received by governments and tourism businesses notable for their conservative proclivities and lock-in effects (Gössling & Higham, 2021). By contrast, the TALC model situates comfortably within the dominant liberal paradigm and is not unduly constrained by its own ideological dogma. Moreover, an extensive record of empirical application appears to validate the model's basic dimensions, giving it utility as an 'ideal type' against which real-life situations can be compared (Weaver, 2020).

We can propose additionally therefore that the TALC is *trustworthy* and has capacities to yield new descriptive and explanatory insights that can facilitate greater tourism sustainability and resilience. It is likely that most if not all destinations have experienced pronounced decline-stage dynamics since 2019, mirroring more or less the global collapse of tourism numbers. The TALC, an iconic tourism model, therefore, offers a highly suitable framework for exploring the tourism effects of the COVID-19 pandemic, an existential threat to the sector. The main objectives of this chapter, accordingly, are to identify the extent to which the TALC has been used to inform academic engagement with the COVID-19 pandemic, and to identify patterns of actual and potential reticulation within the attendant literature.

Methods

Database compilation

To address the two research objectives, the authors created and analysed a database of published academic papers from the COVID-19 era that cited Butler's seminal 1980 paper. We define the 'COVID-19 era' as 2021 or later to consider publication lag effects. Publication in 2021 or subsequently indicates that the editors, reviewers and authors would have been aware of the pandemic and its unfolding devastation of global tourism, at least during the review process. Relevant content, accordingly, could have been accommodated within the manuscript at editor or reviewer insistence, or author initiative. Indeed, editors of some journals (for example, *Journal of Travel Research*) had by then revised their submission guidelines to encourage or require explicit recognition of the pandemic. The second selection criterion was to engage with high-prestige research outlets published in English. Accordingly, the search was confined to peer-reviewed journals in tourism and cognate fields (e.g. hospitality, events) rated at A* or A under the most recent version (2019) of the Australian Business Deans Council Journal Quality List (ABDC, 2022). The A* designation accounts for roughly the top 5% of journals in the field as peer evaluated, while the A designation is assigned, approximately, to the next 15% of journals. Together, the two designations therefore account for the top quintile of tourism journals with regard to peer-perceived outlet prestige.

Google Scholar was selected as the search engine, in part because it is comprehensive, with access to over 389 million records in 2018 (Gusenbauer, 2019). Another consideration is its convenience, with each record accompanied by a link which takes the researcher to all available records that cite the target publication. Our search for the citations of 'Butler (1980)' was done from 1 December to 29 December 2022. To facilitate the search, we instructed Google Scholar to display for further inspection only those records published in 2021 or later. When a qualifying publication was encountered, it was downloaded either as an open-access file or otherwise through the Queensland University of Technology online library. Each article, as a pdf file, was then visually inspected to ensure that Butler (1980) was included in the reference list and actually cited at least once within the text. This process yielded our final database of 87 qualifying articles (Table 5.1).

Table 5.1 Number of qualifying articles by journal

Title	ABDC rating	No. of articles
Current Issues in Tourism	A	12
Journal of Sustainable Tourism	A*	11
Journal of Travel Research	A*	8
International Journal of Tourism Research	A	7
Annals of Tourism Research	A*	6
Journal of Hospitality and Tourism Management	A	6
Tourism Economics	A	6
Tourism Recreation Research	A	6
Tourism Management	A*	5
Tourism Management Perspectives	A	5
Journal of Hospitality and Tourism Research	A	4
Tourism Geographies	A	4
International Journal of Contemporary Hospitality Management	A	2
Journal of Travel and Tourism Marketing	A	2
Asia Pacific Journal of Tourism Research	A	1
Journal of Destination Marketing and Management	A	1
Tourism Analysis	A	1

Article classification and analysis

Each of the 87 articles was then cross-classified against its relationship to the TALC and the COVID-19 pandemic. For the former, Google Scholar's 'find' function for individual pdf files was used to locate each 'Butler (1980)' citation as well as any additional references to the 'TALC' or 'life cycle'. For each such citation, sufficient surrounding text was examined to establish context so that the article as a whole could be classified according to the schemata of Wang *et al.* (2016). Based on an assessment of historical Butler (1980) references, these schemata distinguished between citations that are *knowledge-impeding, knowledge-facilitating* and *knowledge-developing*. Knowledge-impeding citations contain content that is not in the original paper (miscitation) or that treats speculation as assertion (e.g. stating as fact that destinations pass through a predictable sequence of stages). Knowledge-facilitating citations variably acknowledge the TALC's iconic status, treat that content as proposed knowledge (ascription) rather than fact, assess the model, and/or advocate for further evaluation. Finally, knowledge-developing citations, the highest form of engagement, empirically apply, test and/or, based on the presented evidence, alter or extend the model. In situations where multiple citations in an individual article attracted different designations, the overall article was classified according to the highest.

A parallel classification schema was then developed based on the relationship between each article and the COVID-19 pandemic. If the terms 'COVID-19' or 'pandemic' did not appear after a 'find' search of the entire paper, then that article was classified as 'COVID-absent' after further visual inspection to confirm the lack of any reference to the pandemic. If either term was present but the topic was engaged only tangentially, the article was classified as 'COVID-incidental'. Finally, a 'COVID-focal' designation was applied to papers where the research was centred on the pandemic and its effects or after-effects. In empirical papers, this was often manifested in surveys or interviews which included COVID-specific questions. Taken together, the two classification schemes allowed the assignment of each article to one of nine cells within a 3×3 matrix of the three TALC classifications along the x-axis and the three COVID-19 classifications along the y-axis. The classifications were conducted independently by the two authors and then compared. Only six instances of disagreement were encountered and these were all successfully negotiated.

The overall patterns yielded by this final matrix informed the analysis and discussion. 'Primary' or 'core' papers are those that occupy the TALC knowledge-developing, COVID-focal cell, since they represent the highest category of engagement for both topics (see Table 5.2). 'Secondary' papers include those in the TALC knowledge-facilitating, COVID-focal cells, and TALC knowledge-impeding, COVID-focal cells, which display the highest level of engagement with the pandemic but more tangential engagement with the TALC. Also included as secondary papers are those in the TALC knowledge-developing, COVID-incidental cells, and TALC knowledge-developing, COVID-absent cells, which have the opposite trait of high engagement with the TALC but lower or non-engagement with the pandemic. Both sets of secondary papers can facilitate analysis of how the TALC can better inform COVID-focal research, as per our second research objective. To avoid confusion and over-complexity, only papers that contribute to pattern development are used to identify reticulations in this literature.

Results

Overall patterns

COVID-19 was not as much of a topical focus as the authors assumed it would be. Notwithstanding the pandemic's devastating impact on the tourism sector, only 11 COVID-focal papers were identified, accounting for 12.6% of the 87 publications (Table 5.2). COVID-19 is absent altogether in 44 of the papers (50.6%). The remaining 32 COVID-incidental papers (36.8%) mostly confine mention of the pandemic to introductory or concluding text. Here, it is variably framed as a central element of the contemporary research context (e.g. Gazoni & da Silva, 2021; McKercher & Wong, 2021), an opportunity for reform (e.g. Moayerian et al., 2022) or a factor that warrants post-pandemic follow-up investigation (e.g. Szromek et al., 2022). The pandemic in several cases is cited as a research limitation because of the constraints it imposed on data collection, such as substituting telephone interviews for face-to-face encounters (e.g. Rastegar et al., 2022).

As for the level of engagement with the TALC, 24 papers (27.6%) are knowledge-developing while 54 (62.1%) are knowledge-facilitating and nine (10.3%) are knowledge-impeding. Considering the relatively small sample size, these results are not inconsistent with Wang et al. (2016), which respectively assigned 21.9%, 69.8% and 8.3% of 676 individual citations (rather than entire articles) to these three categories.

Table 5.2 Article quantity by COVID-19/TALC engagement mode

	TALC knowledge-impeding (KI)	TALC knowledge-facilitating (KF)	TALC knowledge-developing (KD)
COVID-focal (CF)	1	8	2
COVID-incidental (CI)	3	22	7
COVID-absent (CA)	5	24	15

Core papers   Secondary papers

COVID-focal and TALC knowledge-developing discourse

The two papers that are both TALC knowledge-developing and COVID-focal are described here in detail. Albaladejo *et al.* (2022) contend that the TALC is contextually limited because it describes individual destinations in isolation. Accordingly, in this 'context extension' paper, the model is instead framed within broader geographical and economic contexts of destination competition and interdependency, industry organisation and tourist market structures. Through time, these factors induce tourists to agglomerate or disperse spatially, with agglomeration economies of scale (as per the TALC) eventually creating 'overtourism' effects of inflation, congestion and dissatisfaction that divert tourists to less crowded (dispersed) locations. Factors that induce visitation contraction in one location, in essence, contribute fundamentally to the progression of the tourism development cycle in competing destinations or regions. For empirical evidence, the authors compared the relative flow of international tourists in three sets of competing destinations (Catalonia versus Balearic Islands, Greece versus Turkey, Catalonia versus Madrid). The time frame was prior to and following the Russian invasion of Ukraine, and prior to (2020) and following (2021) the lifting of major restrictions on international travel during the COVID-19 pandemic. The authors found strong support for their 'geography-based dynamic tourism model', which they concluded corroborates but also 'enriches' the TALC by engaging the dynamics of this broader economic and geographical context.

Butler (2022) speculates on the impact of the COVID-19 pandemic on destinations in different stages of the TALC, the essential validity of which is therefore assumed. For simplicity, the six original TALC stages are compressed into early, mid- and late cycles. Butler argues that, all else being equal, tourism is likely to recover quickly to pre-pandemic levels in early-stage destinations since disruptions occur from an already low baseline of visitor numbers and system articulation. In contrast, mid-cycle destinations will experience a longer recovery period due to interruptions and adjustments to multiple elements of established tourism systems. These adjustments include the repatriation of foreign tourism workers and repositioned cruise ships. The worst-case scenario is demonstrated by late-cycle destinations, which would have already been experiencing image and capacity problems prior to the pandemic. Thus, a major post-pandemic challenge is rejuvenating attractions and facilities that were already precarious before COVID-19. This precarity leads to the possibility of tourism abandonment or, more optimistically, recovery to a lower-level equilibrium based on smaller levels of reinvestment. Monitoring how variable local responses to the pandemic will affect these generalised recovery patterns is cited as a worthwhile area of research extension.

COVID-focal and TALC knowledge-facilitating/impeding discourse

Nine papers have a strong focus on COVID-19 but only facilitate (or in one case impede) engagement with the TALC. Thematically, six of the papers inform our reticulation discussion in the next section, as they are dually focused on COVID-19 and the phenomenon of overtourism, which reveals concurrent engagement with the local temporal juxta-position of high and low extremes of tourism intensity. Among these six papers, Kirilenko et al. (2021) propose a method to detect early signs of overtourism in several Florida resort destination hotspots based on pre- and post-pandemic resident perceptions. Visitors surveyed during the pandemic at several Mediterranean hotspots revealed that destination loyalty is significantly affected by their perceptions of how effectively the destination was perceived to adapt to pandemic-induced changes in intensity (Papadopoulou et al., 2022). On the Mediterranean resort island of Santorini, Constantoglou and Thomai (2021) found widespread agreement among residents that COVID-19 provided a chance for a reset of tourism along a more sustainable and just trajectory. This same sentiment is emphasised by Kirilenko et al. (2021), is the central argument of a conceptual paper by Milano and Koens (2022) and is strongly espoused in two empirical papers, by Liberatore et al. (2022) and Szromek et al. (2021), focused on historical city centres in Europe (Florence and Krakow). The Florence focus was on developing indicators to measure carrying capacity to prevent possible decline in a post-COVID-19 future, while surveyed sector stakeholders in Krakow supported post-pandemic tourism dispersal, innovative new products, restrictions on short-term rentals and valuing heritage conservation over profits.

COVID-incidental/absent and TALC knowledge-developing discourse

Twenty-two papers are TALC knowledge-developing but engage either incidentally with COVID-19 or not at all. Not all of these papers provide intuitively useful information for engaging further with the pandemic, in most cases because they investigate pandemic-tangential topics such as online restaurant ratings, sensory perceptions of tourist experiences and mega-event-induced transformation of urban spaces. All the remaining papers are empirical except for one conceptual contribution. Thematically, 12 empirical articles present findings that can assist the post-pandemic recovery of tourism from various administrative, product, resident, market and structural perspectives. Citation and brief descriptions of these 12 additional selected secondary papers are provided in the next section, where the findings from the core and secondary papers are structured and discussed.

TALC/COVID-19 knowledge reticulation

The six secondary papers that are COVID-focal and TALC knowledge-facilitating or -impeding and focus on overtourism share a common narrative that articulates readily into the 'later TALC cycle' scenario of Butler (2022) (see above), which is the most serious scenario of pandemic-induced destination collapse. Thus, as depicted in Figure 5.1 (upper half), these six papers all implicate destination 'hotspots', either urban tourist-historic or coastal resort, where salient 'overtourism' (essentially the *mature* stage following the breaching of local carrying capacities) has dramatically given way to undertourism because of COVID-19. Only two papers (Liberatore *et al.*, 2022; Milano & Koens, 2022) actually use the term 'undertourism', but all share the implied sentiment that some kind of restoration or recovery (i.e. rejuvenation) toward pre-pandemic visitation levels is essential given the longstanding dependence of these locations on tourism-based revenues and employment. This sentiment, however, is not without qualification. All these papers use an allied rhetoric of 'opportunity', 'reset', 'slow tourism' and/or 'just tourism' to advocate for a particular mode of rejuvenation that reflects the deliberate alternative tourism typically displayed in the exploration and involvement stages of the TALC (Weaver, 2000). Associated characteristics espoused within these six papers include more community empowerment, a refocus on authentic local products, reduced seasonality, economic diversification, and migration toward 'high value', longer-stay tourists. This apparent disconnect between the desire for high post-pandemic visitation levels and alternative tourism values can be interpreted as contradictory, but it also suggests implicit support for enlightened mass tourism, a concept which seeks to unite the best characteristics of mass and alternative tourism (Weaver, 2014).

The second set of 12 secondary papers, because they are TALC knowledge-developing but also COVID-incidental or absent, engage with a broader array of TALC stages (see Figure 5.1, lower half). Most of these contributions contain empirically derived knowledge that has potential to positively inform the tourism sector's response to the pandemic. Among those focused on *administrative* knowledge, three papers are specific to China. Yi *et al.* (2021) demonstrate the changing capacities of village tourism committees as the TALC progresses, such that COVID-19 responses that work in early-stage destinations may not resonate in late-stage village destinations. As revealed by Zhang *et al.* (2022), early-TALC forest farms were developing stronger regional interconnections and identities due to tourism. Implications for COVID-19 response are better prospects for integrated regional cooperation, but also more opportunities for pandemic spread. In mature rural destinations, Chen *et al.* (2022) identified the formation of intergenerational solidarity to achieve sustainable outcomes, although this was predicated on meeting the specific needs

Butler (2022) framework (adapted)

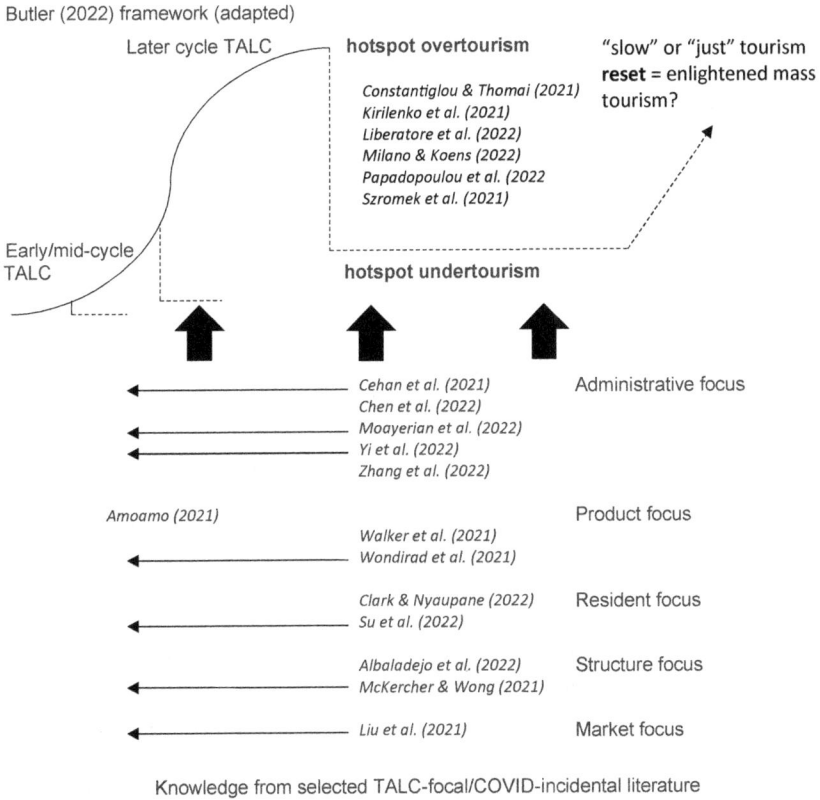

Figure 5.1 TALC and COVID-19 literature: Knowledge reticulation

of each generation. This common focus on rural Chinese destinations is significant in light of policy changes in January 2023, which lifted most COVID-19 restrictions and allowed urban residents to visit their families in vulnerable rural locations during the Lunar New Year holidays.

Administrative capacity is also salient in the community cultural development organisation established in a small one-industry Appalachian town, which has positioned its residents to respond more effectively to external challenges, based on a common identity and shared goals among residents (Moayerian *et al.*, 2022). Like Yi *et al.* (2021), Cehan *et al.* (2021) identified different collaboration networks in early- and mature-stage Romanian towns, with the latter therefore being better positioned to respond to the pandemic because of more reticulated internal organisational networks. Among the *product*-focused papers are reminders how external shocks such as Brexit can stimulate innovation, for example a recommended dark-sky sanctuary for early-TALC Pitcairn Islands (Amoamo, 2021). For the mature destination of Antigua, 'slow tourism'-type products and experiences are advocated by Walker *et al.* (2021) to prevent future decline. Similarly, authentic local culinary experiences are advocated by Wondirad *et al.* (2021) as the primary basis for rejuvenating tourism in smaller Ethiopian cities at various TALC stages.

The two *resident*-focused knowledge papers propose elaborations to the TALC based on deeper understandings of nuance in the surrounding spatial dynamics. Thus, in a rural region of Montana, peripheral residents whose communities were just beginning the cycle tended to be sceptical of tourism rather than euphoric as expected, based on their observations of negative tourism effects in the more tourism-established core of the region (Clark & Nyaupane, 2022). Experiment-based research by Su *et al.* (2022) found that perceived resident quality of life peaks in the growth stage for those residing in the destination core and during maturity for those in the periphery. Nuance is also evident in the *structural* contribution of McKercher and Wong (2021), who contend that destinations experience multiple life cycles (see also McKercher & Wong's Chapter 22 in the present volume). Parallel findings of life cycle interdependency among destinations align this paper with Albaladejo *et al.* (2022) (see above), who also emphasise the idea of interdependency and who are therefore also included as a structural contribution in Figure 5.1. The one *market*-related paper, by Liu *et al.* (2021), found different country-based 'visitation' life cycles to Australia among international stayovers. A common lesson for COVID-19 response from the above nuance-based resident, structural and market knowledge papers is the complexity and interdependence of destinations and their markets, so that 'one size fits all' pandemic response strategies are inadvisable.

Conclusion

Our analysis of high tier pandemic-era papers that cite the classic 1980 TALC model reveals some useful insights into the TALC/COVID-19 research interface. First, very few papers as of late 2022 had explicitly adopted this dual lens. However, the two which do focus on both the iconic original model and the existential threat of COVID offer valuable frameworks around which the secondary papers can be organised. The pandemic-focused secondary papers yield a common emphasis on the overtourism/undertourism juxtaposition, and call for a reset that would in effect lead to enlightened mass tourism because of their advocacy for alternative tourism values as well as high levels of visitation. The TALC-focused secondary papers provide valuable knowledge from administrative, product, resident, structural and market perspectives that can inform engagement with the pandemic. Further reticulation of the TALC and COVID-19 themes in future tourism research is recommended because of the constructive synergies that do or can result from such a dual perspective.

References

ABDC (Australian Business Deans Council) (2022) ABDC Journal Quality List. https://abdc.edu.au/research/abdc-journal-quality-list/.

Al Jazeera (2022) As COVID-hit China opens up to travel, others secure their doors, 27 December. https://www.aljazeera.com/news/2022/12/27/japan-to-require-covid-tests-for-all-visitors-from-china.

Albaladejo, I., Arnaldos, F. and Martínez-García, M. (2022) Tourism distribution at competing destinations: Mobility changes and relocation. *Tourism Economics*. https://doi.org/10.1177/1354816622118991.

Amoamo, M. (2021) Brexit – threat or opportunity? Resilience and tourism in Britain's island territories. *Tourism Geographies* 23, 501–526. https://doi.org/10.1080/1461668 8.2019.1665093.

Butler, R. (2022) COVID-19 and its potential impact on stages of tourist destination development. *Current Issues in Tourism* 25, 1682–1695. https://doi.org/10.1080/13683500.2 021.1990223.

Butler, R. (1980) The concept of a tourist area cycle of evolution and implications for management of resources. *Canadian Geographer* 24 (1), 5–12.

Cehan, A., Eva, M. and Iatu, C. (2021) A multilayer network approach to tourism collaboration. *Journal of Hospitality and Tourism Management* 46, 316–326. https://doi.org/10.1016/j.jhtm.2021.01.006.

Chen, Z., Ryan, C. and Zhang, Y. (2022) Cross-generational analysis of residential place attachment to a Chinese rural destination. *Journal of Sustainable Tourism* 30, 787–806. https://doi.org/10.1080/09669582.2021.1890095.

Clark, C. and Nyaupane, G (2022) Connecting landscape-scale ecological restoration and tourism: Stakeholder perspectives in the great plains of North America. *Journal of Sustainable Tourism* 30, 2595–2613. https://doi.org/10.1080/09669582.2020.1801698.

Constantoglou, M. and Thomai, K. (2021) How much tourism is too much? Stakeholder's perceptions on overtourism, sustainable destination management during the pandemic of COVID-19 era in Santorini Island Greece. *Journal of Tourism and Hospitality Management* 9, 288–313. https://doi.org/10.17265/2328-2169/2021.05.004.

Gazoni, J. and da Silva, E. (2021) System dynamics framework for tourism development management. *Current Issues in Tourism* 25 (15), 2457–247822. https://doi.org/10.1080 /13683500.2021.1970117.

Gössling, S. and Higham, J. (2021) The low-carbon imperative: Destination management under urgent climate change. *Journal of Travel Research* 60, 1167–1179.

Guia, J. (2021) Conceptualizing justice tourism and the promise of posthumanism. *Journal of Sustainable Tourism*, 29. https://doi.org/10.1080/09669582.2020.1771347.

Gusenbauer, M. (2019) Google Scholar to overshadow them all? Comparing the sizes of 12 academic search engines and bibliographic databases. *Scientometrics* 118, 177–214.

Jamal, T. and Higham, J. (2021) Justice and ethics: Towards a new platform for tourism and sustainability. *Journal of Sustainable Tourism* 29, 143–157.

Kirilenko, A., Ma, S., Stepchenkova, S., Su, L. and Waddell, T. (2021) Detecting early signs of overtourism: Bringing together indicators of tourism development with data fusion. *Journal of Travel Research*. https://doi.org/10.1177/0047287521064635.

Liberatore, G., Biagioni, P., Ciappei, C. and Francini, C. (2022) Dealing with uncertainty, from overtourism to overcapacity: A decision support model for art cities. The case of UNESCO WHCC of Florence. *Current Issues in Tourism*. https://doi.org/10.1080/136 83500.2022.2046712.

Liu, Y., Hsiao, A. and Ma, E. (2021) Segmenting tourism markets based on demand growth patterns: A longitudinal profile analysis approach. *Journal of Hospitality and Tourism Research* 45, 967–997. https://doi.org/10.1177/1096348020962564.

McKercher, B. and Wong, I. (2021) Do destinations have multiple lifecycles? *Tourism Management* 83, 104232. https://doi.org/10.1016/j.tourman.2020.104232.

Milano, C. and Koens, K. (2022) The paradox of tourism extremes. Excesses and restraints in times of COVID-19. *Current Issues in Tourism* 25, 219–231. https://doi.org/10.108 0/13683500.2021.1908967.

Moayerian, N., McGehee, N. and Stephenson, M. (2022) Community cultural development: Exploring the connections between collective art making, capacity building and sustainable community-based tourism. *Annals of Tourism Research* 93, 103355. https://doi.org/10.1016/j.annals.2022.103355

Nunkoo, R., Daronkola, H. and Gholipour, H. (2022) Does domestic tourism influence COVID-19 cases and deaths? *Current Issues in Tourism* 25, 338–351.

Papadopoulou, N., Ribeiro, M. and Prayag, G. (2022) Psychological determinants of tourist satisfaction and destination loyalty: The influence of perceived overcrowding and overtourism. *Journal of Travel Research*. https://doi.org/10.1177/00472875221089049.

Papatheodorou, A. (2021) A review of research into air transport and tourism: Launching the *Annals of Tourism Research* curated collection on air transport and tourism. *Annals of Tourism Research* 87. https://doi.org/10.1016/j.annals.2021.103151.

Rastegar, R., Breakey, N., Driml, S. and Ruhanen, L. (2022) Does tourism development shift residents' attitudes to the environment and protected area management? *Tourism Recreation Research*. https://doi.org/10.1080/02508281.2022.2106100.

Sigala, M. (2020) Tourism and COVID-19: Impacts and implications for advancing and resetting industry and research. *Journal of Business Research* 117, 312–321.

Steffen, W., Broadgate, W., Deutsch, L., Gaffney, O. and Ludwig, C. (2015) *The Trajectory of the Anthropocene: The Great Acceleration*. Canberra: ANU Open Research.

Su, L., Yang, X. and Swanson, S. (2022) The impact of spatial-temporal variation on tourist destination resident quality of life. *Tourism Management* 93. https://doi.org/10.1016/j.tourman.2022.104572.

Szromek, A., Kruczek, Z. and Walas, B. (2021) Stakeholders' attitudes towards tools for sustainable tourism in historical cities. *Tourism Recreation Research*. https://doi.org/1 0.1080/02508281.2021.1931774.

Szromek, A., Puciato, D., Markiewicz-Patkowska, J. and Colmekcioglu, N. (2022) Health tourism enterprises and adaptation for sustainable development. *International Journal of Contemporary Hospitality Management*. https://doi.org/10.1108/IJCHM-01-2022-0060.

UNWTO (2022) Tourism recovery accelerates to reach 65% of pre-pandemic levels, 23 November. https://www.unwto.org/taxonomy/term/347#:~:text=International%20 tourism%20is%20on%20track,the%20same%20period%20in%202021.

Walker, T.B., Lee, T.J. and Li, X. (2021) Sustainable development for small island tourism: Developing slow tourism in the Caribbean. *Journal of Travel and Tourism Marketing* 38 (1), 1–15.

Wang, X., Weaver, D., Li, X. and Zhang, Y. (2016) In Butler (1980) we trust? Typology of citer motivations. *Annals of Tourism Research* 61, 216–218.

Weaver, D. (2000) A broad context model of destination development scenarios. *Tourism Management* 21, 217–224. http://dx.doi.org/10.1016/S0261-5177(99)00054-0.

Weaver, D. (2014) Asymmetrical dialectics of sustainable tourism: Toward enlightened mass tourism. *Journal of Travel Research* 53, 131–140. http://dx.doi.org/10.1177/0047287513491335.

Weaver, D. (2020) *Advanced Introduction to Sustainable Tourism*. Cheltenham: Edward Elgar.

Wondirad, A., Kebete, Y. and Li, Y. (2021) Culinary tourism as a driver of regional economic development and socio-cultural revitalization: Evidence from Amhara National Regional State, Ethiopia. *Journal of Destination Marketing and Management* 19. https://doi.org/10/1016/j.jdmm.2020.100482.

Yi, J., Ryan, C. and Wang, D. (2021) China's village tourism committees: A social network analysis. *Journal of Travel Research* 60, 117–132. https://doi.org/10.1177/0047287519892324.

Zhang, C.Y., Knight, D., Li, Y.J., Zhou, Y., Zhou, M. and Zi, M.G. (2022) Rural tourism and evolving identities of Chinese communities in forested areas. *Journal of Sustainable Tourism*. https://doi.org/10.1080//09669582.2022.2155829.
Zhang, H.Y., Song, H.Y., Wen, L. and Liu, C. (2021) Forecasting tourism recovery amid COVID-19. *Annals of Tourism Research* 87, 103149. https://doi.org/10.1080/0955958 2.2022.2155829.

6 A Qualitative and Quantitative Application of the TALC Model to Vietnam Before the COVID-19 Pandemic

Ngoc Trang Vu

The majority of TALC studies have utilised visitor numbers to interpret the development trajectory of the destination analysed. Other attempts have used alternative variables such as tourist segments, marketing and residents' involvement or attitudes towards tourists and tourism development in order to operationalise or modify the model. This chapter discusses a study (Vu, 2021) in the context of Vietnam which examined other variables (or TALC components) quantitatively and qualitatively apart from international tourist volumes. The objective was to test Butler's (1980) TALC model and theory and existing endeavours to operationalise it, utilising the case of Vietnam's inbound tourism. Given the patchy and inconsistent tourism data in the 1990s (Mok & Lam, 1997) and the availability of statistics and national reports on the sector's performance hitherto, the quantitative research scope was up to the onset of the COVID-19 pandemic, and the qualitative part focused on 2015 to mid-2021. (There are now more data available on Vietnam's tourism from 2015, both on the United Nations' and the Vietnamese government's relevant websites.)

The main research question of this study was: To what extent did the TALC model apply to Vietnam's inbound tourism during the period 2015 to mid-2021? In addition, secondary questions were: Where was Vietnam on the TALC curve? And is it possible to forecast its future position(s)?

In virtue of those objectives, the study applied the case study research method, using both quantitative and qualitative analysis, since 'each form of data is useful for […] verification […] of theory' (Glaser & Strauss, 2006: 17–18). First, to establish the TALC curve, Vu carried out desk research utilising data mainly from the United Nations' specialised agencies, such as UNWTO and UNICEF, and the Vietnamese government organisations, including the General Statistics Office of Vietnam (GSOV), Ministry of Culture, Sport and Tourism (MCST), Ministry of

Health of Vietnam (MHV), Vietnam National Administration of Tourism (VNAT) and Tourism Information Technology Center (TITC). Second, she conducted five in-depth interviews with tourism experts and residents in Vietnam to scrutinise other TALC characteristics further. The reason behind the small size of the empirical research sample was the travel restrictions due to COVID-19, which hindered Vu from finding more participants, along with the data saturation she observed after the fifth interview (Vu, 2021: 67–70). While the data were not sufficient to draw any definitive conclusion about the TALC model, some of the main influences were found to be Vietnam's heterogeneity, with over 60 sub-destinations growing at different speeds and the diversity of its international tourist segments, which did not meet the description of any specific TALC stage.

Attempts to Operationalise the TALC

Haywood (1995) was one of the pioneers in the academic endeavour to operationalise the TALC, particularly with his suggestion of using more rigid criteria and a standard deviation to identify different stages and establish the TALC curve. His concerns included: unit of analysis (what is a tourist area?); relevant markets; TALC's pattern and stages, that is, Butler's (1980) bell-shaped curve, *inter alia*; identification of the transition between stages in the model based on, for example, the total annual tourist influx; the unit of measurement (e.g. pure arrivals or various variables to determine carrying capacity, length of stay, tourist dispersion within and throughout the destination, tourist characteristics and seasonality); and relevant time unit (e.g. per year).

It is noteworthy that defining the unit of analysis, or demarcating a tourist area precisely, is usually challenging (Haywood, 2006: 63). Indeed, destinations are 'places with some form of actual or perceived boundary, such as the physical boundary of an island, political boundaries, or even market-created boundaries' (Kotler *et al.*, 2017: 510). For instance, Central America is commonly used as a 'destination' for package tours, even though itineraries often cover only two or three countries (e.g. Costa Rica, Guatemala and Panama), while excluding the others because of political volatility or poor infrastructure (Kotler *et al.*, 2017: 510).

Like the competitive forces that Porter (1979) suggested shape strategies, Haywood (1995: 34) also highlighted some collective features crucial to the success of a tourist area and, particularly, its growth. These impetuses are competition among existing destinations, new entrants to the industry, alternative products/services for the tourism/travel experience, environmentalists taking positions against the industry in question and its development, the bargaining power of various actors (namely, transportation enterprises, tour operators, travel agencies and other suppliers), tourists' perceptions, needs, wants, expectations, price sensitivity, and related public policies and forces (Haywood, 1995: 34–36).

In addition to Haywood's (1995) recommendations, Johnston (2001: 23) suggested a mechanism analysis to identify and justify the critical moments and blurry transitions that distinguish a new stage from the previous one. He categorised events into three groups: additions, alterations and cessations. The first group refers to the events that catalyse tourism growth, such as a new airport, and usually occur at the start of the *development stage*. The second involves replacing nationally owned properties with foreign-owned properties; the last indicates a replacement feature without connection with tourism. Johnston (2001: 16–17) believed the two latter categories occur more often in the later stages.

Johnston applied this *ex post facto* approach to examine Kona (Hawaii) and was able to determine the moment of transition between different stages by defining the 'mechanism of change initiating stage/phase, critical event or blurry transition [...], plus critical junctures' (Johnston, 2006: 202–203). However, it is worth questioning if it is possible to list all significant events, especially when the impacts of some incidents may be invisible. Likewise, how could researchers avoid overlooking some critical facts if the model is applied at a larger scale? Moreover, could ordinary yet frequent events, such as the daily use of the internet, be of any significance to a tourist area's development, regardless of its size?

Coelho and Butler (2012) attempted to comprehensively operationalise the theory and model in light of the 'tourism development index'. In particular, they quantified almost all the significant variables, mathematically positioning the destination in its life cycle. Nevertheless, such a quantitative approach can hardly cover conceptual values, such as tourists' needs, wants and perceptions, or management effectiveness. Furthermore, the proposed list is incomplete as it overlooks marketing and advertising. Despite those weaknesses, Coelho and Butler (2012: 15–16) contributed significantly to the metric of the TALC's *in situ* characteristics (see Table 6.1).

Besides the values and approaches mentioned above, Table 6.1 synthesises numerous supplements from a myriad of TALC applications (i.e. other measurement units and their alternatives). In practice, which measurement units should be used is case-specific, and it is pivotal to emphasise that this list might not be exhaustive because of the dynamics which operate in tourism. Most case studies using the TALC as their conceptual framework have applied a chronological approach to describe and analyse changes in their chosen tourist area relative to the indicators prescribed in Butler's (1980) theory after defining their unit of research (e.g. Chapman & Light, 2016; Collins-Kreiner, 2016; Johnston, 2006). The majority merely utilised available quantitative data to establish the TALC curve.

Nonetheless, whether they conducted quantitative or qualitative research has depended very much on their target indicators. For instance, due to the lack of traditional TALC visitation statistics, Marois and

Hinch (2006) had to collect data through informal semi-structured interviews and participant observation. Likewise, Martin (2006) conducted a questionnaire-based survey to study business leaders', permanent homeowners' and government officers' perceptions of tourism development. In contrast, Johnson and Snepenger (2006) pursued a quantitative approach to analyse residents' 'attitude towards overall benefits and costs of tourism to Silver Valley, Idaho' (Johnson & Snepenger, 2006: 231).

Based on Table 6.1, the case study in this chapter examines Vietnam as the analysis unit, using international visitor data to constitute the TALC curve and discussing visitor segments, sub-destinations, changes in locals' attitudes to tourists and tourism development, and promotion efforts to answer the research question. The initial research (Vu, 2021) examined additional elements to assess or navigate the tourist area's development in the TALC model. However, all findings led to the same conclusion, and thus it was decided to focus on the specific elements mentioned here.

Previous Applications of Butler's TALC to Vietnam

It is noteworthy that previous applications of Butler's TALC theory to Vietnam's tourism neither question its applicability nor examine variables other than visitor data. In particular, Vu and Chijioke (2019) briefly referred to the model as a theoretical basis when searching for the local perception of sustainable tourism development on Phu Quoc Island (a destination in south Vietnam). Bojanic (2005) examined the relationship between the TALC and Singapore's and Vietnam's recovery after the SARS crisis. Mainly based on international arrival numbers, he deduced that while Singapore had already reached the consolidation/stagnation stage, Vietnam was in the involvement phase. However, it is debatable if visitors to the two countries would share the same patterns concerning their consumption behaviours, among other issues; thus, it remains questionable if Bojanic's conclusion is valid. Vu's (2021) investigation of various features of Vietnam's international tourism development stage between 2015 and mid-2021 also sheds light on the validity of previous application efforts.

Vietnam's International Tourism

Vietnam's economy nearly collapsed because of the Vietnam War. International visitors rarely travelled to Vietnam on vacation or business during the 1970s and early 1980s. Then, in 1986, the country launched an economic reform (also known as Đổi mới) to eliminate restrictions on the private sector's investment, initiate foreign investment law, depreciate the official exchange rate and reorganise the banking system (Mok & Lam, 1997: 85–86; Suntikul et al., 2008: 67–80). Afterwards, there was an increase in the number of foreigners visiting Vietnam; international tourism began flourishing in the early 1990s (Bojanic, 2005; Lloyd, 2003:

Table 6.1 Measurements/assessments of Butler's (1980) TALC stages

TALC stage feature/ change trigger	Measurement/assessment
Research unit	Geographically defined regions (Adamiak, 2020; Bao & Zhang, 2006; Boyd, 2006; Camprubí et al., 2009; Corak, 2006; Faulkner & Tideswell, 2006; Haywood, 1995: 31–2; Hazmi et al., 2012; Hovinen, 2006; Johnston, 2001: 11; Johnston, 2006; Marois & Hinch, 2006; Meng et al., 2011; O'Hare & Barrett, 1997; Russo, 2006) Tourism organisation (Haywood, 2006: 67) Tourism products (Collins-Kreiner, 2016; Haywood, 1995: 31–32; Johnston, 2001: 9; Lundgren, 2006) Tourist facilities (such as resorts) (Butler, 1980; Haywood, 1995: 31–32; Hazmi et al., 2012; Johnston, 2001: 11; Malcolm-Davies, 2006; Weaver, 2006)
Tourists/market segments	Bed nights (Lagiewski's (2006) synthesis) Characteristics of tourists, tourist dispersion within and throughout the destination (Haywood, 1995: 33; Hovinen, 2006: 77) Lengths of stay as alternatives (Lagiewski's (2006) synthesis) Market type, distribution method, or market segment (Haywood, 1995: 32) Ticket counts (Bao & Zhang, 2006: 114–115) Tourists' needs, wants, expectations, perceptions and price sensitivity (Haywood, 1995: 36) Visitor arrivals or visitor numbers (both vacationers and excursionists) (Bao & Zhang, 2006: 112–113; Boyd, 2006: 126–127; Dong et al., 2003; Faulkner & Tideswell, 2006; Haywood, 1995: 33; Lagiewski's (2006) synthesis; O'Hare & Barrett, 1997; Russo, 2006 (who also used heritage cities): 143)
Internal characteristics of tourist areas:	
Tourist attractions	Beaches (Johnston, 2001: 11; Lagiewski's (2006) synthesis) Cities (Lagiewski's (2006) synthesis) Islands (Lagiewski's (2006) synthesis; Johnston, 2006) National parks (Boyd, 2006) Plantations (Weaver, 2006) Protected areas (Coelho & Butler, 2012: 15; Lagiewski's (2006) synthesis) Ski mountains (Johnston, 2001: 11; Lagiewski's (2006) synthesis) Cultural resources, such as: Ethnic group (Johnston, 2001: 11) Heritage (Coelho & Butler, 2012: 15; Lagiewski's (2006) synthesis; Malcolm-Davies, 2006; Russo, 2006)
Tourism activities	For example: Agrotourism (Dritsaki, 2009) Cross-country skiing (Lundgren, 2006) (Lundgren also used mountain biking and snowboarding as his unit of analysis) Cultural heritage tourism (Chapman & Light, 2016; Meng et al., 2011) Ethnic tourism (Dong et al., 2003) Mountain biking (Lundgren, 2006) Pilgrimage tourism (Collins-Kreiner, 2016) Residential tourism (Aledo & Mazón, 2004) Snowboarding (Lundgren, 2006) Winter health tourism and mass summer holiday (Corak, 2006)

TALC stage feature/ change trigger	Measurement/assessment
Infrastructure	Houses with water, electricity, and sanitation (Coelho & Butler, 2012: 15–16; Butler, 1980: 8) Internet connections (Coelho & Butler, 2012: 15–16) Accessibility or paved roads (Coelho & Butler, 2012: 16; Butler, 1980: 8, 11; Karplus & Krakover, 2005) Health services (Butler, 1980: 11) Medical staff (Coelho & Butler, 2012: 15; Johnston, 2001: 11) Security services (Butler, 1980: 11) Jail (Johnston, 2001: 11) Police officers (Coelho & Butler, 2012: 15; Johnston, 2001: 11) Wars (Karplus & Krakover, 2005)
Tourism facilities	Airbnb-registered rentals (Adamiak, 2020) Beds, rooms, establishments (Coelho & Butler, 2012: 15; Butler, 1980: 7–9; Dritsaki, 2009; Johnston, 2001: 11; Lawgiewski's (2006) synthesis; Butler, 1980: 8; Hovinen, 2006: 77) Souvenir shops (Butler, 1980) Change in locals' attitudes towards tourists and tourism development (Butler, 1980: 8; Doxey's irridex or index of tourist irritation from Butler, 1980: 10; Johnson and Snepenger, 2006; Martin, 2006) The 'characteristics of both visitors and visited, and the specific arrangements of the area involved' (Butler, 1980: 11) Restaurants (Butler, 1980: 8; Hovinen, 2006: 77) Shopping facilities (Butler, 1980: 8; Marois & Hinch, 2006) Spas (Butler, 1980: 8; Johnston, 2001: 11) Tourism human resources (Butler, 1980: 8; Coelho & Butler, 2012: 15) Tourist enterprises (Butler, 1980: 8; Dritsaki, 2009)
Social, economic, and environmental impacts	Rate of development (Butler, 1980: 11) Tax receipts, dollars spent on work, investment decisions, employment and unemployment, and staff turnover in tourism (Lagiewski's (2006) synthesis)
Seasonality	Tourist season (Butler, 1980: 7–8), e.g. annual (Haywood, 1995: 33–34)
Marketing, advertising, and destination image	For example: Data related to destination images (e.g. brochures, total pictures, destination pictures) (Camprubí et al., 2009) Relational patterns (given a function of a network is to promote destination images) (Camprubí et al., 2009)
'Triggers' (Butler, 2015: 12) or 'social and economic forces' (Haywood, 1995: 34) of a destination's development and change	Bargaining power of transportation companies, tour operators, travel intermediaries, accommodation and suppliers (Haywood, 1995: 35) concerning different levels of organisation in tourist travel arrangements (Butler, 1980: 7) or of involvement in facility planning and provision (Butler, 1980: 8) Competition among existing destinations (Butler, 1980: 8–10; Bao & Zhang, 2006; Haywood, 1995: 34; Johnston, 2001: 11) Environmental advocacy (Butler, 1980: 8, 11; Haywood, 1995: 35) Investments (Karplus & Krakover, 2005) Related public policies and forces (Butler, 1980: 7–10; Haywood, 1995: 35; Johnston, 2001: 11; Martin, 2006) New entrants to the industry (Butler, 1980: 9; Haywood, 1995: 34–36) Alternative products/services for tourism/travel experience (Butler, 1980: 9; Haywood, 1995: 35)

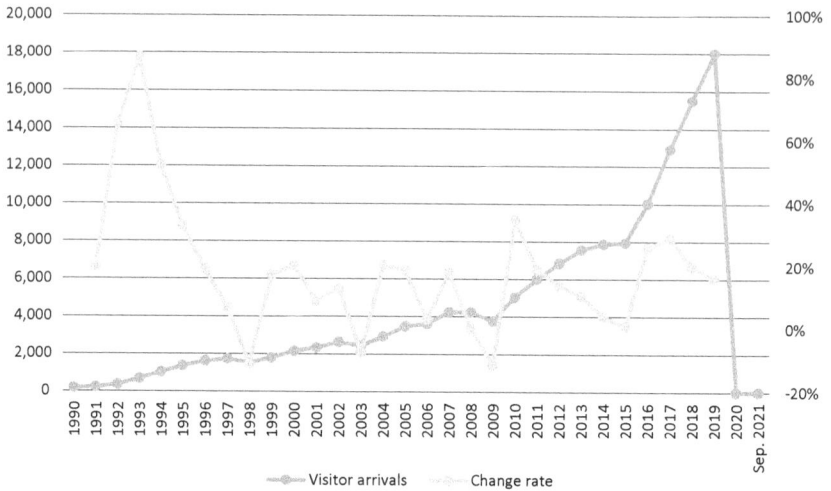

Figure 6.1 Vietnam's visitor arrivals (in 1000s) and change rates (%), 1990–2019

Source: The data include overnight visitors and same-day visitors and are aggregated based on Bojanic's (2005) findings and the statistics available in various UNWTO reports (2008: 856; 2011: 799; 2017: 878; 2015: 808; 2020; n.d.) .

351; Mok & Lam, 1997) and continued rising until 2019 (Bojanic, 2005; UNWTO, 2008: 856; UNWTO, 2011: 799; UNWTO, 2015: 808; UNWTO, 2017: 878; UNWTO, 2020; UNWTO, n.d.).

In January 2020, the COVID-19 pandemic broke out in Vietnam (MHV, 2021). As a result, the country's inbound tourism suffered hefty losses (GSOV, 2021; VNAT, 2020b). In particular, the total number of visitors (measured by bed nights) in 2020 was 97.3 million, 44% less than the previous year (GSOV, 2021). From 22 March 2020, Vietnam's borders were closed to foreign travellers (VNAT, 2021), so no further visitation figures were updated till the end of 2021 (VNAT, 2020a). According to Butler's (1980) TALC theory, Vietnam's inbound tourism had moved toward its demise, for a catastrophic reason.

These temporal shifts are plotted in Figure 6.1.

Sub-Destinations' Diverse Development Stages

Figure 6.2 summarises and illustrates the diverse levels of tourism readiness in Vietnam's 63 official administrative units (58 provinces and 5 municipalities) in 2020 regarding tourism attractions/activities, accommodation facilities, international travel companies, international tour guides, restaurants and shopping malls. Notably, most of these sub-destinations have few or even none of those infrastructure elements, which implies that their tourism development remains in an initial stage (*exploration*).

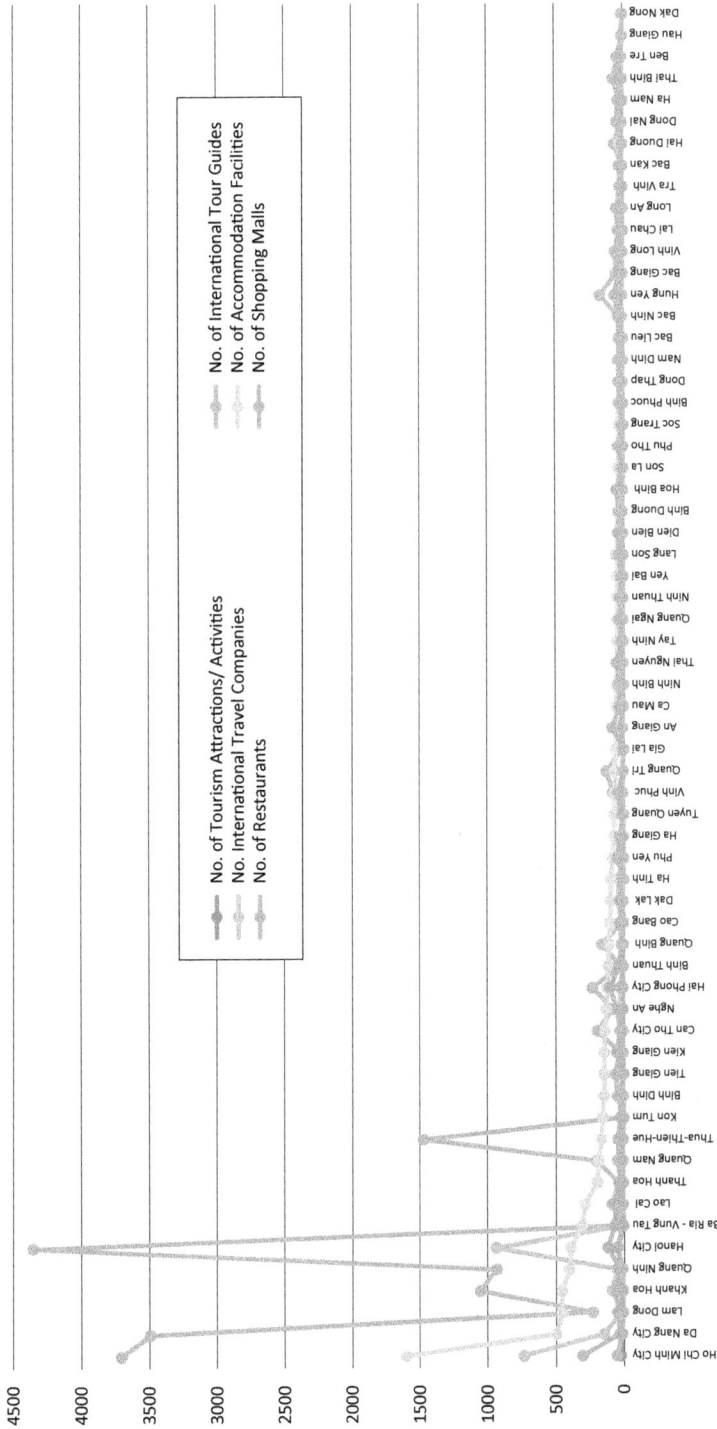

Figure 6.2 Vietnam's 63 cities and provinces by number of tourist attractions/activities, international travel companies, international tour guides, accommodation facilities, restaurants and shopping malls by 2020

Source: The information was aggregated from the database of the Tourism Information Technology Centre (TITC, 2020a–f) and calculated by Vu on 20 July 2021.

Meanwhile, the figures in some regions, such as Ho Chi Minh City, Da Nang, Lam Dong, Khanh Hoa, Quang Ninh and Hanoi, are relatively high, and their tourism developments had surpassed the others significantly and were no longer at the first stage.

Heterogeneity of the Visitor Typology

According to the VNAT's survey of international visitors in 2019, the average length of inbound visitors' stay at commercial accommodation was 8.02 days. An average package tour lasted 8.06 days, and self-arranged visitors stayed 7.98 days on average. The average stay at non-commercial accommodation was higher, at 11.92 days (VNAT, 2019: 12). Though the length of stay is a determinant from which to generalise tourist types, these figures imply a possible assemblage of Cohen's (1972) and Plog's (1974) tourist groups concerning their choice of tour lengths and accommodation types. Such diversity is undoubtedly a pattern of the *development* stage or a more mature one.

The typology appears to be more complex when visitors' origins are considered. According to the UNWTO (2020c), during 2015–2019, Vietnam experienced visitation from several well-defined markets from four continents: Africa, America, East Asia and the Pacific, and Europe. The majority of visitors came from the third group. Europeans were the second-largest market, then Americans. The proportion of African visitors was close to zero (UNWTO, 2020c). Vu's interviewees (various stakeholders) in 2021 elaborated on the characteristics of each group:

In 2019, *Tây* (i.e. Western) backpackers [...] do not need to rent a hotel [...]. In the morning, [they] can make coffee or cook food. (B. A. Tran, in interview 25 July 2021)

[M]any more people [from Europe as well as other countries] have travelled to Vietnam [...] especially with package tours at the beginning. Then their living standards were getting more advanced, so they reached out to people like me, who work more on B2C services and customise tours for them. People are investing more and more money in the quality of their travel. Mass tourism is no longer trendy. (P. A. Tran, in interview 22 July 2021)

[The] European [...] group often has time to wander freely and does not have to visit too many spots like in the old days. (N. T. Nguyen, in interview 27 July 2021)

In 2019, the streets were crowded with thousands of people. Chinese tourists also came in groups. (B. A. Tran, in interview 25 July 2021)

Vietnam still received an influx of Plog's (1974) *allocentrics* or Cohen's (1972) *explorers*, such as *Tây* backpackers, who required fewer arrangements, especially those of poor and mediocre quality, compared with the two previous institutionalised groups and seemed to manage most of their holidays themselves. Furthermore, the destination also experienced Plog's (1974) *mid-centric travellers* or Cohen's (1972) *individual institutionalised tourists*, such as individual European customers, and Plog's (1974) *psychocentrics* or Cohen's (1972) *organised mass tourists*, such as Chinese visitors. In other words, in this regard, patterns of *exploration, development* and *stagnation* stages existed in Vietnam during 2015–2019 (Butler, 1980: 7–9).

In addition, the level of adventure in these tours in practice differs from the attribute description of Cohen's (1972) and Plog's (1974) tourist typologies and is associated with neither the *drifter, explorer* nor *allocentrics*. Indeed, this element usually hinges on travellers' budgets, preferences and possible holiday lengths. For example:

[O]nly young people or adventure lovers went on such routes [...] in the north-east. Because of a collapsed cliff, the road was being repaired and we had to sit in traffic for hours. Several dangerous roads had no light, even though it was 7 or 8 pm. [...] The percentage of people who would go will be lower than in other programmes. Because it is more expensive and requires much more time. (P. A. Tran, in interview 22 July 2021)

Residents' Involvement in International Tourism and Attitude towards Tourists

Another distinguishable attribute is the active interaction between international tourists and locals:

[Local] Kids like my child, aged 12, and even those aged 5–6, are often sent there [to the city centre] to communicate with foreigners and practise English. Thus, the children learn English very quickly. They go by themselves and socialise with foreign visitors. Foreigners are also happy to talk to them. (B. A. Tran, in interview 25 July 2021)

Vietnamese people like to interact with *Tây*. *Tây* also want to interact with Vietnamese people. There is, however, little interaction with Asian visitors. (N. T. Nguyen, in interview 27 July 2021)

It is clear that the contact between the *Tây* group and the locals and their preference for engaging were high; thus, concerning this tourist segment, Vietnam appeared not to be in a mature stage due to such high interaction. However, the situation was complicated because of the lack of engagement between the Asian groups and Vietnamese residents. One possible explanation for the Asian group's meagre communication with the local milieu is that it is a by-product of their tour operators' strategy rather than any local negative attitudes towards tourists. Many Asian tours did not allow much opportunity for such interaction, as '[t]he tours competed based on price, so many trips guided visitors to shopping centres, so the guests did not understand the cultural values of the destination' (V. S. Ha, in interview 9 August 2021). Such a high competition level would suggest a *mature* stage in contrast to the finding with the *Tày* group.

Overall, it remains unlikely that research would be able to determine the specific stage of the analysis unit based on Vietnamese residents' involvement in tourism or their attitude towards tourists. The findings here reflect McKercher's earlier observation that a destination might appear *allocentric* to one market while being *psychocentric* to another (McKercher, 2005: 51). In other words, a tourist area can likely attract more than one of the *psychographic* segments. Likewise, it is possible that a destination can appear in various stages of its life cycle simultaneously, and its categorisation is more market-specific than destination-specific.

The Marketing Factor

According to VNAT's annual reports (2015: 32–38; 2016: 29–37; 2017: 26–32; 2018: 34–41; 2019: 27–35), the Vietnamese government initiated and organised various inbound tourism promotion activities during 2015–2019. Furthermore, this author's interviews in 2021 with multiple tourism stakeholders also revealed some anecdotes about other investments in marketing at the micro-level. For instance:

> companies that still exist have begun to reach customers through social media, on which promoting products is much cheaper or even free. It helps reduce marketing costs in this tough time. However, the competition is getting fiercer as too many companies participate simultaneously. (P. A. Tran, in interview 22 July 2021)

Thus, such efforts confirmed that Vietnam was no longer in the *exploration* stage.

The examination of this element raised several questions concerning the applicability of the TALC, both in the case of Vietnam and likely elsewhere, concerning how to evaluate the impacts of the marketing factor on the destination's development, *inter alia*, and how to utilise this element to determine the research unit's change trajectory, even when the causal link between promotion efforts and tourism results is often proven. These issues should also be considered within the context of the ubiquitous and increasing use of social media, especially Facebook, Instagram and TikTok (Gretzel, 2017: 1–14) since the users of these tools do not necessarily share information with destinations for marketing purposes, nor are they always accurate and factual, yet their posts can have tremendously viral word-of-mouth impacts.

Final Thoughts

Overall, Vu's (2021) study could only eliminate the stage(s) through which Vietnam had passed, and the author remains unable to determine where the destination was situated on the TALC curve before the massive drop in visitation due to COVID-19. Nonetheless, the findings are insufficient to reject the entire theory. First, the incompatibilities between the theory and practice can possibly be attributed to the fact that the original theory describes a resort as a tourist area, and Vietnam is a conglomeration of multiple sub-destinations that are at different stages of economic development. Second, there remains a lack of methodological explanations of how to assess other features in all TALC stages and pinpoint the transition between them, and an analysis based on lexical interpretation triggers more questions than it helps answer the research one. Finally, despite the disputable applicability of the TALC, an attempt to apply TALC to a tourist area produces a detailed inventory of the area's resources, which provides thorough insights that tourism stakeholders could use to make informed decisions in practice.

References

Adamiak, C. (2020) Peer-to-peer accommodation in destination life cycle: The case of Nordic countries. *Scandinavian Journal of Hospitality and Tourism* 20 (3), 212–226.

Aledo, A. and Mazón, T. (2004) Impact of residential tourism and the destination life cycle theory. In F.D. Pineda, C.A. Brebbia and M. Mugica (eds) *Sustainable Tourism* (pp. 26–36). Southampton: Wit Press.

Bao, J. and Zhang, C. (2006) The TALC in China's tourism planning: Case study of Danxia Mountain, Guangdong Province, PRC. In R. Butler (ed.) *The Tourism Area Life Cycle, Volume 1: Applications and Modifications* (pp. 107–115). Clevedon: Channel View Publications.

Bojanic, D. (2005) Tourist Area Life Cycle stage and the impact of a crisis. *ASEAN Journal on Hospitality and Tourism* 4, 139–150.

Boyd, S.W. (2006) The TALC model and its application to national parks: A Canadian example. In R. Butler (ed.) *The Tourism Area Life Cycle, Volume 1: Applications and Modifications* (pp. 119–138). Clevedon: Channel View Publications.

Butler, R. (1980) The concept of a tourist area cycle of evolution: Implications for management of resources. *Canadian Geographer* 24 (1), 5–12.

Butler, R. (2015) Tourism Area Life Cycle. In C. Cooper (ed.) *Contemporary Tourism Reviews, Volume 1* (pp. 183–226). Oxford: Goodfelllow Publishers.

Camprubí, R., Guia, J. and Comas, J. (2009) Managing induced tourism image: Relational patterns and the life cycle. *Tourism: An International Interdisciplinary Journal* 57 (3), 241–258.

Chapman, A. and Light, D. (2016) Exploring the tourist destination as a mosaic: The alternative lifecycles of the seaside amusement arcade sector in Britain. *Tourism Management* 52, 254–263.

Coelho, J. and Butler, R. (2012) The Tourism Area Life Cycle: A quantitative approach of the tourism area life cycle. *European Journal of Tourism, Hospitality and Recreation*, 3 (1), 9–31.

Cohen, E. (1972) Toward a sociology of international tourism. *Social Research* 39 (1), 164.

Collins-Kreiner, N. (2016) The lifecycle of concepts: the case of 'pilgrimage tourism'. *Tourism Geographies* 18 (3), 322–334.

Corak, S. (2006) The modification of the Tourism Area Life Cycle model for (re)inventing a destination: The case of the Opatija Riviera, Croatia. In R. Butler (ed.) *The Tourism Area Life Cycle, Volume 1: Applications and Modifications* (pp. 271–286). Clevedon: Channel View Publications.

Dong, E., Morais, D. and Dowler, L. (2003) Ethnic tourism development in Yunnan, China: Revisiting Butler's Tourist Area Lifecycle. In J. Murdy (ed.) *Proceedings of the 2003 Northeastern Recreation Research Symposium* (pp. 164–169). Newtown Square, PA: US Department of Agriculture, Forest Service, Northeastern Research Station. Available at https://www.fs.usda.gov/ne/newtown_square/publications/technical_reports/pdfs/2004/317papers/dong317.pdf (accessed 26 August 2021).

Dritsaki, C. (2009) The life cycle of agro tourist enterprises. *Tourismos: An International Multidisciplinary Journal of Tourism* 4 (2), 149–154.

Faulkner, B. and Tideswell, C. (2006) Rejuvenating a maturing tourist destination: The case of the Gold Coast, Australia. In R. Butler (ed.) *The Tourism Area Life Cycle, Volume 1: Applications and Modifications* (pp. 306–335). Clevedon: Channel View Publications.

Glaser, B.G. and Strauss, A.L. (2006) *The Discovery of Grounded Theory: Strategies for Qualitative Research*. London: Aldine Transaction. Available at http://www.sxf.uevora.pt/wp-content/uploads/2013/03/Glaser_1967.pdf (accessed 26 August 2021).

Gretzel, U. (2017) Social media activism in tourism. *Journal of Hospitality and Tourism* 15 (2), 1–14.

GSOV (2021) *Vietnam Tourism 2021: Needs Determination and Effort to Overcome Difficulties*. GSOV. Available at https://www.gso.gov.vn/en/data-and-statistics/2021/03/vietnam-tourism-2021-needs-determination-and-effort-to-overcome-difficulties/ (accessed 5 April 2021).

Haywood, K.M. (1995) Can the tourist-area life cycle be made operational? In S. Medlik (ed.) *Managing Tourism* (pp. 31–38). Oxford: Butterworth-Heinemann.

Haywood, K.M. (2006) Evolution of tourism areas and the tourism industry. In R. Butler (ed.) *The Tourism Area Life Cycle, Volume 1: Applications and Modifications* (pp. 51–69). Clevedon: Channel View Publications.

Hazmi, N., Omar, S.I. and Mohamed, B. (2012) Tourism area lifecycle model and its applicability to lodging development of Langkawi Island, Malaysia. In A. Zainal, S.M. Radzi, R. Hashim, C.T. Chik and R. Abu (eds) *Current Issues in Hospitality and Tourism Research and Innovations* (pp. 539–543). London: CRC Press.

Hovinen, G.R. (2006) Lancaster County, the TALC, and the search for sustainable tourism. In R. Butler (ed.) *The Tourism Area Life Cycle, Volume 1: Applications and Modifications* (pp. 73–90). Clevedon: Channel View Publications.

Johnson, J.D. and Snepenger, D.J. (2006) Residents' perceptions of tourism development over the early stages of the TALC. In R. Butler (ed.) *The Tourism Area Life Cycle, Volume 1: Applications and Modifications* (pp. 222–236). Clevedon: Channel View Publications.

Johnston, C.S. (2006) Shoring the foundations of the TALC in tropical island destinations: Kona, Hawaii. In R. Butler (ed.) *The Tourism Ares Life Cycle, Volume 1: Applications and Modifications* (pp. 198–221). Clevedon: Channel View Publications.

Johnston, C.S. (2001) Shoring the foundations of the destination life cycle model, part 1: Ontological and epistemological considerations. *Tourism Geographies* 3 (1), 2–28.

Karplus, Y. and Krakover, S. (2005) Stochastic multivariable approach to modelling tourism area life cycles. *Tourism and Hospitality Research* 5 (3), 235–253.

Kotler, P., Bowen, J., Makens, J.C. and Baloglu, S. (2017) *Marketing for Hospitality and Tourism*. Harlow: Pearson.

Lagiewski, R.M. (2006) The application of the TALC model: A literature survey. In R. Butler (ed.) *The Tourism Area Life Cycle, Volume 1: Applications and Modifications* (pp. 27–50). Clevedon: Channel View Publications.

Lloyd, K. (2003) Contesting control in transitional Vietnam: The development and regulation of traveller cafés in Hanoi and Ho Chi Minh City. *Tourism Geographies* 5 (3), 350–366.

Lundgren, J.O. (2006) An empirical interpretation of the TALC: Tourist product life cycles in the eastern townships of Quebec. In R. Butler (ed.) *The Tourism Area Life Cycle, Volume 1: Applications and Modifications* (pp. 91–106). Clevedon: Channel View Publications.

Malcolm-Davies, J. (2006) The TALC and heritage sites. In R. Butler (ed.) *The Tourism Area Life Cycle, Volume 1: Applications and Modifications* (pp. 162–180). Clevedon: Channel View Publications.

Marois, J. and Hinch, T. (2006) Seeking sustainable tourism in Northern Thailand: The dynamics of the TALC. In R. Butler (ed.) *The Tourism Area Life Cycle, Volume 1: Applications and Modifications* (pp. 250–268). Clevedon: Channel View Publications.

Martin, B. (2006) The TALC model and politics. In R. Butler (ed.) *The Tourism Area Life Cycle, Volume 1: Applications and Modifications* (pp. 237–249). Clevedon: Channel View Publications.

McKercher, B. (2005) Are psychographics predictors of destination life cycles? *Journal of Travel and Tourism Marketing* 19 (1), 49–55.

Meng, Z., Wei, Y. and Yu, Y. (2011) On life cycle of cultural heritage engineering tourism: A case study of Macau. *Systems Engineering Procedia* 1, 351–357. Available at https://www.sciencedirect.com/science/article/pii/S2211381911000543 (accessed 19 October 2020).

MHV (2021) *Chronicle of Covid-19* (Original: Diễn biến dịch, translated by Vu, 2021). Trang tin về dịch bệnh viêm đường hô hấp cấp COVID-19. Available at https://ncov.moh.gov.vn/web/guest/dong-thoi-gian (accessed 24 August 2021).

Mok, C. and Lam, T. (1997) Hotel and tourism development in Vietnam. *Journal of Travel and Tourism Marketing* 7 (1), 85–91. Available at https://www.tandfonline.com/doi/pdf/10.1300/J073v07n01_06?needAccess=true (accessed 19 May 2019).

O'Hare, G. and Barrett, H. (1997) The destination life cycle: International tourism in Peru. *Scottish Geographical Magazine* 113 (2), 66–73.

Plog, S. (1974) Why destination areas rise and fall in popularity. *Cornell Hotel and Restaurant Administration Quarterly* 14 (4), 55–58.

Porter, M. (1979) How competitive forces shape strategy. *Harvard Business Review*. Available at https://hbr.org/1979/03/how-competitive-forces-shape-strategy (accessed 8 August 2021).

Russo, A.P. (2006) A re-foundation of the TALC for heritage cities. In R. Butler (ed.) *The Tourism Area Life Cycle, Volume 1: Applications and Modifications* (pp. 139–161). Clevedon: Channel View Publications.

Suntikul, W., Butler, R. and Airey, D. (2008) A periodisation of the development of Vietnam's Tourism accommodation since the open door policy. *Asia Pacific Journal of Tourism Research* 13 (1), 67–80.

TITC (2020a) *Database of Vietnam's Tourism: Accommodation Facilities* (Original: Cơ sở Dữ liệu Du lịch Việt Nam – Cơ sở Lưu trú, translated by Vu, July 2021). Available at http://csdl.vietnamtourism.gov.vn/cslt (accessed 20 July 2021).

TITC (2020b) *Database of Vietnam's Tourism Destinations* (Original: Cơ sở Dữ liệu Du lịch Việt Nam – Điểm đến Du lịch, translated by Vu, Jul. 2021). Available at http://csdl.vietnamtourism.gov.vn/dest (accessed 20 July 2021).

TITC (2020c) *Database of Vietnam's Tourism: Restaurants* (Original: Cơ sở Dữ liệu Du lịch Việt Nam – Nhà hàng, translated by Vu, July 2021). Available at http://csdl.vietnamtourism.gov.vn/rest (accessed 20 July 2021).

TITC (2020d) *Database of Vietnam's Tourism: Shopping Malls* (Original: Cơ sở Dữ liệu Du lịch Việt Nam – Điểm mua sắm, translated by Vu, July 2021). Available at http://csdl.vietnamtourism.gov.vn/shop (accessed 20 July 2021).

TITC (2020e) *Database of Vietnam's Tourism: Tour Guides* (Original: Cơ sở Dữ liệu Du lịch Việt Nam – Hướng dẫn viên Du lịch, translated by Vu, July 2021). Available at http://csdl. vietnamtourism.gov.vn/hdv/ (accessed 20 July 2021).

TITC (2020f) *Database of Vietnam's Tourism: Travel Companies* (Original: Cơ sở Dữ liệu Du lịch Việt Nam – Doanh nghiệp Lữ hành, translated by Vu, July 2021). Available at: http:// csdl.vietnamtourism.gov.vn/dnlh (accessed 20 July 2021).

UNWTO (2008) *Yearbook of Tourism Statistics, Data 2002–2006* (1st edn). Madrid: UNWTO.

UNWTO (2011) *Yearbook of Tourism Statistics: Data 2005–2009* (1st edn). Madrid: UNWTO.

UNWTO (2015) *Yearbook of Tourism Statistics: Data 2009–2013* (1st edn). Madrid: UNWTO.

UNWTO (2017) *Yearbook of Tourism Statistics: Data 2011–2015* (1st edn). Madrid: UNWTO.

UNWTO (2020c) *Compendium of Tourism Statistics Dataset.* Madrid: UNWTO. Available at https://webunwto.s3.eu-west-1.amazonaws.com/s3fs-public/2020-02/ methodological_notes_2020.pdf (accessed 21 August 2021).

UNWTO (n.d.) *Basic Tourism Statistics.* Available at https://www.unwto.org/statistic/basic-tourism-statistics (accessed 21 August 2021).

VNAT (2015) *Vietnam Annual Tourism Report 2015.* Available at https://titc.vn/ dmdocuments/vn/slide/baocaothuongnien2015/mobile/index.html#p=24 (accessed 15 August 2021).

VNAT (2016) *Vietnam Annual Tourism Report 2016.* Available at: https://titc.vn/ dmdocuments/en/slide/NCTNDLVN2016_EN/mobile/index.html (accessed 15 August 2021).

VNAT (2017) *Vietnam Annual Tourism Report 2017.* Available at: https://titc.vn/ dmdocuments/en/slide/BCTNDLVN%202017_EN/mobile/index.html#p=20 (accessed 15 August 2021).

VNAT (2018) *Vietnam Annual Tourism Report 2018.* Hanoi: VNAT, MCST.

VNAT (2019) *Vietnam Annual Tourism Report 2019.* Hanoi: VNAT, MCST.

VNAT (2020a) *International Visitors to Vietnam in March 2020* (Original: Khách quốc tế đến Việt Nam tháng 3 năm 2020, translated by Vu, 2021). Available at https://www. vietnamtourism.gov.vn/index.php/statistic/international (accessed 2 September 2021).

VNAT (2020b) *Report on Work Summary 2020 – Directions, Key Tasks in 2021* (Original: Báo cáo Tổng kết Công tác năm 2020 – Phương hướng, Nhiệm vụ Trọng tâm năm 2021, translated by Vu, 2021). Hanoi: VNAT, Ministry of Culture, Sports, and Tourism.

VNAT (2021) *Info for travellers on coronavirus in Vietnam.* Official Website Vietnam Tourism. Available at https://vietnam.travel/things-to-do/information-travellers-novel-coronavirus-vietnam (accessed 24 August 2021).

Vu, M.H. and Chijioke, N. (2019) Perception of sustainable tourism development: Insights from stakeholders in Phu Quoc Island, Vietnam. *International Journal of Mechanical Engineering and Technology (IJMET)* 10 (2), 1776–1788.

Vu, N.T. (2021) Butler's Tourism Area Life Cycle – Case study: Vietnam's inbound tourism during 2015–2019 and since the outbreak of the Covid-19 pandemic. Graduate thesis, Fachhochschule Westkueste: Heide, Germany.

Weaver, D.B. (2006) The 'plantation' variant of the TALC in the small-island Caribbean. In R. Butler (ed.) *The Tourism Area Life Cycle, Volume 1: Applications and Modifications* (pp. 185–197). Clevedon: Channel View Publications.

7   The TALC as a Strategic Model

Júlio Coelho

Since 1980, the TALC model (Butler, 1980) has been scrutinised almost to exhaustion. Over this period there have been approaches that have confirmed the evolutionary thesis of destinations, others that have criticised its descriptive effectiveness and still others that have discussed its usefulness as a strategic tool. There have also been those who have sought to give it a quantitative interpretation, to give it greater utility (Coelho & Butler, 2012; Lagiewski, 2006). The work presented in the 2006 multi-volume book edited by Butler (2006a, 2006b) demonstrates the value of the TALC model, highlighting its four dimensions: descriptive; predictive; quantitative; and strategic.

As to its descriptive dimension, one can find clear evidence of the evolutionary characteristics of destinations, with full or partial passages through the six phases proposed in the model. As for its predictive dimension, this has proven difficult to assess because the phases through which a destination will pass are not guaranteed in advance, and nothing guarantees that destinations will go through the six phases sequentially. However, the other two dimensions of the model, its quantification and its usefulness as a strategic model, are still to be developed. The latest quantitative developments pave the way for a consolidation of this dimension, with special emphasis on the different growth rates of the variables considered as measures to identify the different stages of development (Coelho & Butler, 2012). The strategic dimension also remains to be consolidated. While it can be said that the TALC model enables strategies to be developed, these are almost always left to be made only when one enters into the last phase of the model. That is, only when a destination enters the decline phase, and looks for ways to rejuvenate, do strategies arise. But any development model must include a diagnosis phase in its methodology, so that decisions for the future can then be projected.

It has been argued that the TALC model makes it possible to assess the development of tourism. Article 3 of the Statutes of the World Tourism Organization (WTO, 1970, Mexico) states that 'to develop tourism is to contribute to economic expansion, peace and prosperity'. It is also generally agreed that tourism variables are heterogeneous and diverse in nature: social, environmental and economic, in line with sustainable development. This makes it impossible to determine the best variable to identify its growth and consequent development. The original TALC model (1980) proposed that the number of tourists arriving at a destination would be the best, but subsequent works have used other variables, such as occupancy rates, number of visits and number of hotels, among a range of alternatives.

Much has also been said about the importance of tourism for the development of economies, and many economies, particularly the weaker and more limited ones, depend on the growth of tourism to achieve greater levels of economic development. Therefore, developing tourism is also about developing economies, which can be achieved through processes of investment in existing resources, the creation of new resources, and governance decisions and procedures. In a highly competitive world, all economies, and perhaps most of all tourist destinations, fight for the same markets and, to achieve some success, they must be able to choose different policies, or growth strategies (this happens at all stages of the life cycle). Only when one is in the presence of very prolonged periods of stagnation or enters the decline phase is there is a real concern with differentiation and the search for new markets. For any destination, at each stage of its life cycle the degree of competition varies, so in strategic terms it is important to evaluate the scale and stage of the life cycle (Cooper, 1993).

Indeed, tourist destinations must be able to promote and choose development strategies along the same lines as any businesses considered in isolation; that is, at any stage of their evolution, strategies must be appropriately chosen. The TALC model contemplates, in its genesis, the existence of competition or, if we wish, the existence of a competitive context (Butler, 1980), so the different tourist destinations must include this reality in their equations and considerations. In this context, it is legitimate to say that the TALC model can make it possible to assess the development of tourism and, consequently, to assess tourism's contribution to the development of economies. However, there is a question that needs to be asked:

• Can the TALC model contribute to the choice of economic growth strategies, given the different competitive contexts in which we find ourselves?

Or, put another way:

• Can the TALC model be considered a strategic model?

Descriptive Dimension

The original format of the TALC model is suitable for describing the different evolutionary phases of a tourist destination. In essence, the descriptive dimension seeks to characterise the different phases of the development of a destination's evolution in terms of the involvement of tourists in the community, the community's relationship with its visitors, and the carrying capacity of its natural resources.

Researchers have used different indicators, depending on their specific studies and analyses. It is generally agreed by researchers that nothing guarantees that the evolution is common to all destinations, nor that all destinations go through all the stages described in the model (Butler, 1980).

Therefore, it is possible to say that the TALC model is a tool that allows us to evaluate the development of tourism based on which specific indicator that we want to consider. When studies point to alternative models with an alternative number of phases, these are in fact situations as foreseen in the TALC model, from the beginning, rather than being truly alternative models. It is accepted and statistically proven that tourism has been an 'accelerator' for the development of many economies, particularly in the case of small-islands developing states (SIDS). The economic impact of tourism can be seen between 2020 and 2021, when the sudden drop in tourism movements, due to the restrictions resulting from the COVID-19 pandemic, greatly contributed to the declines in economies all over the world.

It is easy to see that tourism contributes to the evolution of economies, and here the TALC model emerges as a potential tool to monitor this evolution, as the variables considered in the model are tourism and economic development. In essence, we can say that the descriptive dimension translates to the diagnostic phase appropriate for a tourist destination, that the TALC model satisfies this capacity and that little or nothing more can be added, other than applying this model to case studies, as has been done many times (see Gore *et al.* in this volume, Chapter 3).

Predictive Dimension

The predictive dimension of the TALC model is limited by its very essence. In other words, not knowing, nor taking for granted that destinations will all pass through the six phases, nor even knowing the nature of the evolution of a tourist destination within each of the phases, it is difficult to use the model to predict what may happen in the future. Any theory must cover all hypotheses or scenarios within the subject it addresses, otherwise it will be only a thesis and applicable only to certain cases. According to Myrdal (1961), a theory should be a set of principles based on empirical evidence that promote the verification of predictions of the functioning of the system. In other words, it is not a simple model or set of hypotheses but, rather, a formal articulation between causes and effects that is repeatedly verified (Echtner & Jamal, 1997).

The TALC model, while it does not have one or more econometric models demonstrating causal relationships to support it, which is very difficult to determine, due to its relational complexity, does not have that forecasting capacity. Considering that a forecast is the result of an analysis of historical data that allows the extraction of trends, we can say that the TALC model allows us only to 'speculate' about a specific pattern of evolution, by considering a certain descriptive historical evolution, or by a comparison with similar situations. Therefore, it will be possible to evolve into prediction only when an econometric or turimetric model is found to support it.

Quantitative Dimension

Although there has not yet been a predictive econometric model that can be applied to the TALC model, this does not preclude the development of a numerical indicator (index) that can be used to identify each phase of the TALC. Some attempts have been made in this direction (Coelho, 2010: 199–200). Therefore, the quantitative dimension is one of those that may still need some evolution, even though the latest developments point towards considering the growth rates of the variables considered as determinants for identifying the different phases of the life cycle (Coelho & Butler, 2012).

Similar to a human being, whose life cycle has its own characteristics for each phase, so too do destinations and economies have this identification. It is important to identify these phases in a more objective way to avoid grey or uncertain areas of the evolution. In other words, it is important to diagnose objectively so that we do not tend to wrongly classify the state of development in which we find ourselves. A wrong classification in terms of diagnosis can lead to wrong decisions in terms of strategy. Therefore, the introduction of quantification can help determine more specifically the stage at which a particular tourist destination is.

Coelho (2010) proposed an index to measure the phases of the life cycle of a tourist destination where all the assumptions of the TALC model were evidenced, and it was demonstrated that this model contemplated all the variants that have been subject to criticism, particularly in the context of the duration of each phase, the number of phases through which a destination passes, and the periods between phases. This proposal not only explains the reason for the existence of the upper asymptote, but also identifies a lower asymptote. The first results from the average saturation of living conditions in a destination as the number of tourists increases. The second results from the decrease in the average living conditions of a destination as the resident population increases.

It has been argued (Coelho & Butler, 2012) that an index that includes variables of a socioeconomic nature (representing social, environmental and economic dimensions), along with the resident population and tourism variables (arrivals, revenue or other), meets the conditions to represent the dynamics of a tourist destination. The index that will be used to measure the TALC model is the following (Coelho, 2010):

$$TALC_{jt}^i = \sum_{v=1}^{n} \frac{1}{n} \left(\frac{\frac{D_{vjt}}{P_{jt}}}{\frac{D_{vTt}}{P_{Tt}}} \right) \times \left(\frac{T_{jt}}{T_{Tt}} \right)$$

D_{vj} represents the variables (v) that are understood as being adequate to evaluate a destination (j) (i.e. variables with an effect on the quality of life of destinations, and which can be aggregated or individual);

D_{vT} represents the totality of variables (v) that exists in the competitive context;

P_j represents the variable resident population of the destination considered (j);

P_T represents the total population that exists in the competitive context;

T_j represents the variable tourists of the destination considered (j);

T_T represents the totality of tourists that exists in the competitive context;

t stands for the time unit.

The use of the ratio $1/n$ is to guarantee an equality of importance for the quality-of-life variables considered.

Originally this index was designated by the Tourism Development Index (Coelho, 2010) but in this work it is designated the TALC Index (TALC^i). If the competitive system is fully balanced (full equilibrium), that is, when all competitors present the same values of the factors considered, this index will have a value of 1 (one).

In order to validate their relevance, numerical models must be able to contemplate two types of data: cross-sectional and time series. In such a situation the proposed index may be used in the context of comparison between destinations, or in an isolated manner comparing the same destination over time. Two papers confirm this dual application (Coelho & Lourenço, 2015; Pêra et al., 2017), as well as the adequacy of the index to assess the evolution of destinations.

This index includes the issues of demography, the existence of tourists (fundamental to the case) and living conditions, as essential factors needed to evaluate the development of tourism in a given destination. It is suggested that the degree of inclination of the tangent to the curve, at the points of change of each of the phases of the life cycle, can be used to complement the differentiation of each of these phases. This is because the degree of slope represents the pace of evolution of the variable(s) considered, in the unit of time considered. In graphical terms, the life cycle curve has time on its abscissa and the index value on its ordinate. It should be noted that the consideration of very long periods of time (many decades or over a century) may distort the results obtained with the proposed index (Athiyaman, 1995). This is because comparisons lose some sense of rationality.

This index proposal may be a contribution to the opening of research in the predictive dimension.

Strategic Dimension

Strategies have to do with success and failure, and according to Athiyaman (1995), businesses (destinations in this case) compete for inputs or for customers, and so require decisions to be made about supply, organisational structure, competitive tactics and internal coordination. In this context, a variety of decision-making tools can be used, such as simulation, game theory, linear programming or statistics. Compared with other industries, tourism has been little developed in terms of strategies, perhaps because it 'hides behind business strategies' (Athiyaman, 1995).

Therefore, knowing in advance at what stage a destination is enables planners and decision makers to develop differentiated strategies, a fact that is of central importance in the current competitive contexts in which different tourist destinations find themselves. For the model to work fully and be generally applicable, it is necessary that the concept of a 'destination' can be whatever is taken to be the site where there are tourists, and this may be at different scales, such as country, region, city or even event. Basically, we will always be in the presence of a specific market, or market segment, as suggested by Haywood (1986).

In order to see different levels of growth, we must include 'investment' in these approaches, for more investment means more wealth for the destination, promoting the increase of visits (Frederick, 1993).

By analogy, one might look at the SWOT model (strengths, weaknesses, opportunities and threats). This model, conceived a long time ago (there are several possible origins for this diagnostic tool, from *The Art of War* to the Harvard School in 1969, or Albert Humphry in the early 1960s), was elaborated by Weihrich (1982). Since then, there have been various approaches to its quantification because of the appreciation that such a step may improve its usefulness (Ghazinoory *et al.*, 2011) and, at the same time, it has been considered useful as a strategic model. Other strategic models that are relevant in the tourist destination context include: Ansoff (1957), who used a market/product analysis to determine diagnosis and strategic choices; Henderson (1970), who used portfolio analysis for strategic development; Porter (1979), with competitive attractiveness analysis for strategy development; and Ritchie and Crouch (1999, 2003), with sequential or hierarchical diagnostic analysis. The first two of these utilised a four-quadrant matrix, while Porter had five inter-related positions and Ritchie and Crouch used five essential conditions for strategy development in tourism destinations.

The strategic models are, as a rule, presented in a double-entry table or through a sequential flow of checks, for easier reading, interpretation and application. With the exception of the Ritchie and Crouch model, which is presented as a model aimed at tourist destinations, all the others are models for application to activities in general and have been applied to tourism activities and territories with varying degrees of adaptation.

In general, strategic models confront organisations within their sector or activity; however, this approach may contain some constraints because the sector is a 'standard', 'representative' or 'average' entity, which may lead to a biased comparison between the competitors themselves. Therefore, it would seem that an approach where an organisation is confronted with its competitors *per se* could be useful.

In other words, if an organisation is faced with the sector in general, the strategy adopted is normally unique to that situation, but if it is faced with each competitor, it may need to apply several strategies simultaneously, or opt for those strategies specifically targeted at a particular competitor. The concepts of cooperation strategies fit into this approach.

Essentially, strategies can be classified as:

- offensive (when the objective is to 'attack' the competition).
- defensive (when the objective is to defend against the 'attacks' of the competition);
- withdrawal (when the existing resources do not allow for keeping up with the competition, or when the entire sector is in effective or imminent decline).

These scenarios may have more or fewer variants and sub-areas, depending on the nature and characteristics of the field under study (generally always in the context of concerns regarding market maintenance or conquest). The offensive strategies are those that require more resources in order to achieve, in a short space of time, differentiating results compared with the competition. Defensive strategies are those that seek to accompany or defend themselves from the competition in its most current dynamics. Normally, the availability of resources is less demanding. Withdrawal strategies should prepare for the exit from markets (e.g. Baum, 2006), minimising commercial losses.

This author's work (Coelho, 2010) verified that the TALC model can also be considered as a model for the development of strategies, both in a sector logic and in a logic of direct confrontation with each of the competitors of that same sector, or area of activity.

Strategies are always developed, in either business or territorial terms, with the aim of improving the situation in the future. As a rule, this is usually achieved with investment measures and, therefore, the development of strategies leads to investment decisions, whatever the plan or field of action. Tourism is not outside this principle; that is, to develop tourism we have to make investment decisions, but this is conditioned by the position a destination may find itself in, and the quantity and quality of the available resources. Therefore, in the first place it is necessary to know where a destination stands at the present and then, according to the competitive context, to decide on the most appropriate strategic solutions to improve that position.

When it comes to strategies, there are no secret formulas with guaranteed success but, rather, options that will seem to be more or less appropriate to the contexts. Entities, territories or companies do not compete with all their competitors at the same time (unless they all have the same or very similar management practices) but, rather, with each one individually. The need to develop strategies results from the fact that destinations, as most enterprises, are normally constrained by their limited financial, human and material resources.

In fact, in terms of tourism, all competitors have to worry about the level of investment, in the variables considered for the effect in question (D, in the equation presented above), along with demographic policies and also with policies or measures to attract tourists. In terms of variables (D), these can involve direct investment, or investment incentives. In the context of the resident population, it is necessary to consider its evolution, through birth, immigration and emigration, and settlement policies, and in terms of tourists, variables can include direct, indirect and induced attraction measures. This situation may result in a mix of strategies, depending on the competitive scenarios in which the destination is set.

Therefore, a destination may exist in the presence of competitive scenarios, where other destinations can be in any of the other stages of the life cycle. This can lead to the need to implement various strategies simultaneously, depending on the desired objective, in terms of positioning or future repositioning of the destination in question. Inevitably, the choice of strategies can never guarantee a given result, since they do not control the strategic choices of competitors, but only enable those which are considered to be the most appropriate and feasible options to be chosen in a given context.

The TALC model illustrates a description of the conditions that characterise a destination in each of the phases of its evolutionary cycle. Therefore, a destination must be able to identify at what stage it is and at what stage its competitors are, to be able to better choose its strategies, in order to strengthen or safeguard its future competitive position.

For a better understanding of the proposal presented here, it is necessary to consider the variables of a socioeconomic nature that ensure quality of life. These are subject to investment for maintenance and improvement and are: the natural and historical-cultural heritage; tourist accommodation; safety and security; accessibility; information and communication systems; urban planning; environmental protection; entertainment and recreational activities; the public health system; and the quality of human resources. However, the model needs to be able to include other types of variables (possibly more or less aggregated), without losing its usability.

In order to improve development levels, there has to be investment in these variables, in addition to appropriate demographic and tourism policies and, clearly, different degrees of investment lead to different levels of development. Thus, in the exploration phase it is likely that all the variables considered are in a very incipient phase, with low levels of presentation and attraction, with a small resident population and low residual values of tourists. As the investments in resources increase, the attraction capacity will be improved, with likely increases in tourist numbers and the resident population of the destination. It is this process of potential continuous improvement, combined with appropriate demographic policies and direct attraction of tourists, which results in a 'typical' life cycle evolution as represented by the S-curve of the TALC model.

Therefore, the subsequent phases (involvement, development, consolidation, stagnation and later post-stagnation) result from this investment dynamic and the reaction that tourists and the resident population have to these policies and decisions. It is the different political or decision-making options, in terms of degree and momentum, that determine the different development strategies.

Thus, it is important to have a model that helps to define these strategies, specifically with regard to tourism development and Figure 7.1 illustrates a possible solution to this problem, where the strategic decisions should depend on the relative position of the destination in question, in relation to its competitive context, when it may have to apply different strategies simultaneously, depending on that same competitive context.

In terms of investment, strategies can be classified in three ways (according to the degree of investment intensity):

- hard strategies;
- soft strategies;
- withdrawal strategies.

$$TALC_{jt}^i = \sum_{v=1}^{n} \frac{1}{n}\left(\frac{D_{vjt}}{D_{vTt}}\right) \times \left(\frac{P_{Tt}}{P_{jt}}\right) \times \left(\frac{T_{jt}}{T_{Tt}}\right)$$

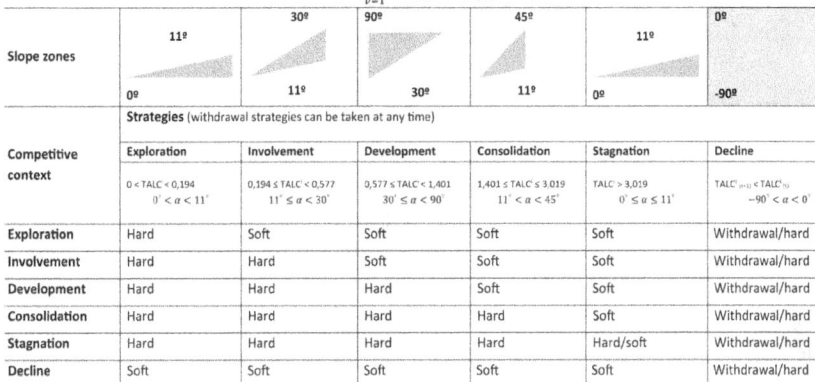

Slope zones						
	11º (0º–11º)	30º (11º–30º)	90º (30º)	45º (11º)	11º (0º)	0º (−90º)

Strategies (withdrawal strategies can be taken at any time)						
Competitive context	Exploration	Involvement	Development	Consolidation	Stagnation	Decline
	0 < TALC < 0.194 0° < α < 11°	0.194 ≤ TALC < 0.577 11° ≤ α < 30°	0.577 ≤ TALC < 1.401 30° ≤ α < 90°	1.401 ≤ TALC ≤ 3.019 11° < α < 45°	TALC > 3.019 0° ≤ α ≤ 11°	TALC (t+1) < TALC (t) −90° < α < 0°
Exploration	Hard	Soft	Soft	Soft	Soft	Withdrawal/hard
Involvement	Hard	Hard	Soft	Soft	Soft	Withdrawal/hard
Development	Hard	Hard	Hard	Soft	Soft	Withdrawal/hard
Consolidation	Hard	Hard	Hard	Hard	Soft	Withdrawal/hard
Stagnation	Hard	Hard	Hard	Hard	Hard/soft	Withdrawal/hard
Decline	Soft	Soft	Soft	Soft	Soft	Withdrawal/hard

Figure 7.1 TALC index/strategy map

The first refers to measures of strong investment levels, above the competition and/or industry average. The second refers to low or moderate levels of investment, comparable to that of competitors or across the sector as a whole. Anything that is disinvestment on an ongoing basis presupposes a withdrawal strategy. This differentiation allows for the identification of the different options faced by decision makers when choosing strategies, according to the current relative position of a destination and what is intended with regard to a future positioning, relative to the markets considered.

It is assumed that decision makers always intend to implement strategies to improve or maintain their position, except in cases of withdrawal. Strategies may follow a normal pattern of evolution or force a more accelerated evolution. This means that destinations have to select different strategic solutions, according to the context of the other competitors in the considered market.

Figure 7.1 allows the following decision-support information to be extracted:

- When a destination is in the same or lower stages than its competitors, in order to reposition itself, it should reinforce its level of investment, except when its competitor is in the decline phase, in which case it will be enough to maintain its normal levels of investment.
- When a destination is in the stagnation phase, either it maintains its level of investment and lets its activities run normally, if it is competing with destinations that are at lower levels, or it tries to anticipate possible future decline (if this is foreseeable), reinforcing its investment and anticipating its market repositioning or rejuvenation, if it is competing with another that is also in the stagnation phase.
- When a destination is in the decline phase, it only has two options: either it withdraws from the market, looking for a new one, or it manages to rejuvenate, within the same market through differentiation and uniqueness policies, which allow it to recover part of the market that is in decline or switch emphasis to a different market. In fact, rejuvenation can be understood as a recovery of the current market of tourists with new and better conditions of attractions and settlement, but it also can be understood as creating or competing for a new market or entering another existing market. Any rejuvenation strategy seeks to place the destination in one of the first three phases of a new cycle.

It is important to note that strategies related to the management of destinations should include not only investment measures in variables considered central to local development, but also measures related to demographics and the direct attraction of tourists, because these also influence the evolution of the destination itself.

Conclusions

It seems clear that the TALC model can and should be considered a strategic model, since it allows the evaluation of different management options, by considering different competitive scenarios. In territorial logic, this model clearly points to the development of the territory and for this to be achieved, 'investment' must be included in any equation.

All strategic models evolve over time, which gives them increased value and more uses. Practically all of them, in addition to their strategic component, are also descriptive. Some have evolved with some quantification, in particular the SWOT model, in order to improve their diagnostic capacity, but in terms of their predictive capacity there are already greater limitations and few developments.

The TALC model shows that a destination has three major strategic options, according to its level of development or the stage of its life cycle:

- hard strategies (strong levels of investment);
- soft strategies (low or moderate levels of investment);
- withdrawal strategies (whenever existing resources do not meet the conditions to maintain themselves in the market, or when that market, as a whole, declines).

Although the approach presented is not particularly innovative, since it translates strategies into investment alternatives, depending on competitive circumstances, it reveals itself as a differentiating approach, given that it refers to the interest in determining the phase of the life cycle in which a destination and its competitors are, so as to optimise the available investment solutions.

Thus, it can be argued that the TALC model is moving towards a 'theory of tourism development'. There is already a 'descriptive', 'quantifiable' and 'strategic' model. As soon as it is possible to introduce a 'forecasting' component into this model, the conditions will be met to establish a true 'theory'.

References

Ansoff, I. (1957) Strategies for diversification. *Harvard Business Review*, 113–124.

Athiyaman. A. (1995) The interface of tourism and strategy research: An analysis. *Tourism Management* 16 (6), 447–453.

Baum, T.G. (2006) Revisiting the TALC: Is there an off-ramp? In R. Butler (ed.) *The Tourism Area Life Cycle, Volume 2: Conceptual and Theoretical Issues* (pp. 219–230). Clevedon: Channel View Publications

Butler, R. (1980) The concept of a tourism area life cycle: Implications for management resources. *Canadian Geographer* 24 (1), 5–12.

Butler, R. (ed.) (2006a) *The Tourism Area Life Cycle, Volume 1: Applications and Modifications*. Clevedon: Channel View Publications

Butler, R. (ed.) (2006b) *The Tourism Area Life Cycle, Volume 2: Conceptual and Theoretical Issues*. Clevedon: Channel View Publications.

Coelho, J.A.S. (2010) Un índice de desarrollo turístico basado en el ciclo de vida de un destino. Unpublished PhD thesis, Universidad de Extremadura, Badajoz, Portugal.

Coelho, J. and Butler, R. (2012) The Tourism Area Life Cycle: A quantitative approach of the tourism area life cycle. *European Journal of Tourism, Hospitality and Recreation* 3 (3), 9–3.

Coelho, J. and Lourenço, P. (2015) A identificação da fase do ciclo de vida de um destino turístico para as escolhas estratégicas: uma proposta de uma ferramenta expedita. *Revista de Estudios Económicos y Empresariales, editada por el Centro Universitario de Plasencia* 27, 15–41.

Cooper, C.P. (1993) The life cycle concept and tourism. In P. Johnson and B. Thomas (eds) *Choice and Demand in Tourism* (pp. 145–160). London: Mansell.

Echtner, C.M. and Jamal, T.B. (1997) The disciplinary dilemma of tourism studies. *Annals of Tourism Research* 24 (4), 868–883.

Frederick, M. (1993) Rural tourism and economic development. *Economic Development Quarterly* 7 (2), 215–224.

Ghazinoory, S., Adbi, M. and Azadegan-Mehr, M. (2011) SWOT methodology: A state-of-art review for the past, a framework for the future. *Journal of Business Economics and Management* 12 (1), 24–48.

Haywood, K. (1986) Can the Tourist Area Life Cycle be made operational? *Tourism Management* 7, 154–167.

Henderson, B. (1970) *The Product Portfolio*. Boston: Boston Consulting Group.

Lagiewski, R.M. (2006) The application of the TALC model: A literature survey. In R. Butler (ed.) *The Tourism Area Life Cycle, Volume 1: Applications and Modifications* (pp. 27–50). Clevedon: Channel View Publications.

Myrdal, G. (1961) *The Political Element in the Development of Economic Theory* (3rd edn). London: Routledge & Kegan Paul (first edn published 1932).

Pêra, C., Fernandes, P. and Veloso, C. (2017) Índice de desenvolvimento turístico: Aplicado à Região Norte de Portugal. *Turismo e Desenvolvimento* 27–28, 85–95.

Porter, M. (1979) How competitive forces shape strategy. *Harvard Business Review* 57, 137–145.

Ritchie, J. and Crouch, G. (1999) Tourism, competitiveness and societal prosperity. *Journal of Business Research* 44 (3), 137–152.

Ritchie, J. and Crouch, G. (2003) *Competitive Destination: A Sustainable Tourism Perspective*. Wallingford: CABI Publishing.

Weihrich, H. (1982) The TOWS matrix – A tool for situational analysis. *Long Range Planning* 15 (2), 54–66.

WTO (1970) *Estatutos da Organização Mundial do Turismo (OMT), México, em 27 de setembro*. Madrid: WTO.

8   Opinions on the Reformation of TALC Studies

K. Michael Haywood

Having grown up in the Caribbean and made numerous visits there over the years, I developed a fascination with tourism. I witnessed the initial phases of start-up, the lead-up to evolutionary growth, followed by stabilised forms of maturity and active pursuit of rejuvenation to counter rapid disruption. Later, as an avid observer and consultant, I witnessed how so many communities-as-destinations and tourism-related enterprises – through their commitments, R&D efforts, plans and strategies – were intent to inspire and aspire, not ire; to gain, not cause strain.

There is nothing delusionary about this. It simply reflects an over-riding belief cemented in the (not always realisable) economics of hope (Pleeging & Burger, 2020), not doom, as well as in the concept of dynamic capabilities as a theory of organisations (Teece, 2022), valuable as a means to helping communities-as-destinations maintain their ability to progress.

Unfortunately, these worldviews regarding tourism do not jive with what some academicians debate as a 'war over tourism' (Butcher, 2020; Higgins-Desboilles, 2021), with tourism often characterised as a commoditised, worrisome phenomenon plundering and overwhelming the commons and sliding into decline, with tourists and tourism often portrayed in derogatory or pejorative terms.

At least that's the impression gleaned by industry insiders, many of whom are trying their utmost to uphold and balance their corporate, societal and sustainability obligations, taking umbrage with those who choose to ignore their contributions, contextual realities and struggles associated with running all types of enterprises – organisations and communities dedicated to serving diverse markets, providing enjoyment, pleasure (Austin, 2022) and sustenance, as best they can, for everyone.

While I have yet to meet and talk with operators or community officials who have shown interest in TALC, that's not to say that they aren't fully aware of tourism's vicissitudes and downside risks. Given the nature of their fixed-capacity, financially leveraged enterprises that are highly vulnerable to the gyrations, cyclicity and seasonality of travel and tourism, they are well versed in the trade-offs between risk mitigation and risk taking. Everyone is seeking resilience, desperately trying to adapt to difficult realities, different mentalities and time-based competition (Stark & Hout, 2023). On the other hand, they instinctively know that travel and tourism's growth is not about to peter out. The constancy of demand, or the desire and need to travel, is everlasting – 'travel and tourism for all' (not just the privileged). That's not to say that economic growth is, or should be, their objective. Operators are savvy enough to realise that growth is simply an outcome of successful win–win performances, the offering of joyful and aesthetic, sensual and resplendent visitor experiences.

But, achieving share-of-heart in competitive marketplaces requires emphasis on earning share-of-market, requiring destinations to spend millions of dollars on marketing and place branding (the power of destinations to attract and inspire). To secure thrive-ability, however, there is growing awareness that success has to be inextricably tied to creative community methods designed to enhance the appeal and success of their communities as a whole … an optimistic outlook associated with prosperity and progress in mind.

And yet, as the proverbial canaries in the gold mine, having sparked concerns about 'overtourism' – the breaching of thresholds (Raworth, 2017) and calls for travel and tourism's 'de-growth' (legitimate or not) – one can gain the impression that more TALC studies must overcome their infatuation with tourism's regress (Haywood, 2022a) seemingly unsympathetic to travel and tourism's relationship-building, hospitable and delightful qualities. Of course, no one is disputing that there are dark undersides to travel and tourism. The facts speak for themselves.

While it has taken time for everyone to catch up with altered realities, progress in the industry's pursuit of sustainability definitely is advancing. But that's not stopping some citizenry groups from demanding a scaling-back of some types of touristic activities and events that seem purposely designed to flood the hot-spot zones in touristic (actually historic, recreation and entertainment) areas … a backlash against annoying behaviours, the car culture, the crush of the crowds and the moneyed interests associated with profiteering.

Similarly, there are certain communities trying to curtail tourism's dominance. Conscious about its power to overwhelm, even destroy the fabric, charm or folkloric aspects of their cultures and nature-based areas, they are promoting locally controlled, community-based tourism … recognition that tourism should address problems associated with poverty (Desmond, 2023) and cultural integrity … requiring attention to diversity, equity and integration (DEI), and a rationing or limitation to access, a stance compatible with the need to secure a sense of normalcy, survival and thrive-ability.

Based on the insights and the critiques contained in this new volume on TALC (which I did not have the opportunity to review), it seems doubtless that TALC studies have a brilliant future. But, it will be conditional on the necessity for more fulsome and deeper-dive assessments so as to fully appreciate and understand the realities and rhythmic flows of touristic activities; the independent nature of (entrepreneurial) stakeholders as they grapple with the need to collaborate, co-create and leverage their interdependencies – recognition that tourism's ecosystem, value and supply chains have to be better integrated and managed for the benefit of all, as everyone strives for prosperity and idealised versions of progress. Deeper dives will provide more valuable and contextually rich knowledge; enhance everyone's abilities to perform and prosper; assist in resource allocation decisions; create meaningful value through mitigation and innovation; improve everyone's mental agility to improvise; adapt to the multiple rhythms of life (Walsh, 2023); and excel through adversity.

As a prelude to further comments, I feel it necessary to provide a glimpse into my initial thinking and sentiment about tourism which have shaped my beliefs regarding tourism's socioeconomic development, and what I have come to consider as its 'Ps' (beyond those commonly associated with marketing) – principled purpose and performance; pride and passion for place; desires for prosperity and progress; a need for partnerships and predictability; favourable policies to achieve an honourable presence; and the will to persevere. As commented at the time (Haywood, 1975: 63–66):

> Tourism development represents a very appealing means by which regions and countries can stimulate investments, earn foreign exchange, and increase employment. Unfortunately, there is an implicit, and sometimes explicit, assumption that the ends of tourists and investors are more important than public welfare.
>
> However, today, we are witnessing a convolution of several factors and forces, especially changes in social values as reflected in environmental sensitivities that are demanding a transcendence of traditional goals of economic life to environmental goals.
>
> Because these environmental goals impose severe constraints on tourism development, the differences between private, public and plural goals require comprehensive planning. Therefore, if tourism development is to be both economically and socially viable, it must be intentionally planned according to performance criteria.
>
> However, the development and use of social performance criteria [clarified in the text] represent a challenge to those involved in tourism development. Further work is required in:
>
> • Identifying those publics or groups that experience the benefits and costs of tourism development.
> • Quantifying the values and attitudes of those publics and groups toward tourism development in order to arrive at an index of social desirability.
> • Interpreting all the analyses and identifying the implications for tourism policy, planning, and development.

While this writer's evaluation of TALC over the intervening years (Haywood, 1986, 1988, 1991, 1992, 1993, 1997, 2006a, 2006b) has expanded on and beyond these early notions, the intent now is not to double down on what has been critiqued or contributed in the past (though the suggestions still apply), but to reveal how the worldwide studies of popularised tourism areas could be advanced and become an integral contributor to, and part of, a new science of progress (Collison & Cowen, 2019; Haywood, 2023).

Review of the Basics

To truly understand the phenomenon of travel and tourism, it's essential to appreciate the roots and links to exploration and trade, transportation and communications, work and leisure, curiosity and cultures. Because very country and region is unique in these regards, all studies of TALC should begin with insightful historical reviews, examining the who, what, when, where and how of tourism development that will lead to an improved understanding of how the future of tourism should or is likely to unfold, and transformation determined as a means of clarifying and highlighting the individuality and identity of communities.

Numerous factors shape and influence an area's unique, attractive and desirable qualities … enhancing, protecting or undermining them. Detailed ecosystem reviews need to explore the relationships among destination's essential input layers, their output and outcome layers, as well as the in-between, often hidden (producing, serving and performing) layers.

For it is these layers and qualities (and interactions among them) that are subject to constant change (improvement or obstruction) from a range of influencers, doers and decision-makers – developers, investors, suppliers, politicians, government agencies, non-governmental organisations (NGOs), citizens, managers, the workforce, industry sector associations, plus a range of other stakeholders, including educators, who either contribute to value-creation or (unwittingly) engage in value destruction.

As for the 'T' in TALC, tourism relies upon and spurs the development of a vast array of resources and complementary enterprises and activities (accommodation, food services, cultural attractions, festivals, events, conference centres, retail establishments, markets, entertainment, transportation, tour operators and so on) to attract and transact with people who reside outside of a community's defined boundaries. Governments, destination management organisations (DMOs) and a host of other organisations all create 'essentialism' about the exciting, exotic and must-see qualities of their destinations. What's interesting about this generalisation (never forgetting travel and tourism's largesse and importance to entire economies, the well-being or 'wellth' of millions of individuals) is that whole communities and many industries, economic, social and cultural sectors are dependent upon and benefit in many ways from this influx of visitors, guests and audiences. Furthermore, hotels, restaurants, attractions and events wouldn't exist at all, or provide valued amenities for local residents and industries, if travel opportunities were minimised or tourism's collaborative and inter-dependent eco-system didn't exist.

Tourism that consists not only of so-called leisure-oriented visitors, but those travelling for vastly different (business and personal) reasons, many of whom reside close by, within local or regional catchment areas … everyone mixing, mingling and moving together in different but inter-secting patterns … patterns that evolve and can be manipulated through decisions (or not) to provide the needed infrastructure, and invest in conference and recreation facilities, sports stadiums, performing arts and cultural centres, including support for small and medium-size enterprises (SMEs) or other entrepreneurial enterprises that allow or permit everyone to flourish.

As for the 'hordes' (many of them local residents) who are invited and descend on destinations to shop, recreate or attend events, any reference to them as being a 'mass' is a misnomer. Visiting groups are highly dif-ferentiated or segmented. People's interests and behaviours are as unique and distinct as their arrival times and lengths of stay, including the disper-sion, location or timing of their activities … all of which provide valuable nuance and variations in the determinacy of seasonally and cyclically determined outcomes associated with the various stages in life cycles and any corresponding shifts in volume.

If only more TALC studies, in explaining the evolution of these segments, paid greater attention to the uniqueness of value being sought by each of them, as well as for other stakeholders (Almquist *et al.*, 2016). Value that can be functional, emotional, social and life-affirming … how value has been identified, evolves, changes and has been incorporated into all of a destination's promises and offerings (or not), including the efforts to improve a destination's quality of life, image and its streetscapes and marketplaces through effective place-making and design, contingent on the need for balance between nostalgia and postalgia (Ybema, 2004).

It's well known that value in all its manifestations is extremely vulnerable to disruption from the outside world, especially when wars, culture wars, climatic calamities and pandemics strike (Haywood, 2020), and geo-political disputes and economic upheavals occur, and similarly within destinations, when they appear unsafe no-go zones, unwelcoming, unfriendly, unkempt and unwilling to upgrade or refurbish. They all give pause or postponement to travel.

Tracking changes in the volume of demand and expenditures is to be expected, but it means little unless the rationale for the change is fully explored, including close examination as to the nature of visitor ex-periences; trends, economic and fashion cycles; the distinctiveness of and differentiation among offerings; host/guest expectations and satisfactions; the remit and ability of local governments and DMOs to carry out their responsibilities; prevailing capacity and capability limitations, especially the necessary infrastructure; the rise or decline in tangible and intangible asset values; the willingness to invest and provide financial capital; the effectiveness of marketing and destination branding efforts (conversion rates); and the effects and influence of word-of-mouth and social media.

To put such concerns into even fuller context, it's useful to undertake comparisons with nearby or comparable destinations, as TALC in one area can influence or be influenced by what's going on in other competing or complementary areas. Consider, for example, the expansion of transportation routes, changes to airlift, competing promotions, tourism-inducing activities, commitments to environmental improvements, even the use of tourism to spur immigration or encourage the development of retirement communities.

As for the 'A' in TALC, clarity as to what constitutes the boundaries of an area can be complicated. In fact, what constitutes a tourism area? What are the criteria? Who decides, based on what intent? Is it based on the number of visitors relative to the local population; or simply an arbitrary designation based on popularity of an area or nodal point, a zoning issue, or simply a means of signifying a historic, cultural or entertainment area?

What if a TALC study was undertaken in the Bahamas? Would it distinguish among the islands? The level, types and timing of activities, including the particular stage of TALC in each of the islands, would be totally different. Of course, if the surrounding seas are included, and the impact from yachting, cruising, watersports, fishing and land-based development was considered, the contextual situation and resulting findings would shift again.

As is well known, the impetus to undertake TALC studies, in large part, originated from an awareness that excessive touristic activity could exceed the carrying capacities of land, water, atmospheric and cultural environments. But why pay sole attention to and blame tourism when a host of additional, contributing factors or forces are likely to be in play? This is made even more problematic when carrying capacities may be unknown, undeterminable or expected to be elastic.

It may seem incongruous, but attention being given to tourism's deleterious impacts has created whole new categories of tourism: eco-tourism, community-based tourism, indigenous tourism, adventure tourism, expedition tourism, dark tourism, cultural tourism, volunteer tourism … in other words, an explosion of niche micro-markets boosting the economies of particular regions of countries and districts of communities. Suffice to say, it has also given rise to numerous NGOs promoting climate-friendly travel, pro-poor tourism, sustainability certification initiatives and programmes, and operators whose programming promotes exclusive and expensive tours in highly fragile and vulnerable areas. One wonders, what have been the impacts from these developments, influences and marketing ploys on the destinations that everyone is trying to protect?

When TALC studies are undertaken for small countries, cities, regional and rural areas, a reader can be confounded when problems related to congestion, overcrowding (with locals mingling with visitors) or environmental impacts are generalised for entire regions or areas, rather than the specific, well-defined areas of overload – beaches, forests, ski slopes, entertainment locales, shopping areas and designated resort areas.

Such problems may (or may not) minimally affect or infringe on neighbourhoods devoid of visitors; districts may, in fact, want visitors, or their share, and could benefit from their presence. Undertourism is often more prevalent than overtourism.

To ensure thoroughness, TALC studies must consider the positive and negative effects of tourism from every angle – on lives, livelihoods, cultures and economies; on the multipliers and support for local businesses (especially the agricultural and artisanal sectors); on quality of life (adequate housing for workers); and, more importantly, the extent to which value-creation or destruction is occurring, has occurred or is likely to occur over time.

No one is disputing the need for TALC studies to focus on carrying capacity assessments. The need for sustainable spatial management is undeniable, but from my point of view, the purpose, possibilities and potential of TALC studies is limited by this singular focus. Ensuring a destination's longevity and thrive-ability has to be multi-faceted. As previously noted, there are a number of ways to determine tourism's inputs and outputs, its economic and social performance (Haywood, 1975).

This leads to the 'L' of TALC (life). It seems presumptuous to assume that tourism and tourism areas proceed through birth-to-death journeys … beginnings that are evolutionary and far from divine; mortality should refer only to the inability of an area to sustain life. Except for extremely remote regions, travel to or from these areas will always be an on-going, on-the-move, mobile phenomenon (of course, requiring system change as everyone adapts to climate change) … so long as the community or locale continues to exist.

Similarly, it's strange to assume that 'Life' applies to a tourism area's categorical components – transportation, accommodation, attractions, and so on – each of which constitute what can be called a product/service class that serves and satisfies people's basic needs. On the other hand, one cannot afford to ignore the constant rate of (technological) change taking place within each product/service class and the corresponding impacts on specific locales.

'Life' is more likely to apply, however, to the variety of product/service forms that exist within each class – budget or luxury hotels, fast food or Michelin-star restaurants, theme parks or museums, for example – because they are likely to exhibit less stability.

As for the brands associated with each product/service form, their lives can be either extremely short or long, and can exhibit undeterminable patterns (beyond the typical S-curve) based on a wide variety of circumstances, particularly financial and managerial decisions that influence the behaviour and choices made by visitors and those operating within the managerial realm of the relevant private, public or plural sectors.

Similarly in regard to the existence of all companies that hold brands in their portfolios: they experience life cycles as well, usually above and beyond their brands. Organisations that are the brand-making machines create new (soft) brands to add to their portfolios, or sometimes sell off some, or at other times using mergers and acquisitions to add or consolidate brands.

In essence, it can be said that the 'Life' of so-called 'tourism areas' isn't simply being determined by the volume of visitors, but by the nature of the decisions and actions of others, a fair number of whom are likely to reside outside of, and may be disconnected from or totally uninterested in, the interests of the community or destination in question.

Given this reality, resentment and tensions could arise if the well-being and prosperity of people, destinations and organisations are at odds and under threat. But, then, would the situation alter if tourism was controlled locally (Higgins-Desbiolles & Bigby, 2023; Kincaid, 1988)? If local citizens represented the labour and policymaking force? TALC studies could be helpful in this regard.

Bringing Clarity to the Cycle in TALC

This brings us to the 'C' in TALC, which, in the literature, suggests that tourism activity levels in destinations proceeds through cyclical patterns commonly associated with the S-curve. Utilising quantitative data, based primarily on visitation rates and expenditures, most TALC studies reveal a starting point in time, leading to take-off, growth, degrees of stabilisation and then the possibility for decline, rejuvenation or renewal of growth, all subject to vastly different time intervals between stages, making it difficult to identify or predict inflection or tipping points.

In typical product/service life cycles, however, sales patterns are studied in comparison with profitability, which has a tendency to falter prior to when sales start to stagnate, which, if detected, can trigger a number of reactions and decisions: discount pricing, launch of a 'new' version of a product/service, a variety of marketing and branding actions, including discontinuation of operations, all of which can defy efficacy and, yet, influence the nature of a destination's cycle.

In destinations (an aggregation of product/service classes, brands, product/service forms and organisations), management of tourism or communities-as-destinations through all their cycles could be called an oxymoron. Sure, there may be certain regulations and rules in place, but DMOs that think they are managing probably aren't. Either they lack agency or their so-called toolbox consists primarily of advocacy and brand positioning strategies (designed to attract a few major segments of the travelling public).

While the mandates of most DMOs are skewed towards marketing (and its funding, which may not be secure), there is a growing realisation that greater effort has to go into ensuring the delivery of community shared value (a Destinations International initiative) from tourism. How this will be determined and play out in the future and affect TALC has yet to be determined, but needs to be studied.

Suffice to say, governance associated with tourism, especially at the level of local destinations, remains a work in progress, though internationally a number of organisations, like US Aid, are attempting to accelerate development and humanitarian progress through partnerships with the private sector in specific locales.

Given the level of complexity associated with cycles, progression through all stages will always be experimental (the timing and direction of each being indeterminate), even when utilising knowledge from destination assessments, strategic research and use of scenarios. Yet that's what can make TALC research interesting.

For an understanding of tourism's early start, most TALC studies have to rely on historical records. Determination of success rests in the hands of the 'movers and shakers' (a mix of entrepreneurial dreamers, corporate giants, zealous politicians and the power they can yield). During this introductory or debut stage, TALC studies need to understand the fantasies, fear, foibles and flaws of start-ups (Ries, 2011), characteristic as well of tourism technology start-ups (Thiel, 2014).

Entrepreneurial start-ups, however, occur at every stage, from inception to decline or rejuvenation. Decisions are made in accord with opportunities (usually related to latent demand) to expand capacities and capabilities, but with no assurance as to the length of their lifespans. Their presence is adjunctive, disruptive or transformational.

In any case, it's essential to be attentive to the nature of decisions, the role of and support from the communities as they evolve as destinations during the take-off, growth and maturity stages. Development during these stages is contingent on accessibility, the ability to form lasting customer connections; to deliver and manage unique, engaging and ever-evolving visitor host/guest experiences; to undertake and constantly perform the necessary chores; to resolve any degenerative conditions; to achieve and maintain competitive and comparative advantage through and by design; to build and maintain brand equity; to promote healthy growth; to embrace, develop and constantly upgrade the appropriate infrastructures.

As is well known, the very nature and composition of 'tourism areas' can shift as disenchantment and displeasure occurs, labour markets disengage, visitor sentiment and expectations are dashed. When service capabilities weaken, the retail mix changes, local patronage is dislocated and inflation causes property values to spike; growth can be stunted, especially when decision-makers are blind to impending problems, compounded by a lack of urgency ... all reactions to uncertainty about the future direction of demand.

Of course, TALC studies, fascinated with the inevitability of the decline stage, can be very useful and valuable. The deleterious impacts associated with travel and tourism need to be identified and avoided. But how, when, from the get-go, awareness and knowledge of these impacts may be unknown, under-rated, or literally hidden and disguised within all preceding stages, or when particular thresholds cannot be easily identified or quantified? These problems need to be resolved, particularly when inducement of decline suddenly comes from calls for tourism's de-growth, and can result in severe socioeconomic dislocations.

These days we are becoming far more aware of the importance of sustainability, regeneration and the impact climatic disruptions are having on destinations. This necessitates greater involvement from governments, ministries and planning departments in preventing and rectifying the devolution of destinations and individual tourism-related enterprises, but with what level of rigour, based on what realisable goals and what immediate and long-term effects?

Similar consideration apply to the impacts coming from the sharing economy (Juul, 2017), online shopping, the connection and caring economies, including the crises nowadays associated with democratic capitalism (Wolf, 2023) and artificial intelligence.

Interestingly, what transpires throughout a destination's development is likely to be a function of its DNA (Bonchek, 2016) – its cultures, predispositions, character, personalities and strategies. If only TALC studies took organisational or community-wide DNA seriously, the uncovering of inherent anomalies and shortcomings (particularly outdated legacy practices) along with the ability (or not) to adapt, evolve, transition and execute – what enables or holds people and organisations back from making or encouraging change – might be better understood.

Particularly when reimagined as contributors to the science of progress, TALC studies could contribute more significantly to our understanding of the machinations within a destination's cycles ... thereby becoming more accomplished in their descriptive analysis, so as to arrive at prescriptions; more circumspect at interpretation, so as to appreciate and clarify intentions; more thorough in depicting problems, so as to identify possibilities and improve performance.

It's one thing for TALC studies to identify a destination's level of vulnerability and exposure from entrenched problems, but it's the shift to identifying preferred outcomes and opportunities that, in the end, truly matters to the destinations themselves. Of course, there are a myriad of problems threatening individual enterprises, industries, communities, regions, countries and the planet, but if prevention is to occur, those vested with the power to make a difference need help if they are to claw their way back from decline and reach new horizons.

Clearly, far greater attention has to be paid to the governance of destinations, how it can be better utilised to manage a destination's growth or stabilise it. The intent: to reverse regress in favour of progress towards 'tourism areas' where all citizens and visitors can have a life, can enjoy the pleasures of life and can benefit from the rewards that tourism offers ... not be sullied by its dislocations.

Reformation

TALC studies cannot afford to be superficial or singular in their emphasis on the decline stage. Throughout this opinion piece, I have identified a number of areas that require attention. But everything is contingent on undertaking 'deep dive' assessments of tourism within specific destinations. Assessments are needed not just to identify or address a wide range of environmental, social, governance (ESG) concerns and other shortcomings (many being ignored because of today's over-riding emphasis on climate), but to clarify and even champion tourism's essentiality, its goodness and benefits (beyond those that are primarily economic). Because if they are ignored, performance, progress and prosperity will stall.

Given the importance of tourism's 'P's, TALC studies need to fathom tourism's purpose – a 'deep purpose' (Gulati, 2022) that will help to clarify the 'why' of tourism for each destination – who it is supposed to benefit, and how. Such studies would determine the degree to which tourism provides and creates meaningful and shared value to all stakeholders, countries, communities and the planet.

Only when there is 'deep purpose' can a bedrock of principles be prudently applied; moral ambiguities addressed; and performance be judged and determined on the basis of carefully conceived and appropriately balanced social, cultural, economic, environmental scoring systems (Fatima & Elbanna, 2020), with performance based, for example, on the Balanced Scorecard (Kaplan & Norton, 1996, 2004). This system is utilised in many businesses, and is considered essential given the need to reflect the value of everything (Mazzucato, 2017); liberate the soul of communities-as-destinations; enhance their allure and anti-fragile qualities (Taleb, 2012); embrace the creator economy; and emphasise place-making that will help amplify its purpose.

Once more inclusive and well-rounded approaches to measuring performance are identified, TALC studies are more likely to contribute to a new science of progress (Collison & Cowen, 2019) ... the beginning of a new era for tourism. To this end, it helps when TALC studies contribute to the historical context, delve into the discoveries that have prompted dreamers who saw potential and possibilities that at the outset may not have been tourism based but, as time moved on, garnered curiosity, attention and the interest of investors and developers.

Collecting and understanding the significance of these preliminary events are more than interesting. One is reminded of books like *The Life and Times of Miami Beach* (Armbruster, 1995) or *A Small Place* (Kincaid, 1988) about tourism in Antigua, which provide fascinating insights and captivating introductions to destinations – narratives that enlighten and can identify interesting and troubling segues to current times, perhaps providing gist to prevailing attitudes towards tourism development, even the eventual unpleasantries associated with untrammelled growth.

In seeking and providing fully fledged oversight, TALC studies are likely to become better balanced in their purview … more likely to redirect the 'mission on messaging' that currently seems to skew negatively in regard to tourism, indeed, to create what could be called a new mission economy (Mazzucato, 20121) that needs to incorporate and include travel and tourism. When more is done to help those involved in the industry to understand tourism within their destination, tourism's leaders will be more inclined to inspire and aspire and, in turn, bring about change and improvement, especially how to foster transitions and turnarounds. By so doing, individual participants and industry leaders will be more inclined: to redefine tourism's role in society to; steer change in tourism's ecosystem; to revise tourism's business models; to restore trust; to manage tensions; and to achieve mastery (Greene, 2013). Mastery is useful in resolving problems (preventing emissions, reducing travel and tourism's carbon footprint, retrofitting buildings) and in pursuing opportunities, opportunities that focus on diversity, inclusion and equity; help build coalitions of stakeholders; develop dynamic capabilities; foster compelling communities; ensure hospitality is inspired; implement Destination International's 'Community Shared Value'; fund efforts that encourage collaborative innovation (green tech, for example); and prioritise comprehensive sustainability, as suggested in the Bridgetown Initiative, put forth by the island of Barbados.

These are all efforts to create transformational improvements and representative governance, essential to ensuring everyone's survival and thrive-ability in an agitated world. Such transformation will demand greater attention to unlocking new value; encouraging corporate support for communities-as-destinations; advancing the importance of innovation and learning how to transition to desired future-forward states – changing the trajectory toward new horizons designed to anticipate and counter disruptions (Blank, 2019).

If everyone is to become truly engaged in ensuring the future of their communities-as-destinations, TALC's cycle must be more attentive and receptive to the up-and-up, active and actionable pursuit of a humanity-centred approach to progress (Haywood, 2023): communities-as-destinations networked, pooling resources and working as a team to tilt the odds in their favour through principled purpose and performance; pride and passion for place; desires for prosperity and progress; a need for partnerships and predictability; favourable policies to achieve an honourable presence; and pushed through the will to persevere.

References

Almquist, E., Senior, J. and Black, N. (2016) The elements of value. *Harvard Business Review*, September, 46–53.

Armbruster, P. (1995) *The Life and Times of Miami Beach*. New York: Alfred Knopf.

Austin, E. (2022) *Living for Pleasure: An Epicurean Guide to Life*. Oxford: Oxford University Press.

Blank, S. (2019) McKinsey's three horizon model defined innovation for years: Here's why it no longer applies. *Harvard Business Review*, February.

Bonchek, M. (2016) How to discover your company's DNA. *Harvard Business Review*, 12 December.

Butcher, R. (2020) The war on tourism. *Spiked* (online magazine), 4 May.

Collison, P. and Cowen, T (2019) We need a new science of progress. *The Atlantic*, 30 July.

Desmond, M. (2023) *Poverty, by America*. New York: Penguin Random House.

Fatima, T. and Elbanna, S. (2020) Balanced scorecard in the hospitality and tourism industry: Past, present and future. *International Journal of Hospitality Management* 91. https://doi.org/10.1016/j.ijhm.2020.102656.

Greene, R. (2013) *Mastery*. London: Penguin Random House.

Gulati, R. (2022) *Deep Purpose: The Heart and Soul of High Performance Companies*. New York: Harper Collins.

Haywood, M. (1975) *New Criteria for measuring the Social Performance of Tourism Development Projects. National and Regional Tourism Development*. IGU Occasional Paper 5. Peterborough: Trent University.

Haywood, M. (1986) Can the Tourism Area Life Cycle be made operational? *Tourism Management* 7 (3), 154–167.

Haywood, M. (1988) Responsible and responsive tourism planning in the community. *Tourism Management* 9 (2), 105–118.

Haywood, M. (1991) Can the Tourism Area Life Cycle be made operational? Ten years of *Tourism Management*. In S. Medlik (ed.) *Managing Tourism* (pp. 31–38). London: Heinemann Professional Publishing.

Haywood, M. (1992) Revisiting the resort cycle. *Annals of Tourism Research* 19 (2), 351–354.

Haywood, M. (1993) Sustainable development for tourism: An organizational perspective. In G. Nelson (ed.) *Sustainable Development – Practices, Problems and Prospects* (pp. 233–241). Waterloo: University of Waterloo.

Haywood, M. (1997) *Business Cycles and Tourism. Economic Geography of Tourism: Theoretical Debates and Perspectives* (pp. 83–98). Philadelphia: University of Pennsylvania.

Haywood, M. (2006a) Evolution of tourism areas and the tourism industry. In R. Butler (ed.) *The Tourism Area Life Cycle, Volume 1: Applications and Modifications* (pp. 51–69). Clevedon: Channel View Publications.

Haywood, M. (2006b) Legitimising the TALC as a theory of development and change. In R. Butler (ed.) *The Tourism Area Life Cycle, Volume 2: Conceptual and Theoretical Issues* (pp. 29–43). Clevedon: Channel View Publications.

Haywood, M. (2020) A post COVID 19 future: Tourism re-imagined, re-enabled. *Tourism Geographies* 22 (3), 599–609.

Haywood, M. (2022a) Tourism's thriveability requires performative change: Foundations. *Good Tourism* blog (online), 13 December.

Haywood. M. (2022b) Tourism's thriveability requires performative change: Changemakers. *Good Tourism* blog (online), 13 December.

Haywood, M. (2022c) Tourism's resilience relies on sustainable, regenerative needs-based models. *Good Tourism* blog (online), 29 August.

Haywood, M. (2023) Tourism in pursuit of progress. *Substack: Tourism's Horizon*, 9 May.

Higgins-Desboilles, F. (2021) The 'war over tourism": The challenges to sustainable tourism in the tourism academy after COVID-19. *Journal of Sustainable Tourism* 29 (4).

Higgins-Desbiolles, F. and Bigby, B.C. (eds) (2023) *The Local Turn in Tourism: Empowering Communities*. Bristol: Channel View Publications.

Juul, M. (2017) *Tourism and the Sharing Economy*. Brussels: European Parliamentary Research Service.

Kaplan, R. and Norton, D. (1996) *The Balanced Scorecard*. Boston: Harvard Business School Press.

Kaplan, R. and Norton, D. (2004) *Strategy Maps*. Boston: Harvard Business School Press.

Kincaid, J. (1988) *A Small Place*. New York: Farrier, Strauss and Giroux.

Mazzucato, M. (2017) *The Value of Everything*. London: Penguin Random House.

Mazzucato, M. (2021) *Mission Economy: A Moonshot Guide to Changing Capitalism*. New York: Harper Business.

Pleeging, E. and Burger, M. (2020) Hope in economics. In S. van den Heuval (ed.) *Historical and Multidisciplinary Perspectives on Hope* (pp. 165–178). Cham: Springer.

Raworth, K. (2017) *Doughnut Economics: Seven Ways to Think Like a 21st Century Economist*. London: Chelsea Green Publishing.

Ries, E. (2011) *Lean Start-Ups*. New York: Crown Business.

Stark, G. and Hout, T. (2023) *Competing Against Time: How Time-Based Competition Is Re-shaping Global Markets*. New York: Free Press.

Taleb, N. (2012) *Anti-Fragile: Things That Gain from Disorder*. New York: Random House.

Teece, D. (2022) The evolution of the dynamic capabilities framework. In R. Adams, D. Grichnik, A. Pundziene and C. Volkmann (eds) *Artificiality and Sustainability in Entrepreneurship* (pp. 113–129). Cham: Springer.

Thiel, P. (2014) *Zero to One*. New York: Crown Business.

Walsh, M. (2023) *Cycles: The Rhythms of Life*. Embodiedfacilitator.com.

Wolf, M. (2023) *The Crises of Democratic Capitalism*. London: Penguin Random House.

Ybema, S. (2004) Managerial postalgia: Projecting a golden future. *Journal of Managerial Psychology* 19 (8), 825–841.

9 Summary: Revisiting the Model – Present Viewpoints

Richard Butler

This chapter addresses some of the points raised in Part 1 of the volume to provide further explanation and hopefully to resolve some criticisms and recommendations made in the preceding chapters.

Assumptions of Growth

As noted earlier, the TALC is a creature of its time, and Keller (this volume, Chapter 10) comments that a 'core societal assumption underlying Butler's TALC is that continued growth is an overarching goal underlying tourism development and indeed all economics'. That is a fair comment, although at that time (1980) such a thought was so fundamental in underlying development in general that it was probably never considered worth commenting on. This writer and others (e.g. Butler & Dodds, 2022; McKercher & Prideaux, 2014) have commented frequently in recent years about the overall priority given to economic arguments over other viewpoints, noting that the 'triple bottom line' of sustainability is rarely if ever equally balanced. In this regard, tourism development is little different from other forms of economic growth and, indeed, for 50 years until the COVID-19 pandemic there had been continuous growth in tourism numbers so that an assumption about increasing growth would have been quite appropriate. In tourism as elsewhere, development meant growth, and while today writers are arguing for degrowth (Andriotis, 2018), to suggest otherwise in the 1960s and 1970s would have been regarded as unusual if not absurd. One might argue still that, to most destinations, overtourism notwithstanding, a decline in business (normally seen in terms of visitor numbers) is viewed as something to be avoided at almost all costs, and the response of virtually all destinations (and other elements of the tourism industry) following the COVID-19 lockdowns (2020–2023) has been to work to restore numbers to their pre-pandemic levels as quickly as possible, and then to focus on increasing them. Thus, the implicit assumption in the TALC model that growth was what every destination wanted was not unjustified, although with hindsight today, such an assumption might well be regarded as short-sighted and responsible for many errors of judgement in marketing and promotion. Commentators such as Andriotis (2018), Dwyer (2022, 2023) and Higgins-Desbiolles *et al.* (2019) have been articulate in arguing for an end to the 'perpetual growth' approach to tourism and for alternatives to viewing success as being represented only by growth.

Infinite Growth: The Las Vegas Puzzle

Even at the time of writing the original article, this writer wondered if Las Vegas (and perhaps other destinations) would prove to be the exceptions to the rule (not exceptions to proving it of course). Could places such as Las Vegas, which in the 1970s seemed capable of endless growth, simply keep growing *ad infinitum* and if they did, would that mean the cycle model was invalid? Having faith in the late Roy Wolfe's thoughts on such a situation, it can be noted that in 1966 he argued that the growth of outdoor recreation was at an unrealistic rate, and he commented:

> this rate simply cannot continue ... I am reminded of the result I obtained when extending the trend line for the growth of visitors to Ontario's Provincial Parks a mere 20 years ahead. I discovered that these visitors would be more than twice as numerous as the whole population of the earth at that time. (Wolfe, 1966: 118)

The possibility of destinations just growing endlessly did remain, giving reason to think the answer to this question lies in appreciating that the Las Vegas of 2020 is not the Las Vegas of 1980. Keller (personal communication in 2020) suggested that Las Vegas had continued to grow because it constantly changed itself, its appeal and its markets; that is, it was, and still is, dynamic, as the model argued. It was perhaps helping to support the model by 'the management of [its] resources' (Butler, 1980: 5), such as they were, as the model argued was necessary. Las Vegas's attractions include sunshine and legalised gambling (for a long time its unique selling point in the USA) and it would appear to have had effective promotion and marketing policies that proved capable of overcoming the loss of its monopoly on legal gambling and subsequent competition from casino-related developments in other destinations. Its willingness to transform its image from just offering gambling to providing other attractions (sporting, music and other events), and even marketing itself, as a family entertainment centre, worked, at least temporarily, although the family centre image appears to have been dropped in recent years. Management through constant change of attractions might well, if appropriately and effectively combined with marketing, prolong the *Development* and *Consolidation* phases of the TALC whenever *Stagnation* appears likely. The graph might then resemble a combination of that of Agarwal (2002) and the sigmoid curves shown in Baum (2006) as discussed in Chapter 23 of the present volume.

The reality is that few places have been as successful as Las Vegas in terms of deliberately managing their visitation, as many of the longest-lasting tourist destinations of the world have relied on unique long-established attributes, such as religious connections and historical/ architectural heritage (e.g. Venice, Rome, Jerusalem), doing little to change their image or to actually manage tourism (with Mecca a rare exception, where the Hajj is heavily managed). Many rely on a regular market and focus any efforts on facility and service provision for that so-far constant market. Las Vegas remains unique in terms of scale and image, and while it has for some years been eclipsed as the gambling centre of the world by Macao (McCartney, 2017), it still has few equals as a tourist destination. The closest comparison is probably to the Disney entertainment parks, where a similar approach to proactive management has been adopted, and the content, if not the overall image, of the destinations has been modified and transformed on an ongoing basis to present an image of an ever-changing but constant fantasy place of dreams. The Disney parks also have the added advantage of being able to discard or change the attractions (rides etc.) without any risk of opposition from destination residents (as there are none) and constantly add replacement attraction on new themes, such as Star Wars or Harry Potter. In such situations, where everything is artificial and authentic only in relation to Disney's own creations, the risk of upsetting 'traditional' visitors is unlikely when such visitors have come precisely to experience fantasies produced in conjunction with Disney's and other image makers' own creations.

Destination Dynamics of Tourist Areas

The starting point for the model was that 'tourist areas' are clearly dynamic, and change, or are changed over time. The term should have been defined more specifically, and this point is addressed later in the volume (Chapter 23). The changes experienced by destinations may be positive or negative, or both, depending on the viewpoint taken and position held, in terms of overall impacts on the destination concerned. It was considered that all destinations are dynamic, albeit at different rates and in differing ways, and that the changes experienced could result from any or all of overuse, obsolescence, removal, replacement, renovation and addition of elements, investment and disasters. Related to the dynamic feature of tourist areas was the assumption that there was a consistent and replicated pattern of development common to most such destinations, as illustrated in the original figure. It is acknowledged that this was a rather arrogant and simplistic assumption, based, as noted above, mostly on the European situation. The original paper did not go into much detail as to the causes of that process, nor the rate at which the pattern developed, but did note that these two characteristics (cause and rate) were likely to vary from one resort to another, while proposing that the overall process was similar in most resorts. Clearly, such comments applied much more directly and meaningfully to European destinations, but they can be seen to be applicable in at least some other parts of the world, including North America and parts of Asia and Australasia (Butler & McDonnell, 2011; Stansfield, 1972).

Visitor Numbers

One criticism of the model has been the use of visitor numbers as the indication of level of development (see Eggli, this volume, Chapter 18). This measure was noted in the original article as being used because of the absence of consistent and reliable alternatives, at least on a global basis, and the fact that at the time of writing, number of visitors was almost always cited as an indicator of growth, if not development. It was never intended by this writer to act as a specific indicator of the *success* of a destination, except in as much as ongoing development (increased visitor numbers) was generally regarded as success at that time. Wilkinson (1996) demonstrated convincingly that increasing visitor numbers alone does not translate into growing economic expenditure, which is what most destinations are desiring. Much depends on the characteristics of the visitors concerned, including their origins, length of stay, behaviour and preferences, some of which are affected in turn by the opportunities to spend in the destination that are offered to them.

The fact remains today, as decades earlier, that numbers of visitors are the data most often recorded in destinations, and normally the only longitudinal data set available to researchers. In specific cases, other data sources may be available and provide a better indication of how tourism is growing (or not) in a specific location. Numbers of building permits for structures related to tourism might be a much better indication of 'development', although definition of what 'related to tourism' really means might be a problem. Bank receipts, credit card expenditures, retail sales would all be more accurate in terms of measuring actual expenditure by tourists in a destination but, again, separating tourist expenditure from other expenditures could be problematic, to say nothing of the privacy issues involved in getting access to and using such data. Data from transportation operators, both to the destination and within it, would be helpful to substantiate visitor numbers as cited by destination management organisations (DMOs) and others and, of course, accommodation usage levels would be particularly valuable, as cost of accommodation can be tied to such figures to provide a measure of actual expenditure on a major item of a tourist's budget (Butler, 1973). All such sources of data could be used instead of simple visitor numbers, but the fact is that for most destinations such data do not exist, particularly not consistently over the long term, which is what the cycle is concerned with. At a national level, relatively little else other than numbers and foreign exchange figures are recorded and these are rarely available at a local level. Most destinations do try to keep a record of what they perceive as numbers of visitors, although in some cases these figures may be as tenuous as numbers of visitors to information bureaux or enquiries, which have been 'converted' into visitors to the destination. They can be useful for identifying trends, which is essentially what the TALC does, but sometimes they are not valid for anything else, owing to inconsistencies in the methods of defining, obtaining and recording such numbers. Thus, in the absence of reliable, consistent alternatives, number of visitors remains the most common and accessible indicator of the nature (growth or decline) of tourism in a destination but, as noted above, with less acceptance that those numbers alone are adequate measures of success of a destination.

Time Dimension

The second axis in the TALC figure, time, also was not discussed in detail, another valid point of criticism. It was noted in the paper that the time scale for a 'cycle' would vary from destination to destination, reflecting the multitude of factors which affected any destination's popularity and attractiveness to markets, including means, modes and levels of access, facilities and services provided, shocks or boosts to the system, political interventions such as subsidies and development aid, and competition. It was deemed impossible to put specific measures on the axis because of such variables. It has been shown that the cycle of some destinations has been longer than a century (e.g. Blackpool and Brighton in England) (Gilbert, 1939; and Jarratt in this volume, Chapter 12), while others may enter and leave tourism within a few decades. Whether this is a weakness of the model or not is debatable, but one has to return to the argument that the model as shown is a generalisation and that it attempts to portray the overall pattern, and both axes of the graph have to be accepted as varying in scale for each destination in reality.

Carrying Capacity

The subject of carrying capacity and its key role in the TALC has, perhaps somewhat strangely to this writer, tended to be either ignored or tacitly accepted in principle or criticised as impractical. With the benefit of hindsight, however, it is surely due for a more rigorous examination. This writer remains a strong supporter of the concept of carrying capacity – the concept that there are limits to the use of resources, beyond which irreparable change or even loss occurs. This seems so obvious that it cannot be realistically challenged if one accepts even the minimum case for sustainable development. Overuse of resources clearly can result in their disappearance (passenger pigeons, dodos and many other species have already disappeared because of humans killing numbers beyond the natural renewal rate of reproduction). Mineral resources (among other natural resources) can be exhausted, forests can be too severely cut to ever regrow to a climax state and water bodies can be drawn down to levels which endanger species present or downstream, or polluted sufficiently to exterminate all life within. Why such a situation could be argued not to occur in a tourist destination remains beyond my understanding.

The argument in the TALC that when carrying capacity levels are exceeded the attractiveness of a destination is reduced (as is its competitiveness) would therefore seem to be justified, even if there is disagreement over the measurement of capacity. It is clear that there is not a realistically accurate and consistent single measure of carrying capacity in the case of a tourist area. This point was noted in the original article ('limits of capacity' in the original figure) and it was argued that there were several forms of capacity, environmental, physical (as in physical plant) and social. The article should have gone on to note that any measures would inevitably have to be dynamic, particularly those in the physical and social spheres, as it is relatively easy, with investment, to increase the capacity of physical plant by adding more rooms, more seats, more spaces and so on. In terms of social capacity, the resident populations of destinations do not remain constant, and different opinions and levels of tolerance and acceptance of the impacts of tourism and tourists emerge over time. Environmental limits are perhaps more difficult to modify, but measures can be taken to reduce impacts, although the modifications necessary might not be acceptable to residents or visitors.

Destinations in widely varying situations and environments are experiencing too many visitors, in some cases in terms of absolute numbers, in other cases in terms of visitors with particular characteristics. Some destinations are taking steps to reverse this situation, so the basic argument that there are at least implicit limits to tourism growth in destinations is surely proven. What has not been proven would appear to be whether such over-visitation, in whole or part, has any actual effect on the attractiveness, popularity or competitiveness of destinations. It would be reasonable to assume it does, but empirical evidence to this effect is lacking. Part of the reason may lie in the argument put forward by Plog (1973) relating to the changing characteristics of visitors to a destination over time and, by implication, that as numbers increase, those sensitive to crowding or excessive numbers are replaced by those who have no or little problem with such levels of visitation. This would suggest that overtourism, then, is predominately a resident and not a visitor issue and that what has been exceeded is the tolerance level (capacity) of residents and not the attractiveness of the destination to visitors. This does not invalidate the inclusion of carrying capacity as a key factor in the TALC model, but it does raise the question of whether excessive visitation alone does result in an eventual decline of a destination, as the model proposed. This is an issue of some fundamental importance to the validity and relevance of the model and it is perhaps surprising that it has not been challenged. Criticism of the inclusion of carrying capacity has normally been related to the impracticality of using the concept in the real world (Lindberg *et al.*, 1997) because of the vast range of types of tourists, in terms of their behaviour, distribution, preferences, spending patterns and cultural characteristics, rather than the argument that over-visitation reduces attractiveness and competitiveness in the overall sense of leading to a decline in visitor numbers.

It might be considered that if and when an overly popular (by some definition) tourist area experiences a decline in tourist numbers, that decline might not be due to a social measure of carrying capacity (resident tolerance, for example) being exceeded, but that measures taken by the area itself to overcome the perceived overtourism are in fact working. If such a situation should emerge, for example, if Amsterdam or Venice were to experience a reduction in visitor numbers that is not clearly related to other factors such as another pandemic, economic recession or a natural disaster, then perhaps, for the first time, major destinations will have shown themselves capable of effective management and limitation of tourist numbers (assuming that is what they were trying to do).

Thus, perhaps the TALC needs some revision to the extent that it is recognised that carrying capacity can be a factor in shaping the curve of visitor numbers, not, or at least much less than originally argued, because excessive numbers have deterred fellow tourists from coming, but because resident intolerance (probably justified) has resulted in measures being taken to reduce the numbers of visitors. To argue that too many tourists make a destination less attractive to other (potential) tourists may be incorrect, at least in the overall sense, although a busy destination may deter those tourists sensitive to crowds, thus changing the overall demographics of visitors. It can be argued that most tourists will be completely unaware that a destination such as Venice may be exceeding its supposed capacity in terms of visitor numbers, or even not care, and thus would not adjust their travel patterns to avoid such a place. One could also argue that a busy or crowded destination may be particularly attractive precisely because of such a level of visitation, as that shows it is a popular destination and presumably worth visiting (and photographing to put online), a key factor in the age of social media.

Conclusion

It might be appropriate to contemplate briefly how the TALC fits in with modern (in the sense of current) tourism and the effect of such agents as www, influencers, social media imagery, virtual reality, 'smart' tourism, the metaverse and fellow travellers. Despite all of these innovations, tourism has continued remarkably unchanged in many respects, in terms of its spatial patterns, markets and overall behaviours. Beaches, cultural heritage, nature and family still dominate the tourism world, as they have for centuries. This is not to argue that nothing has changed – the way tourism is managed, marketed, sold and portrayed have all changed beyond recognition compared with what existed even in 1980. However, there is a danger of being overly influenced by the present and the new and exciting, even if much of that is new only at a superficial level. Inertia is one of the most powerful of those forces influencing all aspects of human behaviour, and tourism is no exception. Thus, while there are shifts in where people go on holiday, the basic patterns of tourism, its major destination and origin countries and its participants' behaviour, are still recognisably similar to those of 1980. China has emerged as a dominant force, both as an attraction for, and as an origin of, a vast number of tourists, but many Chinese tourists travelling abroad go to well-established destination countries, and tourists to China behave as foreign tourists do in almost all countries in terms of 'seeing the sights'. This would suggest that while influences may change, and thus ways of arranging holidays and choosing destinations change, tourist destinations at the macro-scale have remained remarkably consistent and relatively unchanging at their cores. There is perhaps little, therefore, to suggest that the pattern of destination development will not continue much as it has done over the past 40 years and that the TALC model will remain valid, although in a modified form to acknowledge criticisms and suggestions. One might expect that the time for a destination to pass through its initial cycle may be shorter than in previous decades, but it may well be that many destinations will go on to evolve through more than one cycle as they adapt to and adopt new tastes and ways of tourists, a point discussed at more length in the final chapter.

References

Agarwal, S. (2002) Restructuring seaside tourism. The resort life-cycle. *Annals of Tourism Research* 29 (1), 25–55.

Andriotis, K. (2018) *Degrowth in Tourism: Conceptual, Theoretical and Philosophical Issues.* Wallingford: CABI.

Baum, T. (2006) Revisiting the TALC: Is there an off ramp? In R. Butler (ed.) *The Tourism Area Life Cycle, Volume 2: Conceptual and Theoretical Issues* (pp. 219–230). Clevedon: Channel View Publications.

Butler, R. (1973) The tourist industry in the Highlands and Islands. Unpublished PhD thesis, University of Glasgow.

Butler, R. (1980) The concept of the tourist area life-cycle of evolution: Implications for management of resources. *Canadian Geographer* 24 (1), 5–12.

Butler, R. and Dodds, R. (2022) Overcoming overtourism: A review of failure. *Tourism Review* 77 (1), 35–53. https://doi.org/10.1108/TR-04-2021-0215.

Butler, R. and McDonnell, I. (2011) One man and his boat (and hotel and pier...) Henry Gilbert Smith and the establishment of Manly, Australia. *Tourism Geographies* 13 (3), 343–359.

Dwyer, L. (2022) Productivity, destination performance, and stakeholder well-being. *Tourism and Hospitality* 3 (3), 618–633.

Dwyer, L. (2023) Tourism degrowth: Painful but necessary. *Sustainability* 15 (20), 14676. http://dx.doi.org/10.3390/su152014676.

Gilbert, E.W. (1939) The growth of inland and seaside health resorts in England. *Scottish Geographical Magazine* 55, 16–35.

Higgins-Desbiolles, F., Carnicelli, S., Krolikowski, C. *et al.* (2019) Degrowing tourism: Rethinking tourism. *Journal of Sustainable Tourism* 27 (12), 1926–1944.

Lindberg, K., McCool, S. and Stankey, G. (1997) Rethinking carrying capacity. *Annals of Tourism Research* 24 (2), 461–464.

McCartney, G. (2017) Betting on casino tourism resilience: A case study of casino expansion in Macao and the Asia region. In R. Butler (ed.) *Tourism and Resilience* (pp. 195–206). Wallingford: CABI.

McKercher, B. and Prideaux, B. (2014) Academic myths of tourism. *Annals of Tourism Research* 46, 16–28. https://doi.org/10.1016/j.annals.2014.02.003.

Plog, S.C. (1973) Why destinations areas rise and fall in popularity. *Cornell Hotel and Restaurant Association Quarterly* 13, 6–13.

Stansfield, C.A. (1972) The development of modern seaside resorts. *Parks and Recreation* 5 (10), 14–46.

Wilkinson, P.E. (1996) Graphical images of the commonwealth Caribbean: The tourist area cycle of evolution. In L.C. Harrison and W. Husbands (eds) *Practising Responsible Tourism* (pp. 16–40). International Case Studies in Tourism Planning. Toronto: John Wiley and Sons.

Wolfe, R.I. (1966) Recreational travel: The new migration. *Ekistics* 123, 117–123.

Part 2

Relevance

Part 2 of the book focuses on the question of whether the TALC model continues to have relevance four decades after its first publication. The chapters address many of the principal issues raised in the original paper and comment on their applicability in the present context. Keller (Chapter 10) and Gale (Chapter 11) both specifically revisit themes and locations discussed some decades ago through the lens of the TALC. Keller notes the ongoing issue of instability in destinations undergoing a change from one stage of the cycle to another, confirming his conclusions from 1987. Gale similarly re-explores earlier work, examining the multiple forces at work in the formulation and implementation of policy in a destination community and the continued relevance of examining these agents acting on destination development. Jarratt (Chapter 12) uses the example of UK resorts to re-examine the concept of place image and social class and their role in the development, rejuvenation and survival of destinations, and suggests an additional element to consider in the TALC model.

On a different aspect, Romão reviews the implications of 'smart' specialisation in destination development, placing the TALC and its applicability to the current literature on evolutionary economic development. In a more specific context, López-Chávez and Maldonado-Alcudia in Chapter 14 review the application and relevance of the TALC to lifestyle and family businesses, a major element in many tourist destinations. Bolan and Boyd (Chapter 15) examine the way in which developing a new product can rejuvenate an established but declining destination, in their case through the hosting of a major sporting event, which demonstrated how a shift in stage of the life cycle can be achieved. The issue of instability in development is then explored further by Suntikul (Chapter 16) by examining the impacts of political change on destination development in the context of the TALC, in three cases illustrating how important political influence and policy are at all scales of tourism development.

By way of conclusion to Part 2, in Chapter 17 the relevance of the six core elements of the original TALC model in the current day are addressed and, when discussing tourism development in the context of sustainability, the continued need to consider factors such as the question of limits to numbers and the concept of carrying capacity is noted. In that sense, the arguments made in the original article about maintaining the quality of the environment, in both human and environmental contexts (points emphasised by Dodds in Chapter 4), suggest that the overall theme of the original model does have relevance despite the time passing since its initial appearance.

10 Instability and Shifting Control During Stages in Destination Development Revisited

C. Peter Keller

This chapter revisits a proposal made in the 1980s (Keller, 1982), in the context of an investigation of the tourism potential of Baffin Island in northern Canada, explicitly to consider disruptive cycles during progression of the growth curve in Butler's TALC, including an associated shift in industry control. Two arguments are revisited. The proposal suggested periods of instability as demand surpasses capacity to supply along the growth curve, and that these periods of instability would be associated with shifts in power relationships and investments. It was hypothesised that disruptions imply successive transition of development control from local to regional, then national and finally international interests, creating potential for classic centre–periphery conflicts (Hoivik & Heiberg, 1980; Young, 1973). This thinking was guided by the then available literature on tourism as well as field observations when studying tourism growth on Baffin Island.

Four decades on, the opportunity to reflect on this early elaboration of Butler's TALC, notably revisiting two key tenets, is much appreciated. The first tenet to review is the assumption that the politics of regional development has underlying it a gradual transition from local to regional, national and then international control. The second is that there exist disruptive periods of uncertainty in tourism development with associated shifts in investments and power relationships. To place my thinking in context, the chapter begins with observations about general purpose of a model, and specifically Butler's TALC, and this is returned to throughout the chapter. The tourism literature since the 1980s acknowledges the existence of disruptive periods in the growth cycle. It explores the industry's resilience and preparedness to handle them. Case studies make it clear that tourism development studies must pay attention to the reigning policy environments and power relationships when investigating periods of instability. The chapter concludes that Butler's TALC has just the right parsimony to have continued appeal to support this type of investigation, and that this will remain as long as the paradigm of quest for continued growth prevails in economic thinking. The chapter concludes with a brief comment on how tourism on Baffin Island has evolved since the early 1980s.

The Purpose of a Model and Butler's TALC

The purpose of a model is to provide a simplified and generalised representation of a system of interest based on the concept of parsimony. Parsimony can be defined as the judicious trade-off between realism and simplicity. A model should be a sufficiently close approximation to the real system to incorporate most of its salient features. It should have sufficient abstraction and clarity to be easily understood, and be simple enough to allow for evaluation against a wide set of case studies. It should have underlying it both pragmatism and academic appeal. A model devoid of theoretical underpinning will lack foundation. A model so theoretical that it has no practical utility risks being irrelevant.

Butler proposed the TALC as a model to help understand the evolution of a generic tourism destination. His model builds on the product life cycle (also known as the S-shaped curve) as a marketing strategy, published in 1966 (Vernon, 1966), which was by then well established in the economics and business literature (Cao & Folan, 2009). Of course, tourism differs from many other products applicable to the product life cycle, since the tourism product usually is consumed on the site of production and is consumed simultaneously by multiple consumers who interact with the product and each other, in the process often changing the nature of that product. In other words, tourism is more than a consumer product following a simple mode of consumption (Franklin & Crang, 2001; Rojeck & Urry, 1997) since the boundary between what the tourists come to consume and the tourists themselves is blurred (Picard, 1996).

Assuming a continuum from a complex model of complete realism to one of high abstraction, the appeal of both Vernon's product life cycle and Butler's TALC was that they land on the side of high abstraction. Both models are easy to understand and widely applicable. They are elegant frameworks grounded in the theory of economic growth that practitioners can utilise and build on when marketing and advancing product development, and they allow academics to explore if and how the models fit case studies. The fact that Butler's model, introduced in the 1980s, continues to be taught widely in tourism courses, and still attracts debate and a growing body of literature over 40 years later, speaks of its success.

Butler's TALC lends itself to adding layers of complexity to incorporate multidimensional realities of tourism development. One such effort was undertaken by this author while a graduate student of Professor Butler soon after the model was published (Keller, 1982, 1987). Investigating potential for tourism development in Canada's eastern arctic on Baffin Island in what was then known as the Northwest Territories (NWT), I was curious about questions of tourism industry stability and who controls planning, development and service delivery.

Tourism on Baffin Island in the Early 1980s

In the early 1980s the NWT, including Baffin Island, were identified as a peripheral and economically disadvantaged underdeveloped region contemplating increased industrial diversification into tourism to create employment, attract an inflow of capital and facilitate economic growth to increase overall welfare. The region's employment at the time was primarily in traditional occupations, administration, resource extraction and supporting military installations.

This was a period when the parts of the NWT connected by road to the south were beginning to experience independent touring by adventure-seeking individuals, outdoor enthusiasts and those interested in hunting and fishing. Baffin Island was then, and still remains, accessible only by air, boat or non-road overland travel. Apart from visitors for the purposes of business or to visit relatives or friends, Baffin Island was beginning to attract a small number of adventure tourists, supported and serviced by locals. There also was the first evidence of a type of mass tourism, in the form of midnight flights from the south to the town of Frobisher Bay (now Iqaluit) to experience the midnight sun above the Arctic Circle, drink champagne, and buy local arts and crafts before returning to the south for a late breakfast.

Assuming tourism growth according to Butler's TALC, the question arose as to how prepared the NWT and especially Baffin Island were to engage with tourism as a means of economic development on a larger scale. Backed by an emerging literature on tourism development and personal observations, it was argued that investment in tourism did not always yield the nirvana for economic growth it was then made out to be. Given the lack of suitable tourism infrastructure on Baffin Island (accommodation, transportation, dining, attractions and entertainment, etc.) to accommodate growth, investment in the industry would likely need to come from outside. The lack of widespread local awareness of tourism as an economic activity by the communities was noted and it was pointed out that an absence of local labour trained in and familiar with hospitality would imply the need to import those delivering the tourism product, with only the lowest-paid and seasonal jobs going to locals. This led to the realisation that the bulk of tourism expenditures would likely remain with companies located elsewhere but owning and organising the local tourism industry, implying only a small share of tourism expenditures would reach the local and regional economies. Finally, it was argued that, in the absence of tight local and regional control, outside investors driving tourism development and associated infrastructure would do so primarily to suit themselves and the interests of their shareholders.

Stages of Development, Instability and Shifting Control

My field-based observations in the NWT's Baffin Region led me to sympathise with an emerging literature cautioning against uncontrolled tourism development. This literature argued that tourism development in remote and economically underdeveloped regions no doubt brought significant economic potential but also created opportunity for a classic centre–periphery conflict (Hoivik & Heiberg, 1980; Young, 1973). This conflict argued that wealthy and economically developed 'centres' with capacities to generate tourism demand would exploit the economically underdeveloped 'peripheral' regions attractive to tourists.

Butler's TALC had an intuitive appeal to use as a framework to generalise what had been observed. Butler's TALC was combined with the then thinking about tourism typologies advocated by Cohen (1972) and Plog (1972) and the centre–periphery theory, with the hypothesis that during early stages of peripheral tourism, allocentric explorers and drifters would seek authentic experiences while visiting remote places absent of any significant hospitality infrastructure and service. Their needs would be met by locals willing to act as hosts and guides in a basic and traditional format reflecting local values while meeting travellers' needs.

It was argued that when these regions become more discovered, the local communities' capacity to host eventually becomes exhausted, while regional awareness about growing demand for hospitality services and the associated opportunities for economic gain awakens. This represents the first stage of instability and a shift to regional investments to serve primarily regional interests, sometimes at the expense of local interests. This period was linked also to a gradual shift in tourism typology, with the allocentric gradually being replaced by the mid-centric and early individual mass tourists. In other words, the tourism product shifts to take on more of a facilitated and organised nature.

As tourism numbers grow further, it is not unforeseeable that another period of instability will set in when national and international awareness of the destination's tourism potential awaken while regional capacity to handle growing demand is challenged. Another phase change in development can therefore be argued to occur when national and then international investors begin to dominate, with the associated potential for a decline in local and regional control of industry development. This period is linked to another shift in the tourism product as it becomes ever more facilitated and organised, with the emergence of the psychocentric or organised mass tourists beginning to dominate the market.

My research concluded with a caution that the potential evolution from local control over tourism to an economic activity serving primarily outside interests had potential for classic centre–periphery conflicts. Concerning Baffin Island, it was argued that unless carefully managed, tourism may actually be a poor economic development strategy to pursue, and one that might come with significant costs and disappointment to locals.

Forty years later, during the sunset of a long academic career mostly outside tourism, I wondered about the value and relevance of my work on tourism completed as a master's student. How had the literature on tourism development evolved? Did the suggested expansion of TALC to incorporate instability and shift in control make sense? Did Baffin Island manage to develop a thriving tourism industry without classic centre–periphery conflicts?

How Did the Literature on Tourism Development Evolve?

The TALC model and my own early elaboration on it were published in what is viewed as the early days of tourism research. McKercher and Tung (2015), Gursoy and Sandstrom (2016) and Kim *et al.* (2018) note an exponential growth in journals, publication opportunities, papers and collaborations in hospitality and tourism in the past 40 years. This growth spans a broad range of themes, summarised in a number of published literature reviews (Kim *et al.*, 2018) that make it clear that Butler's TALC is widely recognised, referenced and celebrated as one of the leading conceptual models of tourism development, if not *the* leading model. This suggests it has withstood the test of time, striking just the right parsimony.

Relevant to this chapter is the growth of literature exploring the politics of tourism in relation to power relationships and industry control, and what has been written about the industry's susceptibility and response to disruptive periods of instability.

The Politics of Tourism

The model proposed in the early 1980s made the simple assumption that development happens initially at the local scale, then regional, later national and finally global. It did not explicitly address the politics of tourism development related to public policy and planning. The model also did not explicitly consider that social and economic thinking was then in a period of significant shift as we entered the era of the knowledge economies.

The need to recognise and investigate tourism as a political phenomenon was noted in the early 1990s by Richter (1989, 1993), Edgell (1990) and Hall (1994). O'Brien (2011) reviewed how this has led to investigation of tourism as part of public policy and planning (Hall, 1994; Edgell, 1999) and political economy and development studies (Dredge & Jenkins, 2007; Edgell *et al.*, 2008; Hall, 2008; Hall & Jenkins, 1995). This literature does not differentiate explicitly between local, regional, national and international interests and associated power relationships as proposed in the early model (Keller, 1982) but focuses more on the relationships and tensions between private industry, tourism associations and the state. The literature makes it clear that reality is far more complex than suggested back in the 1980s, noting that the tourism industry is an amalgam of the vested players noted above, with sometimes competing interests and demands. These players are in complex relationships and lines of authority, creating ample room for tensions and conflicts irrespective of where the industry in a specific location is in the TALC cycle, and outside the suggestion that conflict arises primarily during disruptive periods of instability and potential crises when demand exceeds capacity to deliver.

Today's literature covering the politics of tourism makes it clear that tourism development is subject to social and economic thinking associated with political beliefs, priorities and realities in any given place at any given time (Butler & Suntikul, 2010, 2017), and that tourism usually is an integral part of broader economic and social development strategies. Butler's TALC was introduced in a period of economic and social thinking sometimes called the post-Fordism era, when the leading global economies shifted to growth of knowledge economies. This is a period when significant capitalist industry restructured away from Fordian mass production of physical tangibles and natural resources, shifting towards growing reliance on commodification of intangible assets, and more recently a growing focus on the human economies emphasising ongoing learning and evaluation of choices to make better decisions (Hart *et al.*, 2010). Since the publication of Butler's TALC we also have entered what Friedman (2005) calls the third period of globalisation, when corporate globalisation has consolidated and we see the emergence of the globalisation of individuals. All this context is relevant to the development, segmentation and marketing of tourism products and the TALC growth curve, evidenced by the fact that in parallel with, and associated with, the above shifts in economic thinking, there has been a move towards the deliberate creation and marketing of tourism as the consumption of experiences, as part of a 'culture of consumption' movement (Featherstone, 1991; Hall, 1994; Urry, 1990).

Reflecting back, therefore, Butler's TALC was introduced during a time when tourism was becoming one of the largest industrial activities in Western economies (Britton, 1991), exemplifying post-Fordism, and when tourism became part of deliberate efforts to market and sell intangible experiences. It was a period when tourism became a key player, to be considered by just about any government considering social and economic development to achieve employment and economic growth. But tourism did not develop and grow in isolation. Hence, as noted, any investigation of tourism development and growth must position itself contextually in the broader social and economic planning and associated policy environments and power relationships surrounding and informing it.

Anne O'Brien, in her 2011 text *The Politics of Tourism Development*, uses Ireland as a case study to highlight the importance of a political lens

on tourism as part of regional and economic development. She demonstrates the complexities of the relationships between private industry,
tourism associations and the state. She highlights the importance of
identifying and acknowledging all the actors with a vested interest in
tourism, understanding their motivations, thinking and actions, addressing the power relationships that exist within and between them,
and managing any existing entrenchments (see also Boyd & Bolan in the
present volume, Chapter 21). Her study shows how complex institutional
politics underpinning government involvement can be in the shaping and
implementation of tourism-related policies as part of broader social and
economic planning. Her work supports Hall's (2008) thesis that government usually plays a central role in the planning, legislation, regulation
and coordination of the tourism industry, as well as holding power to
incentivise entrepreneurial behaviour.

Given all the above, my suggestion of development control transition-
ing from local through regional to national and international was very
much on the highly generalised side of parsimony when modelling tourism
development. It is now known that who controls the industry is very
multifaceted, intricately linked to broader contemporary economic and
political thinking, and subject to complex power relationships. Different
political environments and power relationships create very different
tourism development outcomes. Communities, organisations and government entrenched in protective thinking, where public and private interest
are not aligned, and where policies primarily seek oversight and aim to
control, create a very different development environment from that where
there is consensus among all players on common development goals,
and where policies and associated actions are ambitious, visionary and
constructive towards innovation and growth. The proposed expansion of
TALC simply highlighted and raised awareness about all of the above,
albeit, in hindsight, far too simplistic and too focused on local versus
regional, national and then international control, and too caught up in
the belief that continued growth is a legitimate overarching assumption.

The Assumption of Continued Growth

A core societal assumption underlying Butler's TALC is that continued
growth is an overarching goal of tourism development and indeed all
economics. A thorough discussion of the societal quest for continued
growth to maintain and grow quality of life is beyond this chapter. It will
have to suffice to note that the quest for continued economic growth is
beginning to be challenged by the realisation that our resources really are
finite (Ateljevic, 2020; Bellato *et al.*, 2022; Dwyer, 2021, 2022; Higgins-
Desbiolles *et al.*, 2019), that long-term sustainability is an increasingly
important consideration, and that incomes and standards of living cannot
continue to grow forever without eventually exhausting resources unless

we stabilise and then significantly shrink the population. But accepting the need to stabilise and shrink the population is counter to today's assumption that a growing population is needed to fuel economic growth.

We have to face the reality that, irrespective of social, economic and technological innovations, it is foreseeable that something eventually will have to give as we continue along a path of growth. It is a certainty that the time will come when the paradigm of continued growth and the core assumptions underlying it will, by necessity, have to be replaced. A new paradigm will emerge. It is not a question of 'if', but 'when'.

Continued growth is a fundamental premise on which TALC and all its derivatives are constructed. It is likely that under a new paradigm of social and economic development we will need to abandon TALC when proceeding with conversations about tourism development (Duxbury *et al.*, 2020; Hussain, 2021; Lew *et al.*, 2020). But for now, the assumption of the wish for and need for continued growth looks to hold, despite recognition that our resources are finite. Speculation about the emergence and detail of a new paradigm challenging continued growth that will likely require us to abandon TALC is left for elsewhere and another day.

Growth and Instability

What about the assumption made that disruption and instability arise in tourism development when local capacity to service demand is exceeded as growth continues? This made intuitive sense back in the 1980s when investigating Baffin Island. But today we know from case studies that this is not a necessity. First, there exist many examples of tourism developments starting with non-local investments and non-local control (Weaver, 1988). Second, it is possible to manage continued growth and significant scale change in tourism delivery without disruption and instability as new industry players and investments are introduced, including managing any associated shifts in power relationships.

On the flip side, however, the literature has identified many triggers for disruptive instability and crises in tourism development. Examples include simple shifts in consumer taste, changing perceptions of risk and safety, entry of new competitors, economic recessions, significant shift in exchange rates, loss of social licence to operate by local communities for whatever reason, or emergence of travel barriers caused by events like natural disasters, terrorism, wars or pandemics. Irrespective of cause, the suggestion made in the 1980s holds true that the transition of any tourism development along Butler's TALC will likely encounter explicit periods of instability and possible crises along the way.

A lot can be learned from studies investigating how periods of instability and economic and/or political crises can be moments of intervention leading to change (Hay, 1999), including in tourism development (O'Brien, 2011). This has become the focus of a growing body of tourism literature investigating how resilient tourism is to instability and crises, what strategies exist to prepare for and to handle them, and what the consequences of periods of instability and crises are (Beirman, 2021; Brouder et al., 2017; Butler, 2017; Cheer & Lew, 2021; Hall, 2019; Hall et al., 2018; Hystad & Keller, 2006; Luthe & Wyss, 2014; Saarinen & Gill, 2019). This includes efforts to translate how ecological systems' responses to crises (Holling, 1973) may have relevance in tourism planning (Allen et al., 2014; Farrell & Twining-Ward, 2005; Gunderson & Holling, 2002; Gunderson et al., 2022; Holdschlag & Ratter, 2013; McLeod, 2020). A message that is emerging and becoming amplified is that disruption and crises really are opportunities for change, and that the outcome of crises in tourism should not be assumed simply 'back to before the crisis' and/ or 'more of the same' (Bellini, 2021). This thinking has been amplified by response thinking when emerging from the recent COVID crisis (Lew et al., 2020). Periods of instability are opportunities to make progress on the growing awareness that tourism should be managed sustainably (Hall, 2022) and that tourism should not be allowed to develop and grow without addressing social licence (Baumber et al., 2021; Fan et al., 2019; Jangra & Kaushik, 2022; Mihalič, 2020; Williams et al., 2012). All this is discussed today at some length in the academic literature. Less clear is how much of the knowledge and insights gained is translating into changes in the applied practices of tourism delivery to ensure that the industry is more resilient and better prepared to handle disruptions in the future.

In summary, Butler's TALC assumes smooth growth in tourism along an S-shaped curve. It was proposed that throughout growth there will be significant periods of instability, some translating to crises, and that these periods often are associated with shifts in key actors, investments and power relationships. A growing body of tourism literature looks to be in agreement with this. That literature has identified and investigated the cause for these instabilities, and how resilient and prepared tourism has been to handle them. What becomes clear is that these disruptive periods can lead to significant changes that are likely to change the shape of the hypothesised TALC growth curve. Theoretical models of how to predict, be prepared for and then manage these disruptive periods are emerging (Brouder et al., 2017; Butler, 2017; Hall, 2019). Considerable further work is required to translate these models into what might become applied best management practice.

It was noted earlier that the power of a good model is that it represents a generic case as a benchmark against which to compare reality. TALC has withstood the test of time as a model that meets that criterion. Acknowledging as part of TALC that there will likely be significant disruptive periods along the way that will likely change the shape of the curve was a realistic addition. Where disruptive periods are noted in case studies, they should identify the causes and explore who the key actors and what the associated power relationships were before, during and after the disruption. And where disruptive periods are encountered today, it is timely to ask what opportunities these bring deliberately to manage associated change in the tourism product and its delivery to grow social licence and to re-emerge more sustainable.

What Happened with Tourism in the Northwest Territories and Especially on Baffin Island?

The reader may be curious about what has happened to tourism development in the NWT and on Baffin Island since the 1980s, paying attention whether TALC and the elaboration on the model to address periods of disruption have relevance. Such an analysis is complicated since the NWT split into two separate political entities in 1999, the Northwest Territories and Nunavut (canadahistory.ca, n.d.). Baffin Island is part of Nunavut. Tourism numbers in both the NWT and Nunavut have grown reasonably steadily over the years. There is no evidence of a dramatic 'take-off period' resembling the steep part of an 'S', but a flat and stretched-out beginnings of an 'S' can be argued. Disruptive periods in growth for both regions can be observed. They mirror those encountered elsewhere, notably periods of downturn associated with economic recessions, fuel crises and more recently the COVID pandemic. Visitors attracted to both regions for purposes of business and/or to visit friends or relatives continue to dominate.

Looking specifically at the NWT today (without Nunavut), significant growth has been seen in international visits to the region to experience the northern lights (aurora borealis) (Watson, 2009). This has led notably to significant growth in tourism arrivals in the Yellowknife region, an area readily accessible by plane from the south. The bulk of northern lights tourism tends to be highly organised, aligning with characteristics associated with mass tourism, although it does also attract lone tourists organising their own experience. Fliesser (2019) looked at the development of northern light tourism in Yellowknife and noted a constructive policy environment with reasonable collaboration between community, industry and government. Skilled management and labour to service that industry rely on outside-sourced employment. Northern light tourism is lucrative and therefore highly competitive. The NWT are challenged by tourism opportunities in other regions of Canada as well as Norway, Iceland and Greenland.

Baffin Island has not been a significant player in northern light tourism given its remoteness and associated cost and difficulty of access but has attracted considerable growth in marine tourism, fuelled by climate change progressively opening the Northwest Passage. Marine tourism is attracting the spectrum, from individual explorers and adventurers arriving in private yachts to cruise ships and associated mass tourism (Johnston *et al.*, 2017a, 2017b; Maher, 2010, 2012; Stewart *et al.*, 2010). Johnston *et al.* (2017b) note that steady growth in this tourism sector is raising hope for benefits to the communities, while also causing concern, especially related to crowding and other impacts. The general costs and benefits of cruise ship tourism have been investigated in some detail (Diedrich, 2010; Dowling, 2006; MacPherson, 2008). Overtourism is a concern. In Nunavut, tourist numbers on occasion match or exceed community size when cruise ships are in port, and local capacity to produce arts and crafts cannot keep up with tourism demand. The reality that cruise ships place considerable demands on the local infrastructure while contributing relatively little to the local economies is recognised (Maher, 2010), with Nunavut Tourism (2012) showing that cruise tourists spent less than C$50 per head per day in Nunavut during their cruise in 2011. A growing number of private yachts seeking to navigate the Passage also are very self-sufficient and so contribute relatively little to local economies (Johnston *et al.*, 2017b).

Review of annual tourism reports for both the NWT and Nunavut published over the decades suggest that the two governments are very aware of and proactive about the challenges associated with tourism development, and that Indigenous-led tourism is at the forefront of some of the thinking. Notable over the decades are government investments to raise awareness and to educate the communities about the hospitality industry and what it takes to offer a competitive product, and to offer incentives to local entrepreneurs to invest and participate in tourism.

In summary, the growth of tourism in the NWT, Nunavut and specifically Baffin Island can be modelled using TALC with evidence of a very flat S-shaped curve that is still growing. There have been periods of disruption to growth, and there have been significant shifts in the tourism product, notably the advent of northern lights tourism, and primarily marine-related tourism, associated with the opening up of the Northwest Passage. Significant growth especially in northern light and cruise ship tourism, is associated with outside control and investments, a need for reliance on imported labour, and considerable revenue leakages.

Conclusion

The tourism industry and the academic literature on tourism have come a long way since publication of Butler's TALC and the addition of consideration of disruptive periods during the growth cycle with associated shifts in power relationships and investments in the 1980s. Butler's TALC assumes that tourism is a consumable product, and that growth is a desired overarching goal. Both assumptions have been challenged. But TALC nevertheless continues to attract considerable attention as a starting point of almost any discussion of tourism, given the elegance of its simplicity.

What has become clear over the decades is that case studies examining tourism development should always be placed in the larger context of social and economic development policies, the relevant political and policy environments, and the power relationships that exist between the key players representing industry, government and associations. A reality is that tourism usually is part of broader regional economic and social planning and development, and that this merits explicit consideration.

The literature has demonstrated that the growth cycle modelled by TALC rarely progresses smoothly, in part because of significant disruptive periods. The academic literature has explored the tourism industry's resilience and adaptability to handle such disruptions and how they have sometimes led to significant temporary instabilities. The past assumption may have been that the outcome of disruption should be a return to TALC's growth curve before that disruption. But today there is growing recognition that disruption may also be an opportunity for change, to address growing priorities in tourism development, including sustainability, addressing evidence of overtourism and social licence (Baumber *et al.*, 2021; Bellini, 2021; Williams *et al.*, 2012).

Looking ahead, this chapter suggests that the currently dominant societal paradigm of continued growth driving most economic decisions will eventually be replaced. This, together with more deliberate change management to align tourism development with strategic priorities other than growth, will make Butler's TALC likely less relevant as time goes on.

References

Allen, C.R., Angeler, D.G., Garmestani, A.S., Gunderson, L.H. and Holling, C.S. (2014) Panarchy: Theory and application. *Ecosystems* 17 (4), 578–589. https://doi.org/10.1007/s10021-013-9744-2.

Ateljevic, I. (2020) Transforming the (tourism) world for good and (re)generating the potential 'new normal.' *Tourism Geographies* 22 (3), 1–9. https://doi.org/10.1080/14616688.2020.1759134.

Baumber, A., Schweinsberg, S., Scerri, M., Kaya, E. and Sajib, S. (2021) Sharing begins at home: A social licence framework for home sharing practices. *Annals of Tourism Research* 91, 103293. https://doi.org/10.1016/j.annals.2021.103293.

Beirman, D. (2021) *Tourism Crises and Destination Recovery*. London: Sage.

Bellato, L., Frantzeskaki, N. and Nygaard, C.A. (2022) Regenerative tourism: A conceptual framework leveraging theory and practice. *Tourism Geographies*, 1–21. https://doi.org/10.1080/14616688.2022.2044376.

Bellini, N. (2021) 'Back to normal' vs. 'new normal': The post-pandemic recovery of Italian tourism. *Symphonya. Emerging Issues in Management* (symphonya.unicusano.it) 2, 26–37. https://dx.doi.org/10.4468/2021.2.04bellini.

Britton, S.G. (1991) Tourism, capital, and place: Towards a critical geography of tourism. *Environment and Planning D: Society and Space* 9, 451–478. https://doi.org/10.1068/d09.

Brouder, P., Clavé, S.A., Gill, A. and Ioannides, D. (2017) *Tourism Destination Evolution*. London: Routledge.

Butler, R. (1980) The concept of a Tourist Area Cycle of evolution: Implications for management of resources. *Canadian Geographer* 24 (1): 5–12. https://doi.org/10.1111/j.1541-0064.1980.tb00970.x.

Butler, R. (2017) *Tourism and Resilience*. Wallingford: CABI.

Butler, R. and Suntikul, W. (2010) *Tourism and Political Change*. Oxford: Goodfellow Publishers.

Butler, R. and Suntikul, W. (2017) *Tourism and Political Change* (2nd edn). Oxford: Goodfellow Publishers.

Canadahistory.ca (n.d.) https://www.canadashistory.ca/explore/politics-law/the-creation-of-nunavut accessed 1/13/2023

Cao, H. and Folan, P. (2011) Product life cycle: The evolution of a paradigm and literature review from 1950–2009. *Production Planning and Control* 23 (8), 1–22.

Cheer, J.M. and Lew, A.A. (2021) *Tourism, Resilience and Sustainability: Adapting to Social, Political and Economic Change*. London: Routledge.

Cohen, E. (1972) Towards a sociology of international tourism. *Social Research* 39 (1), 164–182.

Diedrich, A. (2010) Cruise ship tourism in Belize: The implications of developing cruise ship tourism in an ecotourism destination. *Ocean and Coastal Management* 53, 234–244.

Dowling, R.K. (2006) *Cruise Ship Tourism*. Wallingford: CABI.

Dredge, D. and Jenkins, J. (2007) *Tourism Planning and Policy*. Brisbane: John Wiley.

Duxbury, N., Bakas, F. E., Vinagre de Castro, T. and Silva, S. (2020) Creative tourism development models towards sustainable and regenerative tourism. *Sustainability* 13 (1), 2. https://doi.org/10.3390/su13010002.

Dwyer, L. (2020) Tourism development and sustainable well-being: A beyond GDP perspective. *Journal of Sustainable Tourism* 28, 1–18.

Dwyer, L. (2022) Tourism contribution to the SDGs: Applying a well-being lens. *European Journal of Tourism Research* 32, 3212. https://doi.org/10.54055/ejtr.v32i.2500.

Edgell, D.L. (1990) *International Tourism Policy*. New York: Van Nostrand Reinhold.

Edgell, D.L. (1999) *Tourism Policy: The Next Millennium*. Urbana: Sagamore Publishing.

Edgell, D.L., DelMastro, M., Allen, M., Smith, G. and Swanson, J.R. (2008) *Tourism Policy and Planning: Yesterday, Today and Tomorrow*. Oxford: Butterworth Heinemann.

Fan, D.X., Liu, A. and Qiu, R.T. (2019) Revisiting the relationship between host attitudes and tourism development: A utility maximization approach. *Tourism Economics* 25 (2), 171–188. https://doi.org/10.1177/1354816618794088.

Farrell, B. and Twining-Ward, L. (2005) Seven steps toward sustainability: Tourism in the context of new knowledge. *Journal of Sustainability Tourism* 13, 109–122. https://doi.org/10.1080/09669580508668481.

Featherstone, M. (1991) *Consumer Culture and Postmodernism*. London: Sage.

Fliesser, U.E. (2019) Tourism around Yellowknife: A brilliant development. MA thesis, Trent University, etd:674, TC-OPET-10637.

Franklin, A. and Crang, M. (2001) The trouble with tourism and travel theory. *Tourist Studies* 1 (1), 5–22.

Friedman, T.L. (2005) It's a flat world, after all. *New York Times Magazine*, 3 April.

Gunderson, L.H., and Holling, C.S. (eds) (2002) *Panarchy: Understanding Transformations in Systems of Humans and Nature*. Washington, DC: Island Press.

Gunderson, L.H., Allen, C.R. and Garmestani, A.S. (eds) (2022) *Applied Panarchy*. Washington, DC: Island Press.

Gursory, D. and Sandstrom, J.K. (2016) An updated ranking of hospitality and tourism journals. *Journal of Hospitality and Tourism Research* 40 (1), 3–18. http://doi.org/10.1177/1096348014538054.

Hall, C.M. (1994) *Tourism and Politics: Policy, Power, and Place*. London: John Wiley.

Hall, C.M. (2008) *Tourism Planning: Policies, Processes and Relationships* (2nd edn). Harlow: Prentice Hall.

Hall, C.M. (2019) Resilience theory and tourism. In J. Saarinen and A.M. Gill (eds) *Resilient Destinations and Tourism: Governance Strategies in the Transition Towards Sustainability in Tourism* (pp. 34–47). London: Routledge.

Hall, C.M. (2022) Sustainable tourism beyond BAU (Brundtlund as usual): Shifting from paradoxical to relational thinking? *Frontiers in Sustainable Tourism* 1. https://doi.org/10.3389/frsut.2022.927946.

Hall, C.M. and Jenkins, J.M. (1995) *Tourism and Public Policy*. London: Routledge.

Hall, C.M., Prayag, G. and Amore, A. (2018) *Tourism and Resilience: Individual, Organisational and Destination Perspectives*. Bristol: Channel View Publications. https://doi.org/10.21832/HALL6300.

Hart, K. , Laville, J.L. and Cattani, A.D. (2010) *The Human Economy*. Cambridge: Polity.

Hay, C. (1999) Crisis and the structural transformation of the state: Interrogating the process of change. *British Journal of Politics and International Relations* 1 (3), 317–344.

Higgins-Desbiolles, F., Carnicelli, S., Krolikowski, C., Wijesinghe, G. and Boluk, K. (2019) Degrowing tourism: Rethinking tourism. *Journal of Sustainable Tourism* 27 (12), 1926–1944. https://doi.org/10.1080/09669582.2019.1601732.

Hoivik, T. and Heiberg, T. (1980) Centre–periphery tourism and self-reliance. *International Social Science Journal* 32 (1), 69–98.

Holdschlag, A. and Ratter, B.M.W. (2013) Multiscale system dynamics of humans and nature in the Bahamas: Perturbation, knowledge, panarchy and resilience. *Sustainability Science* 8 (3), 407–421. https://doi.org/10.1007/s11625-013-0216-6.

Holling, C.S. (1973) Resilience and stability of ecological systems. *Annual Review of Ecology, Evolution and Systematics* 4, 1–23.

Hussain, A. (2021) A future of tourism industry: Conscious travel, destination recovery and regenerative tourism. *Journal of Sustainability and Resilience* 1 (1). https://digitalcommons.usf.edu/cgi/viewcontent.cgi?article=1008&context=jsr.

Hystad, P. and Keller, C.P. (2006) Disaster management: Kelowna tourism industry's preparedness, impact and response to a 2003 major forest fire. *Journal of Hospitality and Tourism Management* 13 (1), 44–58.

Jangra, R. and Kaushik, S.P. (2022) Understanding tribal community's perception toward tourism impacts: The case of emerging destinations in western Himalaya, Kinnaur. *Asian Geographer* 39 (1), 69–92. https://doi.org/10.1080/10225706.2020.1830134.

Johnston, M.E., Dawson, J., de Souza, E. and Stewart, E.J. (2017a) Management challenges for the fastest growing marine shipping sector in Arctic Canada: Pleasure crafts. *Polar Record* 53, 67–78.

Johnston, M.E., Dawson, J. and Maher, P.T. (2017b) Strategic development challenges in marine tourism in Nunavut. *Resources* 6, 25.

Keller, C.P. (1982) Development of peripheral tourism destinations: Case study Baffin region. Unpublished MA thesis, Department of Geography, University of Western Ontario.

Keller, C.P. (1987) Stages of peripheral tourism development: Canada's Northwest Territories. *Tourism Management* 8 (1), 20–32.

Kim, C.S., Bai, B.H., Kim, P.B. and Chon, K. (2018) Review of reviews: A systematic analysis of review papers in the hospitality and tourism literature. *International Journal of Hospitality Management* 70, 49–58. https://doi.org/10.1016/j.ijhm.2017.10.023.

Lew, A., Cheer, J.M., Haywood, M., Brouder, P. and Salazar, N.B. (2020) Visions of travel and tourism after the global COVID-19 transformation of 2020. *Tourism Geographies* 22 (3), 455–466.

Luthe, T. and Wyss, R. (2014) Assessing and planning resilience in tourism. *Tourism Management* 44, 161–163. https://doi.org/10.1016/j.tourman.2014.03.011.

MacPherson, C. (2008) Golden goose or Trojan horse? Cruise ship tourism in Pacific development. *Asia Pacific Viewpoint* 49 (2), 185–197.

Maher, P.T. (2010) Cruise tourist experiences and management implications for Auyuittuq, Sirmilik and Quttinirpaaq National Parks, Nunavut, Canada. In C.M. Hall and J. Saarinen (eds) *Tourism and Change in Polar Regions: Climate, Environments and Experiences* (pp. 119–134). London: Routledge.

Maher, P.T. (2012) Expedition cruise visits to protected areas in the Canadian Arctic: Issues of sustainability and change for an emerging market. *Tourism* 60, 55–70.

McKercher, B. and Tung, V. (2015) Publishing in tourism and hospitality journals: Is the past a prelude to the future? *Tourism Management* 50 (2). http://doi.org/10.1016/j. tourman.2015.03.008.

McLeod, M. (2020) Tourism governance, panarchy and resilience in the Bahamas. In S. Rolle, J. Minnis and I. Bethell-Bennett (eds) *Tourism Development, Governance and Sustainability in the Bahamas* (pp. 103–113). London: Routledge. https://doi. org/10.4324/9781003032311.

Mihalič, T. (2020) Conceptualising overtourism: A sustainability approach. *Annals of Tourism Research* 84, 103025. https://doi.org/10.1016/j.annals.2020.103025.

Nunavut Tourism (2012) *Nunavut Visitor Exit Survey (2012).* Iqaluit: Nunavut Tourism and CanNor.

O'Brien, A. (2011) *The Politics of Tourism Development: Booms and Busts in Ireland.* Basingstoke: Palgrave Macmillan.

Picard, M. (1996) *Bali: Cultural Tourism and Touristic Culture.* Singapore: Archipelago Press.

Plog, S.C. (1972) Why destination areas rise and fall in popularity. Paper presented to the Southern Chapter of the Travel Research Association, October.

Richter, L.K. (1989) *The Politics of Tourism in Asia.* Honolulu: University of Hawaii Press.

Richter, L.K. (1993) Tourism policy making in South-East Asia. In M. Hitchcock, V.T. King and M.J.G. Parnwell (eds) *Tourism in South-East Asia* (pp. 179–199). London: Routledge.

Rojeck, C. and Urry, J. (eds) (1997) *Touring Cultures.* London: Routledge.

Saarinen, J. and Gill, A.M. (eds) (2019) *Resilient Destinations and Tourism: Governance Strategies in the Transition towards Sustainability in Tourism.* London: Routledge. https://doi.org/10.4324/9781315162157.

Stewart, E.J., Draper, D. and Dawson, J. (2010) Monitoring patterns of cruise tourism across Arctic Canada. In M. Lück, P.T. Maher and E.J. Stewart (eds) *Cruise Tourism in Polar Regions: Promoting Environmental and Social Sustainability?* (pp. 133–146). London: Earthscan.

Urry, J. (1990) *The Tourist Gaze* (1st edn). London: Sage.

Vernon, R. (1966) International investment and international trade in the project cycle. *Quarterly Journal of Economics* 80 (2), 190–207.

Watson, P. (2009) Bright lights, big northern dreams. *Toronto Star,* 10 October.

Weaver, D. (1988) The evolution of a 'plantation' tourism landscape on the Caribbean island of Antigua. *Tijdschrift voor Economische en Sociale Geografie* 79 (5), 319–331.

Williams, P.W., Gill, A.M., Marcoux, J. and Xu, N. (2012) Nurturing 'social license to operate' through corporate–civil society relationships in tourism destinations. In C.H.C. Hsu and W.C. Gartner (eds) *The Routledge Handbook of Tourism Research* (pp. 196–214). London: Routledge.

Young, G. (1973) *Tourism: Blessing or Blight?* Harmondsworth: Penguin.

11 Revisiting Rhyl and the TALC: A Study of Land Use, Value and Cover, and Tourism Policy in a Traditional Seaside Resort, 1990–2023

Tim Gale

This chapter revisits and updates research first reported in Gale (2005), which uses a case study of Rhyl, in North Wales, to examine the causes and consequences of the decline of British seaside resorts as holiday destinations in the context of local politics and broader transformations to economy and society in the late 20th century. Taking Butler's (1980) Tourist Area Life Cycle (TALC) as its starting point, it proposes a 'stratified ontology' of resort decline that links 'surface appearances' (changes to the built environment and representations of Rhyl) to 'external threats' (competition from cheap foreign package holidays and domestic city and countryside breaks) and 'internal problems' (an ageing and expensive-to-maintain product in need of repair and repurposing for contemporary tourists' tastes), underpinned by the 'generative mechanisms' of economic restructuring and cultural change (new forms of employment and uses for leisure time). Drawing on time-series analysis of business property data, visual (semiotic) analysis of brochures, posters and other marketing collateral, and document analysis of the minutes of local authority committee meetings held in county archives, the original study describes Rhyl's rise and fall as a destination of choice for holidaymakers living in the industrialised conurbations of nearby Lancashire, Merseyside and the West Midlands, and offers some lessons for the TALC (which are summarised later in the chapter). The original study concluded in the year 2000.

Much has happened in the early part of this century, in Rhyl and in British seaside resorts generally. In Britain, coastal tourism is growing once again – challenging the narrative of decline – with an estimated £17.1 billion tourism spend from 27 million overnight visits plus 217 million day visits supporting 285,000 jobs, mostly in small- and medium-sized enterprises (National Coastal Tourism Academy, 2016). Disruptive technology and sharing platforms have upended the tourist accommodation, table and counter-service restaurant, and taxi and private hire industries; for example, Airbnb penetration in coastal areas of England and Wales is now three times the rate of that in non-coastal areas, with the number of entire places available for short-term rent up by 56% between 2019 and 2022 (Blood & Duncan, 2022). The COVID-19 pandemic and associated restrictions on personal mobility and liberty then led to an estimated £9.7 billion loss in tourism spend at the coast in 2020 and a £6.6 billion loss in 2021 (reductions of 57% and 39% on 2019, respectively), with at least 7% of coastal businesses closing permanently; as of October 2022, only two-thirds (67%) of businesses were back to profitability (National Coastal Tourism Academy, 2023).

It is timely, therefore, to return to the subject of seaside resorts and to re-examine the TALC as a concept and a tool for understanding the past, present and (potential) future(s) of these much-changed destinations. As for Rhyl, with the release of data used to calculate business rates for the period 2010–2023 for non-domestic properties in England and Wales, by the UK government's Valuation Office Agency (VOA), and new tools and technologies such as Google Street View (which allows remote users to view a location as it appears in the present day and at various points in the recent past), there is an opportunity to return to this particular resort – albeit virtually – and to update information on land use, cover and value captured for and summarised in Gale (2005).

The Rise and Fall of Seaside Resorts in Britain

Historically, British seaside resorts were destinations for long holidays, that is, of four or more nights away from home. Their appeal was founded on the distinct natural qualities of the coastal environment (the sea, sandy beaches, picturesque topography and an agreeable climate), fused with the unique pleasures afforded by piers, theatres, ballrooms, funfairs, aquariums, botanic gardens, bandstands and various other amenities. They were a paradox: on the one hand, a setting for 'rational recreation' or travel with a serious or higher purpose in mind – namely the renewal of the body, mind and spirit – and on the other hand, a liminal space in which tourists or trippers could break with everyday routines and expected behaviours and 'let their hair down', having fun with family and friends building sandcastles, playing ball games or paddling in the sea, among other things.

When the seaside was first discovered by painters, amateur geologists and health seekers in the mid-18th century, travel for recreation was limited to royalty and the aristocracy and was well beyond the reach of the ordinary man or woman. Initially, spa towns such as Cheltenham and Tunbridge Wells were the destination of choice for these wealthy tourists, but this changed as the spas became overly popular and medical practitioners started to advocate seawater as a cure and a restorative for those in poor health. In the 19th and early 20th centuries, coastal resorts were transformed into holiday centres for the masses (Towner, 1996; Walton, 2000), as changes associated with the Industrial Revolution led to rising incomes and available time (initially the Sabbath and then whole weekends and public holidays). The expanding railway network provided an affordable means by which residents of industrial towns and cities could escape to the seaside, principally on organised excursions and later by making their own travel arrangements. This seasonal, mass migration was supported by the state, the church and factory owners, recognising the benefits of permitting and promoting short periods of leave from work, for example boosting morale, efficiency and productivity, and attendance. Few international visitors to Britain ever made it to the seaside, preferring to stay in London or to take a circular tour through England and into Scotland, stopping in historic towns like Oxford or Edinburgh and areas of outstanding natural beauty such as the Cotswolds and Lake District. Seaside resorts were, and to a large extent still are, destinations for domestic tourists.

Peaking in the 1950s and 1960s, these resorts were challenged by post-Second World War improvements in surface and air transport. The growth in car ownership and the national network of motorways and trunk roads freed holidaymakers of the strictures of the railway timetable and the set days of arrival and departure imposed by the holiday camps and guest-houses, while charter flights brought much of southern Europe and '3S' (sun, sea and sand) holiday destinations within reach for many Britons. Initially, this did little to stem the flow of staying visitors to the British seaside, lending the impression that things were 'back on track' after years of conflict and austerity. However, the groundwork was laid for a seismic shift in holiday-taking habits, while resorts themselves missed opportunities to build resilience for the future (Demetriadi, 1997).

The writing was on the wall. Between 1979 and 1988, visitor nights at British seaside resorts declined by 39 million, or 27% (Wales Tourist Board, 1992, cited in Gale, 2005). A combination of reduced revenues from tourism, poor-quality accommodation and tired attractions, and image problems served to undermine resorts' *raison d'être* (to shelter and to entertain tourists). The local state and private enterprise responded with various measures, investing in new attractions and 'wet weather' facilities such as indoor bathing pools, upgrading accommodation and conserving the best of the historic built environment – including some outstanding Victorian, Edwardian and Art Deco architecture – while enhancing the remainder. Efficiencies were realised by restructuring of businesses and organisations to make them lean and more productive. Examples included the rationalisation of Butlin's portfolio of holiday villages in the UK, the employment of 'fringe' workers on seasonal contracts at visitor attractions and the growth of self-catering accommodation and self-service restaurants as an expression of the desire to reduce labour costs in the hospitality industry (Agarwal, 2002). To extend the season, special events were staged in the shoulder months, most famously Blackpool's illuminations, while in the larger resorts the conferences and exhibitions market was targeted with significant investment in new venues, such as the Bournemouth International Centre, which opened in 1984.

These measures met with modest success but could not overcome some undeniable realities. Seaside resorts, with few exceptions, are far removed from the main centres of industry and commerce, and opportunities for economic development and diversification beyond tourism were limited, thereby locking them into the tourist trade. Landowners and tenants were burdened with property – much of it dating to the previous century – that was expensive and difficult to maintain. (Wind-blown sand and salt water are a problem for stone and metal structures like piers, and buildings and signs become bleached in the sunshine and need regular painting.) Changes to the way people work in the late 20th century, brought on by the outsourcing of manufacturing to other countries and a move into service and information industries, profoundly affected leisure time and choices, and undermined the symbiotic link between resorts and their market areas. Videocassette recorders, computer games consoles and satellite television led to an increase in the consumption of leisure and entertainment in and around the home, hastening the demise of the seaside funfair and the 'end of the pier' show. Cheap and widely available medicines offered an instant fix for aches, pains and various ailments that would once have necessitated a holiday by the sea, to 'take the waters' and inhale the briny air.

This somewhat fatalistic account of the recent history and contemporary standing of resorts is challenged by developments in the first two decades of the 21st century. New leisure markets have been attracted to the seaside, including seniors and the under-35s, in search of health and wellness, adventure, slow food and travel. Upmarket hotel chains and celebrity chefs are taking up residence by the sea, such as Hilton in Bournemouth and Rick Stein and his collection of seafood restaurants in Padstow, Cornwall. Art galleries like the Turner Contemporary at Margate and pop-up installations such as Weston-super-Mare's 'See Monster' appeal to the cultural tourist and help put these forgotten destinations 'on the map'. Outdoor fitness parks and paths offer opportunities for exercise and self-improvement, harking back to the days of resorts as health centres. Moreover, the number of international visitors – though comparatively small – is growing, especially from Germany, the Netherlands and France, a trend accelerated by the devaluation of the pound after the Brexit referendum. Although the COVID pandemic initially cut off the supply of tourists to resorts just as they were preparing for the 2020 holiday season, there was a later rise in domestic tourism to the seaside and the countryside as the travel restrictions were lifted and visitors flocked to nearby beaches and the countryside, where the risk of transmission was very low.

Hence, there are signs of recovery and perhaps even a renaissance for the Great British seaside holiday. In saying that, while resorts in general might be growing, the rate of growth does not match that of the visitor economy nationally. Also, the fortunes of individual resorts depend on their size; the largest and smallest resorts have critical mass and distinctiveness respectively, whereas those resorts that belong to the 'squeezed middle' have neither and are faced with thinking the unthinkable, that is, whether to exit the tourism industry or at the very least give up pretentions to be a holiday destination (Baum, 1998). One such resort is Rhyl, North Wales.

The Rhyl Case Study

Described by the writer and food critic A.A. Gill (2002) as 'a town only a man driving a crane with a demolition ball would visit with a smile', Rhyl is a good example of a post-mature destination nearing the end of the tourist area life cycle. Home to over 25,000 people, it is located on the North Wales coast, making it one of the few north-facing resorts in the UK. From the 1850s through to the 1950s, Rhyl was popular with staying visitors from north-west England and the Midlands, who arrived via the Chester–Holyhead railway. Large hotels were constructed in the second quarter of the 19th century, followed by various public utilities such as a waterworks and gas supply, and flagship attractions, including a pleasure pier in 1867, a fairground to the west of the resort in 1895 and the 1000-seat Pavilion Theatre in 1908. Built at a cost of £16,500, the last was an impressive structure that dominated the seafront and became a motif for 'Sunny Rhyl', the centrepiece of which was a huge, illuminated dome flanked by terraces picked out in locally produced yellow brick. Along with Rhyl's Victoria Pier, the Pavilion Theatre was demolished in the early 1970s because it was deemed to be in too poor a state of repair and too dated an attraction for a modern resort. It would likely have received listed building status had it survived into the 1980s, when interest in the UK's industrial heritage, and in saving it for future generations, grew dramatically.

These lost attractions were replaced with indoor facilities such as the Sun Centre and the New Pavilion Theatre, and the Rhyl Library, Museum and Arts Centre. Designed by Gillinson Barnett and Partners and consisting of three pools, a wave machine, water slides, an overhead monorail and a licensed bar and restaurant, the £4.25 million Sun Centre opened in 1980 to great acclaim and was the 'number one' attraction in Wales for many years thereafter, attracting 500,000 visitors a year by 1985 (Saumarez Smith, 2019). It was part-financed by a grant from the European Regional Development Fund (ERDF) and built to produce a trading profit that could be used to offset the substantial running costs and trading losses of the New Pavilion Theatre, which was constructed adjacent to the Sun

Centre and opened in 1991. The Rhyl Library, Museum and Arts Centre represented a different kind of investment in culture-led regeneration and is possibly best known for containing a mock-up of the former pier, with iron railings and wooden decking. (The irony of the local state simulating past attractions that it deemed fit to demolish, at least under previous administrations, is not lost on the author!)

The Skytower and Children's Village opened in 1988 and 1995, respectively, part of a comprehensive redevelopment of the promenade. However, these and other investments did little to resurrect tourism; between 1989 and 1995, bedspaces declined by 36% and 53% in the serviced and self-serviced categories, according to figures produced by the local council (Gale, 2001). In addition, Rhyl was in danger of losing its distinctive sense of place at this time and becoming much like any other town in Britain (except this one happened to be by the sea). For example, the White Rose Shopping Centre and newly pedestrianised High Street (and, more recently, out-of-town developments such as the Marina Quay Retail Park, which was built on the site of the former Ocean Beach Funfair), possessed the same chains, store designs and street furniture as similar sites 'back home', reducing Rhyl to the status of a 'clone town'.

Tourism policy at this time focused on safeguarding serviced accommodation through the land use planning system, presuming against development that would see the conversion of existing hotels and guesthouses to other uses within Rhyl (and neighbouring Prestatyn). In addition, Rhuddlan Borough Council in partnership with the Welsh Development Agency commissioned a master plan for Rhyl promenade and, separately, a feasibility study for the redevelopment of the Foryd Harbour, to the west, resulting in the designation of co-terminous 'tourism redevelopment areas' where there was a presumption in favour of major tourist attractions and facilities that complemented existing development at those sites. However, these interventions achieved next to nothing; if anything, they proved to be counterproductive. They did not stop hotel and B&B accommodation from closing and merely acted as a block on finding an alternative use for the property or the land, meaning buildings were left empty and boarded up and became a magnet for squatting and vandalism. As for the areas zoned for tourism uses, the private sector showed little interest either in expensive new-build developments or in moving into untenanted property (e.g. retail units in the Children's Village). It is little wonder, therefore, that the successor authority, Denbighshire County Council, has pursued a more 'pragmatic' land use policy over a much-reduced area.

In the period since 2000, the Sun Centre and above-mentioned Ocean Beach Funfair have been closed and demolished. Of the three great Victorian hotels that survived into the 21st century – the Westminster Hotel (1878), the Hotel Marina (1889) and the Palace Hotel (1899) – only the first remains. Derelict buildings and façade gaps have emerged on the promenade along West Parade, though new developments have appeared on some of these sites, including a budget hotel and pub. A waterpark and adventure sports area, dubbed 'SC2' (Sun Centre Two), has been constructed near to the existing Skytower, which was revitalised together with the New Pavilion Theatre on the East Parade. Demolition of the dilapidated Queen's Buildings began in 2021, clearing the way for a £12.6 million market hall and events space, the latest step in Denbighshire County Council's plan to create, through compulsory purchase, land clearance and reconstruction, 'a modern, distinctive seaside town that meets the needs of its community' (Denbighshire County Council, 2020). Indeed, the local authority has responsibility for a large and mostly rural area, but it is continuing to invest in and to secure investment for the resorts of Rhyl and Prestatyn as two of the main 'crowd pullers' in the county (alongside the Clwydian Range and Dee Valley Area of Outstanding Natural Beauty, Llangollen and the Vale of Clwyd). This investment, alongside the promotion of selected 'discovery themes' (e.g. active and adventure, heritage, and food and drink tourism), is seen as essential to achieving Denbighshire County Council's three key outcomes for tourism in the area: to spread the season; to increase length of stay; and to encourage more spending (Denbighshire County Council, 2023).

The life cycle of Rhyl is summarised in Table 11.1, which highlights key developments in the history of the resort that align with what is known of the various stages of the TALC. It should be noted that estimates of when the resort entered and exited each stage are to the nearest decade, and therefore imprecise; no one event is, by itself, a turning point and transitions between stages are likely to be gradual and not visible until after the fact.

Rhyl's status and prospects as a destination for tourists and day trippers are perhaps best summed up not by Gill's putdown but rather by the name of an early Victorian submarine that sank off the coast in 1880, the *Resurgam*, which translated from the Latin means 'I will rise again'. Certainly, recent investments give cause for optimism but that was also true of prior developments such as the Children's Village and Drift Park Water Play Area on the promenade, which have done little to win back the tourist trade. Suffice to say, for 'hope' we should substitute 'facts on the ground' and be guided by the available evidence, which in this case takes the form of property data (indicating land use and value) and digital photography (land cover).

Changes to Land Use, Value and Cover in Rhyl since 1990

One of the challenges of using the TALC as a tool to describe, never mind predict, the development of a destination over time is the difficulty of obtaining reliable estimates of tourist arrivals over a sufficiently long period and at the right scale, which is the variable used for the vertical or y axis in Butler's (1980) original model. Rhyl is no exception in this regard.

Table 11.1 Rhyl's passage through the TALC

Stage of the TALC	Key events	Estimate of when Rhyl entered/ exited this stage
Exploration	Sea marsh drained	1810s
	Paddle steamers and horse-drawn coaches	
Involvement	First hotels	1820s–1840s
	Sea bathing observed	
	Large auction of land for development	
Development	Railway station opened and later extended	1850s–1950s
	Promenade improvements	
	Installation of drainage, sewers, water supply and street lighting	
	Fire service and policing	
	More hotels built (e.g. Westminster Hotel, Hotel Marina, Palace Hotel)	
	New visitor attractions (e.g. Victoria Pier, Winter Gardens, Marine Lake and Pleasure Grounds, Pavilion Theatre, Open Air Bathing Pool, Royal Floral Hall)	
Consolidation	Some activities deemed unfashionable and disappear (e.g. ballroom dancing, brass bands)	1960s–1970s
	Pier and principal theatre demolished	
Stagnation	Eroding sense-of-place, 'identikit' developments (e.g. White Rose Shopping Centre)	1980s
	Image divorced from environment in promotional material (e.g. annual municipal brochure)	
Decline	Reduction in serviced and self-catering accommodation (in 1989 respective bedspaces totalled 2890 and 2396; in 1995 they totalled 1857 and 1129)	1990s–2010s
	Growing number of HMOs (houses in multiple occupation), converted from hotels and B&Bs	
	Boarded up, derelict property in core visitor areas	
	Attractions closed (e.g. Ocean Beach Funfair)	
Rejuvenation	Replacement attractions and amenities (e.g. Sun Centre, Rhyl Library and Museum/ Arts Centre, Skytower, Sea Life Centre, New Pavilion Theatre, Events Arena, Children's Village, SC2)	1980s – to date
	Chain hotels opened (e.g. Premier Inn, Travelodge)	
	More car parking	
	Land clearance, redevelopment (Queen's Market)	

The most recent volume and value data are for the county of Denbighshire as a whole, which includes the market town of Llangollen and the rural hinterland as well as Rhyl and the nearby resort of Prestatyn. These data, generated by the Scarborough Tourism Economic Activity Model (STEAM), suggest that 5.99 million visitors – 1.59 million staying and 4.40 million day visitors – were attracted to the county in 2019, spending around £552.35 million (Conwy and Denbighshire Public Services Board, 2023). This represents an increase on the 5.93 million visitors and £490.35 million spend recorded for 2017, which, in turn, was up by 25% and 70% respectively on the comparative figures for 2007 (*Rhyl, Prestatyn and Abergele Journal*, 2018). Going back further, to 1993, there were an estimated 1.7 million staying and 2.5 million day visitors to Rhyl and Prestatyn combined, spending in the region of £200 million (Denbighshire County Council, 1995). However, these estimates do not include the rest of Denbighshire (i.e. beyond the two main resorts) and so cannot be compared with the STEAM estimates to establish the temporal trend.

It makes sense, therefore, to use proxy data to measure destination development that are easier to obtain, more reliable and which permit comparisons over many years and not just a few. Demand-side data are, by definition, volatile and are likely to be derived from 'finger in the wind' estimates and the application of multipliers, whereas supply-side data such as hotel bedspaces are relatively stable and based on real numbers yet reflect changes in demand (even though there may be a lagged response). These data often lie behind a paywall. Fortunately, there are exceptions that are available in the public domain, including statistics on rateable value (RV), which are used to calculate business rates in England and Wales. An RV is assigned to each non-domestic property or 'hereditament' (defined as buildings, premises within buildings or non-building properties), which takes into consideration various factors, including use, location, age, services and facilities, quality and floorspace. Since 1990, RVs for all of England and Wales have been compiled into Rating Lists that are searchable by street name and town and updated every five to seven years. A line of data in those lists will include the address of the property/ hereditament, a description of the land use accompanied by a special code, and the RV. In Gale (2005), these data were scraped from the 1990, 1995 and 2000 lists for hereditaments located along streets that were deemed to comprise Rhyl's recreational business district (RBD). The RBD corresponds to Barrett's (1958) blueprint or 'bird's eye view' of a typical seaside resort and comprises the promenade and the streets leading off it, where most hotels, theatres, gift shops and restaurants are to be found. The subsequent publication of Rating Lists for 2005 (not available to the author), 2010, 2017 and 2023 permits a comparison of the number and mean rateable value of hereditaments in Rhyl's RBD for different land uses up to the present day, a much longer period than that covered by the original study.

Table 11.2 Number and mean rateable value of non-domestic hereditaments in Rhyl's Recreation Business District (RBD) by land use category, at current and constant (April 1988) prices

		Rating list											
		1990		1995		2000		2010		2017		2023	
Land use category	Primary use codes	No.	Mean RV	No.	Mean RV	No.	Mean RV	No.	Mean RV	No.	Mean RV	No.	Mean RV
Serviced accommodation	CH, CH2	54	£3,281.72	39	£4,946.79	36	£4,926.25	21	£4,452.38	18	£5,116.67	18	£15,708.33
					£3,722.47		£3,205.32		£2,201.21		£2,098.20		£5,519.64
Self-catering accommodation	CH1	14	£2,762.50	12	£2,797.08	11	£2,657.18	1	£5,100.00	2	£8,350.00	4	£4,156.25
					£2,104.81		£1,728.92		£2,521.38		£3,424.10		£1,460.43
Eating out	CR, CR1	11	£9,055.45	9	£10,705.56	9	£10,130.56	6	£10,445.83	6	£10,141.67	5	£11,540.00
					£8,055.95		£6,591.55		£5,164.30		£4,158.81		£4,054.96
Licensed trade	CL, CL1, CL2	5	£13,250.00	6	£23,583.33	6	£22,958.33	5	£25,850.00	4	£19,187.50	2	£81,862.50
					£17,746.51		£14,938.08		£12,779.95		£7,868.24		£28,765.07
Retail	CS	33	£9,122.58	33	£10,671.36	27	£11,452.41	19	£10,775.00	14	£10,831.79	11	£10,640.00
					£8,030.22		£7,451.63		£5,327.04		£4,441.81		£3,738.71
Office	CO	7	£8,150.00	7	£9,647.86	6	£14,225.00	3	£28,666.67	3	£39,708.33	3	£34,316.67
					£7,260.03		£9,255.64		£14,172.48		£16,283.25		£12,058.28
Miscellaneous commercial	CA, CG, CM, CP, CW	20	£3,863.00	18	£4,528.06	20	£5,456.50	13	£12,861.92	13	£9,332.69	10	£13,307.50
					£3,407.37		£3,550.33		£6,358.79		£3,827.07		£4,676.03
Commercial leisure	LT, LT1, LT2, LT4, LX	14	£35,081.79	12	£44,979.17	13	£43,211.54	9	£50,627.78	11	£41,472.73	10	£36,105.00
					£33,846.92		£28,116.04		£25,029.80		£17,006.78		£12,686.67
Municipal leisure	EM1, LC2, LX	4	£71,425.00	4	£47,320.00	4	£55,275.00	5	£56,430.00	4	£31,312.50	5	£102,925.00
					£35,608.40		£35,965.25		£27,898.35		£12,840.36		£36,166.06
Other	IF3, IX, MH2, MT1, MX	16	£9,136.88	20	£8,291.00	19	£9,422.89	19	£8,021.05	15	£11,751.00	16	£13,173.44
					£6,238.99		£6,131.10		£3,965.52		£4,818.75		£4,628.92

Table 11.2 summarises for each available Rating List from 1990 to 2023 the total number of hereditaments and mean RV for 10 categories of land use in Rhyl's RBD, at current and *in italics* constant (1990) prices; the latter was determined using the Retail Prices Index (RPI), the oldest measure of inflation in the UK. The land use categories are per Gale (2005) for the sake of consistency: serviced accommodation; self-catering accommodation; eating out; licensed trade; retail; office; miscellaneous commercial (advertising rights, car parks and garages mostly); commercial leisure (amusement arcades, cinemas and private-sector attractions such as the Sea Life Centre); municipal leisure (libraries, swimming pools and sports centres run by or for the local authority); and 'other' (industry, private members' clubs, surgeries and hospitals, public toilets, etc.). Several trends can be discerned:

- A significant decline in the number of hereditaments in the serviced accommodation, retail and miscellaneous commercial categories (the top three land uses in the 1990 list, on this measure). This is down to the consolidation of separate properties into one property, as with the amalgamation of neighbouring amusement arcades to form larger entertainment centres, plus the exit of many small- and medium-sized enterprises such as guest houses that had been replaced by the time the 2023 list was published with corporate chains such as Travelodge and Premier Inn (which each count as one hereditament but contain many rooms/beds).
- A sharp uptick between the 2017 and 2023 lists in mean RV for the municipal leisure, licensed trade and serviced accommodation categories. This can be attributed to significant capital investment (the two budget hotels mentioned above plus two chained pubs on or near these premises, and the SC2 complex), fuelled in large part by private-sector development pressure that was conspicuously absent in earlier rounds of investment (which were funded from council reserves, annual rate levies and ERDF grant-in-aid).
- Six categories are worth less in real terms in the 2023 list than they were in the 1990 list (self-catering accommodation, eating out, retail, commercial leisure, municipal leisure and 'other').

Figure 11.1 displays the total number of hereditaments in Rhyl's RBD and the total RV, over the period covered by the Rating Lists. It suggests a shrinking product, though, as noted above, the capacity of the resort to accommodate, to refresh and to entertain tourists – as measured in bedspaces, covers, seats in venues and the like – may not have fallen as much as these data suggest. What has fallen, however, is the cumulative value of commercial property in the RBD; this may have bottomed out after the 2017 list, but only a small recovery is noted after taking inflation into account. Of course, the 2023 revaluation is the first to be conducted after the pandemic, but this has no bearing on the latest values because state support for struggling businesses has been provided through rates relief rather than by favourable assessments of RV.

Figure 11.2 provides a more granular picture of change over time, depicting variations in the mean RV for each of the land use categories adjusted for inflation and converted to index numbers to aid comparison (1990 = 100). From this we can make out a cluster of underperforming sectors: leisure (both commercial and municipal), eating out and retail, joined by self-catering accommodation, which had previously been on an upwards curve. In contrast, the mean RV for the licensed trade and serviced accommodation categories has shot up, although this based on a small number of hereditaments in the 2023 list (relative to the 1990 list).

There are two things to note here:

• The effect of new-build developments on RV, namely the 69-room Premier Inn and Brewers Fayre pub (sister brands and subsidiaries of Whitbread p.l.c.) and the 70-room Travelodge and nearby Marston's pub (the product of a UK-wide joint venture between the two companies, instituted in 2009 in the wake of the 'credit crunch' and its impact on the pub trade).
• Non-tourism land uses have performed reasonably well, suggesting the resort is or could be home to more than just tourism businesses going forwards. The competitive disadvantage of Rhyl's remote coastal location relative to inland towns in north-east Wales that have had more success in attracting light industry and commercial tenants, such as Wrexham, has been mitigated to some extent by the opportunities presented by the internet to work and trade remotely. Thus, diversification beyond tourism may be possible, though these data alone cannot confirm this.

While the Rating Lists permit an analysis of land use and value over time, they can only take us so far in understanding changes to the built environment of a resort like Rhyl. In Gale (2005), analysis of RV data was supplemented by traditional fieldwork and field and archive photography, to capture and represent Rhyl's changing touristscape. Two decades on, this research can be conducted at a distance with Google Street View (GSV) images captured using omnidirectional cameras mounted on cars. Ever since 360° panoramas were added to Google Maps in the 2000s, starting with major cities but quickly spreading to cover much of the world accessible by road, there has been a trickle of academic studies that use GSV as a method or tool (Uribe-Toril et al., 2021). Until recently, very few studies have made use of the ability to 'go back in time' in GSV and view earlier images of a given site where they exist. For Rhyl, GSV imagery has been captured periodically since around 2009 (typically every three years), allowing 'before and after' comparisons of sites and properties of interest.

Figure 11.3 is an extract from Google Maps showing roads in Rhyl's RBD covered by GSV; Google's terms of service allow the map to be

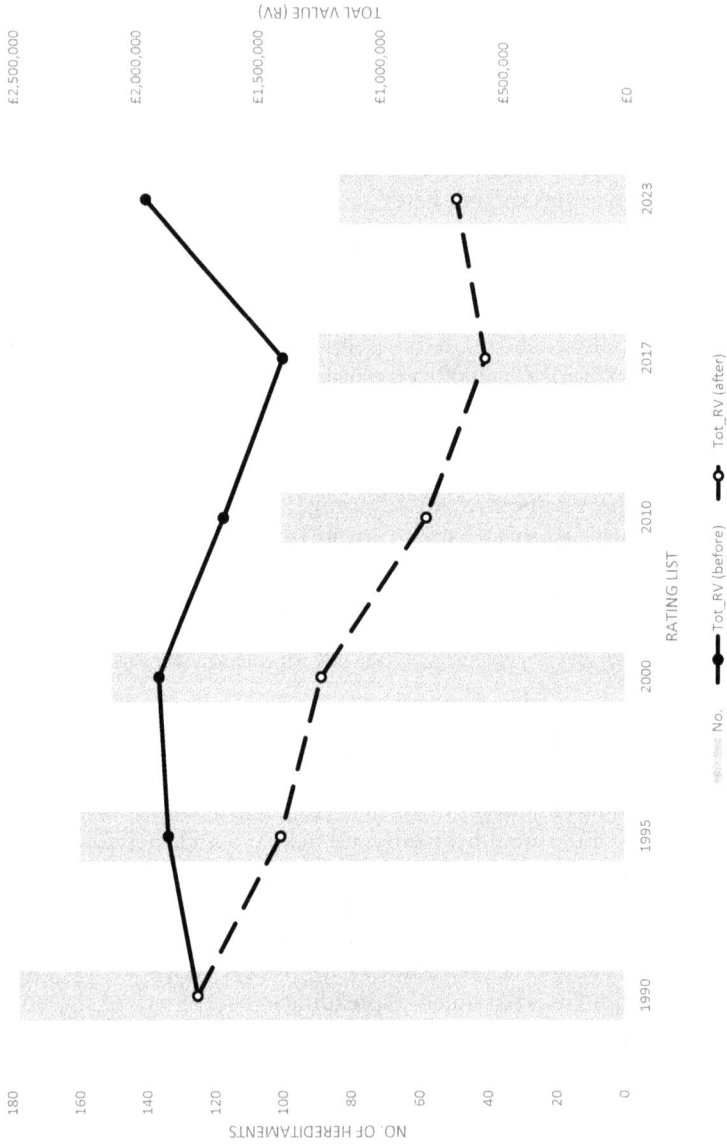

Figure 11.1 Number and total rateable value of non-domestic hereditaments in Rhyl's RBD, before and after allowing for inflation (RPI)

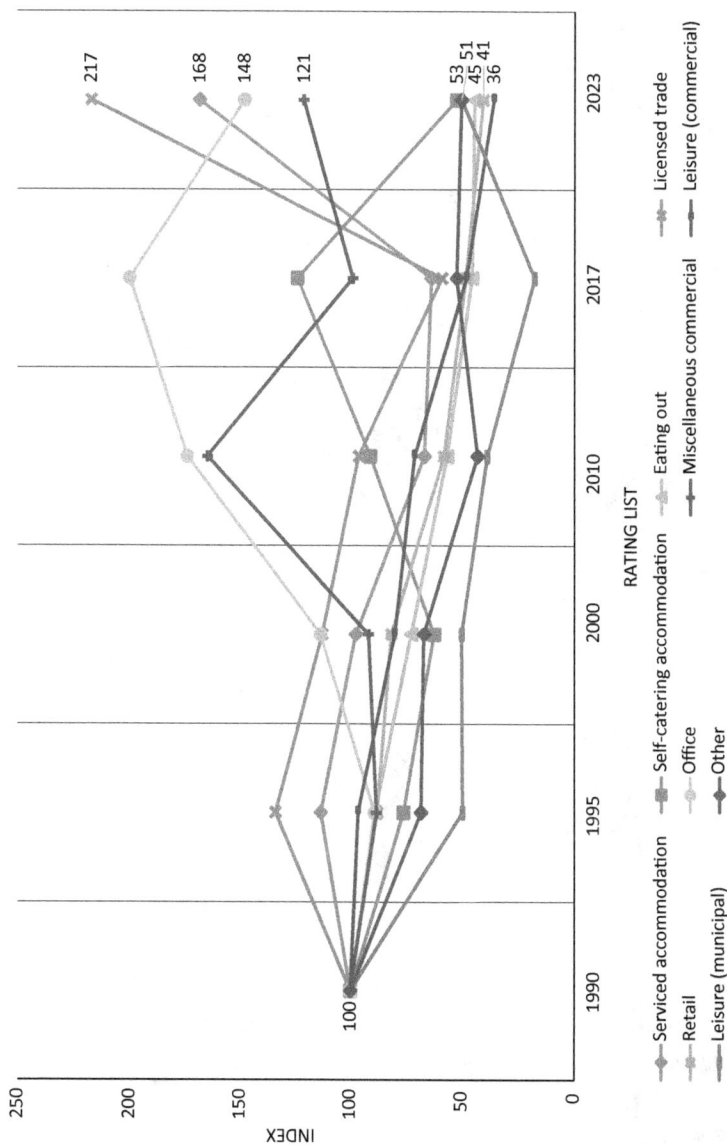

Figure 11.2 Rateable value indices for non-domestic hereditaments in Rhyl's RBD by land use, after allowing for inflation (RPI)

Figure 11.3 Map of West Parade and adjoining streets, Rhyl (Google Maps)

reproduced here with the correct attribution, but not GSV images themselves (at least not in print). Hence, no such images have been included in this chapter, but they are easily accessible by searching Google Maps and using the Street View facility (located in the bottom right of the map). Using GSV, the author observed locations in Rhyl where significant construction, demolition or modification had taken place, partly to help visualise changes to the properties and their characteristics captured in the Rating Lists, and partly to understand the changing aesthetics and aesthetic qualities of the resort from a 'tourist-eye view'. Example addresses include: 21–26 West Parade (Premier Inn and SC2); the junction of East Parade and Conwy Street (Sun Centre and New Pavilion Theatre); and the area around 60 Queen Street (Queen's Buildings). A visual assessment of these sites reveals material transformations that tally with known indicators of decline and rejuvenation (as suggested by Gonçalves & Aguas, 1997, in Shaw & Williams, 2004), including a move out of tourism activities (boarded up properties and façade gaps along the promenade, and the removal of signs advertising facilities and amenities for tourists) and a renewal of the product (new hotels, visitor attractions and landscaped areas).

From these data we can conclude that Rhyl has experienced a significant loss of 'tourism function' since its heyday as a holiday destination in the 1950s and 1960s, but that it continues to appeal to certain tourists and markets (principally families taking short breaks or day trips, and young adults attracted by the night-time economy). Environmental improvements on the seaward side of the B5118 road (West Parade and East Parade), and the replacement and refurbishment of property dating back to the mid-19th century on the landward side, have gone some way to rehabilitating the resort as a tourist site/sight, in turn helping to attract private investment, not just from SMEs, as in the past, but crucially from chained businesses that are adding (or replacing lost) capacity and introducing greater consistency in service standards; this is a basis on which to build for the future. There are also welcome signs of a more diverse tourism product, focusing on sport and adventure among other things, including the opening of a kite-surfing school and ninja assault course. 'Declinism' appears to be in retreat, at least for the time being.

Lessons for the Life Cycle

There are several conclusions that can be drawn from this analysis for the TALC itself. The original study of Rhyl (Gale, 2005; also Gale & Botterill, 2005) advanced various criticisms of the model, most notably the fallacy of using the number of tourists as a measure of development when such numbers are hard to come by, the absence of clear breaks or turning points that would help to identify the end of one stage and the start of the next, and the simplicity of the asymptotic curve which, in suggesting a constant conjunction between arrivals and time elapsed since discovery, fails to account for the influence of contemporaneous events or the fact that destinations are not homogeneous but, rather, comprise many products and markets, each with their own life cycle that may be at odds with the overall trajectory of growth or decline.

This last point is explored in Chapman and Light's (2016) study of the seaside amusement arcade sector. They propose that resorts are a 'mosaic' of elements, each element corresponding to a particular sector of the visitor economy. Their analysis suggests that the arcade sector in resorts was growing when the resorts themselves were in decline; paradoxically, arcades now seem to be declining thanks to the rise of home computing and the impact of gambling legislation, while resorts are experiencing something of a revival. Thus, global, national and local processes combine to enable and to constrain demand for this element and for all the elements of the resort mosaic, favouring some and disadvantaging others. In this chapter, the analysis of property data for Rhyl discriminates between land uses as opposed to sectors, but the principle is the same; some categories of use are in ascendancy and others are retreating at any given time (as seen in Figure 11.2). Thus, a more 'granular' understanding of resort development is obtained than that permitted by blanket applications of the TALC.

Furthermore, change in destinations is 'revolutionary, not evolution-ary' (Gale & Botterill, 2005: 167). The story of the rise and fall of British seaside resorts like Rhyl is very much of its time. This was a period char-acterised by peace in Europe, rising incomes, car ownership, television and video, de-industrialisation, the diminishing power of the church and the state, and artificially cheap food and travel, which cut the umbilical cord between resorts and the urban areas where their visitors lived and worked, and opened up new places to visit and possibilities beyond these shores for the masses, including the rapidly expanding service classes (see Urry, 1990; also Agarwal, 2002, on resort restructuring and the shift from a Fordist to a post-Fordist regime of accumulation). The TALC, therefore, is a description of a particular period in the history of tradi-tional tourism places, rather than a foretelling of what may happen when all manner of destinations grow old and lose their competitive edge over younger rivals.

That said, if it were not for the TALC, an answer (or answers) to the question of why resorts rise and fall in popularity would continue to elude us. It is an excellent jumping-off point for studies that seek to understand the changing fortunes of named destinations and destination types. The biological metaphor works well, too, even if Ravenscroft and Hadjihambi (2006: 152) dismiss it as 'little more than a heuristic, useful in reducing complex relationships to a simple linear form in which changes are pre-dominantly a function of time elapsed since "birth"'. It is easy to imagine resorts as entities that are conceived, grow up, mature and ultimately decline, much like living things. Indeed, we can extend the metaphor and think of the resort as the 'patient' and different sectors of the visitor economy or different land uses as the 'organs'. Even in an ailing resort, one or more of these sectors or uses may be functioning well, but decline is likely to be swift and terminal in the event of 'multiple organ failure'.

Conclusion

Rhyl has not yet reached the end of the TALC. There is no 'exit' from tourism (*per* Baum, 1998), and Rhyl may even be enjoying an extended period of life as a tourist destination due to a change in both *polity* and *policy*. Local authority restructuring in April 1996 saw the replacement of smaller district councils in England and Wales with larger unitary authorities, ending the tenure of Rhuddlan Borough Council and heralding a new era under Denbighshire County Council. Concurrently, there was a change in direction as regards tourism and economic development, from the local state as 'entrepreneur' (commissioning new amenities and improvements to infrastructure paid for with cash reserves and regional development match-funding), to the local state as 'enabler' (identifying parcels of land for redevelopment and clearing dilapidated and derelict buildings to make way for large hospitality and retail chains). This is bearing fruit, attracting lost trade back to Rhyl as well as new markets, and leveraging private-sector investment at levels rarely seen previously in the resort.

Going forwards, Rhyl is likely to be affected for better or worse by external factors such as Brexit (e.g. the loss of the ERDF as a potential means of part-funding capital projects), volatile energy and commodity prices in an era characterised by conflict between and within nation states (driving up costs for businesses and softening demand), and new technologies that disrupt tourism demand and supply (e.g. sharing platforms, and automation and artificial intelligence). Foreign holidays may become prohibitively expensive and socially unacceptable, as the true cost of long-distance travel for the environment and its contribution to the climate crisis is recognised through higher prices and taxation and flight-shaming, leading to a wholesale switching (back) to domestic tourism and resorts like Rhyl. (Ironically, an increase in surface temperatures might make the Welsh weather more agreeable for beach tourism in the fullness of time.) Conversely, in a post-carbon society the practice of 'demolish and rebuild' will become harder to justify because of the embodied carbon in buildings, obliging developers and local authorities to find new users and uses for existing property. This could involve 'pop-up' sites and events, as with the former Tropicana open-air swimming baths on the seafront at Weston-super-Mare, which has hosted Banksy's Dismaland and the above-mentioned 'See Monster', an oil rig repurposed as a temporary public artwork and visitor attraction (see Pimentel Biscaia & Marques, 2022; Gale, 2022).

Whatever the future may bring for Rhyl and for British seaside resorts in general, and whether the TALC can adequately convey what transpires, it would be interesting to come back in another 20 years and repeat the study again. One thing is for certain: change is the only constant in life (and in tourist destinations), meaning there will always be a place for theories and concepts – even those that have been around for 40-plus years at the time of writing – that help us make sense of the passage of time and how it affects tourism spaces and places.

References

Agarwal, S. (2002) Restructuring seaside tourism: The resort lifecycle. *Annals of Tourism Research* 29 (1), 25–55.

Barrett, J.A. (1958) The seaside resort towns of England and Wales. PhD thesis, University of London.

Baum, T. (1998) Taking the exit route: Extending the tourism area life-cycle model. *Current Issues in Tourism* 1, 167–175.

Blood, D. and Duncan, P. (2022) Alarm over sharp rise in Airbnb listings in coastal areas of England and Wales. *The Guardian* (online), 18 October. Available at https://www.theguardian.com/technology/2022/oct/18/sharp-rise-airbnb-listings-coastal-areas-england-wales?CMP=share_btn_tw (accessed 31 March 2023).

Butler, R. (1980) The concept of a tourism area cycle of evolution: Implications for resources. *Canadian Geographer* 24 (1), 5–12.

Chapman, A. and Light, D. (2016) Exploring the tourist destination as a mosaic: The alternative lifecycles of the seaside amusement arcade sector in Britain. *Tourism Management* 52, 254–263.

Conwy and Denbighshire Public Services Board (2023) *Key Employment Sector – Tourism*. Available at https://conwyanddenbighshirelsb.org.uk/home/english-wellbeing-assessment/english-key-employment-sector-tourism/#_ftn5 (accessed 1 April 2023).

Demetriadi, J. (1997) The golden years: English seaside resorts, 1950–74. In G. Shaw and A. Williams (eds) *The Rise and Fall of British Coastal Resorts* (pp. 49–75). London: Pinter.

Denbighshire County Council (1995) *Prospectus, November 1995*.

Denbighshire County Council (2020) Extra funding secured for Queen's Buildings development. Available at https://www.denbighshire.gov.uk/en/news/news-detail.aspx?article=3c3d0c5c-49a0-4834-9f10-4e5cbb3e5247 (accessed 1 April 2023).

Denbighshire County Council (2023) *Denbighshire County Council Tourism Strategy, 2019–2022*. Available at https://www.denbighshireambassador.wales/wp-content/uploads/2016/03/Denbighshire-County-Council-Tourism-Strategy-2019-2022.pdf (accessed 31 March 2023).

Gale, T. (2001) Late twentieth century cultural change and the decline and attempted rejuvenation of the British seaside resort as a long holiday destination: A case study of Rhyl, North Wales. PhD thesis, University of Wales. Available at https://figshare.cardiffmet.ac.uk/articles/thesis/Late_twentieth_century_cultural_change_and_the_decline_and_attempted_rejuvenation_of_the_British_seaside_resort_as_a_long_holiday_destination_A_case_study_of_Rhyl_North_Wales/20359545 (accessed 1 April 2023).

Gale, T. (2005) Modernism, post-modernism and the decline of British seaside resorts as long holiday destinations: A case study of Rhyl, North Wales. *Tourism Geographies* 7, 86–112.

Gale, T. (2022) Weston-super-Mare's See Monster: The good and the bad of pop-up attractions. *The Conversation*. Available at https://theconversation.com/weston-super-mares-see-monster-the-good-and-the-bad-of-pop-up-attractions-192196 (accessed 12 October 2022).

Gale, T. and Botterill, D. (2005) A realist agenda for tourist studies, or why destination areas really rise and fall in popularity. *Tourist Studies 5*, 151–174.

Gill, A.A. (2002) Wales: An apology. *The Guardian*, 19 October. Available at https://www.theguardian.com/uk/2002/oct/19/britishidentity.guardianleaders (accessed 1 April 2023).

National Coastal Tourism Academy (2016) *Coastal Tourism in 2016*. Available at https://coastaltourismacademy.co.uk/resource-hub/resource/2016-coastal-tourism (accessed 31 August 2019).

National Coastal Tourism Academy (2023) *Coastal Tourism Business Survey 2021 Wave 3 Results*. Available at: https://coastaltourismacademy.co.uk/uploads/Business_Survey_2021_Wave_3_national_results.pdf (accessed 1 April 2023).

Pimentel Biscaia, M.S. and Marques, L. (2022) Dystopian dark tourism: Affective experiences in Dismaland. *Tourism Geographies* 24, 306–325.

Ravenscroft, N. and Hadjihambi, I. (2006) The implications of Lamarckian theory for the TALC model. In R. Butler (ed.) *The Tourism Area Life Cycle, Volume 2: Conceptual and Theoretical Issues* (pp. 150–163). Clevedon: Channel View Publications.

Rhyl, Prestatyn and Abergele Journal (2018) Tourism up by 70 per cent since 2007. *Rhyl, Prestatyn and Abergele Journal* (online), 5 September. Available at https://www.rhyljournal.co.uk/news/16689301.tourism-70-per-cent-since-2017 (accessed 1 April 2023).

Saumarez Smith, O. (2019) The lost world of the British leisure centre. *History Workshop Journal* 88, 181–203.

Shaw, G. and Williams, A.M. (2004) *Tourism and Tourism Spaces*. London: Sage.

Towner, J. (1996) *An Historical Geography of Recreation and Tourism in the Western World 1540–1940*. Chichester: John Wiley.

Uribe-Toril, J., Ruiz-Real, J.L., Galindo Durán, A. and de Pablo Valenciano, J. (2021) How to use Google Street View for a time-lapse data collection methodology: Potential uses for retailing. *Journal of Ambient Intelligence and Humanized Computing* 14, 2199–2209.

Urry, J. (1990) *The Tourist Gaze*. London: Sage.

Walton, J.K. (2000) *The British Seaside: Holidays and Resorts in the Twentieth Century*. Manchester: Manchester University Press.

12 The Role of Place Image in the Decline and Rejuvenation of Traditional English Seaside Resorts

David Jarratt

This chapter considers the interplay between place image, class and the Tourism Area Life Cycle model (TALC) at the traditional coastal resorts of England. These mature destinations have long been associated with a blanket narrative of decline, seemingly in line with TALC (Butler, 1980). Yet not all have faced the same fate; simply put, the place image of working-class resorts suffered more acutely, especially in the late twentieth century. They came to represent poor taste in comparison with more exclusive resorts and other leisure/tourism options; they slipped down the Leisure Spaces Hierarchy (Urry, 1995a). So, place image is a relevant variable and even a 'trigger' (Butler, 2006: 286) which impacts the fortunes of these tourist places, as depicted in the stages of the TALC model.

'Place' can be approached on three levels – descriptive, social-constructionist or phenomenological (see Cresswell, 2015: 56). This chapter aligns primarily with the first but also the second level; it details specific places but also discusses social processes and the gazes of social groups. So, this chapter accepts the relational and subjective nature of places and the meanings that are attached to them, but it is not especially concerned with the ontological baggage which often seems to accompany discussions of place. Nor is the focus on the mechanics of place branding or marketing. Instead, this chapter concentrates on place image more generally, that is, place reputation and identity, linking directly to resort popularity in terms of tourism (Walton, 2000: 42) and issues of class in terms of how resorts are symbolically represented in society and media (Urry, 1995a, 1997).

Butler's model dates back to the start of the 1980s – perhaps the darkest decade for the English seaside. Urry's observations on the consumption of seaside tourism date back to the 1990s, when rejuvenation was often either in its early stages or merely a plan. Tentatively, this chapter observes that the seaside's decline phase now appears to be ending. It seems appropriate to revisit these works as the rejuvenation of traditional English resorts is underway and the seaside appears to be moving back up the Leisure Spaces Hierarchy. So, the TALC model (Butler, 1980) and Leisure Spaces Hierarchy (Urry, 1995a) are considered first, as they provide the theoretical context for this chapter; then, the place image of the traditional seaside resort and implications for the TALC model are discussed.

The TALC Model

Butler's (1980) Tourism Area Life Cycle (TALC) model has been at the centre of academic debate within tourism studies for decades. Its clarity and flexibility mean that it has informed discussions of the fortunes and futures of tourism destinations. Like the product life cycle (PLC), on which it is based, it is useful for informing planning and change management but less so for forecasting (Coles, 2006). This much-valued model has been critiqued (Agarwal, 1997, 2005) and alternatives offered, including the application of chaos theory, in acknowledgement of some intervening factors (Russell, 2006), and work by Baum (1998), which considered a resort model with sigmoid curves, meaning that as a tourist area is reinvented, old products sit in tandem with the new. All have their advantages and, importantly, illuminate a complex set of circumstances. Indeed, place image, as discussed in this chapter, could be considered one of the many variables characterising tourism places, meaning that their evolution is both linear and complex, with both predictable and unpredictable outcomes (Russell, 2006). These critiques, amendments and models have one thing in common with each other and Butler (1980): they leave many established destinations in the stagnation or post-stagnation phase; the difference between the two can be difficult to ascertain. In other words, tourist areas are left in a state of uncertainty.

One suggestion from Ravenscroft and Hadjihambi is that another way to consider resorts might be with reference to the process of evolution rather than to a life cycle: 'the development of resorts takes place over a number of iterations, each reflecting a change (improvement) on the last' (Ravenscroft & Hadjihambi, 2006: 150). They point out that the TALC and PLC models are based on Darwinism, which assumes a decline/death stage, and instead consider a Lamarckian approach to evolution, which does not. This implies that resorts may simply adapt into modified forms based on what has gone before rather than face decline. Indeed, some destinations have second lives after reaching maturity (Agarwal, 1997, 2005); Butler's model allows for this in the rejuvenation stage, which can be considered a positive reaction to the threat of decline. Nevertheless, one can question the extent to which the TALC and PLC rely on inevitability, especially as products and destinations are not biological as per Darwin's work on life cycles. So, resorts in stagnation or decline need not be subject to an inevitable fate. A focus on Lamarckian evolution or a move away from an assumption of potential decline is not without issue though (Ravenscroft & Hadjihambi, 2006). The onwards and upwards Lamarckian approach, where a resort evolves – that is, each iteration reflects an 'improvement' on the previous version (Ravenscroft & Hadjihambi, 2006: 150), does not necessarily tally with the experience of older tourism areas, which, in many cases, have experienced a decline as described by Butler (1980).

English seaside resorts are some of the clearest examples of tourism decline as depicted in TALC, largely because they were among the earliest mass tourism areas – the first wave, as it were. Mass tourism took hold in the Industrial Revolution of the 19th century and with the dawning of the railways in particular (Brodie, 2019). While this story of early mass tourism development is not exclusive to England, one could look to Coney Island in the USA or Rhyl in Wales (see Gale in this volume, Chapter 11) for instance, they seem to offer a good example of widespread decline following growth and, to a varying extent, stagnation (Butler, 1980). However, various mitigating circumstances complicate this narrative of decline. There is a myriad of micro-factors, the local history, governance and particular characteristics of specific resorts and their markets which are difficult to account for and add complexity (Agarwal, 2005). Connected to this is the importance of place image, which has been linked to spirals of decline, sealing the fate of seaside resorts (Jarratt, 2019) – this does not necessarily contradict TALC but offers one explanation for this variance between resorts and why forecasting can be problematic. To put it another way, challenges of place image facing these resorts are not only a result of decline but are also a trigger factor which can bring it about.

The Leisure Spaces Hierarchy

In the second half of the 20th century, a pattern of decline in reputation and tourism provision was established in the predominantly working-class seaside resorts. They were subject to a seemingly inevitable decay as they moved through their apparent life cycle. However, Urry (1997: 103) suggests that the TALC model does not 'sufficiently interrogate changes in fashion, style and taste which have transformed British social life'. Urry suggests these cultural processes leave the resorts less valued than they once were and largely visited by poorer as well as older people and those with few other choices. In essence, he argues that the middle classes led the way in labelling resorts as tasteless on the one hand and rural areas (including those on the coast) and cultural sites as tasteful on the other (Urry, 1995b, 1997). Resorts were rejected by a range of visitors as increasingly they were considered old-fashioned, tacky or worse.

Morgan and Pritchard (1999) also stress the significance of class at the seaside and write about the hierarchy of destinations in Devon and the struggle between different socioeconomic groups. They suggest that tourism is a cultural arena in which ideas of superiority and inferiority are played out and predict that social tone is likely to remain a shaper of tourism development for the foreseeable future. Such distinctions within tourism are tied to identity and ego (Munt, 1994) and are encapsulated by Waterhouse (1989: 18) when he writes about the development of travel in the railway age – 'I am a traveller, you are a tourist, he is a tripper'.

Urry (1995a) suggests a social hierarchy of seaside resorts; for example, Lytham on the Fylde Coast may be considered much more upmarket than nearby Blackpool, while St Anne's would be literally and symbolically in-between. However, this has been largely superseded by the Leisure Spaces Hierarchy, which includes a much wider range of destinations, coastal or otherwise, both in the UK and abroad. So, seaside resorts now must compete with a variety of places in this hierarchy, many of which will be newer and 'organized in terms of more variegated distinctions of taste and fashion' (Urry, 1997: 104). Here, Urry borrows from Bourdieu's (1984) 'distinction' essentially to see taste (linked to the consumption of symbolic goods – such as holidays) as a way to distinguish between social groups or classes. This is an activity often associated with the middle class, which Urry refers to as the service class. Bourdieu explains how this group denigrates the working class and their 'lower, coarse, vulgar, venal, servile – in a word, natural – enjoyment' (1984: 7), not least through leisure and tourism practices. Visiting artistic and cultural sites plays a key role in maintaining this social differentiation. During the late 20th century, traditional resorts were generally seen to focus on such 'natural' enjoyments and to be the negation of culture. Urry points out that good taste might allow a member of the service class to pass through as a voyeur, or perhaps in some ironic fashion, but not to stay as a regular tourist. These resorts were considered undesirable and for those with poor taste; this was wrapped in a portrayal of decline. This declinism and its implications for these places, as they move through their life cycle, is now explored.

Decline: Not Just a Phase But a Narrative

The fate of the English seaside is not only about infrastructure life cycle, investment and so on but also about place image and reputation, which may be ill-informed at times. Yet, it is powerful, bolstered by the media, and often very difficult to change. Resorts may well have socio-economic problems to contend with, some of which may be acute, but even so we can see long-running narratives and placeism (that is discriminatory practices against a locality) which go beyond this.

The traditional British seaside resorts are often described in a context of long-term decline, first brought on by the advent of cheap package holidays to the Mediterranean in the 1960s. While there is some truth to this, the story is more nuanced. For many families in Britain, especially working-class ones, it was likely to be the early 1980s before such holidays would become commonplace (Walton, 2000). Much of the burgeoning competition from the 1960s onwards was from domestic destinations, such as rural areas with good road connections, rather than relying on railway connections. Holiday habits changed but the seaside resorts could still attract large numbers of visitors. For instance, Blackpool's popularity remained largely unchecked until the 1980s. Most traditional resorts struggled during that decade, and many seaside attractions and guest houses were lost in the 1980s and 1990s.

Such losses were particularly acute for medium-sized resorts, which were neither small enough to be exclusive nor big enough to sustain major attractions or to compete against larger, often longer-established resorts (Jarratt, 2019; Walton, 2000). Examples of this squeezed middle, which often included resorts that had grown rapidly in the first half of the 20th century but were to face sharp decline, included Clacton and Bognor Regis. We now turn to one such resort, Morecambe, before considering its larger neighbour, Blackpool.

Hassan (2003: 254) writes, 'Morecambe suffered a calamitous fall in visitor spending from £46.6 million in 1973 to £6.5 million in 1990, expressed in constant values'. In the 20th century, through boom and bust, resorts like Morecambe became increasingly associated with the working classes, something not reflected so much in their earlier histories. The factors impacting decline were not always global or national but could be local; for Morecambe, these included environmental pollution, over-reliance on one geographical market and more competitive resorts nearby (Hassan, 2003; Jarratt, 2019). In the 1970s this resort, dubbed the Costa Geriatrica, was increasingly associated with the elderly; it was the place where seagulls don't land anymore and where they don't bury their dead but prop them up in bus shelters, according to TV comedian Colin Crompton, who had a routine based on the resort. In *The Kingdom by the Sea* (1983), writer Paul Theroux failed to see how anyone could travel to Morecambe for pleasure. In 2003 it was even designated the third crappiest town in the UK by public vote and subsequently listed third in the popular *Idler Book of Crap Towns* (Jordinson & Kieran, 2003).

The public perception of Morecambe (the more recent fortunes of which are explored later in this chapter) as well as of more boisterous seaside resorts such as Blackpool, had changed dramatically in the second half of the 20th century:

> the celebrations of the gregarious virtues of the 'people' on holiday from the 1890s to the 1950s have given way in the 1980s and 1990s to revulsion at a perceived dominant combination of bloated bodies, alcohol abuse, junk food, litter, and aggressive behaviour. (Walton 2000: 13)

Walton goes on to cite several examples of unnecessarily negative journalistic coverage which fuelled these perceptions. One example is a tongue-in-cheek portrayal by an Italian who writes that the English working class do not need to go to Spain to behave like beasts as they do it perfectly well in Blackpool (Severgnini, 1992).

Blackpool divides opinion in England today. Along with Scarborough, it is the most visited seaside resort and home to many popular attractions, yet for many it is the epitome of bad taste, wrapped up in a decline narrative, despite the high visitor numbers and significant investment. Mazierska (2020a: 1) agrees with that portrayal and observes, despite these successes, that there is a widespread perception that Blackpool is in decline and unappealing. She states that this is partly because of its reputation as a working-class northern town. Film representations of the resort, for example, tend to paint an unattractive picture (Mazierska, 2020b). This is also reflected in post-war music: prevalent themes include class and decline as well as nostalgia (Gillon, 2020).

A good example of image problems was Blackpool's 2010 application for UNESCO World Heritage status (Department for Culture, Media and Sport, 2010); the bid failed and much of the public reaction was negative. The BBC's online coverage of the story was inundated with negative comments and jokes made at the expense of the resort. Reactions of disbelief and hilarity met claims that the birthplace of mass tourism deserved to be preserved as a heritage site (Walton & Wood, 2009). This is despite the town having an impressive amount of seaside heritage, including the world's only fully intact Winter Gardens complex, Blackpool Tower and three piers (see Figure 12.1) – to name only the best-known

Figure 12.1 One of Blackpool's three piers. Photograph by Jenny Steele, reproduced with permission

examples. An article in *The Guardian* at the time, entitled 'Blackpool: Profile of a ghost town' (Moss, 2010), while in some ways sympathetic to the bid and the resort, did nothing to dissuade stereotypes and declinism. There are numerous examples of similar negative press coverage over the years (Mazierska, 2020a; Walton, 2000).

So, underpinning the oversimplistic and long-running narrative of decline was a negative appraisal of and, sometimes, snobbery towards largely traditional and working-class traditional seaside resorts, which had fallen out of fashion over many years for vast swathes of the British population.

Survival and Rejuvenation

While economic restructuring and decline certainly took place in the second half of the 20th century, the story was far more nuanced and less universal than is often suggested. Some smaller resorts like Salcombe and Lynton in Devon or Grange-over-Sands in Cumbria continually catered for relatively wealthy visitors and retirees. According to Walton (2000: 42), they became

> fixed in an early stage of the 'resort cycle' (thereby undermining its viability as a concept) and, with their strong identities and reputations, remained less vulnerable to changing fashions than their more dynamic but unstable rivals.

Here, Walton recognises the importance of place image and identifies exceptions to the TALC model, although this does not necessarily undermine the concept. He also points out that the function of coastal communities is not fixed; for instance, Brighton became a successful city by the sea in the late 20th century, with tourism only part of its more diversified economy. Furthermore, Blackpool and Scarborough have continually operated as hugely popular traditional and fully functioning resorts. Even so, there have been notable changes, such as the rise of the caravan (static trailer) economy (especially along the east coast of England) and a relative decline in the popularity of traditional break and breakfasts. In short, the UK seaside resorts have adapted and survived despite becoming more culturally marginal in the late 20th century.

Of late, various developments, notably Brexit and the international travel restrictions associated with COVID-19, have meant a boost in domestic tourism for British resorts. Yet the default declinist position of press coverage remains evident, although it was now more likely to take the form of historical context; recent tourism successes are framed by a persistent decline narrative. Nevertheless, there is little doubt that a movement towards the seaside is taking place. Seaside resorts are no longer places *of recovery*, but places *in recovery* as they move back into the cultural mainstream (Steele & Jarratt, 2019). Elborough (2010) observes that our rapprochement with the seaside has been underway since the start of the 21st century, when the artist Tracey Emin sold her Whitstable beach hut to Charles Saatchi for £75,000 – which would soon reflect the real-world inflation of beach hut prices in southern England. He also points to the popular BBC TV series *Coast*, which was first aired in 2005. Gentrification is now well established in many coastal resorts, especially those within commuting distance of major economic centres, as the middle class move in (Shah, 2011). This does not, though, necessarily diminish the serious socioeconomic challenges facing residents in many coastal communities.

A cultural rapprochement with the traditional seaside resort seems to be gathering momentum. Those which had struggled saw regeneration attempts, most notably perhaps at Margate. An important part of this rapprochement is that the built environment of the seaside resorts has been increasingly valued (Jarratt, 2022). Since around the turn of the century onwards, Historic England has recognised the value of England's much-diminished seaside heritage (Brodie, 2018; Historic England, 2023). Perhaps as these sites grow older, such recognition, underpinned by a nostalgic appeal, is more readily accepted. Nostalgic images associated with the seaside are instantly recognisable as 'part of England's collective consciousness, our folk memory' (Elborough, 2010: 7). The decline of resort infrastructure can, of course, lead to physical demolition but, before this, resorts can adopt a faded grandeur that some people find attractive, affirming, deeply nostalgic and even an expression of Englishness (Elborough, 2010; Jarratt & Gammon, 2016). Such decay marks a stage further back; it allows a connection to a *golden age* – not just for the resort but for individuals too (Jarratt, 2022).

In this case, elements of decline can be considered a positive aspect of place image, through nostalgia and built heritage which is increasingly considered as heritage (Light & Chapman, 2022). This complicates the TALC model's applicability a little but, in fairness, this meme is only just starting to take shape and placeism against working-class seaside resorts is still the norm. Furthermore, one might argue that the emergence of heritage pales in comparison with the problems associated with an ageing infrastructure. Yet heritage assets are significant, not only for their own sake but symbolically; they can help facilitate a more positive place image and attract new markets. Indeed, the acceptance of seaside heritage within the Authorised Heritage Discourse (Light & Chapman, 2022) could be equated with movement up the Leisure Spaces Hierarchy. For, as we have seen, heritage and culture are associated with good taste. Linked to this, seaside heritage is also important because it offers a distinctiveness that sets these resorts apart from other places (Jarratt, 2015). So, any new developments in resorts that wish to be popular destinations should wherever possible be distinct from today's *blandscapes* and foster their appeal as somewhere else (Shah, 2011).

So, chronological distance need not only mean decline but can facilitate the emergence of heritage tourism assets. Furthermore, changes in place image are slow to materialise and difficult to predict for several reasons, including cultural change and successful regeneration efforts (Smith, 2001, 2005). To demonstrate these points, it is useful to return to Morecambe, where we now see a reopened landmark hotel, TV tourism linked to ITV's *The Bay*, and improved transport links. Also, the Eden Project has started work on a new site in the town which is set to transform the local visitor economy – a flagship of the government's levelling-up agenda (Eden Project, 2023). None of these things would be easy to predict at the turn of the last century, when the resort's place image was so problematic. Increased belief in the potential of the resort has been building over the last two decades or so. The antecedents of this can be traced back to the late 20th century, when, following serious flooding, new coastal defences were built and, as part of it, a new promenade featuring a series of statues. At the centre of the Tern project, which opened in 1999, is a statue of a once-popular comedian who took his name from the town – Eric Morecambe. The statue seemed to symbolise the town and its history and, at the very least, gave the new promenade a photographic focal point [in much the same way as a statue of the comic character Desperate Dan from *The Dandy*, published by the Dundee-based publisher DC Thomson, has been used to push that city's tourist appeal – editor's comment].

Morecambe's new promenade, brought about by necessity, can be considered the start of various efforts at regeneration, but it saw setbacks, notably the closure of the Frontierland theme park in 2000. Yet, in 2008, the once derelict and architecturally important Midland Hotel reopened; it became an important symbol of hope for a brighter future (Jarratt, 2022) and was reported positively in the media. Very slowly, the image of the resort improved. Visitors, who enjoyed the coastal strip and the stone jetty, also saw the potential and noted the lack of attractions, while enjoying a wistful nostalgia and seaside heritage (Jarratt, 2022; Jarratt & Gammon, 2016). Meanwhile, neighbouring Blackpool has seen significant investment from the private and public sectors, record visitor numbers and will soon be home to a museum of seaside entertainment.

It is important to remember that regeneration/rejuvenation can be transformative, in terms not only of the physical environment but also of place image. Consider the Barcelona effect, for example. The Spanish city saw re-imaging initiatives and, consequently, more attractive meanings became associated with it. Visitors came to know the city not just for its features but for a series of synecdoches; it came to be seen as a cosmo-politan, cultural and lively destination (Smith, 2005). It was successful because, within the symbolic economy (Urry, 1995a, 1997), any efforts at image enhancement should be holistic and seek to be symbolic rather than purely functional and operational (Smith, 2001). This allows attrac-tive, coherent representations and meanings to become attached to places

Figure 12.2 The Midland Hotel, Morecambe, during the popular Vintage by the Sea Festival. Photograph by Jenny Steele, reproduced with permission

(Smith, 2005). We have also seen in recent decades the regeneration of former industrial cities in northern England not far from Blackpool and Morecambe, such as Manchester and Liverpool. In the 1990s, a pioneering developer, Urban Splash, started to transform the Manchester city centre through regeneration, at a time when the city was not considered the success story it is today. It was the same developer, Urban Splash, which saw the rapprochement with the seaside and the potential in Morecambe; it started work on the grade 2 listed Midland Hotel, which reopened in 2008 (see Figure 12.2). Both cases illustrate a shift in place image, from drab to desirable.

Conclusion

There are many complexities which impact TALC (Agarwal, 2005; Russell, 2006); one of these is place image, partly informed by issues of class and social change. Many traditional English seaside resorts have faced severe blows to their place image but, over many decades, this has changed. One reason for the slow recovery of working-class resorts in particular was a persistent blanket narrative of decline and placeism. Here we see the interplay between class, place image and tourism success. So, a change in place image can be seen as a precursor of the transition between TALC stages; it is a trigger. Tourism is, after all, about selling places and the experiences they afford – so the image is vitally important, especially if targeting higher-spending and more-demanding tourists.

Given the importance of the symbolic economy (Urry, 1995a, 1997), any efforts at image enhancement should seek to be symbolic and holistic rather than purely functional/operational (Smith, 2001, 2005). In other words, rejuvenation should try to transform how places are seen, rather than stressing what they have (facilities etc.). With this in mind, practitioners need to focus on seaside events and attractions which complement any positive elements of place image – especially those that are more symbolic and have the potential to improve place image, such as the retro, vintage, nostalgic aspects of traditional seaside resorts, much like Vintage by the Sea Festival in Morecambe (see Figure 12.2) or Dreamland Theme Park in Margate. Seaside heritage is important here as an attraction, venue or backdrop, as it offers a distinctive and unique *genus locus*. The main challenge for seaside heritage has been its physical survival and, linked to this, its recognition. Other options include purpose-built cultural or environmental attractions which can tickle the middle-class palette, with the most obvious examples being perhaps the Turner Contemporary Art Gallery in Margate and the Eden Project in Morecambe, both of which reflect the cultural/environmental attributes of the sites on which they are situated.

Butler's model is still very useful in understanding the challenges facing tourist areas. The seaside resorts discussed here are among the oldest mass tourism areas, and are in the final stage of rejuvenation. Looking at the future – how long will it last, how much will tourism grow in these resorts and at what point stagnation? And then what? These are the same questions that were asked the first time around. It makes one think that this is an ongoing process (Baum, 1998); the question might be whether we can do it better the second time around – can we control tourism in a bid to ensure longer-term economic sustainability and viability? Recent debates on so-called overtourism, chronic staff shortages and the impact of Airbnb on rental and house prices suggest that those challenges may require different solutions, or at least more effective ones. Nevertheless, we should learn, as a minimum, that tourism needs better-informed and longer-term focused management, leadership and decision-making. Meanwhile, the small and medium-sized tourism businesses that dominate English resorts are, understandably, and as ever, more concerned with visitor figures for the next season.

References

Agarwal, S. (1997) The resort cycle and seaside tourism: An assessment of its applicability and validity. *Tourism Management* 18 (2), 65–73.

Agarwal, S. (2005) Global–local interactions in English coastal resorts: Theoretical perspectives. *Tourism Geographies* 7 (4), 351–372.

Baum, T. (1998) Taking the exit route: Extending the TALC model. *Current Issues in Tourism* 1 (2), 167–175.

Bourdieu, P. (1984) *Distinction: A Social Critique of the Judgement of Taste*. London: Routledge.

Brodie, A. (2018) *The Sea Front*. Swindon: English Heritage Books.

Brodie, A. (2019) *Tourism and the Changing Face of the British Isles*. Swindon: English Heritage Books.

Butler, R. (1980) The concept of a tourist area cycle of evolution: Implications of management resources. *Canadian Geographer* 24 (1), 5–12.

Butler, R. (2006) The future and the TALC. In R. Butler (ed.) *The Tourism Area Life Cycle, Volume 2: Conceptual and Theoretical Issues* (pp. 281–291). Clevedon: Channel View Publications.

Coles, T. (2006) Enigma variations? The TALC, marketing models and the descendants of the product life cycle. In R. Butler (ed.) *The Tourism Area Life Cycle, Volume 2: Conceptual and Theoretical Issues* (pp. 49–66). Clevedon: Channel View Publications.

Cresswell, T. (2015) *Place: An Introduction*. Chichester: Wiley-Blackwell.

Department for Culture, Media and Sport (2010) UK tentative list of potential sites for World Heritage nomination: Application form [Blackpool]. Available at https://assets.publishing.service.gov.uk/government/uploads/system/uploads/attachment_data/file/78258/WHAF_Blackpool.pdf (accessed 1 February 2023).

Eden Project (2023) The Eden Project Morecambe, UK. Available at https://www.edenproject.com/new-edens/eden-project-morecambe-uk (accessed 7 July 2023).

Elborough, T. (2010) *Wish You Were Here: England on Sea*. London: Hodder & Stoughton.

Gillon, L. (2020) Nostalgia and simulacra: Blackpool in song. In E. Mazierska (ed.) *Blackpool in Film and Popular Music* (pp. 83–101). Cham: Palgrave Macmillan.

Hassan, J. (2003) *The Seaside, Health and The Environment in England and Wales since 1800*. Aldershot: Ashgate.

Historic England (2023) Historic England's research into seaside resorts. Available at the Historic England website, https://historicengland.org.uk/research/current/discover-and-understand/coastal-and-marine/seaside-resorts (accessed 7 April 2023).

Jarratt, D. (2015) Sense of place at a British coastal resort: Exploring 'seasideness' in Morecambe. *Tourism: An International Interdisciplinary Journal* 63 (3), 351–363.

Jarratt, D. (2019) The development and decline of Morecambe in the nineteenth and twentieth centuries: A resort caught in the tide. *Journal of Tourism History* 11 (3), 263–283.

Jarratt, D. (2022) The importance of built heritage in the English seaside experience. In R. Sharpley (ed.) *The Routledge Handbook of the Tourist Experience* (pp. 481–498). Abingdon: Routledge.

Jarratt, D. and Gammon, S. (2016) 'We had the most wonderful times': Seaside nostalgia at a British resort. *Tourism Recreation Research* 41 (2), 123–133.

Jordinson, S. and Kieran, D. (2003) *The Idler Book of Crap Towns: The Fifty Worst Places to Live in the UK*. London: Pan Macmillan.

Light, D. and Chapman, A. (2022) The neglected heritage of the English seaside holiday. *Coastal Studies and Society* 1 (1), 34–54.

Mazierska, E. (2020a) Introduction: The changing fortunes of Blackpool. In E. Mazierska (ed.) *Blackpool in Film and Popular Music* (pp. 1–27). London: Palgrave Macmillan.

Mazierska, E. (2020b) Blackpool fantasy narrative in *Bob's Weekend*, *The Harry Hill Movie* and *Miss Peregrine's Home for Peculiar Children*. In E. Mazierska (ed.) *Blackpool in Film and Popular Music*. Cham: Palgrave Macmillan (pp. 65–83).

Morgan, N.J. and Pritchard, A. (1999) *Power and Politics at the Seaside: The Development of Devon's Resorts in the Twentieth Century*. Exeter: University of Exeter Press.

Moss, S. (2010) Blackpool: Profile of a ghost town. *The Guardian*, 27 August. Available at https://www.theguardian.com/travel/2010/aug/27/blackpool (accessed 17 February 2023).

Munt, I. (1994) Eco-tourism or ego-tourism? *Race and Class* 36 (1), 49–60.

Ravenscroft, N. and Hadjihambi, I. (2006) The implications of Lamarckian theory for the TALC model. In R. Butler (ed.) *The Tourism Area Life Cycle, Volume 2: Conceptual and Theoretical Issues* (pp. 150–163). Clevedon: Channel View Publications.

Russell, R. (2006) Chaos theory and its application to the TALC model. In R. Butler (ed.) *The Tourism Area Life Cycle, Volume 2: Conceptual and Theoretical Issues* (pp. 164–179). Clevedon: Channel View Publications.

Severgnini, B. (1992) *L'inglese: lezioni semiserie*. Milan: Rizzoli.

Shah, P. (2011) Coastal gentrification: The coastification of St Leonards-on-Sea. PhD thesis, Loughborough University.

Smith, A. (2001) Sporting a new image? Sport-based regeneration strategies as a means of enhancing the image of the city tourist destination. In C. Gratton and I. Henry (eds) *Sport in the City: The Role of Sport in Economic and Social Regeneration* (pp. 127–148). London: Routledge.

Smith, A. (2005) Conceptualizing city image change: The 're-imaging' of Barcelona. *Tourism Geographies* 7 (4), 398–423.

Steele, J. and Jarratt, D. (2019) The seaside resort: Nostalgia and restoration. In E. Speight (ed.) *Practising Place: Creative and Critical Reflections on Place* (pp. 132–150). Sunderland: Art Editions North, University of Sunderland.

Theroux, P. (2003) *The Kingdom by the Sea: A Journey Around the Coast of Great Britain*. London: Hamish Hamilton

Urry, J. (1990) *The Tourist Gaze: Leisure and Travel in Contemporary Societies*. London: Sage.

Urry, J. (1995a) *Consuming Places*. London: Routledge.

Urry, J. (1995b) A middle-class countryside. In T. Butler and M. Savage (eds) *Social Change and the Middle Classes*. London: UCL Press.

Urry, J. (1997) Cultural change and the seaside resort. In G. Shaw and A. Williams (eds) *The Rise and Fall of British Coastal Resorts: Cultural and Economic Perspectives* (pp. 102–117). London: Mansell.

Waterhouse, K. (1989) *The Theory and Practice of Travel*. Sevenoaks: Hodder and Stoughton.

Walton, J.K. (2000) *The British Seaside: Holidays and Resorts in the Twentieth Century*. Manchester: Manchester University Press.

Walton, J.K. and Wood, J. (2009) Reputation and regeneration: History and the heritage of the recent past in the re-making of Blackpool. In L. Gibson and J. Pendlebury (eds) *Valuing Historic Environments* (pp. 15–137). Aldershot: Ashgate.

13 Smart Specialisation and the Life Cycle of Destinations: An Evolutionary Approach

João Romão

The Tourism Area Life Cycle (TALC) (Ma & Hassink, 2013) and the specialisation processes within regional economic systems (Boschma *et al.*, 2016) can both be perceived as evolutionary, path-dependent processes, where time and space matter. This chapter discusses the interrelations between these two place-based mechanisms, with a focus on the principles of smart specialisation (Foray *et al.*, 2012), which constitutes a major source of inspiration for contemporary regional innovation plans. The aim is to provide a framework for the analysis of the integration of the tourism industry within smart specialisation strategies, with consideration of the characteristics of each stage of destination development.

The conceptual framework proposed by evolutional economic geography (EEG) (Boschma & Martin, 2010) is a tool that can be used to address this problem, as it integrates historical and institutional perspectives with analysis of the spatial allocation of economic activities. This framework may help systematise how tourism can establish different types of relations with other economic activities within regional economic structures (Brouder & Eriksson, 2013) along the evolution of the life cycle of destinations (Sanz-Ibáñez & Clavé, 2014).

Describing economic specialisation as a spatial and path-dependent process is the starting point for this analysis, with a general description of the conditions needed for the emergence of new economic activities and a discussion on different types of spatial agglomeration, concluding with a synthesis of the processes of agency and 'bricolage' – with the related sources of path-dependence – that can be developed in each region.

Next, tourism development is presented as a spatial and path-dependent process. The specific case of tourism is analysed in terms of the types of relatedness, proximity and spatial agglomerations developed by this industry, concluding with a systematisation of the relations between path-dependent processes, the life cycle of destinations (Butler, 1980) and the types of proximity and variety in which tourism can be involved. Table 13.1 synthesises this analysis.

Finally, a connection between the life cycle of destinations and smart specialisation strategies is established, by describing how smart specialisation assumes that regional resources and capabilities are mobilised to address market opportunities and societal challenges through bottom-up processes of innovation. The analysis continues with a discussion of the role of technologies in tourism and specialisation processes, and concludes with a systematisation of the different roles and tasks of tourism planning along the life cycle of destinations, as synthesised in Table 13.2.

This chapter concludes by defining how the framework proposed can be applied to the empirical analysis of different cases where tourism assumes a relevant role within regional economic structures, implying that the sector has reached a stage of development that justifies a central position within smart specialisation strategies.

Specialisation as a Spatial and Path-Dependent Process

Emergence, resources, capabilities and relatedness

The study of how and why new economic activities emerge, and the study of innovation processes, enlarge the scope of traditional economic studies, by considering the historical evolution and interactions between institutions, education, culture, policy frameworks or governance (Neffke *et al.*, 2009).

The interactions potentially contributing to the creation of new ideas, initiatives or innovations that favour spatial agglomerations and regional development processes are normally rooted in their relatedness (Balland *et al.*, 2019), which can be defined as the cognitive proximity between them (Boschma & Gianelle, 2014; Aarstad *et al.*, 2016). Interactions do not depend exclusively on geographical aspects but also on other types of proximity: cultural, institutional or based on shared knowledge.

The different types of proximity and relatedness coexisting in the same territory may lead to the development of different varieties resulting from the emergence of new activities and branches within regional economic systems (Boschma *et al.*, 2013; Davids & Frenken, 2018). Interactions and spillover effects tend to spread faster within organisations that are in close proximity. However, unrelated variety tends to protect economic structures from negative external shocks, by preventing the diffusion of a potentially recessionary impact (Content *et al.*, 2019) – which is important to notice in the case of tourism (Aarstad *et al.*, 2016), considering its high vulnerability to external shocks of different types (Hall *et al.*, 2020).

The available resources in each region also constitute an important determinant of the regional specialisation and diversification patterns. Local resources that open opportunities for innovation can eventually be difficult to find in other places. Natural and cultural resources are normally more difficult to move, but also other types of community resources – like labour qualifications and skills, accumulated knowledge, research activities or governance institutions – can also be territorially embedded, implying transaction and mobility costs (Krugman, 1996).

Moreover, the technological and broader societal developments that may influence patterns of consumption and production also affect how externalities are generated and spread, with the related implications for location and agglomeration processes. In particular, the emergence of the creative economies characterising post-Fordist societies (OECD, 2014; Scott, 2007) has had deep implications for both the dominant type of externalities and the type of spatial concentration of activities. Similarly, tourism activities are also changing, in a process that can be seen as independent of the life cycle of destinations.

These aspects tend to assume a more crucial relevance in the case of tourism services due to the characteristics of their provision: the consumption must be made in the place of production (spatiality), implying a simultaneous (temporal) interaction between consumers and producers (co-terminality) (Romão, 2018). Place-based determinants of innovation and development of tourism services assume a more central role than for most other economic activities. This embeddedness of tourism services within the territory also promotes a closer connection with companies from other sectors operating in the same location (Romão, 2020b).

Processes of agglomeration

A different type of concern relates to how and why economic activities concentrate in a specific location, adding the importance of place and location to economic analysis (Martin, 2014). Demographic, cultural, technological, institutional and political factors – along with their interdependences – must also be taken into account in the historical process of evolution in destination planning and management, in the case of tourism.

Knowledge and technology were increasingly considered to explain economic performance, and knowledge creation and diffusion were seen as core drivers of economic growth, justifying the importance attached to education, and to research and development (Lucas, 1988; Romer, 1986).

There is also an evolution in the type of externalities dominating agglomeration processes. The Marshall–Arrow–Romer (MAR) type were predominant since the early stages of the Industrial Revolution, when knowledge was perceived as industry-specific, justifying the concentration of similar industries around the same location. Differently, the Jacobs type (urbanisation or diversification externalities) reflects how knowledge may spill over between complementary industries, justifying the importance of a diversified economic structure (Henderson, 1997).

When looking at tourism, it is possible to distinguish which of these types of externalities predominate. The 'resort type' of development, with a spatial concentration of tourism-related activities in a specific location, eventually isolated from the local communities, can be perceived as an industrial district, where companies (hotels, restaurants, entertainment facilities, tours and activities, travel agencies or souvenir shops) benefit from MAR-type externalities. This type of agglomeration is easily identified in coastal or mountain areas oriented to the exploitation of natural resources (Lazzeretti *et al.*, 2016; Romão & Neuts, 2017). Conversely, urban tourism – a very strong development in the last few decades – relies on the second (Jacobs) type of externality, by integrating a wide diversity of possible experiences with the supply of services, not necessarily concentrated in a specific location (even though tending to concentrate in some areas of a city, say, historical). In this case, a diversified local economic structure – in particular when looking at the creative economies, as defined by OECD (2014) – clearly favours the supply of tourism services.

Agency, bricolage and sources of path dependence

The emergence and development of new development paths ('path creation') in a specific location can be perceived as a work of 'bricolage' (Boschma *et al.*, 2017), where different types of actors act jointly in organised networks to create the conditions for the emergence or development of new industries.

Thus, 'agency' and the related 'agents' (Neffke *et al.*, 2018) – which are not exclusively private companies operating in the market but also other institutions with relevance to the dynamics of the economic system – assume a central role within innovation and development processes. As will be discussed, the diversity of agents involved in the provision of tourism services is normally very large, clearly changing over the life cycle of tourism destinations.

Keeping in mind the path-dependency of all of these development processes – and how the policies and solutions to be implemented in the future depend on the existing conditions and the options and paths built in the past – this chapter concludes with a summary of the sources of path dependency in tourism development, departing from the general description and systematisation proposed by Martin (2014).

In the case of tourism, obvious causes of path-dependence are the natural resources, which often determine the type of services and the type of tourism that can be developed. Specific examples are beaches, mountains or other forms of nature-based tourism, like natural parks for eco or rural tourism. This was systematically observed by Romão (2021) in southern European regions that tended to develop forms of tourism in regions with high ecological value, generating relatively low value-added. Cultural resources, not only related to the built environment (monuments, museums, etc.) but also to intangible aspects (events, festivals, music, local knowledge and handicrafts, or gastronomy), may also exert a strong influence on the development of tourism services. Moreover, when prioritising tourism within regional development strategies, the existence of sunk costs (e.g. those related to large-scale investments in infrastructures for transport) clearly reinforces the importance of the sector. This may lead to the creation of agglomeration economies, benefiting from the externalities resulting from the co-location of tourism-related companies and organisations; thus, even though the value-added generated by tourism in southern European regions was relatively low, this sector was still mobilising significant amounts of local resources for investment (Romão, 2021).

This proximity can be expressed at different levels, eventually leading to the emergence of specific forms of knowledge spin-off, development of skills and technological lock-in processes (related to high degrees of specialisation in a specific sector) that eventually create obstacles to the emergence of different paths. This was observed in different case studies undertaken in regions with high levels of tourism, like the Spanish islands (Capó *et al.*, 2007), the south of Portugal (Romão *et al.*, 2016) and some regions of Croatia (Kožić, 2019). These aspects will be contextualised within the evolutionary process of destination development in the next section.

Tourism Development as a Spatial and Path-Dependent Process

Tourism: A place-based decentralised and unbalanced value chain

The supply of tourism products and services in a destination is largely dependent on the existing relevant local resources. These create a high potential for tourism services to develop interactions and synergies with other local economic activities with relevance to the provision of different experiences (Tussyadiah, 2014). This territorial embeddedness is reinforced by the aspects of co-spatiality, co-temporality and co-terminality that characterise the provision of tourism services, leading to the creation of a continuous process of interaction and exchange of information between consulters and producers (Romão, 2018).

With the development of digital technologies and the related implications for the capacity to generate, store and analyse data, these fluxes of information constitute a potential source of innovation based on co-creation processes where user-generated data (obtained in different ways and often raising issues about awareness and privacy protection) support the development or improvement of products and services, while contributing to establishing a better link between strategies of destination differentiation and market segmentation. These interactions can start long before tourists travel (when they are still selecting, planning or purchasing their services) and they can last until after tourists return home (when they still can share experiences on social media or travel websites). Thus, they can support the development of personalised products and services adjusted to specific needs and motivations, and they can also help to bring the right visitors to the right places (Binkhorst & Dekker, 2009).

These technological developments supporting and enhancing production processes oriented to personalised forms of consumption are not exclusive to tourism – in fact, they are a common characteristic of the contemporary 'creative economies', where consumers are often looking for unique 'experiences' (Currid-Halkett & Scott, 2013). In the case of tourism, this uniqueness is commonly related to the specific characteristics of each place, including unique lifestyles and traditions. In this context, tourism and tourists increasingly use the same spaces and services as local residents. The concept of 'live like a local' represents this new tendency, but the emerging urban conflicts between tourists and residents are also a sign of the limits of this type of development, as broadly documented by Colomb and Novy (2017).

A tourism destination can be perceived as a decentralised value chain, where different services (including a variety of attractions, amenities, facilities or infrastructures) are provided by wide a range of diverse companies. Although each destination can be seen as a large 'repository of information' about travel behaviour, exploring co-creation opportunities requires technological capacity to accumulate and to analyse data, implying that larger organisations are in a better position to explore these technological opportunities.

In a broader sense, these digitally mediated interactions and fluxes of information at the destination level include producers, distributors, consumers, regulators and other organisations involved in the tourism industry, like the press, non-governmental organisations (NGOs) or other community-based organisations (mostly when the destination reaches the stages of development or afterwards). In this context, the concept of 'smart tourism' emerged. The term describes co-creative processes of product development and permanent innovation, and also the possible implementation of collaborative governance systems supported by systematic and informed monitorisation of impacts and participatory methods engaging local stakeholders (Boes et al., 2016).

Tourism, relatedness, proximity and spatial agglomerations

The tourism system and the related networks emerging between organisations and their stakeholders evolved in a similar way (Malakauskaite & Navickas, 2010). Until the end of the 20th century, it was still common to observe agglomerations of tourism-related activities in specific locations linked to tourism attractions. Sharing similar markets and with a close cultural and institutional proximity, accommodation and other touristic services were frequently concentrated around these areas.

The emergence of the 'creative economy' and the increasing importance of the search for personalised and diversified unique experiences also implied a renewed relevance of cities as tourism destinations, with a significant growth of urban tourism observed since the beginning of the 21st century (UNWTO, 2012). Currid-Halkett and Scott (2013) note that the demand for and supply of cultural and creative facilities converge in big cities, with a high concentration of a highly educated population with high income (demand) coexisting with a large number of theatres, music halls, museums and other educational and entertainment services (supply). In this sense, scope and variety converge in large urban centres (Scott, 2017), which reinforces their tourist appeal. However, this can also constitute a source of negative economic externalities, eventually leading to gentrification processes and sociopolitical conflicts, as documented by Zerva et al. (2019) or Romão et al. (2023) for Barcelona.

Its place-based character and the importance of path dependence for tourism's historical development suggest that each destination may have its own characteristics, leading to a specific evolutionary process. That specificity also influences the type of connections with other economic activities or the processes of agglomeration that can emerge. In this sense, the integration and role of tourism within regional economic structures will depend on the behaviour and decisions of the agents involved, in a process of bricolage that always relies on the local resources and existing opportunities. The framework proposed by the Tourism Area Life Cycle (TALC) can help in understanding how these processes evolve over time. In fact, both the TALC and the processes of emergence diversification and specialisation of regional economies can be seen as evolutionary processes. A proposal for the integration and systematisation of these aspects is presented next.

TALC, path dependence, proximity and variety

The purpose of this synthesis is to propose a framework for the analysis of the relations between the historical evolution of a tourism destination and the different types of relations that the tourism industry can establish with other local activities in the different stages of its life cycle. This formulation can constitute a framework to be tested in further empirical studies.

It is clear that, in the first stages of the life cycle of destinations, the few emerging tourism services tend to be concentrated in the traditional hospitality services (accommodation, food and drink). As demand increases, related services sharing the same markets and requiring similar skills may appear, taking advantage of the geographical, cultural and institutional proximity with the pre-existing activities. The agents of these slow transformations are normally local small companies, and there is no systematic institutional destination planning, marketing or management.

As the destination becomes more attractive, moving towards the development stage, emergent transportation services and tourism activities may establish connections with less related activities (from a technological point of view), even though they can share the same markets. Eventually, larger companies from outside the region start to operate at the destination, creating some forms of power imbalance between stakeholders and requiring new forms of regulation (see Keller, in this volume, Chapter 10).

At this stage, public institutions may become more active, in terms not only of tourism planning and management, but also of supporting and investing in public infrastructure and amenities. Other types of organisation may also become active, both when there is a perception that opportunities in tourism should benefit local communities) and when there are perceived negative impacts on the daily life of local communities.

Following the process of the development of a destination – and the related increasing number of visitors – new opportunities for innovative products and services may emerge, eventually leading to the creation of connections to much less related activities (Erkus-Öztürk, 2016). In particular, the emergence of new consumption patterns related to the 'creative economies' may support the creation of innovative relations between tourism service providers and different types of creative agents in the destinations, thus enlarging the scope of the supply. These aspects become even more crucial in the later stages of the cycle, in case destinations face a risk of decline and need to rejuvenate the supply by adding new products and services. This process can be much faster in cities, as information and knowledge can quickly flow between different activities in order to generate innovative products and services. The very rapid growth of urban tourism in the last two decades, supporting a wide variety of tourism experiences, suggests not only that the exploration of synergies between different activities can be more intense and faster, but also that evolution within the life cycle of the destination itself can also be faster.

In the later stages of the cycle, after stagnation, it is common for large companies originating from outside the region to leave the destination, in search of more attractive opportunities. Similarly, some activities will tend to reduce or disappear when tourism demand declines. However, more innovative approaches – probably less related to the traditional tourism and hospitality services – may emerge when a destination adopts a strategy of rejuvenation.

Table 13.1 summarises these ideas, as a starting point for the discussion of the potential role of tourism, during the different stages of the life cycle of a destination, within regional smart specialisation strategies.

Smart Specialisation, Tourism and the Life Cycle of Destinations

Opportunities and societal challenges

The smart specialisation approach (Foray et al., 2012) to regional innovation strategies also emphasises the evolutionary, path-dependent and

Table 13.1 TALC, path dependency, agency, proximity and variety: Dominant characteristics

TALC	Source of path dependence	Agent	Services	Type of proximity	Variety
Exploration Involvement	Natural and cultural heritage	Local small companies engaged in related activities	Traditional hospitality	Geographic, markets, skills	Related
Development	Sunk costs	Added: large foreign companies; public regulatory institutions (DMO); NGOs	Added: transports, ICT, tours, and activities; events; support	Added: knowledge, cultural, institutional, technological	Added: unrelated
Consolidation Stagnation	Knowledge; technology; inter-regional linkages				
Decline		Suppressed: international companies	Suppressed: tours and activities		
Rejuvenation	Natural and cultural heritage	Companies and organisations undertaking creative unrelated activities	Diversification of creative experiences	Suppressed: markets, skills, knowledge	Increasing: unrelated

Source: Author

place-based character of the development processes. The implementation of these strategies should rely on a limited number of priority sectors, in order to concentrate regional efforts and resources in the activities with higher opportunities and potential to generate spillovers within related sectors. Proximity, knowledge and relatedness are central characteristics shaping these strategic orientations. Considering its clear territorial embeddedness and the high potential to establish links with different types of economic activities, the tourism sector can assume a central role within smart specialisation strategies (Balland *et al.*, 2019).

From a technological point of view, it is expected that these priority sectors can mobilise local resources and capabilities in order to develop new and innovative combinations and solutions with higher value-added. In the case of tourism, the generally small scale of the local businesses acting during the first stages of the destination life cycle constitutes a potential obstacle to their involvement in these processes. However, when reaching the development stage, the integration of tourism companies can be easier, taking into account the expectation of business development and also the arrival of larger companies in a destination (Romão, 2020a).

Apart from commercial opportunities, smart specialisation also aims at mobilising local economic systems to provide solutions to the societal challenges affecting contemporary societies. As such, aspects like ageing populations or climate change are expected to mobilise local knowledge and resources. In the particular case of tourism, mostly when the development stage corresponds to large flows of visitors, aspects related to carbon emissions generated by air transport, transports and mobility at the destination, or high energy or water consumption, can certainly be addressed by networks of organisations that include local companies. Moreover, the development of innovative solutions and services in these fields can constitute an important commercial opportunity.

Tourism has a high potential to establish connections with a large variety of different activities, eventually leading to different types of innovation, branching and reconfiguration of local and regional economic systems (Weidenfeld, 2018). However, it is also extremely vulnerable to the impacts of negative external shocks, in many cases impossible to control at the destination level. Looking only at the last two decades, the diversity of shocks is impressive: security problems after the 9/11 terrorist attacks, several relatively small-scale pandemics, a global international crisis and a massive global pandemic with COVID-19 (Hall *et al.*, 2020). All these events had significant impacts on tourism and reveal the importance of promoting and maintaining a diversified local economic structure, rather than relying on such a vulnerable sector.

Moreover, when considering reflectively long series of data, several authors identified important limitations to the contributions of tourism for regional economic growth, with reducing impacts over time, or even a negative long-term impact, at least when compared with the performance of non-touristic regions, oriented to activities with greater incorporation of technology and skilled labour, leading to higher levels of productivity and value-added (Adamou & Clerides, 2010; Romão, 2020a). During the stage of development, high levels of tourism demand can make the sector extremely attractive for investment and employment, eventually leading to the decline of other activities and to a long-term deterioration of the technological capabilities and levels of education and skills. As such, promoting the development of economic activities unrelated to tourism appears as a strategic option that could increase the levels of regional resilience in places where tourism achieves the stage of development.

Information and communication technologies, key enabling technologies and the smart tourism ecosystem

Smart specialisation strategies assume two types of interactions between the regional priority sectors and technologies: one is related to the intensification of the utilisation of Information and Communication Technology (ICT) and the other is related to the development of Key Enabling Technologies (KET) that share some forms of knowledge proximity (Romão, 2020b).

The potential of tourism to establish strong connections with ICT is well documented in the literature: these technologies have had a deep impact on all stages of travelling, providing multiple types of information for decision-making, allowing for bookings and reservations, enabling different payment methods, and opening opportunities for co-creative interactions between providers and consumers of tourism services, while providing active and diversified support to the travel experience in many different ways – including the combination of real and virtual information, from augmented reality to the recent developments with the 'meta-verse'. Moreover, processes of automation, robotisation and utilisation of contactless methods of interaction were greatly developed during the COVID-19 pandemic.

The tourism ecosystem of a destination in the development stage has a high potential to develop into a smart system (Boes et al., 2016), where destination planning and management can take advantage of these fluxes of data and information already circulating in the digital sphere. Other types of technological developments related to the use of sensors and the 'internet of things' enhance this potential for a rich data-based and informed destination management, including opportunities to create different forms of participatory governance, by reinforcing the collaboration and decision-making processes involving local tourism stakeholders and local communities (Sigala & Marinidis, 2012). However, these processes do not rely solely on technological aspects: they also depend on cultural and political factors.

Moreover, digital technologies can also promote a deep, permanent and fruitful connection between tourism providers and the other creative activities in a destination, by supporting the creation, development, promotion and distribution of new services and experiences based on local heritage, knowledge and lifestyles (Binkhorst & Dekker, 2009). Even though these activities are often not oriented to the tourism market, the presence of tourists may constitute a new opportunity, by creating a new demand for services that can be used by both tourists and non-tourists.

Similarly, key enabling technologies can benefit from these new market opportunities and they may also exert deep impacts on the development of new tourism services (along with a potential contribution to a more efficient management and use of resources). This can have an impact on economic performance and also on environmental protection, mostly when applied to some sensitive impacts created by tourists (e.g. mobility and transport, congestion, water and energy consumption). The development of innovative solutions for tourism can help to create new technological solutions to be applied in other activities and places.

It is also noteworthy that both ICT and KET can be mobilised in the later stages of the destination cycle, when trying to create new tourism development paths for rejuvenation. At this level, technologies can help to promote an innovative reconfiguration of the tourism systems in order to develop new services and experiences based on the local and regional resources.

However, the vulnerability of the tourism sector should be also considered along with the importance of developing other sectors – with the related technological solutions – that do not depend on tourism flows. By developing clusters of activities unrelated to tourism, local and regional economies can be more resilient when facing negative tourism-related external shocks. As such, the focus on concentrating resources on the development of related activities (and the corresponding technologies) proposed by the smart specialisation approaches should be carefully – and critically – considered when tourism is one of these priority sectors. Romão (2020a) suggests that many different patterns of specialisation can coexist with the choice of tourism as a regional priority.

Tourism planning and development

Regional smart specialisation strategies are innovation plans that aim at mobilising all the regional economic system in a sustainable process of development. However, tourism has other types of instruments for planning, marketing and management that are normally tourism-specific and oriented to specific purposes. Destination management organisations (DMOs) may have their own plans about the future development of the tourism sector, eventually defined at the same territorial level as the smart specialisation strategies. On other occasions, however, these territorial levels may differ. In order to give clear indications and guidelines to the private sector, it is important that these public strategic documents are consistent, pointing out similar or compatible orientations. It is noteworthy that all these planning tools have different roles, purposes and impacts during the life cycle of destinations. This chapter discusses the specific case of smart specialisation strategies, which could define a position for the tourism industry within the overall regional economic and innovation systems. However, when defining this position, there are other implications, opportunities and restrictions that have to be considered. For example, determining that tourism will assume a central role in the regional specialisation process often implies a continuous growth in the number of visitors, eventually leading to the problems of 'overtourism' that have been systematically identified over the last decades. The systematic failure to address these problems (Dodds & Butler, 2022) justifies special attention.

Among the problems created by overtourism, there are several issues calling for economic regulation and planning the development of infrastructure and public facilities. Congestion in public spaces or on public transport requires investments to accommodate new demand. Utilisation of short-term rental houses may create scarcity and inflation in the housing market, thus imposing or accelerating the displacement of local people. In all these cases, residents may have to endure additional costs and eventually poorer living conditions. Moreover, investments in infrastructure and facilities to address these problems – or to stimulate tourism development in general terms – imply a reduction in the resources available for other public functions (e.g. education and health).

The diversity of impacts of tourism development and the path-dependent character of the evolution of destinations justify the implementation of different types of policies that go much beyond the scope of the stakeholders involved in tourism. These policies will certainly impact how tourism interacts with other economic activities and the broad regional economic system, and also with daily life and the infrastructure and facilities that support the living conditions of local populations. These problems do not have the same magnitude and impact over the life cycle of destinations, as Table 13.2 summarises.

It should be noted that tourist destinations may comprise different products and services, with different life cycles, eventually creating difficulties in trying to identify one specific and unique cycle. Moreover, smart specialisation strategies (and other regional development planning tools) are often defined at a relatively large territorial scale, which may itself impose new complexities on the analysis of each particular case.

Conclusion

These analyses, aimed at describing the life of destinations and the regional patterns of specialisation as path-dependent evolutionary

Table 13.2 TALC, smart specialisation and other governance tools

TALC	Smart specialisation		Tourism marketing	Tourism management	Other
	Priority	Relatedness			
Exploration Involvement	None	High proximity (traditional hospitality)	None	Development of small-scale local services and facilities	None
Development Consolidation	High	From high to lower proximity; progressive involvement of diverse creative activities;	Defining products, positioning, targeting and promoting	Product development based on local resources; progressive diversification of services; development of tourism and transport infrastructure	Planning public infrastructure and facilities; regulation of housing markets
Stagnation	Low	support of activities unrelated to tourism			
Decline	None	High proximity; strong support of activities unrelated to tourism	Concentration in core products and markets	Minimising private costs of decay	Minimising social costs of tourism decay
Rejuvenation	High	Low proximity; support of activities unrelated to tourism	Diversification of products and/or markets	Suppressed: markets, skills, knowledge	Planning public infrastructure and facilities; regulation of housing markets

Source: Author

processes, are highly dependent on local and historical conditions. It seems clear that the TALC model constitutes a very relevant tool to analyse and to frame the type of relations that the tourism industry can establish with other economic sectors according to the different stages of tourism development and the different position of destinations along the life cycle.

Being aware that each place and moment has specific and unique characteristics, it is possible to propose a framework to define how, given the different types of relations based on diverse forms of proximity, tourism can become established within regional economic systems, with the consequent processes of spatial agglomeration. From this, it is also possible to suggest roles for tourism within smart specialisation strategies over the evolution of the life cycle of destinations.

Considering its high potential to interact with the rest of the economy and to integrate different types of ICT, tourism can assume a central role within smart specialisation strategies from the stage of development, when it reaches a relevant scale influencing regional economic structures. Within these strategies, tourism can start by promoting inter-relations within hospitality services that are in close proximity; however, as time passes, other opportunities will emerge, with potential interactions with sectors that are in less close proximity, like those related to creative activities, transport and mobility, or energy production and consumption. Interaction with sectors with less proximity will be even more relevant in cases when a region reaches a stage of rejuvenation.

Other types of planning tools are also required, however, during the life cycle of destinations. Apart from the usual plans for tourism marketing and management promoted by DMOs and the companies directly involved in the provision of tourism services, other plans to regulate the large impacts of tourism on the daily life and living conditions of local populations must be implemented from the development stage of the life cycle. In particular, the consequences of overtourism (like inflationary pressures on housing costs) must be addressed beyond smart specialisation strategies and the conventional tourism marketing and management.

Considering the time- and place-dependence of tourism destinations and regional economic systems, the framework proposed in this study can be tested and improved in different cases and conditions. The TALC model and the conceptual frameworks adopted in this study from the evolutionary economic geography approach seem useful and flexible tools to operationalise these types of studies in the future.

References

Aarstad, J., Kvitastein, O.A. and Jakobsen, S. (2016) Related and unrelated variety in a tourism context. *Annals of Tourism Research* 57, 234–278.

Adamou, A. and Clerides, S. (2010) Prospects and limits of tourism-led growth: The international evidence. *Review of Economic Analysis* 3, 287–303.

Balland, P.A., Boschma, R., Crespo, J. and Rigby, D.L. (2019) Smart specialization policy in the European Union: Relatedness, knowledge complexity and regional diversification. *Regional Studies* 53 (9), 1252–1268.

Binkhorst, E. and Dekker, T. (2009) Towards the co-creation tourism experience? *Journal of Hospitality Marketing and Management* 18 (2–3), 311–327.

Boes, K., Buhalis, D. and Inversini, A. (2016) Smart tourism destinations: Ecosystems for tourism destination competitiveness. *International Journal of Tourism Cities* 2 (2), 108–124. https://doi.org/10.1108/IJTC-12-2015-0032.

Boschma, R. and Gianelle, C. (22014) *Regional Branching and Smart Specialisation*. Policy S3, Policy Brief Series No. 06/2014. Seville: European Commission Joint Research Centre.

Boschma, R. and Martin, R. (2010) The aims and scope of evolutionary economic geography. In R. Boschma and R. Martin (eds) *The Handbook of Evolutionary Economic Geography* (pp. 3–39). Cheltenham: Edward Elgar.

Boschma, R., Minondo, A. and Navarro, M. (2013) The emergence of new industries at the regional level in Spain: A proximity approach based on product relatedness. *Economic Geography* 89, 29–51.

Boschma, R., Coenen, L., Frenken, K. and Truffer, B. (2017) Towards a theory of regional diversification: Combining insights from evolutionary economic geography and transition studies. *Regional Studies* 51 (1), 31–45. https://doi.org/10.1080/00343404.2016.1258460.

Brouder, P. and Eriksson, R. (2013) Tourism evolution: On the synergies of tourism studies and evolutionary economic geography. *Annals of Tourism Research* 43, 370–389.

Butler, R. (1980) The concept of a Tourism Area Life Cycle of evolution: Implications for management of resources. *Canadian Geographer* 24 (1), 5–12.

Capó, J., Font, A. and Nadal, J. (2007) Dutch disease in tourism economies: Evidence from the Balearics and the Canary Islands. *Journal of Sustainable Tourism* 15 (6), 615–627.

Colomb, C. and Novy, J. (eds) (2017) *Protest and Resistance in the Tourist City*. London: Routledge.

Content, J., Frenken, K. and Jordaan, J.A. (2019) Does related variety foster regional entrepreneurship? Evidence from European regions. *Regional Studies* 53 (11), 1531–1543. https://doi.org/10.1080/00343404.2019.1595565.

Currid-Halkett, E. and Scott, A. (2013) The geography of celebrity and glamour: Reflections on economy, culture, and desire in the city. *City Culture and Society* 4 (1), 2–11. doi:10.1016/j.ccs.2013.01.003.

Davids, D. and Frenken, K. (2018) Proximity, knowledge base and the innovation process: Towards an integrated framework. *Regional Studies* 52 (1), 23–34.

Dodds, R. and Butler, R. (2019) *Overtourism: Issues, Realities and Solutions*. Berlin: De Gruyter.

Erkus-Öztürk, H. (2016) (Un)related variety, urban milieu and tourism-company differentiation. *Tourism Geographies* 18 (4), 422–444.

Foray, D., Goddard, J., Beldarrain, X., Landabaso, M., McCann, P., Morgan, K. and Ortega-Argilés, R. (2012) *Guide to Research and Innovation Strategies for Smart Specialization*. Brussels: S3P – European Union, Regional Policy.

Hall, C.M., Scott, D. and Gössling, S. (2020) Pandemics, transformations and tourism: Be careful what you wish for. *Tourism Geographies* 22(3), 577–598. https://doi.org/10.1080/14616688.2020.1759131.

Henderson, V. (1997) Externalities and industrial development. *Journal of Urban Economics* 42 (3), 449–470.

Kožić, I. (2019) Can tourism development induce deterioration of human capital? *Annals of Tourism Research* 77, 168–170.

Krugman, P. (1996) Urban concentration: The role of increasing returns and transport costs. *International Regional Science Review* 19 (1–2), 5–30.

Lazzeretti, L., Capone, F. and Innocenti, N. (2016) The impact of related variety on tourist destinations: An analysis of tourist firms clustering. In F. Capone (ed.) *Tourist Clusters, Destinations and Competitiveness Theoretical Issues and Empirical Evidences* (pp. 62–80). Abingdon: Routledge.

Lucas, R. (1988) On the mechanics of economic development. *Journal of Monetary Economics* 22, 3–42.

Ma, M. and Hassink, R. (2013) An evolutionary perspective on tourism area development. *Annals of Tourism Research* 41, 89–109.

Malakauskaite, A. and Navickas, V. (2010) Relation between the level of clusterization and tourism sector competitiveness. *Engineering Economics* 21 (1).

Martin, R. (2014) Path dependence and the spatial economy. In M. Fischer and P. Nijkamp (eds) *Handbook of Regional Science* (pp. 609–629). New York: Springer.

Martin, R. and Sunley, P. (1998) Slow convergence? The new endogenous growth theory and regional development. *Economic Geography* 74 (3), 201–227.

Neffke, F., Henning, M. and Boschma, R. (2009) How do regions diversify over time? Industry relatedness and the development of new growth paths in regions. *Economic Geography* 87 (3), 237–265.

Neffke, F., Hartog, M., Boschma, R. and Henning, M. (2018) Agents of structural change: The role of firms and entrepreneurs in regional diversification. *Economic Geography* 94 (1), 23–48. https://doi.org/10.1080/00130095.2017.1391691.

OECD (2014) *Tourism and the Creative Economy*. Paris: OECD Publishing.

Romão, J. (2018) *Tourism, Territory and Sustainable Development: Theoretical Foundations and Empirical Applications in Japan and Europe*. Singapore: Springer.

Romão, J. (2020a) Tourism, smart specialization, growth and resilience. *Annals of Tourism Research* 84, 102995.

Romão, J. (2020b) Variety, smart specialization and tourism competitiveness. *Sustainability* 12, 5765. https://doi.org/10.3390/su12145765.

Romão, J. (2021) Nature, tourism, growth, resilience and sustainable development. In A. Mandić and L. Petrić (eds) *Mediterranean Protected Areas in an Era of Overtourism: Challenges and Solutions* (pp. 297–310). Berlin: Springer.

Romão, J. and Neuts, B. (2017) Territorial capital, smart tourism specialization and sustainable regional development: Experiences from Europe. *Habitat International* 68, 64–74.

Romão, J., Guerreiro, J. and Rodrigues, P. (2016) Tourism growth and regional resilience: The 'beach disease' and the consequences of the global crisis of 2007. *Tourism Economics* 22 (4), 699–714.

Romão, J., Domènech, A. and Nijkamp, P. (2023) Tourism in common: Policy flows and participatory management in the Tourism Council of Barcelona. *Urban Research and Practice* 16 (2), 222–245. https://doi.org/10.1080/17535069.2021.2001039.

Romer, P. (1986) Increasing returns and long-run growth. *Journal of Political Economy* 94 (5), 1002–1037.

Sanz-Ibáñez, C. and Clavé, S.A. (2014) The evolution of destinations: Towards an evolutionary and relational economic geography approach. *Tourism Geographies* 16 (4), 563–579.

Scott, A.J. (2007) Capitalism and urbanization in a new key? The cognitive-cultural dimension. *Social Forces* 85 (4), 1465–1482.

Scott, A.J. (2017) *The Constitution of the City*. Cham: Palgrave Macmillan.

Sigala, M. and Marinidis, D. (2012) E-democracy and Web 2.0: A framework enabling DMOS to engage stakeholders in collaborative destination management. *Tourism Analysis* 17 (2), 105–120.

Tussyadiah, I.P. (2014) Toward a theoretical foundation for experience design in tourism. *Journal of Travel Research* 53 (5), 543–564.

UNWTO (2012) *Global Report on City Tourism*. Madrid: UNWTO.

Weidenfeld, A. (2018) Tourism diversification and its implications for smart specialisation. *Sustainability* 10, 319.

Zerva, K., Palou, S., Blasco, D. and Donaire, J.A.B. (2019) Tourism-philia versus tourism-phobia: Residents and destination management organization's publicly expressed tourism perceptions in Barcelona. *Tourism Geographies* 21 (2), 306–329. https://doi.org/10.1080/14616688.2018.1522510.

14 From Start-Up to Maturity: Integrating the TALC Model With the Tourism Family Business Life Cycle in a Coastal Destination

Beatriz Adriana López-Chávez and
César Maldonado-Alcudia

Tourism family-owned businesses contribute to tourist destination development through their sociocultural roots in the territory since they seek to survive at a trans-generational level. However, only a small percentage transcend to the stage of maturity. Life cycle models for family businesses do not consider aspects of the industry in which they operate, which is crucial for their long-term development. This chapter aims to integrate the Tourist Area Life Cycle (TALC) model with the evolution of family businesses in the hotel industry in a traditional coastal destination located in north-west Mexico. The findings support the applicability of the TALC model for the business axis for family-owned hotels, from start-up to maturity, and long-term destination development requires internal decision-making.

Tourism is one of the most important industries in contemporary society and makes a vital economic contribution. According to the United Nations World Tourism Organization (2023), tourism flows for 2022 indicate that international travel had recovered to 80–95% of its pre-pandemic levels, which shows tourism's high resilience.

Small and medium-sized family-owned companies are a large component of the tourism industry (Getz & Carlsen, 2005; Hjalager, 2010). The management types of these organisations, however, is made more complex face by the interaction of family and business systems, which develop socioemotional dynamics (Zellweger *et al.*, 2010). Nevertheless, the tourism family business has contributed to the development of tourist destinations by fostering collaboration and cooperation between various actors, who are oriented towards long-term survival. This can help overcome the disadvantages of limited size and resources (Kallmuenzer

& Peters, 2018), while supporting local development and identity (Hallak & Assaker, 2013), coping with high seasonality to maintain the local economy (Banki *et al.*, 2016) and being resilient to economic crises and natural disasters (Ismail *et al.*, 2019; Rienda *et al.*, 2020). Despite these positive effects, little research has been conducted on the dynamics of family tourism businesses, particularly in traditional coastal destinations in emerging economies.

Between 80% and 90% of the world economy is made up of family businesses. In Latin America, they represent 85% (González & Olivié, 2018). One of main objectives of a family business is to survive through its generations; however, the percentage that reaches the third generation is low, in the case of Mexico only 10% (Grabinsky, 2016), and two out of three businesses die in the first six years (Olguín *et al.*, 2016). Therefore, a large number of these organisations do not go beyond the first stage of their life cycle when they face decline.

Given the importance of family businesses in the world economy, particularly for developing tourist destinations, it is vital to analyse how they evolve to contribute to strategic decision-making. One of the most commonly used models for this is the life cycle. However, the models focused on family businesses do not consider the industry in which the company operates, even though it is crucial for the long-term development of the business (Lumpkin & Dess, 2001). For this reason, this chapter aims to integrate the life cycle model of tourist areas (Butler, 1980) into the analysis of the evolution of family tourism hospitality businesses in a traditional destination on the north-west coast of Mexico. The chapter is structured as follows. First, the theoretical framework that discusses the usefulness of life cycle models is described. The necessary elements are presented to integrate the basis of the TALC model into the study of family businesses. Then, the methodology is presented (comparative case studies of four hotels in the coastal destination), followed by the results, which socio-historically contextualise the destination through the life cycle stages, with an analysis of and across the cases. Finally, the conclusions are drawn.

Theoretical Background

Life cycle models help analyse the landscape and guide decision-making about resources; the most widely used in the field of tourism is Butler's (1980) proposal, which focuses on understanding the evolution of tourist areas. It is most commonly used to address the development of destinations (Butler, 2014; Segrado *et al.*, 2011; Silva & Almeida, 2015) as well as for various analysis units (Haywood, 1986), such as tourism market studies (Duffus & Dearden, 1990; Tomljenović & Getz, 2009) and at the company level, such as the hotel sector in coastal destinations (Dorta, 2016; Rodríguez & Conejero, 2011; Vera-Rebollo *et al.*, 2010).

Other models used in the organisational field are those of Greiner (1972) and Daft (2011). The first describes periods of growth, called evolution, and, between them, periods of crisis, called stages of the revolution, where it will be necessary to apply specific strategies to overcome the crisis and continue the subsequent development. The occurrence of further stages of growth and revolution will depend on the industry's growth rate. If the company operates in a rapidly expanding market, it will need to expand its structure (Greiner, 1972).

Daft's model (2011) affirms that throughout the development of organisations, there are changes in their structures, control systems, innovation and goals that they pursue. According to that model, the stages of evolution are entrepreneurial, collectivity, formalisation and elaboration. Each phase has its characteristics in its structure, goals, management style, products and services offered, and drive for innovation.

For family businesses, the three-dimensional evolutionary model of Gersick *et al.* (1997) is the most cited. It is made up of the axes of family, property and business, each evolving over time. The family dimension concerns the involvement of the different members, from the moment they enter the business, working together and passing on the baton. The ownership axis shifts from a controlling founder to a sibling partnership and finally to a cousin consortium. Lastly, the axis of the business begins at start-up, and goes through expansion to maturity.

Among the criticisms of these models, it is pointed out that they assume companies necessarily grow in size and structure (Churchill & Lewis, 1982), something that does not always occur in small and medium-sized family tourism companies since there are businesses in which the size is part of the product offered, mainly in the hospitality sector, where old houses or buildings are converted into lodging establishments (Andersson *et al.*, 2002; Getz & Peterson, 2005; Liu & Cheng, 2018).

The models focus on employee numbers and annual sales, and ignore the added value or the rate of change of the products and production processes (Churchill & Lewis, 1983), that is, of their capacity for innovation to maintain the quality of the service and their competitiveness in the market.

López-Chávez and Maldonado-Alcudia (2022) propose that mature family tourism businesses go through precise stages of development on the business axis, which is based on the Butler (1980) model, as a result of their ability to adapt to the changing environments of tourism from technological and social innovations. The stages of the model are:

- *Development*, which indicates an increase in occupancy, market loyalty and new niches, as a notable adaptation to technological and social changes through various innovations, planning and strategic projection of the business.
- *Consolidation*, which refers to moderate growth in employment,

strong market loyalty and identification of new niches, notably adaptation to technological and social changes through innovations, and business planning.
- *Rejuvenation*, which implies a recent improvement in occupation, adaptation to technological and social changes through various innovations, internal structural changes and planning, and improvement of facilities.
- *Stagnation*, which indicates that the occupancy rate has reached its maximum. It sees little or no business planning, and physical facilities show moderate signs of wear. It depends mostly on repeat customers.
- *Decline*, which reflects a sustained drop in occupancy rates, and there is not enough adaptation to technological and social changes. It has a development perspective that is far from reality. There is little or no planning. The physical facilities appear worn out. This stage is all about competing through cheap rates and extended stays.

Methodology

Through a qualitative methodology and a comparative case study method, information was collected from four family-owned hotels in a coastal tourist destination in north-west Mexico. Qualitative studies are necessary to understand the complex dynamics of the tourism industry (Kallmuenzer *et al.*, 2021; Pikkemaat *et al.*, 2018). Case studies provide new and valuable perspectives on family businesses (De Massis & Kotlar, 2014).

The cases presented here were instrumental, meaning they were selected to illustrate a particular issue or phenomenon (Creswell, 2012; Stake, 1999). Through simple observation, two cases were identified that complied with diversified innovations, while the other two did not. All of them are small and medium-sized family-owned hotels in operation for more than 20 years, which suggests that they had already gone through the start-up and formalisation stage and to maturity (Gallo, 1998), allowing enough time to analyse how each operation has developed in the life cycle stages. All cases are on the seafront since the attraction they offer is associated with the primary destination product, namely, the coast in a coastal destination.

In total, eight narrative interviews with owners and managers were carried out, in addition to four observation guides, one per establishment. The field work was carried out from December 2020 to April 2021 in Mazatlán, Sinaloa, Mexico. A pilot test was carried out to reduce possible biases in the interview guidelines. Some questions were taken from other studies that addressed the development of family tourism businesses in the lodging sector (Andersson *et al.*, 2002; Kallmuenzer *et al.*, 2019; Liu & Cheng, 2018). The non-participant observation guides helped analyse the conditions of the physical facilities of the hotels. According to De Massis and Kotlar (2014), combining interviews with non-participant observation is an elementary strategy to reduce bias and triangulate information, which complements the rigour of qualitative research in family businesses.

Content analysis of the interview information used Atlas.ti 9 software and abductive inference within a particular theoretical context (Krippendorff, 2004). Firstly, in a deductive way, the main categories of the study were established, which are the stages of the life cycle, as well as a series of codes pre-identified in the literature; subsequently, during the analysis, other codes and subcategories emerged inductively and were integrated into the results. In addition, reduction, visualisation, categorisation and contextualisation techniques proposed by De Massis and Kotlar (2014) were followed to carry out the qualitative analysis of the study cases.

Results

The research results are presented in three sections (Creswell, 2012; Stake, 1999). First, the contextualisation of the tourist destination is illustrated, followed by the description of the cases individually and their cross-case analysis.

Contextualisation: The development of Mazatlán as a tourist destination

Mazatlán, Sinaloa, is a traditional tourist destination located on the north-west coast of Mexico (see Figure 14.1). During its pre-tourist stage, it was a commercial and fishing port where sailors of different nationalities met and needed places to stay. The tourist dynamics resulted from the inertia of the commercial activity, which gave way to the beginnings of the life cycle as a tourist destination, which are described below according to the Butler (1980) model.

During the exploration stage, in the first years of the 20th century, there basic hosting infrastructure appeared that facilitated visitors' stay; public water and energy utilities and a rubbish collection service were established. Regarding transportation, the South Pacific Railroad linked Mazatlán with the north-west of the country and the US border. This new land connection triggered a new economic dynamism (Espinoza, 2010).

In the involvement phase, international-category hotels were promoted in the Olas Altas area, the first urban tourism area, which began in 1922 with the opening of the first hotel facing the sea. In transportation, the railway connections to the country's south grew, attracting national visitors, while 200 Americans arrived by sea each year (Espinoza, 2010). By air, a flight from Mexico City to Los Angeles, California, with a stopover in Mazatlán began operations (Ruiz, 2015). Given the tourist boom in Mazatlán, more significant international and regional investment was promoted for the construction of more hotels and the institutionalisation

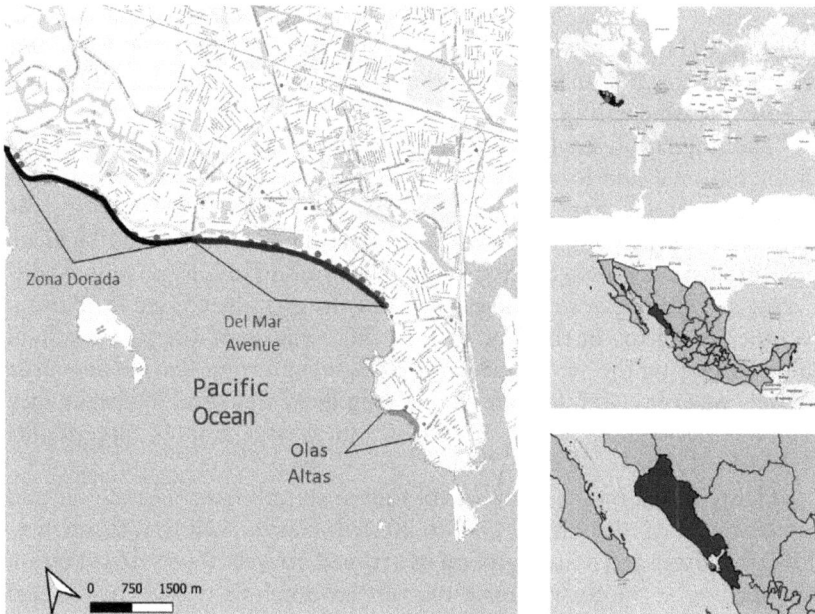

Figure 14.1 Location of Mazatlán, Sinaloa, Mexico (Source: Authors' elaboration)

of the promotion of tourist activity, evidence of the economic relevance that it denoted.

The development stage came after the end of the Second World War in 1945. The construction of hotels up to 12 storeys high with more technology continued, in parallel with road expansion, in two tourist areas, Av. Del Mar and Zona Dorada, reaching 1300 hotel rooms and an occupancy rate of 65% annually. In terms of transportation, the technological innovation in aviation allowed the arrival of trips on jet planes (Ruiz, 2015). It incorporated the industrialisation of tourism, with an offer of packages that included transportation, accommodation and complementary services, characteristic of Fordist production (Latiesa & Álvarez, 2000). At the end of 1970, there were already 161 tourism companies, surpassing fishing businesses (Espinoza, 2010).

During the consolidation stage, between 1972 and 1985, Mazatlán was Mexico's second most important tourist destination (behind Acapulco). The fishing entrepreneurs began investing in the hotel industry. The expansion of the Zona Dorada was evident. With high-class hotels, mostly locally owned, the number of rooms reached 5238 in 1980, with an average occupancy of 65% (Barbosa & Santamaría, 2006). The urban development was mostly on the coast, towards the northern part of the city. Tourism demand was dominated by the foreign market, mainly Americans and Canadians. However, during this stage, the Mexican government began implementing two planned centres elsewhere: Cancún and Los Cabos. Years later, these would represent serious problems for traditional destinations because they captured most public funds and private investments.

The stagnation stage started in 1986, when there was a recessive cycle in the national and local tourism sectors. There was a decrease of 10% from the previous year (Santamaría, 2005). Among the leading causes was American tourism moving away due to the overvaluation of the Mexican peso against the dollar, the negative publicity of actions against drug trafficking and the Mexican policies of seizing drugs at the border, in addition to other problems in the city, such as the collapse of the water system in 1987. During the 1990s and until 2004, a significant decline in tourist arrivals was observed, the offer of lodging decreased, and the occupancy rate was between 47% and 37%, with an average stay of three nights (DATATUR, 2023).

Figure 14.2 shows the numbers of tourist arrivals from the national and international markets from 1964 to 2021. It can be seen that through to 2014, there was a sustained growth in national arrivals. It was derived from the opening of motorway infrastructure in north-east Mexico, coupled with a series of renovations, starting in 2016, of public spaces, such as the boardwalk, the historic centre, parks and investment in hotels by international chains, and the construction of condominium buildings and residences. Except for 2020, due to the COVID-19 pandemic (DATATUR, 2023), domestic tourism flows consolidated activity in the destination, while international tourism remained lower.

In 2020, Mazatlán registered 249 lodging establishments (Instituto Nacional de Geografía y Estadística, 2022). Of these, 51 were located on the beachfront from Olas Altas to the Zona Dorada, corresponding to

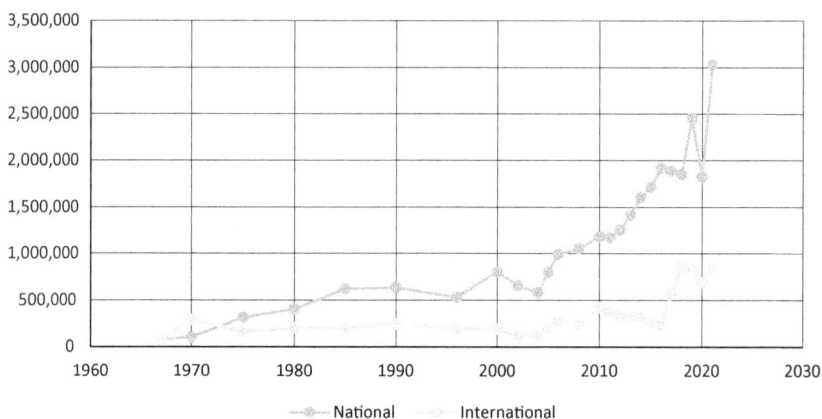

Figure 14.2 Tourist arrivals to Mazatlán 1964–2021 (Source: Own elaboration based on DATATUR, 2023)

three of the four main areas of the destination. Of the establishments, 26 were family-owned hotels with more than 20 years of belonging to the same family, distributed among 22 families. According to a state agency, in 2021, Mazatlán occupied the third national position in tourist arrivals at beach destinations, with more than 3.8 million (Consejo para el Desarrollo Económico de Sinaloa, 2022).

Based on the stages of TALC, the growth of Mazatlán as a tourist destination can be traced through its urban expansion from south to north. Olas Altas, the oldest part of the city, marked the stage of involvement in the activity, while the Del Mar Avenue and Zona Dorada characterised the development stage (see Figure 14.1). After a decline in Mazatlán's competitive position relative to other beach destinations, the growth of the Marine and Cerritos Zones contributed to a recovery in economic and investment terms.

Case Analyses

Case A

This hotel has 50 rooms and 22 employees. Only one family member works in the business: the founder's son and current director.

- *Start-up*. In 1990, mother and son started a lodging establishment, transforming their home into 16 rooms equipped with only a fan and a bed.
- *Expansion*. Between 2006 and 2015, the hotel experienced significant room growth, from 16 to 50. They added additional services such as television and air conditioners, improving the physical design.
- *Maturity*. After 2015, the hotel has maintained its services and size, relying on cheap rates for customers who make frequent business trips. A regional economic crisis made them lower their rates or apply monthly rates. In 2014, the increase in tourism flows due to the opening of a motorway allowed changes in rates and continuous improvements to physical facilities and rooms. At the time of the research, a stagnation stage was identified in the hotel's life cycle. As a result of the pandemic, the market to which it was directed had decreased considerably at the destination, and the business had not implemented strategies to adapt to new niches (López-Chávez & Maldonado-Alcudia, 2022).

Case B

This hotel has 101 rooms and 25 employees. Four family members work on the management team. Decision-making is concentrated in the current chief executive and founder of the business.

- *Start-up*. The establishment was an investment of a North American company in 1960. In 1970 it was bought by the current director and his brother, both accountants by profession with no experience in the tourism industry. Their business interests led them to experiment in this sector. Initially, it had 31 rooms and some amenities.
- *Expansion*. Between 1975 and 1993, they expanded the number of rooms to 56 and added some services, such as a restaurant and parking.
- *Maturity*. Between 2014 and 2016, the establishment expanded to 101 rooms. Over the following years, it went through various stages, reflecting the ups and downs of the national economy. At the time of this research, a stagnation stage was identified due to the failure to adapt to the changes brought about by the pandemic (López-Chávez & Maldonado-Alcudia, 2022).

Case C

This hotel has 58 rooms and 30 employees. A second-generation controlling owner runs it. He is the only family member in the business and the current director.

- *Start-up*. The establishment was founded by an American investor in 1952 in the oldest part of the destination. In the 1960s, it was bought by two Mazatlán businessmen, and later one of them obtained 100% ownership.
- *Expansion*. From 1970 to 1985, expansion was achieved by acquiring another lodging establishment in a newer tourist area in the Zona Dorada and with the involvement of the owner's two sons in the business's management.
- *Maturity*. In the 1990s, and with the father's death in 2000, a sibling partnership took over the establishment, but the performance of the hotels was very different. The one located in the old area lacked sufficient attention and was focused on a market with low purchasing power and extended stays. Years later, the brothers decided to divide the ownership of the hotels, each remaining as the owner of one establishment, so the property passed from a brothers' partnership to a controlling owner. So, this hotel underwent revolutionary changes in management and operation, with a structural renewal of functions, market orientation, physical remodelling, new amenities and new services, respecting the traditional design form and focusing on quality. Hence, the stages of decline and rejuvenation of this case during its maturity are identified, and in 2021 experiencing a consolidation stage (López-Chávez & Maldonado-Alcudia, 2022).

Case D

This hotel has 120 rooms, 40 flats and 25 employees. The history of the establishment dates back to 1922, when it was founded by an investor of American origin. It was the destination's first hotel built facing the sea, and is currently run by the fourth generation.

- *Start-up*. The family that owns the hotel acquired it in 1965, and there have been few changes in its services and physical facilities.
- *Expansion*. Expansion was observed with the introduction of the pool and new rooms.
- *Maturity*. The maturity stage is characterised by a stagnation in the supply of quality services, due to the modification of the rooms for extended-stay markets, primarily for Americans. In 2009, it came under the ownership of siblings, but conflicts arose due to a lack of defined roles and functions, affecting the services. In 2020, it passed into the hands of one of the owners, and gradual changes began, such as using social networks and improving some physical facilities. However, the owner's sudden death nine months later and a lack of a succession plan left the business without an official owner. As a result of these problems, a decline stage was identified (López-Chávez & Maldonado-Alcudia, 2022).

Cross-Case Analysis

Among the cases, the three stages of development of the business axis can be observed based on the Gersick *et al.* (1997) model. In addition, it is possible to identify substages along this axis related to the life cycle of Butler's (1980) model. For example, within the start-up stage is the involvement of one (Cases C and D) or several (Cases A and B) family entrepreneurs who invest in the tourism industry, either for economic reasons or lifestyle, as reported in other studies (Ahmad & Muhammad, 2016; Andersson *et al.*, 2002).

In the formalisation expansion stage, it is possible to relate this to the growth in rooms (Cases A, B and D) or the introduction of new amenities such as a swimming pool, car park and restaurant, among others (Cases A, B, C and D), the added value Churchill and Lewis (1983) mention. At this time, the owners took advantage of rapid market growth (Greiner, 1927) to reinvest in the business.

In the maturity phase, multiple stages are observed, especially in older hotels (Cases C and D). It was identified that they went through stages of stagnation, marked by a decrease in their occupancy rates and even a change from rooms to flats (Case D) related to the late stages of the TALC (Butler, 1980). A decline is observed with the drop in the occupancy rate related to the regional economic crisis, which required structural changes

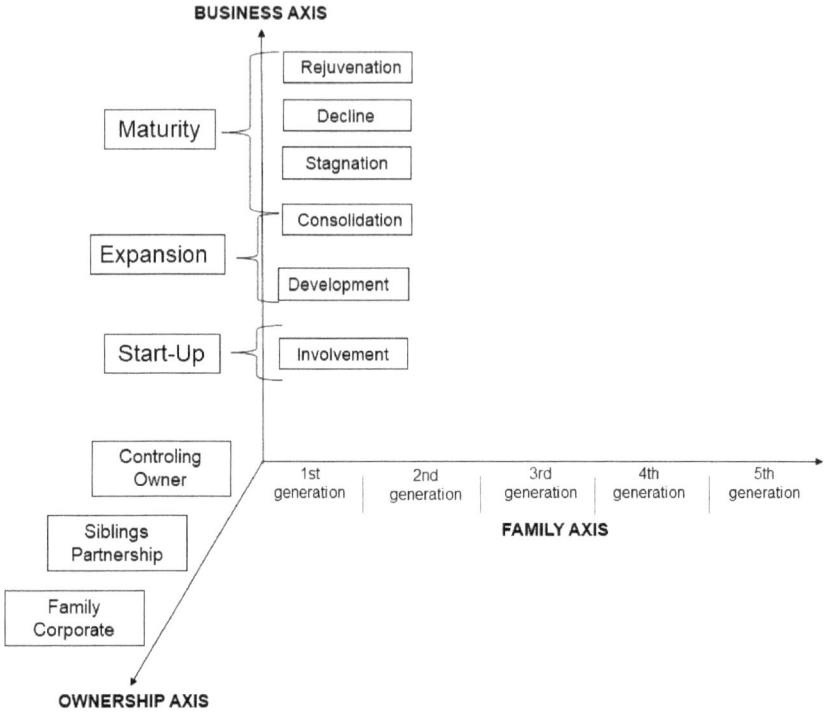

Figure 14.3 Life cycle models of hotels family-owned from start to maturity (Source: Authors' elaboration based on results and Butler, 1980; Gersick *et al.*, 1997; López-Chávez & Maldonado-Alcudia, 2022)

to achieve rejuvenation and later consolidation (Case C) or adaptive changes to continued stagnating (López-Chávez & Maldonado-Alcudia, 2022). Therefore, consolidation can be related to both the expansion and the maturity phases. Figure 14.3 shows the model's stages of the business axis that were found in these cases, both those indicated by Gersick *et al.* (1997) and those identified from Butler's proposal for tourist areas (1980). The unit of analysis is the lynchpin of the family-owned hotel business.

As noted, three of the lodging establishments of them were initially ventures of foreign residents, integrated into the offer during the stage of involvement (Case A) and development of the destination (Cases C and B) and later acquired by families and Mexican companies during the development stage, characterised by a high-growth market (Butler, 1980; Greiner, 1972).

On the other hand, the dynamics of the destination's evolution have implications for internal decision-making in family businesses. In times of stagnation and decline in destination indicators, hotels implemented strategies to sustain themselves. These included decreased rates, monthly rents, and the introduction of new services, something documented in other studies (Banki *et al.*, 2016; Ismail *et al.*, 2019; Rienda *et al.*, 2020). As well, there was the postponement of the final disposition of the business in view of better seasons and capital gains in the area in a period of more significant investments (Case A).

Conclusions

Given the accelerated transformations of the tourism industry, destinations and companies must use tools to manage their resources and cope with changes through adaptation. This research analysed the development of family-owned hotels in their business axis and found that, in addition to the phases of the Gersick *et al.* (1997) model, it is possible to identify specific substages based on those proposed by Butler (1980) for tourist areas. This research thus provides knowledge that reaffirms the validity of life cycle models to understand the development of tourist areas. In particular, the Butler (1980) model has helped understand the evolution of Mazatlán as a tourist destination. Applied to a specific unit of analysis (Haywood, 1986), namely the family-owned hotel business, it is possible to identify the substages, which are: involvement, growth, consolidation, stagnation, decline and rejuvenation, throughout the start-up, expansion and maturity phases. These substages make sense in the interrelation of the business with the tourism industry.

Among the study's limitations, it is important to mention that, due to the research characteristics, qualitative multiple case studies do not seek the generalisation of the findings but rather explore their relationship with other possible realities. In this sense, the results could be helpful to relate them to the reality of other family tourism businesses in coastal destinations in emerging economies. Further studies are necessary for family hotels with other levels of seniority, with greater family involvement in the business and other lines within the tourism industry, as well as integrating the guests' vision in the perception of the quality of the service.

References

Ahmad, S. and Muhammad, A. (2016) Entrepreneurial characteristics, motives, and business challenges: Exploratory study of small- and medium-sized hotel businesses. *International Journal of Hospitality and Tourism Administration* 17 (3), 286–315. https://doi.org/10.1080/15256480.2016.1183550.

Andersson, T., Carlsen, J. and Getz, D. (2002) Family business goals in the tourism and hospitality sector: Case studies and cross-case analysis from Australia, Canada, and Sweden. *Family Business Review* 15 (2), 89–106. https://doi.org/10.1111/j.1741-6248.2002.00089.x.

Banki, I., Ismail, H. and Muhammad, I. (2016) Coping with seasonality: A case study of family owned micro tourism businesses in Obudu Mountain Resort in Nigeria. *Tourism Management Perspectives* 18, 141–152. http://dx.doi.org/10.1016/j.tmp.2016.01.010.

Barbosa, A. and Santamaría, A. (2006) *Estudio Comparativo de Playas: Mazatlán, Acapulco, Cancún y Los Cabos (1970–2005)*. Mexico: Universidad Autónoma de Sinaloa.

Butler, R. (1980) The concept of the tourist area life-cycle of evolution: Implications for management of resources. *Canadian Geographer* 24 (1), 5–12. https://doi.org/10.1111/j.1541-0064.1980.tb00970.x.

Butler, R. (2014) Coastal tourist resorts: History, development and models. *ACE: Architecture, City and Environment* 9 (25), 203–228. https://doi.org/10.5821/ace.9.25.3626.

Churchill, N. and Lewis, V. (1983) The five stages of small business growth. *Harvard Business Review* 61, 30–50. https://hbr.org/1983/05/the-five-stages-of-small-business-growth.

Consejo para el Desarrollo Económico de Sinaloa (Codesin) (2022) *Sinaloa en números: llegada de turistas y ocupación hotelera en Sinaloa, durante enero a diciembre 2021.* https://bit.ly/3KbnyiD.

Creswell, J. (2012) *Qualitative Inquiry and Research Design: Choosing Among Five Approaches*. New York: Sage.

Daft, R.L. (2011) *Leadership*. Mason, OH: Thompson Higher Education.

DATATUR (2023) *Compendio Estadístico del Turismo en México. Actividad Hotelera: Porcentaje de Ocupación en Establecimientos de Hospedaje de Categoría Turística.* https://datatur.sectur.gob.mx/SitePages/ActividadHotelera.aspx.

De Massis, A. and Kotlar, J. (2014) The case study method in family business research: Guidelines for qualitative scholarship. *Journal of Family Business Strategy* 5 (1), 15–29. https://doi.org/10.1016/j.jfbs.2014.01.007.

Dorta, A. (2016) El proceso de renovación de la oferta alojamiento turístico en destinos consolidados: el caso de Puerto de la Cruz (1955–2009). *Cuadernos de Turismo* 38, 115–145. https://doi.org/10.6018/turismo.38.271381.

Duffus, D. and Dearden, P. (1990) Non-consumptive wildlife-oriented recreation: A conceptual framework. *Biological Conservation* 53 (3), 213–231. https://bit.ly/3KeeoSO.

Espinoza, Y. (2010) La competitividad de Mazatlán como destino turístico frente al mercado norteamericano 1945–1987. Master's thesis, Universidad Autónoma de Sinaloa. https://www.academia.edu/7896642/La_competitividad_de_Mazatl%C3%A1n_como_destino_tur%C3%ADstico_frente_al_mercado_norteamericano_1945_1987.

Gallo, M. (1998) *La sucesión en la empresa familiar*. Barcelona: Caja de Ahorros y Pensiones de Barcelona.

Gersick, K., Davis, J.A., Hampton, M.M. and Lansberg, I. (1997) *Generation to Generation: Life Cycles of the Family Business*. Boston: Harvard Business School Press.

Getz, D. and Carlsen, J. (2005) Family business in tourism. State of the art. *Annals of Tourism Research* 32 (1), 237–258. https://doi.org/10.1016/j.annals.2004.07.006.

Getz, D. and Peterson, T. (2005) Growth and profit-oriented entrepreneurship among family business owners in the tourism and hospitality industry. *International Journal of Hospitality Management* 24 (2), 219–242. https://doi.org/10.1016/j.ijhm.2004.06.007.

González, E. and Olivié, C. (2018) *Empresa Familiar, Emprendimiento e Intra-emprendimiento*. Madrid: EAE Business School. https://www.aref.es/sites/default/files/archivos/SRC_Emprendimiento_EmpresaFamiliar.pdf.

Grabinsky, S. (2016) *Empresas Familiares en México: aspectos sucesorios. Cuadernos de gobernabilidad y fiscalización.* http://sug.unam.mx/docs/publicaciones/cuaderno_3_v2.pdf.

Greiner, L. (1972) Evolution and revolution as organizations grow. *Harvard Business Review* 50. https://mgeiscee.files.wordpress.com/2010/01/b3-greiner.pdf.

Hallak, R. and Assaker, G. (2013) Family vs. non-family business owners' commitment to their town: A multigroup invariance analysis. *Asia Pacific Journal of Tourism Research* 18 (6), 618–636. https://doi.org/10.1080/10941665.2012.695286.

Haywood, K.M. (1986) Can be the tourist-area life cycle be made operational? *Tourism Management* 7 (3), 154–167. https://doi.org/10.1016/0261-5177(86)90002-6.

Hjalager, A.M. (2010) A review of innovation research in tourism. *Tourism Management* 31 (1), 1–12. https://doi.org/10.1016/j.tourman.2009.08.012.

Instituto Nacional de Geografía y Estadística (INEGI) (2022) *Directorio estadístico nacional de unidades económicas, DENUE.* https://www.inegi.org.mx/app/mapa/denue/default.aspx.

Ismail, H.N., Mohd Puzi, M.A., Banki, M.B. and Yusoff, N. (2019) Inherent factors of family business and transgenerational influencing tourism business in Malaysian islands. *Journal of Tourism and Cultural Change* 17 (5), 624–641. https://doi.org/10.1080/14766825.2018.1549058.

Kallmuenzer, A. and Peters, M. (2018) Entrepreneurial behaviour, firm size and financial performance: The case of rural tourism family firms. *Tourism Recreation Research* 43 (1), 2–14. https://doi.org/10.1080/02508281.2017.1357782.

Kallmuenzer, A., Kraus, S., Peters, M., Steiner, J. and Cheng, C-F. (2019) Entrepreneurship in tourism firms: A mixed-methods analysis of performance driver configurations. *Tourism Management* 74, 319–330.

Kallmuenzer, A., Tajeddini, K., Gamage, T.C., Lorenzo, D., Rojas, A. and Schallner, M.J.A. (2021) Family firm succession in tourism and hospitality: An ethnographic case study approach. *Journal of Family Business Management.* https://doi.org/10.1108/JFBM-07-2021-0072.

Krippendorff, K. (2004) *Content Analysis: An Introduction to Its Methodology.* New York: Sage.

Latiesa, M. and Álvarez, A. (2000) *El turismo en la sociedad contemporánea: diversificación, competitividad y desarrollo.* Granada: Proyecto sur de ediciones, S. L.

Liu, C.W. and Cheng, J.S. (2018) Exploring driving forces of innovation in the MSEs: The case of the sustainable B&B tourism industry. *Sustainability (Switzerland)* 10 (11), article 3983. https://doi.org/10.3390/su10113983.

López-Chávez, B.A. and Maldonado-Alcudia, C. (2022) Exploring the life cycle of family-owned tourism businesses in maturity. *Journal of Family Business Management.* https://doi.org/10.1108/JFBM-10-2021-0126.

Lumpkin, G. and Dess, G. (2001) Linking two dimensions of entrepreneurial orientation to firm: the moderating role of environment and industry life cycle. *Journal of Business Venturing* 16, 429–451. https://doi.org/https://doi.org/10.1016/S0883-9026(00)00048-3.

Olguín, M., Gonzales, J. and Patiño, I. (2016) Elementos críticos para la sucesión de la empresa familiar. *Vinculatégica EFAN* 1, 2185–2205.

Pikkemaat, B., Peters, M. and Chan, C.S. (2018) Needs, drivers and barriers of innovation: The case of an alpine community-model destination. *Tourism Management Perspectives* 25, 53–63. https://doi.org/10.1016/j.tmp.2017.11.004.

Rienda, L., Claver, E. and Andreu, R. (2020) Family involvement, internationalisation and performance: An empirical study of the Spanish hotel industry. *Journal of Hospitality and Tourism Management* 42, 173–180. https://doi.org/10.1016/j.jhtm.2020.01.002.

Rodríguez, I. and Conejero, A. (2011) *Renovación de destinos turísticos maduros, expertos y grupos de interés, discurso global–local y escenarios de futuro: el caso de Benidorm.* Universidad de Alicante. http://rua.ua.es/dspace/handle/10045/20508.

Ruiz, M. (2015) *50 años Aeropuertos y Servicios Auxiliares. Biblioteca Mexicana del Conocimiento.* https://www.gob.mx/publicaciones/articulos/50-anos-aeropuertos-y-servicios-auxiliares?idiom=es.

Santamaría, A. (2005) *Del alba al anochecer, el turismo en Mazatlán (1972–2004).* Mexico: Ed. Universidad Autónoma de Sinaloa.

Segrado, R., Amador, K., Jiménez, J. and Arroyo, L. (2011) Etapas del ciclo de vida del destino turístico Cozumel (México). In J. Fernando Vera Rebollo (ed.) *Seminario Internacional Renovación y Reestructuración de Destinos Turísticos Consolidados del Litoral [Recurso electrónico]: comunicaciones.* Alicante: Universidad de Alicante, Instituto Universitario de Investigaciones Turísticas. http://rua.ua.es/dspace/handle/10045/20809.

Silva, J. and Almeida, P. (2015) La identificación de la fase del ciclo de vida de un destino turístico para las escuelas estratégicas: Una propuesta de una herramienta expedita. *Estudios Económicos y Empresariales* 27, 15–41. https://core.ac.uk/download/pdf/72046663.pdf.

Stake, R. (1999) *Investigación con estudio de casos* (2nd edn). Madrid: Ediciones Morata S.L.

Tomljenović, R. and Getz, D. (2009) Life-cycle stages in wine tourism development: A comparison of wine regions in Croatia. *Tourism Review International* 13 (1), 31–49. https://doi.org/10.3727/154427209789130666.

United Nations World Tourism Organization (2023) Tourism set to return to pre-pandemic levels in some regions in 2023. https://www.unwto.org/news/tourism-set-to-return-to-pre-pandemic-levels-in-some-regions-in-2023.

Vera-Rebollo, F., Rodríguez I. and Capdepón M. (2010) *Reestructuración y competitividad de destinos maduros de sol y playa: la renovación de la planta hotelera de Benidorm.* Instituto Universitario de Investigaciones Turísticas. http://rua.ua.es/dspace/handle/10045/14180.

Zellweger, T.M., Eddleston, K.A. and Kellermanns, F.W. (2010) Exploring the concept of familiness: Introducing family firm identity. *Journal of Family Business Strategy* 1 (1), 54–63. https://doi.org/10.1016/j.jfbs.2009.12.003.

15 Applying Golf Tourism to the TALC Model and as a Catalyst for Coastal Rejuvenation: The Case of The Open, at Royal Portrush, Northern Ireland

Peter Bolan and Stephen Boyd

Golf is the world's largest sports-related travel market. More tourists travel in relation to golf each year than any other sport (Hudson & Hudson, 2014). Something which for a long time from its inception was an activity mostly played in the vicinity of the participants' place of residence (Butler, 2019) has now become a significant and highly lucrative form of tourism. Such a change began to occur from the 1950s and 1960s, with increases in disposable income, leisure time and developments in transport coinciding with the increasing popularity of golf as a leisure activity and as a spectator sport (Butler, 2019; Gelan, 2003; Hudson & Hudson, 2014; Priestly, 2006). The concept of golf tourism can be defined as 'travel away from home to participate in or observe the sport of golf, or to visit attractions associated with golf' (Hudson & Hudson, 2014: 5). This form of tourism is also extremely lucrative, with golf tourists typically spending two to three times as much as other types of tourist (Hariss & Lepp, 2011; Hudson & Hudson, 2014; Wilson & Thilmany, 2006). In global terms this accounts for a significant source of revenue with golf tourism valued at some US$30 billion, with over 50 million golf tourists travelling the world to play on some of the estimated 40,000 courses (Hudson & Hudson, 2014: 3).

'Cold water' resorts such as those around the UK and Ireland have arguably seen something of a decline across a similar timeframe to golf's growth in popularity (especially from the 1970s onwards). According to Kennell (2010), many such seaside towns (due to increasing competition from warmer package holiday destinations and other market dynamics) were left with a legacy of unemployment, social problems, outdated infrastructure and redundant urban spaces. By the early 2000s the need for regeneration was becoming all too evident (Agarwal, 2002). The response to such decline from the 1980s through to the 2010s often involved attempts to reposition these seaside towns within the tourism marketplace through a process of rebranding and product development, often with very limited success. Many such seaside towns, however, have a golf course (in some cases multiple courses). If that is a course of some standing, used for higher-profile tournaments and events (from the scale of The Open and the Ryder Cup down to a European Tour event such as an Irish Open or a Scottish Open) then those coastal resort towns have an added potential to use golf's popularity and worldwide appeal as an opportunity to attract investment and act as a catalyst for regeneration (Bolan *et al.*, 2015).

The golf tourism literature, in particular, shows a lack of research focus and investigation with regard to coastal resort regeneration and rejuvenation, in relation to community impact and involvement, and with regard to tourism development modelling. This chapter reappraises Butler's tourist area cycle of evolution, best recognised as the Tourism Area Life Cycle (TALC) (Butler, 1980), through the case of The Open Golf Championship at Royal Portrush (Northern Ireland) in 2019, and the utility of such modelling of a singular catalyst event for rejuvenation given that this prestigious tournament is due to return to Royal Portrush in 2025.

Golf Tourism

According to Gelan (2003: 406), 'Major sporting events have become one of the fastest-growing segments of the tourism industry'. Most significant is the sport of golf, which provides a source of revenue that many tourist destinations have found difficult to resist (Palmer, 2004; Readman, 2003). The phenomenon of golf tourism falls under the umbrella of sports tourism. Many regions around the world have been 'using a sport like golf as central to a strategy for encouraging inward investment' (Harris & Lepp, 2011: 66). This is because certain sports and sporting events can make an important contribution to a region's economy (particularly a sport like golf, which is known for its high-spending clientele). Indeed, potential benefits of certain sporting events go beyond tangible economic outcomes and include 'psychic income', enabling even a small community to celebrate its uniqueness, develop local pride and promote a stronger image of place (Gelan, 2003).

Golf tourism in today's world attracts high-spend travellers, contributing the equivalent of some US$30 billion in economic terms (Hudson & Hudson, 2014). Much of this is fuelled by golf events, particularly golf's annual majors (The Open, The Masters, The US PGA, The US Open) and the Ryder Cup (which takes place every two years and pits the best golfers from Europe against the best golfers from the USA). The 2016 Open Championship at Royal Troon generated £110 million economic benefit – £64 million direct and £46 million in AVE (advertising value equivalency) for that region of Scotland (see www.theopen.com). The Irish Open (a European Tour event) in 2012 at Royal Portrush brought a direct £12 million economic impact for that region of Northern Ireland, 28,000 bed-nights and a television reach of over 400 million households globally (see www.tourismni.com).

The image and reputation of any destination, or for that matter a particular golfing region or course, is formed in multilayered constructs created through time, which can include everything from word-of-mouth recommendations, to quality, value for money and even course design (Correia *et al.*, 2009; Humphreys, 2011; Wilson & Thilmany, 2006). These elements, known as 'golfographic variables', create the 'push and pull factors' that not only influence the golfer but also the general tourist in generating the tangible and intangible elements that shape the motivations and perceptions about those places (Correia *et al.*, 2009; Harrison-Hill & Chalip, 2006; Hinch & Higham, 2004; Hudson & Hudson, 2014; Kim *et al.*, 2008; Petrick, 2002). There is a 'lifestyle image associated with golfing holidays', which can provide powerful 'status and prestige' motivations (Weed & Bull, 2004: 68). Humphreys, expanding on Bourdieu's notion of social and cultural capital, describes the concept of 'golfing capital' as a way players can 'enhance their standing within golf-related social networks as well as enjoy the benefits of these networks more extensively' (Humphreys, 2011: 109).

Golf, and by extension golf tourism, also has an important social impact. This is particularly the case when it comes to golf events which have demonstrated a considerable positive charitable impact on society. In the USA alone, 'golf generates $3.9 billion for charitable causes each year' (Hudson & Hudson, 2014: 255). For instance, the Irish Open (an annual European Tour event) is supported by the Rory Foundation (a children's charity run by former world number one golfer Rory McIlroy) and has an important financial impact for children's charities each year. More widely, regular golf tourism improves quality of life for residents through infrastructure changes, development of existing and creation of new businesses and services, rising property values and a general sense of civic pride.

Golf in Northern Ireland

The island of Ireland currently has 430 golf clubs affiliated to the GUI (Golfing Union of Ireland). 'Ireland has worked hard to develop its golf profile and has capitalised on the Irish diaspora in North America' (Harris & Lepp, 2011: 67). Golf tourism is particularly popular with the American market and Ireland has strong links with North America.

There are two different forms or categories of golf course: 'links' courses and 'parkland' courses. Golf tourists predominantly prefer to play on links courses. Links golf courses are those which are situated in coastal locations, on areas of sand dune topography, characterised by undulating terrain, sandy soil and indigenous grasses such as marram and sea lyme (Hudson & Hudson, 2014; R&A World Golf Museum, 2022). Northern Ireland has some 90 golf clubs, with 13 of these classified as links courses and the remainder parkland courses. Two of Northern Ireland's courses regularly feature in listings of the world's top 10 links courses: Royal Portrush (founded in 1888) and Royal Country Down (founded in 1889). One of these, Royal Portrush, has hosted The Open on two occasions to date. The first in 1951 and latterly in 2019. Northern Ireland has also gained further prominence due to the extremely high profile of its top golfers in the past 15 years. From Rory McIlroy (US Open winner in 2011, US PGA winner in 2012 and 2014, winner of The Open in 2014 and regularly ranked world number one golfer) to Graeme McDowell (US Open winner in 2010) and Darren Clarke (winner of The Open in 2011). Northern Ireland, for such a small country and population, has achieved great success on the global golf stage.

While a number of Northern Ireland's golf courses prove popular with visiting golf tourists (Royal Portrush, Royal County Down, Portstewart, Ardglass, Castlerock, Ballycastle, Galgorm Castle, Lough Erne), it is Royal Portrush that proves the greatest draw, thanks not just to its quality and dramatic coastal landscape, but also its pedigree in regularly hosting many high-profile golf tournaments and events, most notably The Open (Bolan, 2021). According to Butler (2019: 237):

> One of the unusual features of golf as a sporting activity is the fact that 'ordinary' golfers (i.e., those who play golf, often at a relatively poor level of performance, for enjoyment and not as an occupation) are able to play golf on many of the same courses that the elite golfers play on in tournaments.

For the golf tourist, then, to be able to play on the same course that they have seen their golf idols play on in major tournaments is a huge motivating factor.

There are several reasons why links courses generally appeal more to golf tourists than parkland courses: links golf is the original form of golf (the activity having begun at St Andrews in Scotland on a links course); links golf is seen as more challenging than its parkland counterpart; and on a global basis there are many fewer links courses than parkland courses (Bolan *et al.*, 2015), with only 246 of the former (Peper & Campbell, 2010). Consequently, this form of golf holds a certain status and appeal that fuels its popularity. The island of Ireland as a whole has 58 links courses (almost a quarter of the global total) and Northern Ireland alone has 13 of these (including the two top world ranking courses), which is hugely significant in terms of golf tourism potential.

The economic impact of golf tourism in Northern Ireland in 2019 was put at a figure of £52 million by Tourism NI (up £9.5 million from

The Economic Impact of golf tourism for Northern Ireland in 2019 is:

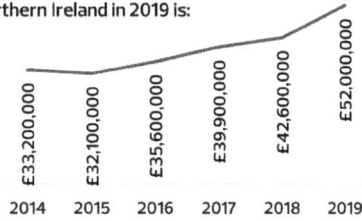

2019 = £52,000,000
2018 = £42,600,000
2017 = £39,900,000
2016 = £35,600,000
2015 = £32,100,000
2014 = £33,200,000

£33,200,000   £32,100,000   £35,600,000   £39,900,000   £42,600,000   £52,000,000

2014   2015   2016   2017   2018   2019

The number of golfing visitors to Northern Ireland is:

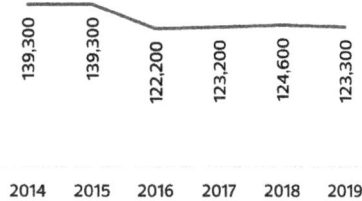

2019 = 123,300
2018 = 124,600
2017 = 123,200
2016 = 122,200
2015 = 139,300
2014 = 139,300

139,300   139,300   122,200   123,200   124,600   123,300

2014   2015   2016   2017   2018   2019

Figure 15.1 Golf tourism's impact in Northern Ireland (Source: Tourism NI, 2020)

the previous year), with the highest proportion of spend among overseas markets coming from North America (Tourism NI, 2020). In the same survey report, the top key reasons for choosing Northern Ireland as a golf destination were: quality and reputation of courses; home to an Open venue; and awareness of major winners from Northern Ireland (see Figure 15.1).

While destinations in all forms of tourism were severely hit by COVID in 2020 and 2021, more recently published survey data on golf tourism reveal that the number of 'tee times' booked by visitors to Northern Ireland in 2022 was 30% higher than pre-COVID levels (with the vast majority of such bookings now coming through specialist tour operators, whereas before the pandemic the majority were travelling independently). Green fee revenue for clubs in 2022 was up 153% on 2019 (Golf Business News, 2023), creating a highly positive picture for golf tourism's potential in Northern Ireland to expand and develop further, especially with The Open due to return to Royal Portrush for its 153rd tournament in 2025.

Impact from Golf Events

Golf tournaments and events have the potential to bring significant economic impact both in the short term, through initial visitation, and in the longer term, through the high level of television and wider media coverage such events receive (Gelan, 2003; Priestly, 2006). Tournament revenues come from a variety of sources, including fees generated by selling the broadcast rights, corporate sponsorship of the event, spectator ticket sales and merchandise sales. This is increased by visitor spend in the host region from spectators, media staff and the competing golfers (and their entourage) on accommodation, food and drink, retail and visiting nearby tourist attractions (Domínguez-Gomez & Gonzalez-Gomez, 2017; Hudson & Hudson, 2014).

As well as major tournaments in the USA, there are 120 international professional golf tournaments across Europe, the Middle East and Africa, and some 35 professional events in Japan. These all bring hugely significant economic benefits (Hudson & Hudson, 2014). Hudson and Hudson (2014) discuss how the Ryder Cup is watched on television by a billion people worldwide and The Open (golf's original major) regularly achieves audiences of around 600 million. European Tour events such as the Irish Open also receive widespread media coverage (in excess of 400 million television viewers globally) and have seen a surge in interest since the sell-out 2012 tournament at Royal Portrush, which ignited a renaissance for the event (Bolan et al., 2015).

In the events world reputation in everything (Hudson & Hudson, 2014. In a wider 2011 study by Humphreys 'reputation was highlighted by the interviewees as being highly influential in their decision making process' (Humphreys, 2011: 115). This is borne out in the survey findings from Tourism NI (2020), in which the 'quality and reputation of courses' was cited by golf visitors as their number one reason for choosing Northern Ireland as a destination.

The rationale for hosting large-scale sporting events is that they leave a legacy such that their impact will 'remain longer than the event itself' (Preuss, 2007: 211). This is something that the Royal & Ancient (R&A, organisers of The Open) now actively champion and pursues. Each year it provides £100,000 to community groups and organisations to support projects and initiatives that will have a positive and long-lasting impact on the local environment and communities where The Open is staged.

Ramasamy et al. (2022) suggest that hosting annual events may be preferable to hosting a single mega-event. However, when it comes to some sports, and most notably golf, this is not always feasible, especially for the highest-level tournaments such as a major. The one golf major which always takes place in the same venue is The Masters, which is always played at Augusta National in Georgia (USA). The other majors rotate through a number of key venues. Once on the rota as a successful host, however, such venues are guaranteed to host the event on a regular basis, for anything from 5 to 10 years.

The Open

While there are a number of prestigious annual golf tournaments around the globe, The Open is the world's oldest and golf's original championship. Played since 1860 on iconic links courses, it is the sport's

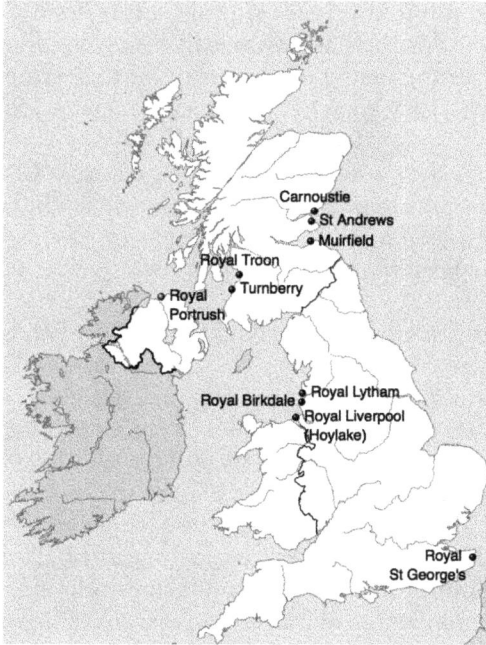

Figure 15.2 Open golf venues in the modern era (Source: R&A, 2023)

most international major championship, with qualifying events on every continent (R&A, 2023). The tournament is organised each year by the R&A, which was founded in 1754 and is based at St Andrews in Scotland (the home of golf). Another element of uniqueness is that while The Open rotates around various courses in the UK, it does not utilise any parkland course venues. It is only ever played on a links course.

Beyond St Andrews, four other Scottish courses are current venues on the championship host rota (see Figure 15.2): Carnoustie and Muirfield on the east coast and Turnberry and Royal Troon on the west coast. English host venues are mostly west coast: Royal Liverpool (Hoylake), Royal Birkdale and Royal Lytham, with only Royal St George's on the east coast. One other host venue has returned to the modern rota and that is Royal Portrush in Northern Ireland. As the oldest golf championship in the world and arguably the most prestigious, the opportunity to be a host venue on a regular basis is hugely significant.

Royal Portrush first hosted The Open in 1951, when it was the venue for the 80th Open Championship, the first time the tournament had taken place outside Scotland or England, marking a milestone for Northern Ireland and for the town of Portrush. Already a golf course of some renown (having existed since 1888), its potential as a possible Open venue was helped when one of the town's own golfers, Fred Daly, won the 1947 Open

Championship at Royal Liverpool (Hoylake). This drew the attention of the golfing world to Portrush, as Daly was the first golfer from the island of Ireland to win The Open and the first to play in a Ryder Cup. He remained the only Northern Irish winner of a major until Graeme McDowell (also a Portrush native) won the US Open in 2010 (followed thereafter by further Northern Irish successes with Rory McIlroy and Darren Clarke from 2011 onwards). While it was hoped that Royal Portrush might host The Open again in the 1960s, growing civil unrest ended any such chances. The venue had to wait for almost another 70 years before it got the opportunity for The Open to return.

A key catalyst for change in golfing terms was when Royal Portrush was selected to host the Irish Open in 2012. This was a milestone in itself, as it was the first time in almost 60 years that this golf event had taken place in the North. The tournament was a huge success, with a record attendance of 112,000 over the four main days, and 131,000 over all six days of the event. It was the first time a European Tour event had sold out prior to play on all four main days and was the highest attendance ever recorded on the European Tour (European Tour, 2013). Portrush (and the surrounding region) proved that it could successfully host a large-scale golf event in the modern era to a level that garnered a high level of praise with significant media coverage (the tournament was watched by a television audience of 412 million). The organisers of The Open (the R&A) took note and it was announced in June 2015 that Royal Portrush would host the 148th Open Championship in 2019.

The return of golf's oldest event to Northern Ireland's north coast was a resounding success. Portrush set a new record for any Open venue outside of St Andrews, with some 237,750 spectators (see Figure 15.3). In comparison, the previous year's venue of Carnoustie in Scotland had achieved 170,000 spectators (R&A, 2019). It was also the first time the event had ever been a sell-out in terms of ticket sales, with £106 million of direct economic benefit generated from the hosting of the tournament and a further £23.7 million in terms of AVE from media coverage and exposure. Very significantly, from when it was announced in 2015

Key Impact Factors
- First sell-out Open Championship
- 237,750 spectators
- £106 million direct economic benefit
- £23.7 million AVE
- 36,000 bednights
- Over 600 million reach on television (150 countries)
- £17.5 million Regeneration programme
- £100,000 R&A Legacy Fund
- £35,000 R&A funded school golf programme

THE OPEN
148" ROYAL PORTRUSH

Figure 15.3 Impact of the 148th Open at Royal Portrush (Source: R&A, 2019)

that Royal Portrush would host the event, the coastal resort town of Portrush and surrounding region received £17.5 million for a regeneration programme. Some £5 million of that went towards a new train station in the town (highly appropriate for a seaside town that first really began to grow as a tourist resort as a result of the railway arriving there in the 1850s).

Tourism Development Models

Tourism development is a complex process that involves interactions between tourists, destinations and various stakeholders. While over the years a number of models have been proposed to aid in understanding the dynamics of tourism development, a prominent example is the Tourism Area Life Cycle (TALC) introduced by Butler in 1980. The model provides insight into the evolution and development of tourism destinations over time, while also offering a framework for sustainable tourism planning and management.

Butler (1980) argues that tourist areas go through predictable stages of development, each characterised by distinct aspects. These stages include exploration, involvement, development, consolidation, stagnation and decline or rejuvenation. The decline stage of Butler's model is typically where the destination experiences a decrease in visitor numbers, has ageing infrastructure and sees a decline in economic benefits. Such a stage may be caused by changing tourist preferences, increased competition and environmental degradation or decay. These are symptoms that clearly fit with many UK seaside resorts. As Butler himself points out, decline does not necessarily mean the end of a destination however, as, through focused planning and rejuvenation efforts, destinations can transition into a new phase of growth and development.

The authors here propose that golf tourism, particularly through high-profile golf events (such as The Open), can act as a catalyst and provide the means to enable declining coastal resorts to transition into a new regenerative phase. Indeed, some researchers such as Lim and Patterson (2008) have also advocated that golf tourism can help redefine and rejuvenate resorts that have stagnated or declined. Although they allude to this in their work on the impact of a mega golf event on island destinations such as Jeju Island (Korea), their research does not specifically address in any detail how golf tourism can achieve this.

Coastal Resort Regeneration

Coastal resort regeneration in the UK has become an increasingly important issue in recent years, as many seaside towns have faced economic decline, outmoded infrastructure, rising unemployment and a variety of social problems (Agarwal, 1999, 2002; Kennell, 2010). Many of these once popular and thriving destinations have struggled to adapt to changing tourism patterns and other economic shifts, resulting in a decline in their attractiveness and tourism appeal. Dynamics of resort decline can be both internal (loss of competitiveness, loss of uniqueness) and external (consumption and production-related processes, intensified competition), with clear symptoms, such as declining visitor numbers, poor image and lack of investment (Agarwal, 2002). Such seaside towns still have a unique charm, however (harking back to what first made them popular), which, combined with the generally natural scenic beauty of their surrounding locales, and in many cases their historical significance, mean they still have potential to attract visitors and boost local economies.

Portrush on Northern Ireland's north coast was typical of such UK seaside towns. Having enjoyed a boom time in the late Victorian and early Edwardian period as a fashionable seaside watering place for its health benefits (Young, 2002), by the 1970s its was already seeing its tourism fortunes and appeal decline. The seaside town had gone through Butler's (1980) *exploration* stage between 1750 and 1826, prior to that having had no real evident relationship with tourism. Portrush's *involvement* stage was between 1827 and 1854, with construction of the harbour commencing in 1827 and its completion in 1837 marking a milestone for the town, alongside the opening of the first hotel (the Antrim Arms) in 1838 (Bolan, 1995). Indeed, as Mullin (1982: 99) states, 'Portrush remained merely a small fishing village until a proper harbour was built in the early 19th century'. The *development* stage for the seaside town was from 1855 to 1882, a turning point being the arrival of the railway in 1855 as well as new steamboat connections to Glasgow and Liverpool thanks to the relatively new harbour (Bolan, 1995). Portrush's *consolidation* stage ran from 1883 to 1905, another turning point being the opening of the world's first electric tramway between the seaside town and Bushmills (a town around the coast and home to the world's oldest licensed whiskey distillery, operating since 1608). The electric tramway was extended to the Giant's Causeway in 1887, at which time a golf course also opened in Portrush under the name the Country Golf Club, renamed the following year as Royal Portrush Golf Club. By 1900, steamers were not only running to places like Glasgow but also regularly to Boston and New York (Bolan, 1995). It is believed Portrush had as many as 17 hotels in this period (Mullins, 1982). Contrastingly, when The Open arrived in 2019, the town had only four hotels.

Between 1906 and 1949 Portrush's fortunes were not so great – the town's *stagnation* stage – with all steamboat connections ending during the First World War. After the war, many could not afford to travel and a further source of tourists from southern Ireland dried up after Partition in 1921. The General Depression through the 1920s, followed by the Second World War, further reduced the numbers of visitors. However, during the 1920s and 1930s some seeds for future success were planted (Bolan, 1995).

One of these was the opening in 1926 of Barry's Amusements (a large outdoor and indoor amusement park). In 1929 the North West 200 motorcycle race event began (an international road race which is currently the largest annual outdoor sporting event on the island of Ireland). The mid- to late 1930s saw the opening of the Arcadia Dance Hall on the seafront and of the town's first cinema, the Majestic. Butler (1980) proposes that at such a stage, the resort image becomes divorced from its geographic environment (which was the original principal draw for tourists). Partly as a result of these innovations, however, Portrush entered a period of *rejuvenation* between 1950 and 1969, when such attractions came to the fore and visitor numbers to the region improved, a period when the town became known as the 'Brighton of the north' (Bolan, 1995). The local urban council created summer programmes of events, and the mid-50s saw the opening of a conference centre with business visitors granted free use of the town's tennis courts, bowling greens and putting greens.

A turning point of a different kind then appeared. The cheaper overseas competition that all UK seaside towns faced then took hold and that was further exacerbated by the outbreak of 'the Troubles' in Northern Ireland. As a result, the resort then entered its *decline* stage, which, like many UK cold water resorts, continued for several decades. When the Irish Open golf tournament was announced for Royal Portrush in 2012, the town was given £400,000 by the Northern Ireland government to invest in infrastructure and regeneration. The town's long association with golf (since 1888) was a potential means of rejuvenation for the resort. Agarwal (2002) argues that coastal resort regeneration should take a holistic approach, addressing physical, economic, social and environmental factors. She posits that focusing on just one aspect, such as infrastructure development or tourism promotion, is not sufficient to create significant and sustainable change.

When the R&A announced that Royal Portrush was to host the 148th Open in 2019, the town received a much larger injection of funding for regeneration projects, this time to the tune of £17.5 million. The very successful hosting of the Irish Open in 2012 suggested that golf tourism might provide the means to meaningful regeneration. While most of the spend went on infrastructure (a new train station and coastal pathways) some of the funding (including a further £100,000 from the R&A as part of its Legacy Fund) was devoted to aspects of a more social and community nature, which would benefit the local population. A further £35,000 was given by the R&A (see Figure 15.3) as part of its schools golf programme to encourage and support more young people playing golf. Since 2019, through private-sector investment (mostly from North America), a number of new four- and five-star spa hotels were created in and around the town. The success of golf tourism in general, but highlighted by The Open in particular, has helped attract further investment to the resort. With The Open set to return to Royal Portrush in 2025 for its 153rd tournament, the potential for continued regeneration is very high.

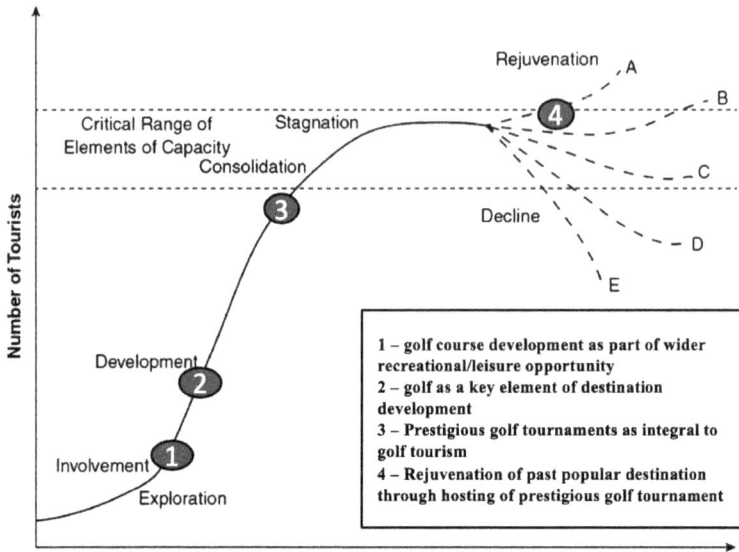

Figure 15.4 Application of golf course development, golf tourism and tournament hosting to the Tourist Area Life Cycle (TALC)

The authors here have modified Butler's (1980) TALC model by applying golf course development, golf tourism and golf tournament/event hosting it, to show how it can provide the means to deter decline and bring about rejuvenation for ailing resort towns (see Figure 15.4).

At Point 1 in Figure 15.4, the development of a golf course helps in the *exploration* and *involvement* stages of the resort from a recreational and tourism perspective (typical of many UK seaside towns in the late 1800s and early 1900s). In the case of Portrush (see also Boyd & Bolan in this volume, Chapter 21), it would be hard to envision that the early elite travellers across the Victorian and Edwardian era did not also take in the opportunity to play on the course given its development in 1888; taking in the sea air, cold-water bathing and exercising outdoors playing golf were all part of wellness (as understood at that time), with which Portrush quickly became identified. As golf becomes more of a draw for visitors to the resort it becomes a key component aiding destination development at Point 2 in the revised model. Again, in the case of Portrush, this equates to when the opportunity came to host the Irish Open in 2012 as part of a tourism development opportunity for Northern Ireland as a whole; it also coincides with that year being positioned by Tourism NI as the tipping point where tourism at a Northern Ireland level was exhibiting characteristics of a destination region that was well into the *development* stage (see Boyd & Bolan in this volume, Chapter 21). If the resort is successful through its golf product in attracting and hosting prestigious golf tournaments and events (such as an Irish Open or a Scottish Open) then, as at Point 3, this can keep fuelling tourism growth. When applied to Portrush and Northern Ireland more broadly, the successful hosting of the Open in 2019 took place against a wider context of multi-niche tourism opportunity and attraction offer (the screen, food and events). Boyd and Bolan (Chapter 21) argue that across the north coast, issues of sustainability were being called into question and so the region was close to entering the capacity zone of the TALC model, and the numbers that attended the 148th Open added to that pressure.

In the scenario where a resort has stagnated or even headed into decline (as typical of many UK seaside towns), the hosting of prestigious golf tournaments, especially of the scale and prominence of The Open, can truly bring about core aspects of regeneration (Point 4 on the revised model), which, if embraced and nurtured, can lead to rejuvenation of the resort. In the context of Portrush and the wider north coast region, if a non-COVID-19 scenario is played out, by the time of the hosting of the 153rd in 2025 it would not have been inconceivable that the growing pressures of anticipated increasing tourism numbers of tourists into Northern Ireland would have placed further strain on the region, by then potentially well into Butler's 'critical zone of capacity'. However, considering COVID-19, the authors here posit that the return of the Open in 2025 will be of critical importance in post COVID-19 recovery and, as Boyd and Bolan (Chapter 21) suggest, act as a major fulcrum to facilitate wider 'redevelopment' of tourism for Northern Ireland, accepting that recovery will come from a lower base.

Conclusion

Seaside towns around the UK and Ireland have been experiencing many challenges from the 1970s to the present day (Agarwal, 1999, 2002; Kennell, 2010). Golf tourism presents a compelling opportunity for coastal resort regeneration. By leveraging the allure of golf and the higher-spending visitors it brings, some seaside towns have the means to revitalise their economies, create employment, develop and improve infrastructure, promote sustainability and enhance their overall tourism appeal. The authors have shown here how this can present opportunities in the final stages of Butler's (1980) TALC to transition into a rejuvenation phase. By investing in golf infrastructure and attracting golf tourists, suitable seaside resorts can diversify their revenue streams and create new employment. Golf courses require regular maintenance, clubhouses need staff and local businesses can benefit from increased tourism, including hotels, restaurants and retail establishments, ultimately creating a more sustainable economic base for the community.

In addition, golf tourism can contribute to the preservation and enhancement of natural landscapes. Responsible course design and management practices can help to conserve dune systems, wetlands and wildlife habitats in such coastal locales where links courses are found. Such integration of golf and nature can enhance the overall appeal of such seaside resorts, attracting visitors who are both health and environmentally conscious.

Furthermore, golf tourism can foster community development and social cohesion. Coastal resorts that embrace golf tourism can create opportunities for local residents to engage with visitors and promote cultural exchange. Such interactions can help the development of local arts, crafts and culinary offerings. Golf tournaments and events can also help unite communities, by fostering a sense of civic pride and identity. In such a way, the shared experience of golf and what it brings can strengthen community bonds, generating a sense of belonging and collective ownership of the regeneration process. With its unique blend of leisure, sport and natural scenic beauty, golf can attract enthusiasts from all over the world, more so with the prestige of hosting high-profile tournaments, and this can create a range of benefits that can revitalise coastal communities.

References

Agarwal, S. (1999) Restructuring and local economic development: Implications for seaside resort regeneration in Southwest Britain. *Tourism Management* 20 (4), 511–522.

Agarwal, S. (2002) Restructuring seaside tourism: The resort cycle. *Annals of Tourism Research* 29 (1), 25–55.

Barnett, T. (2011) Golf tourism: Economic benefits vs. environmental impacts. TourismReview.com.

Bolan, P. (1995) The lifecycle concept in tourism: A study of the coastal resort of Portrush. MSc dissertation, University of Ulster.

Bolan, P. (2021) Golf tourism can be a key driver for the Northern Ireland economy. *The Chronicle*, September, 7–8.

Bolan, P. and Hutchinson, K. (2012) *The Irish Open Golf Championship: A Dual Impact Perspective*. International Conference on Tourism and Events: Opportunities, Impact and Change, June, Europa Hotel, Belfast.

Bolan, P., Hutchinson, K. and Crossan, M. (2015) *Golf Tourism in Ireland: Strategic Impact and Potential – A Framework for Success*. 11th annual Tourism Hospitality and Research in Ireland Conference (THRIC), June, Letterkenny.

Butler, R. (1980) The concept of the tourist area cycle of evolution: implications for management of resources. *Canadian Geographer* 24, 5–12.

Butler, R. (2019) Contributions of tourism to destination sustainability: Golf tourism in St Andrews, Scotland. *Tourism Review* 74 (2), 235–245.

Correia, A., Oliveira, N. and Silva, F. (2009) Bridging perceived destination image and market segmentation – an application to golf tourism. *European Journal of Tourism Research* 2 (1), 41–69.

Domínguez-Gomez, J.A. and Gonzalez-Gomez, T. (2017) Analysing stakeholders' perceptions of golf-course-based tourism: A proposal for developing sustainable tourism projects. *Tourism Management* 63, 135–143.

European Tour (2013) 'Irish Open Success at Portrush', European Tour presentation at Royal Portrush Golf Club, March 2013, Portrush, Northern Ireland.

Gelan, A. (2003) Local economic impacts: The British Open. *Annals of Tourism Research* 30 (2), 406–425.

Golf Business News (2023) https://golfbusinessnews.com/news/management-topics/revenue-club-reports-8-increase-in-green-fee-income-for-uk-ireland-clubs, accessed 10 March 2023.

Harris, J. and Lepp, A. (2011) Golf, tourism and the 2010 Ryder Cup: (De)constructing images of Wales. *Journal of Sport Tourism* 16 (1), 55–73.

Harrison-Hill, T. and Chalip, L. (2006) Marketing sport tourism: Creating synergy between sport and destination. In H. Gibson (ed.) *Sport Tourism: Concepts and Theories. An Introduction* (pp. 86–105). Oxford: Routledge.

Hinch, T. and Higham, J. (2004) *Sport Tourism Development* (1st edn). Clevedon: Channel View Publications.

Hudson, S. and Hudson, L. (2014) *Golf Tourism* (2nd edn). Oxford: Goodfellow Publishers.

Humphreys, C. (2011) Who cares where I play? Linking reputation with the golfing capital and the implication for golf destinations. *Journal of Sport and Tourism* 16 (2), 105–128.

Kennell, J. (2010) Rediscovering cultural tourism: Cultural regeneration in seaside towns. *Journal of Town and City Management* 1 (4), 364–380.

Kim, S., Kim, J.H. and Ritchie, B.W. (2008) Segmenting overseas golf tourists by the concept of specialization. *Journal of Travel and Tourism Marketing* 25, 199–217.

Lim, C.C. and Patterson, I. (2008) Sport tourism on the islands: The impact of an international mega golf event. *Journal of Sport and Tourism* 13 (2), 115–133.

Mullin, J.E. (1982) *The Causeway Coast*. Belfast: Belfast University Press.

Palmer, C. (2004) More than just a game: The consequences of golf tourism. In B.W. Ritchie and D. Adair (eds) *Sport Tourism: Interrelationships, Impacts and Issues* (pp. 117–134). Clevedon: Channel View Publications.

Peper, G. and Campbell, M. (2010) *True Links: An Illustrated Guide to the Glories of the World's 246 Links Courses*. New York: Artisan.

Petrick, J.F. (2002) Experience use history as a segmentation tool to examine golf travellers' satisfaction, perceived value and repurchase intentions. *Journal of Vacation Marketing* 8 (4), 332–342.

Preuss, H. (2007) The conceptualisation and measurement of mega sport event legacies. *Journal of Sport and Tourism* 12 (3), 207–228.

Priestly, G.K. (2006) Planning implications of golf tourism. *Tourism and Hospitality Research* 6 (3), 170–178.

R&A (2019) History of the Open Championship. R&A seminar at Ulster University, Coleraine, Northern Ireland, May.

R&A (2023) https://www.randa.org/en/championships/the-open-championship, accessed 13 March 2023.

R&A World Golf Museum (2022) https://www.worldgolfmuseum.com, accessed 10 March 2023.

Ramasamy, B., Wu, H. and Yeung, M. (2022) Hosting annual sporting events and tourism: Formula 1, golf or tennis? *Tourism Economics* 28 (8), 2082–2098.

Readman, M. (2003) Golf tourism. In S. Hudson (ed.) *Sport and Adventure Tourism* (pp. 165–201). New York: Haworth.

Tourism NI (2020) *Golf Tourism in Northern Ireland – 2019: Final Report*. Wisley: Sports Marketing Surveys.

Weed, M. and Bull, C. (2004) *Sports Tourism: Participants, Policy and Providers*. London: Elsevier Butterworth-Heinemann.

Wilson, J. and Thilmany, D. (2006) Golfers in Colorado: The role of golf in recreational and tourism lifestyles and expenditures. *Journal of Travel and Tourism Marketing* 20 (3–4), 127–144.

Young, A.F. (2002) *Old Portrush, Bushmills and the Giant's Causeway*. Mauchline: Stenlake Publishing.

16 National and International Political Influences on the TALC

Wantanee Suntikul

Tourism and politics are intertwined in many ways. At the quotidian level, destinations are affected by laws and regulations at the local, national and international scales, which affect the economics of tourism development, accessibility of places to tourist markets, perceptions of destinations among tourists and the degrees of freedom and constraint that travellers experience on site. The relationship between politics and tourism is reciprocal. Just as political situations frame the landscape within which tourism develops, tourism also plays a role in international diplomacy, formal and informal, and can be both an instrument for maintaining and developing political relations between nations and a bellwether of the status of political relations between nations linked by tourism patterns and dependencies, such as source/host, or supplier/consumer. As such, radical changes in the political climate and context, from the destination level to the international geopolitical level, can have a profound impact on tourism patterns and practices (Butler & Suntikul, 2010, 2017).

In the past half century, the world has seen such major geopolitical events as the dissolution of the Soviet Union and the effects of changing borders and alignments across Eastern and Central Europe, tragedies such as the 2002 Bali bombings and the September 11, 2001 terrorist attacks in the USA and the rise of global terrorism that they heralded, the opening up – in both the political and tourism accessibility sense – of formerly less accessible countries such as China and Vietnam, the fleeting Arab Spring and the subsequent reinstatement of despotism in many countries in the Middle East and North Africa, the expansion of the European Union and the UK's withdrawal from same, the Russian occupation of Ukraine, and ongoing internal conflicts in countries such as Syria, Sudan and Peru.

As a generalised model, the TALC presents a conceptualisation of the stages of development of attractions that has stood the test of time, and which has been affirmed and elaborated upon by numerous studies in the more than four decades since its first publication (Lagiewski, 2006). As a process that unfolds over time, and in interaction with a multitude of contextual factors, the specifics of the nature of a tourism area's progression through its life cycle are conditioned by the macro- and micro-level vagaries of that tourism area's political situation, and the overall geopolitical situation in which it is embedded, and changes therein.

Just as the development of tourism is a process, as elaborated by the TALC, the political context of a location is also characterised by change, over time. In politically stable democracies, such change is generally incremental and afforded by established processes for elections, administrative handover and new legislation. Despotic regimes seek to maintain continuity of the status quo of autarchic rule through various means. Both cases represent a degree of predictable continuity in the political milieu of tourism at a given destination. However, such stability is not guaranteed and radical political change can divert the expected trajectory of all aspects of social and economic development in an area, for example as witnessed following the fall of the Berlin Wall (see below).

To the extent that political change can also be associated with an increase in violence, or a change in economic policy or paradigm, or different alliances and alignments, there are many ways in which it can affect the parameters that affect tourism development. It can lead to acceleration or deceleration, truncation or detouring of the path of development outlined by the TALC. Emerging economies, which are projected (as destinations) to account for 57% of tourist arrivals by 2030 (World Economic Forum, 2015), run a higher risk of political instability. It is not just changes in the local political context that affect the developmental path of tourism destinations. For example, travel restrictions or political turmoil in tourist source markets can cut-off the supply of visitors, and politically driven interruptions in access to oil by petroleum-producing countries affect the price of travel on a global scale.

This chapter investigates the ways in which the TALC has been affected by different types of political change in recent years, by way of example, focusing on three cases of different types of political change – the handover of Macao from Portugal to China, the Russian annexation of Crimea in Ukraine, and Berlin in the context of German Reunification. It focuses both on the ways in which political change can trend towards more openness and removal of barriers and constraints, and on the other hand how it can also impose barriers and constraints on tourism and disincentivise travel to affected places.

Macao: Tourism and Handover

The territory of Macao, at the mouth of the Pearl River on China's south-east coast, was a Portuguese entrepot and colony from the mid-16th century until its handover back to Chinese control in 1999, two years after Britain's handover of neighbouring Hong Kong. As a Special Administrative Region (SAR), like Hong Kong, Macao retains a high degree of autonomy and individual identity within greater China. It is best known in the present day as a major destination for gambling tourism.

Gambling has been legally practised in Macao since it was first legalised by the Portuguese government in 1850, as a source of government revenue. The territory became a significant gaming destination from 1962, when the government granted a monopoly on gambling operations to the Sociedade de Turismo e Diversões de Macau syndicate of Macanese and Hong Kong business interests, which aggressively developed the sector (Chan, 2000). However, 37 years into the gambling monopoly, in terms of the stages identified in the TALC, tourism in Macao could be said to have reached *stagnation* and early *decline* by the time of the handover of the territory from Portugal to China. The number of tourist arrivals had been fluctuating around 7–8 million since 1995, with 7.44 million in 1999, the year of the handover. Receipts from tourism had been declining steadily, from $3.23 billion ($417 per tourist, 45.88% of GNP) in 1995 to $2.60 billion ($349 per tourist, 39.68% of GNP) in 1999 (worlddata.info, n.d.).

In 2002, the government of Macao, which had been returned to China three years earlier, ended the 40-year gambling monopoly in the territory and opened the casino development market to international investors, leading to a proliferation of casinos and the entry of international gaming concerns into Macao (McCartney, 2010). Two Las Vegas casino groups, Sands and Wynn, were granted the first licences, in 2002, and the Sands Macao and Wynn Macao casinos opened for business in 2004 and 2006, respectively. The Venetian Macao on the Cotai Strip followed in 2007.

By virtue of its designation as the only legal gambling destination in China, post-handover Macao was put in a special position that changed its fortunes. Rather than one foreign gambling destination among many for Chinese tourists, it gained privileged access to the Chinese domestic market. The fact that Macao had recently been repatriated to Chinese rule also opened up this gambling tourism destination to the Chinese market at a time of growing affluence and mobility and a growing middle class. While Chinese citizens require permits to enter the SAR of Macao, accessibility was eased by the Chinese government in 2003 through the Individual Visit Scheme, which allowed travellers from selected cities in mainland China to visit Macao and Hong Kong on an individual basis, rather than having to travel with group tours or on a business visa, as had been previously required. This greatly facilitated independent travel and by 2004 1.8 million tourists had taken advantage of the scheme to visit Macao (Xinhua News, 2004).

Macao has thus come to serve a unique role as a heterotopia (Foucault, 1971) within greater China, under Chinese control but operating under special rules. Simpson (2021) has even proposed that the Chinese government sees Macao as a training ground for the creation of the 'quality consumers' and sophisticated speculators who conform to the valorised model of the ideal Chinese citizen.

Such has been the success of the development of the gambling sector in Macao that it currently accounts for 40% of GDP and fully 80% of government revenues in the territory. Despite, and indeed because of, the boon that gambling has brought to the city in the post-handover period, this over-reliance on tourism has been said to constitute a dimension of vulnerability in Macao's economy, as became apparent when President Xi Jinping's crackdown on corruption in 2012 led gaming junkets to be displaced from Macao to other Asian destinations such as Vietnam, the Philippines, Cambodia and South Korea (Fraser, 2015; Hamdi, 2021). There was also a drastic drop in visits to Macao in 2020 due to the COVID pandemic, resulting in a 55% drop in Macao's GDP per capita from $76,958 in 2019 (compared with $65,120 for the USA) to $34,561 in 2020. Over the same period, the per capita GDP of China increased from $10,143 to $10,408 (World Bank, 2021a, 2021b, 2021c).

Tourists greatly outnumber the local population in the SAR, and while a good many Macao citizens draw their livelihood from the tourism industry and benefit from the economic, infrastructural and entertainment dividends brought by the development of gaming tourism, tourism is also responsible for high prices, social ills and conflicts over resources, leading to some disillusionment with the territory's gambling-centric economy and tourism industry within the local society (Lei *et al.*, 2023), symptomatic of a looming *stagnation* phase of the TALC and raising the spectre of potential *decline* if a strategy for achieving *revitalisation* is not identified.

Ukraine: Tourism and Occupation

In February–March 2014, Russian forces occupied the Crimean Peninsula in Ukraine, and the annexation of the invaded territories was formally declared on 18 March 2014. These events are considered to mark the beginning of the Russo-Ukrainian War, which escalated with Russia's full-scale invasion of the country in February 2022. In typical fashion for the effects of armed conflict on tourism, the ongoing war in Ukraine has been responsible for many changes in tourism volume and patterns in Russia, Ukraine and beyond, including disruption of air traffic patterns, effects on the global price of oil and therefore of international travel, and a decline in both inbound and outbound travel for Russia and Ukraine (Nicolova, 2022).

From the turn of the 21st century up to the 2008 financial crisis, the Ukraine tourism industry had experienced a constant and steepening increase, from just under 11 million international arrivals in 2000 rising to nearly 29 million in 2008. After a fall to 24 million in 2009, arrivals again began to climb, more slowly but steadily, to 26 million in 2013. In terms of the TALC, this description demonstrates hallmarks of a transition from *development* to *consolidation*.

Ukraine's overall tourism receipts also had been on a steady growth trend in the years leading up to the invasion. Between 2013 and 2014, tourism receipts in Ukraine plummeted from US$5.9 billion to US$2.264 billion, falling even further in 2015, to US$1.662 billion. This was followed, however, by a steady growth, increasing by 17.18% from 2016 to 2017, 12.38% from 2017 to 2018 and 14.37% from 2018 to 2019. The tourism receipts fell steeply, by 73.53%, from 2019 to 2020, with the impact of the COVID pandemic, declining from US$2.595 billion to US$687 million (World Bank, 2023). The two pronounced dips in these historical perspectives are patently attributable to two cataclysmic events, one human-made and one natural.

With the beginning of the Russian invasion and occupation, international tourism arrivals to Ukraine fell by nearly half, from an all-time high of 26 million in 2013 to around 13 million in 2019 (World Bank, 2023). The provision and use of tourism infrastructure decreased as well, with the number of hotels decreasing from 3,582 in 2013 to 2,644 the following year, with numbers of room reservations declining accordingly (Kiptenko *et al.*, 2017).

Within the greater context of Ukraine, however, the country's principal tourism area – Crimea – has deviated from the trends of the country, as a whole, during the war period. Statistics since 2013 have tallied visitor numbers for Crimea and for the rest of Ukraine separately. Both of these numbers show a similar drop between 2013 and 2014, the year of the beginning of the Russo-Ukraine War with the Russian occupation of Crimea, with visitors to Crimea decreasing from 5.9 million to 3.8 million (a decline of 35.59%), and visitor numbers for the rest of Ukraine falling from 18.8 million to 12.7 million (a 32.45% drop). However, the aftermath of Russia's annexation of Crimea saw very different trends for these two regions. While visitor numbers to the non-Crimea areas of the country rebounded by 11.81%, to 14.2 million, over the next five years until 2019, Crimea saw a steep increase of 97.74%, to an unprecedented 7.4 million visitors over the same period.

The Russian annexation of Crimea saw a decimation of travel to that region from most countries, with international visitor numbers falling 85–90% (Westerman, 2022). Several cruise lines stopped calling in Crimean Black Sea ports, including Odessa, Sevastopol and Yalta (World Economic Forum, 2015). The Ukrainian government has been explicitly and publicly discouraging foreign tourists from visiting the country for as long as hostilities continue (Fingar, 2022), even while promoting the country's attractions to the international market in hopes of readying a rapid recovery of the tourism industry after the hoped-for end of conflict (Shehadi & Fingar, 2022). Thus, any growth in tourism numbers outside of Russian-held areas is attributable to changes in domestic travel.

However, during the occupation period, the number of Russian tourists visiting Crimea has grown substantially. Russia has invested billions of dollars in upgrading the tourism-related infrastructure of Crimea, including new airport terminals and renovation of hotels and other facilities. The rapid development of infrastructural projects, including the bridge across the Kerch Strait and the Tavrida Highway, created direct links between Crimea and Russia, facilitating the development of Crimea into what Tanner (2021) has termed 'the main center of Russian auto-tourism', spurring growth in demand for tourism-related services. The Russian government also launched an aggressive campaign since 2015 to bring tourists to Crimea and increased the number of flights between Russia and other members of the CIS (Commonwealth of Independent States) and this tourism destination area. It is predicted that tourism numbers in Crimea will continue to grow if the region remains under Russian control (Tomczewska-Popowycz & Quirini-Popławski, 2021).

Crimea has been a popular resort area for Russians since the Soviet era, and is thus familiar to the Russian populace. However, historically, it has served as a destination primarily for the elite and well-to-do among Russian tourists. Tourism to Russian-occupied Crimea, on the other hand, has been dominated by lower-income, low-spending Russian tourists (Marusyak, 2021). This can be seen as accelerating the transition of a *consolidating* tourism area to one that exhibits some of the warning signs of impending *decline*, particularly in terms of a reliance on low-price, low-value tourism with reduced length of stay and per-tourist expenditures in a tourism area whose prior development was characterised by a degree of exclusivity [similar, perhaps, to Plog's (1973) suggested cycle of changes in tourists, from allocentric to psychocentric – editor's comment].

Berlin: Tourism and Reunification

The Reunification of Germany was a process that began on 9 November 1989 with the announcement of the abolition of bans on travel to the West by citizens of the communist German Democratic Republic (GDR) (the 'fall of the Berlin Wall') and was completed on 15 March 1991, when the Unification Treaty formally came into force. Two important milestones in this process were the abolition of the GDR currency (the East German Mark) in July 1990, and the formal dissolution of the German Democratic Republic on 3 October of the same year. These two initiatives contributed considerably to an immediate and drastic shift in the profile of tourists to the eastern part of the country, including Berlin, as tourists from socialist countries were faced first with the prohibitively high prices caused by the introduction of the Western Deutschmark as currency (Hill, 1993) and then with the difficulty of acquiring a visa to a destination that had fallen out of the Eastern bloc. Whereas in 1989 6.5 million of the 8.8 million visitors to the GDR came from socialist countries, in 1990 these countries accounted for only 1 million visitors.

Prior to the Reunification, East and West Berlin were separate, and very different, destinations. Tourists to East Berlin were a mix of East German citizens – typically brought on propaganda-toned government-organised tours – and Westerners brought by tour operators from Western Europe, welcomed for the exchange currency that they brought into the country but tending to present their customers with an unflattering view of the East in their tours. By nature of its tenuous geographical and political situation, much of the tourism image of West Berlin centred on the very precarity of its situation, with the Berlin Wall figuring as a central experience of a visit to the city.

The German federal government provided extensive financial support for the development of the tourism infrastructure in the repatriated eastern parts of the now reunified country. Of the 20 billion German marks invested in tourism development in the territory of former East Germany between 1990 and 1998, 7.6 billion marks was provided by governmental funds (equivalent to US$4.3 billion of US$11.3 billion, by the 1998 exchange rate). In 1991 alone, 500 tourism projects were thus supported. Over these years, this development is estimated to have created or protected 43,000 hotel and catering jobs and 7,000 jobs in other tourism-related services (Benthien, 2000). This financial support was accompanied by knowledge transfer to improve tourism practices in the newly incorporated eastern Länder to bring them up to Western standards (Godau, 1991).

In the years immediately following the fall of the Berlin Wall, the term 'Reunification tourism' (*Vereinigungstourismus*) was coined to refer to the phenomenon of travellers motivated to travel to the city to experience the aftermath of one of the 20th century's most significant political turning points, at the place where it most tangibly came to a head. Topping many lists of tourist sites in the city (returned as the capital of Germany in 1999) is the restored and modernised Reichstag (parliament) building, which sat largely vacant during the Cold War but was once again anointed as the seat of the German parliament (Bundestag) in 1999. Such tangible markers of the new beginning heralded by Reunification, as well as relics of the communist East – such as the Television Tower (Fernsehturm) on Alexanderplatz – and museums and memorials to this period of history – such as the Checkpoint Charlie Museum and the Berlin Wall Memorial – ensure that the Cold War era and its abrupt and spectacular cessation are still elements of the image and tourist experience of Berlin.

Even as such sites remain as reminders of an important but receding period in Berlin's history, the trajectory of development of the city in the 1990s took on a much more pronounced forward-looking tack, as it became poised to become once again the political centre of the country and an internationally significant hub of business, media, technology, culture and tourism. Some of the most substantial relics of the divided city were eradicated from its fabric, including the 2008 demolition of the Palast der Republik – the East German Parliament building – and most of the Berlin Wall itself had been demolished by the end of 1990, to make way for developments such as the gleaming Daimler Benz/Sony high-rise development on Potsdamer Platz.

This concerted programme of selective erasure and memorialisation of relics of the recent past (compare the similar process that occurred in Northern Ireland, described by Boyd and Bolan in Chapter 21 of this volume – editor's note) and normalisation of Berlin as a future-focused united metropolis set the stage for the image of the city that is presented to visitors today. As a tourism area, Berlin has blossomed from a divided destination embedded in the *stagnation* phase, into one of Europe's most popular urban destinations. On the eve of the pandemic, in 2019, Berlin was surpassed only by London and Paris among European cities in visitor numbers, with 34 million overnight stays by 14 million visitors (Berlin Tourismus & Kongress GmbH, 2023). The TALC phase of *rejuvenation* would seem to apply here, par excellence, as the best-case progression from the *stagnation* phase, and the absolutely pivotal role of political change in driving this development is clear.

Conclusion

This chapter has demonstrated how the development of tourism areas can be substantially affected by the appropriation of these areas into political agendas in the context of political change. It has brought forward examples of such dynamics in the solidification and validation of Russian political claims and economic influence on occupied Crimea, the integration of Macao into greater China as an economic engine and a 'bracketed out' gambling heterotopia for Chinese citizens, and the promotion of Berlin as a symbol of reunified Germany and anchor for the image of the nation to the world. In all these examples, it has become apparent, on the one hand, how the introduction of such political schisms into the mix of tourism area development can skew or divert the progression of a tourism area through the stages of the TALC and, on the other hand, has reaffirmed the usefulness of the TALC model in articulating the nature of these disruptions and the implications for the future of these areas.

The three cases of Berlin, Crimea and Macao have several factors in common. In all three cases, political change has brought with it a marked change and increase in the metrics of tourism development, including tourist arrivals, tourism revenues and tourism infrastructure. Secondly, and directly related, the development of all three of these tourism areas was facilitated by governmental policies and plans by virtue of these locations playing a strategic role in the respective governments' economic, social and political agendas.

Thirdly, in all three cases, the political change experienced by each of these places brought a shift in the accessibility and attractiveness of the destination to a changed, and often more lucrative, set of tourist source markets. With the handover of Macao to China, the territory became the most accessible (and only domestic) gambling destination for the vast and increasingly mobile and affluent population of mainland China, at the same time maintaining its accessibility to the global market and opening up to casino development by world-class gaming consortia. The German Reunification moved Berlin from a divided city, with high political significance for both the West and the East, but limited in its tourism development, to a pivotal place in the political and cultural self-image of the reunified country, with high accessibility and high drawing power to the international tourism market. Russia's annexation of Crimea has brought growth in numbers to that area, but in a way that decreases the diversity and value of the tourism sector.

In a world that is still experiencing significant political change on an almost annual, if not more frequent basis in some areas, the influence of that change on tourism, both internationally and domestically, will inevitably continue. The resulting dynamism produced in destination areas from these political changes will cause them to move in unexpected directions at unanticipated rates and continue to affect their progress through their life cycles.

References

Benthien, B. (2000) Tourism in Germany ten years after Reunification – Problems and results of transformation. In A. Mayr and W. Taubman (eds) *Germany Ten Years after Reunification*. Leipzig: Institute für Länderkunde.

Berlin Tourismus & Kongress GmbH (2023) Berlin hosts the world: Facts and figures. Visit Berlin website https://about.visitberlin.de/en/current-figures.

Butler, R. and Suntikul, W. (2010) *Tourism and Political Change*. Woodeaton: Goodfellow Publishers.

Butler, R. and Suntikul, W. (2017) *Tourism and Political Change* (2nd edn). Woodeaton: Goodfellow Publishers.

Chan, S.S. (2000) *The Macau Economy*. Macau: Publications Centre, University of Macau.

Fingar, C. (2022) 'We're planning now for the recovery': In conversation with Ukraine's Tourism Minister Mariana Oleskiv. Investment Monitor website https://www.investmentmonitor.ai/interviews/ukraine-tourism-minister-mariana-oleskiv-investment-recovery.

Foucault, M. (1971) *The Order of Things*. New York: Vintage Books.

Fraser, N. (2015) Junket operators look beyond Macau to sidestep Beijing's crackdown. *South China Morning Post*. https://www.scmp.com/news/china/policies-politics/article/1813110/junket-operators-look-beyond-macau-sidestep-beijings?module=perpetual_scroll_0&pgtype=article&campaign=1813110.

Godau, A. (1991) Tourism policy in the new Germany. *Tourism Management* 12 (2),145–149.

Hamdi, R. (2021) Casinos made Macau one of the wealthiest places in the world – but they also brought heightened inequality and crime. Now China is cracking down. Insider website https://www.businessinsider.com/macau-gambling-beijing-cracks-down-future-in-question-casinos-2021-11.

Hill, R. (1993) Tourism in Germany. In W. Pompl and P. Lavery (eds) *Tourism in Europe: Structures and Developments* (pp. 219–241). Wallingford: CAB International.

Kiptenko, V., Lyubitseva, O., Malska, M., Rutynskiy, M., Zan'ko, Y. and Zinko, J. (2017) Geography of tourism of Ukraine. In K. Widawski and J. Wyrzykowski (eds) *The Geography of Tourism of Central and Eastern European Countries* (pp. 509–551). Cham: Springer International.

Lagiewski, R.M. (2006) The application of the TALC model: A literature survey. In R. Butler (ed.) *The Tourism Area Life Cycle, Volume 1: Applications and Modifications* (pp. 27–50). Clevedon: Channel View Publications.

Lei, W.S., Suntikul, W. and Chen, Z. (2023) Tourism development induced social change. *Annals of Tourism Research: Empirical Insights* 4 (1).

Marusyak, B. (2021) Occupied tourism: How have tourist numbers in Crimea changed? Promote Ukraine website https://www.promoteukraine.org/occupied-tourism-how-have-tourist-numbers-in-crimea-changed.

McCartney, G. (2010) Stanley Ho Hung-sun: The 'King of Gambling'. In R. Butler and R. Russell (eds) *Giants of Tourism* (pp. 170–181). Wallingford: CABI.

Nicolova, M. (2022) How Russia's war on Ukraine impacts travel and tourism. Emerging Europe website https://emerging-europe.com/news/how-russias-war-on-ukraine-impacts-travel-and-tourism.

Plog, S.C. (1973) Why destination areas rise and fall in popularity. *Cornell Hotel and Restaurant Association Quarterly* 13, 6–13.

Shehadi, S. and Fingar, C. (2022) Support Ukraine by visiting us: The rebuilding of Ukraine's tourism industry is already under way. Investment Monitor website https://www.investmentmonitor.ai/interviews/rebuilding-ukraines-tourism-industry-under-way.

Simpson, T. (2021) Interiorized urbanism in Macau: Model city for post-Mao China. In M. Mitrašinović and T. Jachna (eds) *The Emerging Public Realm of the Greater Bay Area: Approaches to Public Space in a Chinese Megaregion* (pp. 98–108). London: Routledge.

Tanner, D.A. (2021) Tourism in Crimea: Record number of guests. Tourism Review News website https://www.tourism-review.com/tourism-in-crimea-reports-huge-success-news12203.

Tomczewska-Popowycz, N. and Quirini-Popławski, Ł. (2021) Political instability equals the collapse of tourism in Ukraine? *Sustainability* 13, 4126.

Westerman, A. (2022) With Ukraine at War, Officials Hope to Bring Tourism Back to Areas Away from Fighting. NPR (National Public Radio) website https://www.npr.org/2022/10/01/1125495184/ukraine-russia-war-economy-tourism

World Bank (2021a) GDP per capita (constant 2015 US$) – Macao SAR, China. World Bank website https://data.worldbank.org/indicator/NY.GDP.PCAP.KD?locations=MO.

World Bank (2021b) GDP per capita (current US$) – China. World Bank website https://data.worldbank.org/indicator/NY.GDP.PCAP.CD?locations=CN.

World Bank (2021c) GDP per capita (constant 2015 US$) – United States. World Bank website https://data.worldbank.org/indicator/NY.GDP.PCAP.CD?locations=US.

World Bank (2023) International tourism, number of arrivals – Ukraine. World Bank website https://data.worldbank.org/indicator/ST.INT.ARVL?locations=UA.

World Economic Forum (2015) *Growth Through Shocks*. Travel and Tourism Competitiveness Report 2015. Geneva: World Economic Forum.

SwitzerlandWorlddata.info (n.d.) Tourism in Macao. World Data website https://www.worlddata.info/asia/macao/tourism.php.

Xinhua News (2004) Anniversary of individual visit scheme highlights market success in Macao. Gale Business website https://go-gale-com.uc.idm.oclc.org/ps/i.do?p=GBIB&u=ucinc_main&id=GALE%7CA119859778&v=2.1&it=r&sid=summon&aty=ip.

17 The TALC: Relevance 40 Years On

Richard Butler

The focus in this chapter is on whether the TALC model and its key elements (as discussed earlier) have relevance some four decades after their appearance. The easy answer to such a question might be to list the number of citations of the model and the number of examples of its application in a wide range of settings, as shown by the review of literature by Gore *et al*. in Chapter 3 of this volume. While such metrics generally are of dubious value in this writer's opinion, along with H factors and other measures so attractive (and unfortunately often essential) to modern researchers and journals striving to prove their worth, they do suggest there is continued interest and use of the model by researchers in the present day. This chapter will review the key elements of the model and suggest whether they are still meaningful in the context of current research. The question of whether the model is relevant, indeed, whether it has ever been relevant in the applied 'real' world beyond academia, is not discussed in this chapter, as it has been commented on elsewhere in this volume, particularly Chapter 8, by Haywood.

Perhaps the strongest support for the ongoing relevance of the TALC model is the continuing dynamics in tourism, as shown by the continuous appearance of new tourist areas (in the widest sense of the term) and new tourist destinations (in the more specific context). Over the four decades since the publication of the original model, new tourist destinations include parts of China, of Brazil, of the extreme south of Argentina and Chile, southern Pacific islands and even Antarctica. These have begun to attract what seem to be ever increasing numbers of visitors, many by cruise ship. Almost all international travellers to such new destinations are tied to air travel to reach such locations or the starting point for cruises thereto. Interventions such as World Heritage Site designation and similar distinctions such as National Parks, Wildlife Reserves, Game Parks and National Historic Sites, as well as deliberately created facilities, including winter sports venues, annual cultural and sporting events, and dark tourism sites, have all acted as triggers for the identification and subsequent promotion of locations as tourist attractions and destinations.

How and why such places emerge as tourist sites, what their growth pattern is, what agencies are involved, how they are marketed and promoted, and by whom, and the impacts that new or increased tourism creates or accentuates, are all worthy of study, and the TALC provides one framework or model on which such studies can be based. Given the large number of case studies of destinations that have used the TALC in such a way, there are comparisons and contrasts that can be drawn between new destinations to determine if a common pattern of development and growth is being followed. For those destinations in which that is not the case, such aberrations justify further study, either to adjust the TALC model or to identify alternative development pathways that might be being followed or that are likely to emerge. It is relevant in that context to note the more recent interest in development pathways, as illustrated in papers in the special issue of *Tourism Geographies* (16 (4)) in 2014, several of which deal with path dependency and tourism area development and reference the TALC model (Gill & Williams; Sanz-Ibáñez & Clavé; Ma & Hassink). This emerging interest in an evolutionary approach to development is discussed in Chapter 23 of the present volume.

If the TALC is to have continued relevance, one would expect that it would be meaningful and useful in the context of at least some of the current issues in tourism, which are the foci of the following discussion.

Overtourism

The issue of most direct relevance to an increasing number of destinations at the current time is that of overtourism (Dodds & Butler, 2019; Milano *et al.*, 2019; Mihalič, 2020), a relatively recently coined term (Ali, 2016) but an issue which has bedevilled tourist destinations for centuries (Koens *et al.*, 2018). It would be inappropriate to ignore the long history of tourism in its many forms (pilgrimage, economic ventures, romantic voyages, dark or memorial visits and purely hedonistic pursuits) and the correspondingly long list of issues and problems faced by both visiting and visited populations. Complaints of the 'wrong type' of and too many tourists certainly date back to at least the 19th century, when arguments against the then increasing popularity of Venice were voiced by the art critic John Ruskin (see Ruskin, 1980). More recently, the oft-cited Irridex of Doxey (1975) demonstrates that the opposition of local residents to increasing numbers of visiting tourists is not limited to contemporary complaints by residents in Barcelona, Venice, Dubrovnik and Edinburgh against cruise ships and sheer numbers of visitors these places are now experiencing (Dodds & Butler, 2019).

The term 'overtourism' did not exist in 1980, but it was clearly anticipated by the importance given in the TALC model to carrying capacity and potential limits to development in destinations. While the social implications of development, and particularly overdevelopment, had already been discussed (Butler, 1974), in the original TALC paper more focus was given to the carrying capacity of services and facilities, along with environmental issues, than the impacts on local residents, although this was clearly an issue anticipated to become a problem. That point has gained increasing relevance with the growing number of protests and opposition to current and particularly further tourism developments in some destinations. Tourism brings with it many related problems, rarely deliberately and often unanticipated, but in recent years there have been calls for a more critical turn in tourism studies (Tribe, 2008), as seen in arguments to change the way in which success is perceived by destinations (see, for example, Dwyer, 2023).

Limits

The emergence of overtourism in the public and academic minds in recent years, notwithstanding the subject being totally dismissed during the COVID pandemic, is inevitably and inexorably related to the topic of limits on numbers of visitors and carrying capacity. Ways of measuring capacity and defining what are too many visitors is discussed elsewhere in this volume, but it is clear that some destinations are facing real problems in terms of two elements: numbers and types of visitors. The latter was barely discussed, although was perhaps implicit, in the 1980 paper; the former was, as noted above, central to the idea of appropriate management of tourism. The relevance of overtourism remains high, despite the fact that over the past half century or so the notion has faced constant criticism and calls for rejection of the concept in the context of tourism (United Nations World Tourism Organization, 2018). Some of the powerful proponents of tourism, such as the World Tourism Organization, have consistently denied the issue of overtourism or excessive numbers of tourists and, with that denial, challenged the concept of defining limits to tourist numbers, either globally or at specific destinations. The arguments proposed for such a viewpoint are generally based on suggesting it is not absolute visitor numbers that are the problem but their distribution (spatially and temporally). The rejection of carrying capacity was initially based on the idea that it was not feasible to produce figures on how many visitors were too many for a site, and then criticism moved more correctly to arguing that the same approach did not fit easily in a tourist setting because of the vast range of differences in characteristics and behaviour within a typical destination's population of visitors, and in particular the level of tolerance of crowding (e.g. McCool & Lime, 2001).

While the argument presented in the 1980 paper was that there was a 'critical range of elements of capacity', shown on the original model, the implication drawn, incorrectly, tended to be that one figure could be used to represent the carrying capacity of a destination, akin to the maximum number of tourists that should visit the location at any one time. This is unrealistic given the heterogeneity of both destinations and visitors, and also because of the dynamics of both elements, which mean any measure would quickly become out of date. This point was made in the original paper, which discussed '*levels* of carrying capacity' (Butler, 1980: 7, emphasis added) and it went on to note:

> These [levels] may be identified in terms of environmental factors (e.g. land scarcity, water quality, air quality), of physical plant (e.g. transportation, accommodation, other services), or of social factors (e.g. crowding, resentment by the local population).

The paper concluded (reflecting again on the importance of setting limits to numbers) that carrying capacity involved more than one factor:

> Tourist attractions are not infinite and timeless but should be viewed and treated as finite and possibly non-renewable resources. They could then be more carefully protected and preserved. *The development of the tourist area could be kept within predetermined capacity limits, and its potential competitiveness maintained over a longer period.* (Butler, 1980: 11, emphasis added)

As noted above, the relevance of limits to numbers has become an issue of concern in an increasing number of destinations because overall tourism numbers had increased annually until the outbreak of the COVID pandemic in 2019. While arguing about the possibility of establishing a single figure to represent the maximum number of tourists that should visit a destination at any point in time is pointless and even counter-productive, and no longer relevant given what is known about changes in resident attitudes, technological change and changes in visitor preferences, it can be argued strongly that it would be more relevant for destinations to examine the unavoidable problems arising where capacity has clearly been, or is about to be, reached. These may be simple, such as car parking spaces, a problem which can be overcome by the physical development of further infrastructure, or much more complex, such as where residents or tourists have expressed opposition to current, let alone greater, numbers of visitors on the basis of their personal levels of tolerance of crowding.

Alleviating pressure on one or more such elements may well prove successful in resolving problems in other areas. The problem of limits reflects the dynamic nature of many, if not all, of the elements involved, and the question of how many tourists are appropriate is as relevant today, if not more so, as when the original paper was presented.

Patterns of Development

The life cycle model, on which the TALC was based, remains of mixed value. In the business and management literature there is little doubt, from the large number of case studies, that many destinations have followed such a growth pathway during their development, and that this pattern appears likely to continue. One element which is less relevant, or perhaps misleading, is the assumption that there is only one life cycle for tourist destinations. That assumption is the result of the necessity when creating models to oversimplify reality and to reduce a wide range of complex issues and forces to a single, usually simple, characterisation. The pattern or course of development is still relevant as it allows researchers to compare specific cases against a generalised norm, and to identify different patterns of growth and development which may have implications for the economic well-being of the destination, as well as being meaningful for other impacts that location may experience. It is likely, however, that, as McKercher and Wong discuss in this volume (Chapter 22) and elsewhere (McKercher & Wong, 2021), many destinations have more than one life cycle operating at any point in time, and thus the single curve shown in the 1980 article can be argued to be, if not irrelevant, perhaps misleading. This point is discussed in Part 3 of this volume in terms of revisions to the model, but that does not deny the relevance of modelling the development process of destinations, particularly in order to identify the forces at work that shape that pattern.

Management

To discuss the management of tourism and tourism destinations implies, if not demands, that there be agencies with such a responsibility and ability, and also suggests that it is possible to think of tourism as an entity. Those assumptions are very wide of the mark. Many of the problems faced by tourism and by destinations relate to the absence of these characteristics; thus, the part of the title of the 1980 article that reads 'implications for management of resources' is perhaps more relevant than at any other time since 1980. Dredge (2016) noted the oxymoronic title of destination management organisation (DMO), a type of organisa-tion that is found in many tourism communities, as such organisations are most often promotion and marketing bodies, and can do little to manage tourism or tourists, even if they feel that to be part of their mandate. Tourism management is most effectively practised where there is a single entity with responsibility for that role, and such a situation rarely exists in tourist destinations, where there are generally large numbers of individual enterprises most often in competition for business (tourists) and unlikely to agree to actions that might impinge or limit their own ability to do as they wish to increase or maximise their return on investment. Destina-tion communities are rarely homogeneous in terms of their outlook, for example, on growth or limitation, preservation or conservation, develop-ment or protection, and fewer or more services and facilities, so unanimity over development pathways is unlikely, and even where agreement can be found, circumstances are likely to change and affect intents (Gill & Williams, 2011). Furthermore, tourism itself is not homogeneous – the difficulties of identifying one carrying capacity figure demonstrates that clearly – and thus talking of managing tourism really means managing many forms of tourism at different scales and with different impacts.

Thus, the implications for management of resources and communities are still highly relevant and in most cases increasing in importance as tourism continues to grow, particularly in the rapid recovery phase after the COVID pandemic. Far greater attention needs to be paid to determining how management can become effective and how intended plans and appropriate controls can actually be implemented. It has long been argued (Dodds & Butler, 2010) that it is the non-implementation of appropriate measures that has resulted in the almost total failure to develop truly 'sustainable tourism'. The result has been that the term has become another oxymoron in the tourism literature. To achieve any significant move towards sustainability, management is not only relevant but crucial, and thus examination and scrutiny of how or whether there has been management in tourist destinations is more relevant than ever.

Spatial Elements

One can argue that the spatial elements of the TALC are less important than those of carrying capacity and management, but in terms of the relevance of the model for looking to the future of specific destinations, they remain significant. While the TALC was not created with the idea of being a predictive model, in response to a question raised when the paper was first presented, it was noted that the model could be used in a predictive manner. That response was meant to suggest not a quantitative application to predict exact numbers of visitors but, rather, to anticipate the overall pattern and process of development. Others (Berry, 2006; Manente & Pechlaner, 2006) have shown that, in fact, the model can be used in a predictive manner, for example by illustrating potential movement from one stage of development to another. It should be possible also to look forward in a broader context to the spatial spread of tourism around and related to destinations and thus the anticipated regional growth and development of tourism. This would need to include detailed information on future developments beyond a specific destination, such as transportation services, resource availability (such as land and water) and, particularly, resident attitudes towards tourism growth.

Several models of the different spatial patterns of tourism development have been discussed in the tourism literature (see Pearce, 1995) and it is clear that much depends on the geography of the area under consideration. The distribution of attractions such as beaches, of features such as rivers and mountains (which can be both attractions and obstacles), micro-climates, shoreline characteristics, seasonality and distance from markets all greatly influence the nature and scale of development, as well as the precise location. The situation is also complicated by the need to take into account issues such as land ownership, Indigenous rights and views for or against development (Butler & Carr, 2024). Thus, consideration of spatial factors remains important, and increases as the level of accessibility to previously unvisited or sparsely visited areas increases through transportation developments that also influence the likely future spatial pattern of development.

Forces of Change

As was noted earlier, forces of change, or triggers, do not specifically feature in the TALC model and that is clearly an oversight and is addressed by Bolan and Boyd (Chapter 15), Gale (Chapter 11), Jarratt (Chapter 12), Keller (Chapter 10), Peters and Schönherr (Chapter 20) and Suntikul (Chapter 16). These forces remain highly relevant, however, because to understand the pattern and process of development of destinations it is essential to identify and understand the forces that have brought about and shaped that pattern, in other words, what has triggered the changes experienced in the destinations being examined. Simply commenting on changes, in scale, in character, in timing and in demands and pressures exerted by visitors, without identifying the causes of those changes, is interesting but hardly helpful to understanding the process of tourism destination development.

The absence of discussion of triggers in the model may be one factor which explains its recognition but limited application beyond academia (Haywood, in Chapter 8 of this volume). Merely describing a pattern is not of great value if it is not explained and followed by a discussion of what actions might be implemented as a result. Any examination of change requires at least some consideration of how and why such changes have come about, for example whether they are the result of the intervention of entrepreneurs (Russel & Faulkner, 1999; Peters & Schönherr in Chapter 20 of this volume), of actions by local or other political players, of external forces, or even by chance. It is vital not only to identify the agents or triggers of change, but also to clarify the linkages and relationships between them, both in the destinations themselves and further afield, for, as Weaver and Oppermann (2000) demonstrated, external agents can be as, or even more, important than internal forces in shaping a pattern or process of development at the local scale. Short-term local triggers, such as local elections and changes in political direction – as recorded by Martin (2006) and Dodds (2007) – illustrate how local policies can easily be revoked when political forces combine to change something they oppose. Similarly, changes of policy at the national or international level can also serve to override local policies and wishes to fit a desired bigger picture (Suntikul, Chapter 16 of this volume), a situation many Indigenous communities have become familiar with when their traditional priorities and ways of operating become changed to fit external preferences (Butler & Carr, 2024). Whether such triggers can be anticipated, forestalled or modified will depend on circumstances, and possibly on the stage of the development cycle a particular destination is in, again suggesting that adding such an element as triggers to the TALC model would increase its relevance and potential use.

Conclusion

Whether the TALC model, in its entirety, or perhaps some specific elements of it, is relevant four decades after publication is a question better answered by others, and some of the contributors to this volume have done so. This chapter can perhaps be best concluded by noting that the frequent (more than weekly) citation of the original paper, mostly positively, in the context of its application or its use in supporting a point suggests that it is seen as still being relevant to many researchers today. Rather to my surprise, the TALC model now features in high-school teaching on tourism in Britain and elsewhere. The surprise is twofold: first, that tourism has finally been recognised as something important enough to take its place in school-level education; and second, that the TALC model was included in the relevant literature. It is considered to be a suitable model to use in education about tourism (Butler, 2021) as it encompasses many key elements that should be included in that subject area, in particular the way we can learn from the past, what forces bring about change and innovation, what broad societal changes influence development, how development impacts places and people, and what might we learn about future trends and implications.

A good example of this is provided on a website (www.coolgeography. co.uk) that includes an interesting example of the TALC model, using the major English tourist resort of Blackpool (www.coolgeograhy.co.uk/GCSE/AQA/Tourism/Lifecycle). Figure 17.1 plots the number of tourists against time from 1800 to 2000, and also shows the population of the town, various forces that have acted on tourism to Blackpool and periods of decline and rejuvenation. The graph is not dissimilar to parts of that of Figure 21.2 (Boyd & Bolan, this volume). Blackpool makes an excellent case study, as it reveals many of the elements of destination development discussed by the contributors to this volume, and particularly because it is currently experiencing a second period of growth, despite suffering from a bad press and particularly its fall in social status discussed by Jarratt in Chapter 12 of this volume, whereby it is seen as a low-class destination and inappropriately pictured as the worst case of British resort decline. Haslam (2023) notes that Blackpool, despite such a negative image, received almost 19 million visitors in 2021, making it the largest resort in terms of visitation in the UK, and on a par with Venice and other much

Tourist visits to Blackpool between 1800 and 2010

In 19th Century rich people went to Blackpool to visit its 7 mile beach.

During interwar years (1918-1939)Blackpool was recognised as one of Europe's leading coastal resorts, helped by a new law giving workers holidays with pay

After the Second World War from 1960 onwards Blackpool began to stagnate & then decline because of package holidays, cheap air transport and better climate (e.g. the Mediterranean)

£300million rejuvenation project launched in 2000

In 1870s workers were given annual holidays.

The Tower opened 1894.

South Shore's Fairground 1904 - advertised as the Pleasure Beach 1905.

Central Pier opened 1868.

Blackpool has run-down areas and is mainly popular with stag and hen parties.

In 1846 the railway was built, cutting the costs and time. It became cheaper to travel so many working class visitors began coming to Blackpool every weekend.

The practice of sea bathing to cure diseases was becoming fashionable among the wealthier classes who began making the trek to Blackpool for that purpose

1. Exploration

2. Involvement

3. Development

4. Consolidation

5. Stagnation

Decline

Rejuvenation

ESTIMATES

Number of tourist visitors (millions)

20 18 16 14 12 10 8 6 4 2 0

Date

1800   1850   1900   1950   2000

Blackpool's Population	473	2,500	14,000	47,000	47,000	147,000	142,284	142,064

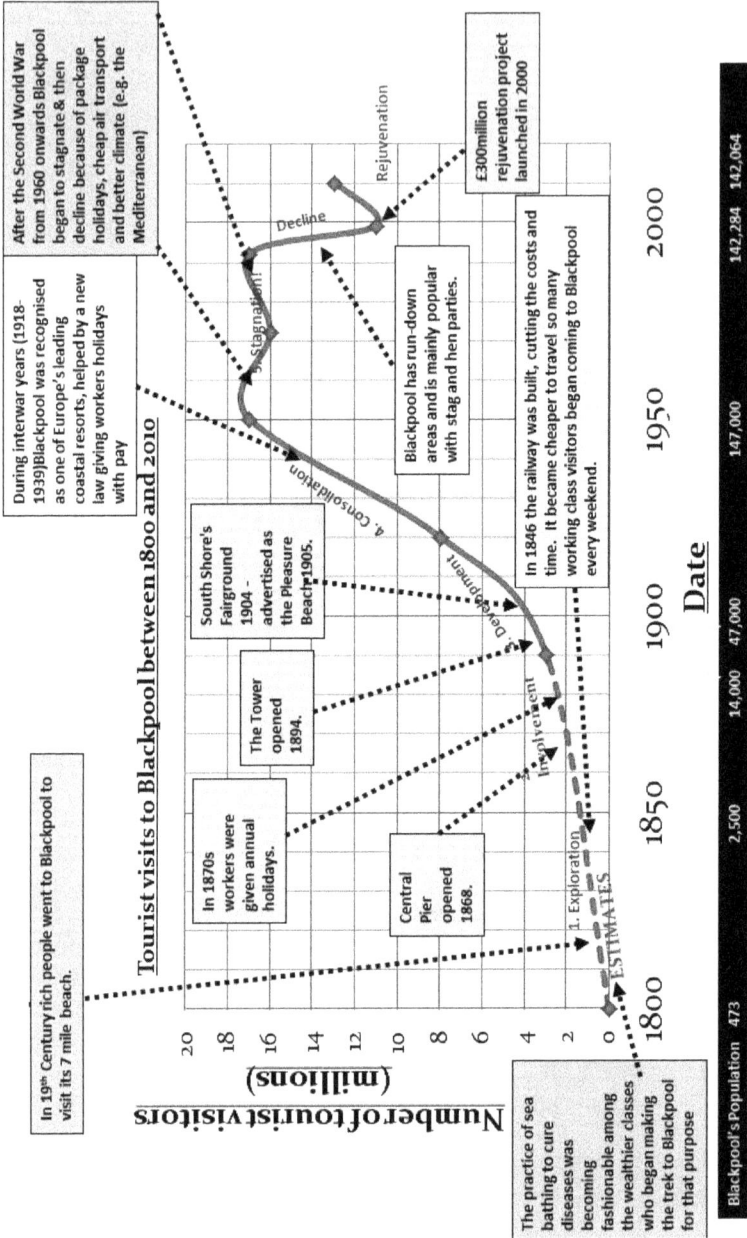

Figure 17.1 Blackpool's tourist history applied to the Butler model

more highly regarded tourist magnets. It has certainly undergone decline. In 1911 its railway station was the busiest in the world (Haslam, 2022: 2) and its population peaked at 147,000 in 1910 but was down to 142,000 in 2001 – though that is much less of a decline than that of Venice (Visentin & Bertocchi, 2019). Interestingly, in the British media to date, there do not appear to have been any records of complaints about overtourism in Blackpool, perhaps a reflection of the social class issue and perhaps because Blackpool is not pretending to be anything other than a tourist destination. It is, of course, a destination catering almost entirely for UK domestic tourists, a feature in common with many UK coastal tourist communities. Such a position, perhaps, may stand it in good stead in recovering from COVID-19, as it suffered less than many other resorts, especially those dependent on foreign visitors, some of whom at least faced problems of quarantine on arrival in a host foreign country and again on returning to their home country. Future illustrations of the TALC applied to Blackpool in the post-COVID-19 era could reveal whether such an argument has any validity, and may be taken as further evidence of its continued relevance and potential value.

It would be absurd to ignore the criticisms of the model, both the more valid ones actually based on what was written in the model, and others which resemble the 'almost one in ten … [that] are mis-citations or un-warranted assertions' that were discussed by Wang *et al.* (2016). Some of these issues and criticisms are discussed in Part 3 of the book in terms of revisions to the original model. That discussion and subsequent changes may make the model more relevant in the future after it has been adjusted to take into account the massive amount of research carried out in tourism in the four decades since its publication, particularly that relating to evo-lutionary economic geography and other aspects of product development and evolution in a sustainable context (Brouder, 2017).

How we, as researchers, select topics, look at specific things and places, make judgements and reach conclusions very much reflects the times we are operating in. There can be little argument that the TALC was a product both of its period of intellectual development (the late 1960s and 1970s) and my own experiences and mind-set. If no such article had appeared in 1980, writing an article on the development of tourist destinations today would almost certainly produce a different type of paper, in terms of both approach and content. It would inevitably contain empirical data and probably complex statistical analysis to support its basic argument(s). It is unlikely that it would present the same discussion and model and it might or might not prove as resilient, and possibly as relevant, as the TALC. Such is the nature of academic research; relevance is sometimes less important than the intellectual arguments which result from publication, and perhaps in that context at least the TALC has made a contribution that is still useful.

References

Ali, R. (2016) Exploring the coming perils of overtourism. Skift.com.

Berry, T. (2006) The predictive potential of the TALC model. In R. Butler (ed.) *The Tourism Area Life Cycle, Volume 2: Conceptual and Theoretical Issues* (pp. 253–279). Clevedon: Channel View Publications.

Brouder, P. (2017) Evolutionary economic geography: Reflections from a sustainable tourism perspective *Tourism Geographies* 19 (3), 438–447.

Butler, R. (1974) The social implications of tourist development. *Annals of Tourism Research* 2 (2), 100–111.

Butler, R. (2021) Overtourism, education and the tourism area life cycle mode. In H. Séraphin and A.C. Yallop (eds) *Overtourism and Tourism Education Strategies for Sustainable tourism Futures* (pp. 7–23). London: Routledge.

Butler, R. and Carr, A. (2024) *A Handbook of Indigenous Tourism*. London: Routledge.

Dodds, R. (2007) Sustainable tourism and policy implementation: Lessons from the case of Calvia, Spain. *Current Issues in Tourism* 10 (1), 296–322.

Dodds, R. and Butler, R. (2010) Barriers to implementing sustainable tourism policy in mass tourism destinations. *Tourismos* 5 (1), 35–52.

Dodds, R. and Butler, R. (2019) *Overtourism: Issues, Realities and Solutions*. Berlin: De Gruyter.

Doxey, G.V. (1975) A causation theory of visitor–resident irritants: methodology and research inferences. In *Proceedings of the Travel Research Association 6th Annual Conference* (pp. 195–198). San Diego: Travel Research Association.

Dredge, D. (2016) Are DMOs on a path to redundancy? *Tourism Recreation Research* 41 (3), 348–353.

Dwyer, L. (2023) Tourism development to enhance resident well-being: A strong sustainability perspective. *Sustainability* 15, 3321. https://doi.org/10.3390/ su15043321.

Gill, A. and Williams, P. (2011) Rethinking resort growth: Understanding evolving governance strategies in Whistler, British Columbia. *Journal of Sustainable Tourism* 19 (4–5), 629–648.

Gill, A. and Williams, P. (2014) Mindful deviation in creating a governance path towards sustainability in resort destinations. *Tourism Geographies* 16 (4), 546–562.

Haslam, C. (2023) Blackpool's unlikely bounce back – and why you'll want to go this summer. *The Times*, 22 September 22. https://www.thetimes.co.uk/article/the-surprising-seaside-star-in-the-best-value-holiday-stakes-w2wmzxz3p, accessed 23 September 2023.

Koens, K., Postma, A. and Papp, B. (2018) Is overtourism overused? Understanding the impact of tourism in a city context. *Sustainability* 10 (12), 4384. https://doi.org/10.3390/su10124384.

Ma, M. and Hassink, R. (2014) Path dependences and tourism area development: The case of Guilin, China. *Tourism Geographies* 16 (4), 580–597.

Manente, M. and Pechlaner, H. (2006) How to define, identify and monitor the decline of tourist destinations: Towards an early warning system. In R. Butler (ed.) *The Tourism Area Life Cycle, Volume 2: Conceptual and Theoretical Issues* (pp. 235–253). Clevedon: Channel View Publications.

Martin, B. (2006) The TALC model and politics. In R. Butler (ed.) *The Tourism Area Life Cycle, Volume 1: Applications and Modifications* (pp. 222–236). Clevedon: Channel View Publications.

McCool, S. and Lime, D. (2001) Tourism carrying capacity: Tempting fantasy or useful reality? *Journal of Sustainable Tourism* 9 (5), 372–388.

McKercher, B. and Wong, I.K.A. (2021) Do destinations have multiple life cycles? *Tourism Management* 82, 104232.

Mihalič, T. (2020) Conceptualising overtourism: A sustainability approach. *Annals of Tourism Research* 84, 103025.

Milano, C., Cheer, J.M. and Novelli, M. (2019) *Overtourism: Excesses, Discontents and Measures in Travel and Tourism*. Wallingford: CABI

Pearce, D.G. (1995) *Tourism Today: A Geographical Analysis*. Harlow: Longman.

Ruskin, J. (1980) *The Stones of Venice, Volume 2*. Chicago: Wiley.

Russel, R. and Faulkner, B. (1999) Movers and shakers: Chaos makers in tourism development. *Tourism Management* 20 (4), 411–423.

Sanz-Ibáñez, C. and Clavé, S.A. (2014) The evolution of destinations: Towards an evolutionary and relational economic geography approach. *Tourism Geographies* 16 (4), 563–579.

Tribe, J. (2008) Tourism: A critical business. *Journal of Travel Research* 46 (3), 245–255.

Wang, X., Weaver, D.B., Xiang, L. and Zhang, Y. (2016) In Butler (1980) we trust? Typology of citer motivations. *Annals of Tourism Research* 21, 216–218.

Weaver, D.B. and Oppermann, M. (2000) *Tourism Management*. Melbourne: Wiley.

Visentin, F. and Bertocchi, D. (2019) Venice: An analysis of tourism excesses in an overtourism icon. In C. Milano, J.M. Cheer and M. Novelli (eds) *Overtourism Excesses: Discontents and Measures in Travel and Tourism* (pp. 18–38). Wallingford: CABI.

United Nations World Tourism Organization (2018) *'Overtourism'? Understanding and Managing Urban Tourism Growth Beyond Perceptions*. Madrid: UNWTO.

Part 3

Revision

Part 3 of the book looks to the future, in the sense of identifying and discussing revisions and additions that could or should be made to the TALC model, and its more general role and place in destination development. It begins (Chapter 18) with Eggli's argument that there is a need to revise the conceptual approach of the TALC by discussing more than tourist numbers and impacts and broadening the model to focus on interactions between all people in a destination. In a similar manner, Séraphin *et al.* (Chapter 19) argue for the need to reframe the TALC model, along with academics' approach to tourism in general, to include specific consideration of future generations, namely children, and how their tourism activities, desires and needs relate to the TALC.

Peters and Schönherr (Chapter 20) examine the role of entrepreneurs in different stages of the TALC, explaining how this group of stakeholders become agents of development and how their role and significance vary through the different stages as they act as triggers to change, from exploration to rejuvenation and decline. Boyd and Bolan (Chapter 21) use the tortuous example of Northern Ireland to illustrate how many of the elements of the TALC combine in the context of rises, falls and rises following conventional development, political crises, conflict and COVID-19, resulting in a wave-like cycle of development and decline and redevelopment. The pattern and number of life cycles in a destination are discussed by McKercher and Wong (Chapter 22), who use previous research to argue for there being more than one form of life cycle for destinations, including one similar to that suggested by Boyd and Bolan.

The concluding chapter summarises the suggestions for and criticisms of the TALC made over the past 40 years, and notes how the changed context for tourism makes the model's simplicity vulnerable, as change has shifted from being mostly evolutionary towards being increasingly revolutionary (i.e. at a much faster rate). Despite this, my overall conclusion is that there is still value in the model, albeit in a modified and expanded form. The volume concludes with the presentation and discussion of a modified TALC figure that is more accurate, if perhaps less elegant, in illustrating the general pattern of tourism destination development.

18 The Need to Revise the Conceptual Approach of the TALC Model

Florian Eggli

The discussion on overtourism, which was predominant in the pre-COVID era, as well as the sudden cessation of tourism due to the pandemic, were respectively triggered by either excessive or insufficient visitor numbers. This quantitative line of argument underpins the narrative of either *too many* or *too few* tourists and stems from the conceptual thinking of the Tourism Area Life Cycle (Butler, 1980), which takes the element of 'visitor numbers' as the decisive factor in assessing the different stages of tourism development. This is certainly not wrong but, as this chapter argues, 'visitor numbers' is only one of many factors counting towards the condition of a destination. This chapter suggests that *people, practices* and *place* also need to be considered in assessing the current state of a tourism destination.

The chapter presents a new approach to the basic concept of the TALC in three distinctive ways. First, it argues that the binary view of tourists on one side and residents on the other falls short in adequately capturing the often confused and confusing maze of people mingling in a tourist place. Second, the chapter argues that it is not only the number of tourists which is decisive in capturing the carrying capacity of the place but also the practices of the inhabitants. Their distinct forms and characteristics of 'practising space' must also be considered when discussing the upper limits of a place. Finally, it is argued that a place has different facets and fragments, which all differ in their respective maturation phase, with distinct phases taking place simultaneously in time and space and performed in parallel by different actors in different situations, constantly producing the tourist place. The distinct phases a place is made up of are all interwoven with each other, which makes it hard to define a tipping point for a destination as such.

The chapter therefore concludes that the discussion on tourism development should go beyond the concept of carrying capacity. There is not a clear threshold which determines decline or rejuvenation. It is a constant maze of people, an ongoing entanglement of practices which

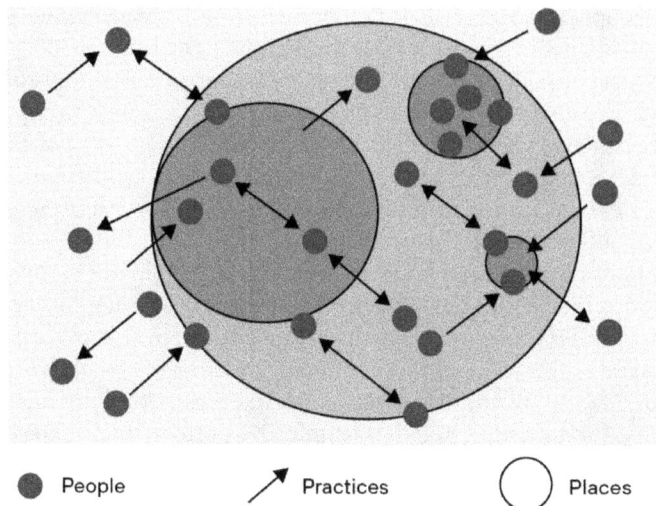

Figure 18.1 Conceptualisation of place as practised by people (Eggli, 2021: 45)

steadily shapes the places and thus determines how tourism is dealt with. Therefore, the conceptualisation proposed in this chapter goes beyond measuring the number of visitors at a certain time and in a certain location to draw conclusions about the carrying capacity of a tourism destination. It argues, moreover, that, in addition to a consideration of visitor numbers, searching questions need to be asked about what kind of *people* are visiting, inhabiting and sharing the place, how these people *practise* their life-worlds and what kind of *place* unfolds out of the co-creation of these manifold practices (Figure 18.1).

Such additional information leads to a more nuanced and differentiated view of what is going on in a tourist destination. With such qualitative considerations, more adequate measures to govern tourism places can be developed. Such measures mostly go beyond what currently is applied by city governments, local authorities and destination management organisations (DMOs) (UNWTO, 2018, 2019). Prevailing measures, for example, include diverting tourism flows towards unexploited areas, imposing visitor caps at peak times and prolonging tourism exploitation in former resting (off-season) periods. Within this chapter an approach will be developed which goes beyond such quantitatively informed measures. Instead of focusing on the numerical carrying capacity of a place, ideas are developed about how 'living with tourism' can become a more mutually beneficial and enriching experience.

The presented insights in this chapter were developed in a PhD thesis called 'Living with tourism in Lucerne' (Eggli, 2021), for which more than 80 people were interviewed in city strolls in Lucerne, Switzerland, in 2019/2020. This mobile method (Büscher *et al.*, 2011; Urry, 2007) enabled the gathering of many subjective perspectives along the way and combining them into a holistic view. These strolling interviews were accompanied by a picture camera, serving to visualise an urban ethnography of the place. Furthermore, many artefacts were gathered, assembled and included in the empirical data, which led to an overall comprehension of how a place deals with all the different aspects of tourism.

The findings presented in the PhD thesis are condensed in this chapter. It concludes that it is a *with-tourism scenario* (or at least *a-not-possible-without-tourism scenario*) which determines how a tourist place performs, rather than (as the dominant discourse suggests) an *over- or undertourism scenario*. The following three sections develop this thinking and provide a rationale for a more engaged, dynamic and performative conceptualisation of the way tourism destinations develop.

People: It Is About All Kinds of Different People Inhabiting a Place

Early studies on overtourism, such as a McKinsey & Company report commissioned by the World Travel and Tourism Council (WTTC) in 2017, identified *tourism density* (the number of tourists per square kilometre) and *tourism intensity* (the number of visitors per resident) as key metrics to assess the alienation of local residents. These quantitative metrics are both openly accessible and easily comparable from destination to destination. But on the downside, these numbers do not reveal much about the qualitative nature of people visiting the place. While such figures provide statistical evidence of the number of people entering a destination and the local population, they do not indicate anything about who is engaging with the place. Furthermore, the binary view of hosts on the one hand and guests on the other is an oversimplification of reality, which needs to be overcome for a better understanding of what is going on in a tourism destination. By opening-up consideration of various different actors, projects and mobilities this duality can be surmounted, and a more nuanced view of tourism can be established.

Actors at tourism destinations are becoming increasingly diverse, changeable and multifaceted. Tourist places now tend to be inhabited by different sorts of people sourced from varied backgrounds, mingling with all kinds of interests and agendas. Sheller and Urry (2006: 207), for example, include '[a]sylum seekers, international students, terrorists, members of diasporas, holidaymakers, businesspeople, sports stars, refugees, backpackers, commuters, the early retired, young mobile professionals, prostitutes, armed forces and many others' in the set of actors who fill 'the world's airports, buses, ships, and trains'. These actors are not reducible to a dichotomy of hosts on one side and guests on the other. International students, for instance, fit both categories at the same time. Being new to a place, discovering the many sides and sights and often speaking a foreign language, such inhabitants are often (mis)judged as tourists. But at the same time, international students feel and act as hosts, when welcoming their friends and families to their new temporary home and sharing local knowledge and anecdotes. They often even take over local habits to distinguish themselves as 'non-tourists' when overtly showing their newly acquired skills. Similarly, commuters, who would not call the place they commute to their primary home and statistically do not count as hosts, nevertheless have a feeling of belonging towards the particular place. Such people are, notwithstanding, have some claim on the image, organisation and governance of a destination.

These two examples show that the binary view of host and guest is not sufficient to accurately capture *tourism density* or *tourism intensity* or to discuss the alienation of local residents. Rather, such examples call for a more fluid and lucid conceptualisation of a place, which opens up to a more differentiated and nuanced view of the people inhabiting a destination. A wide range of people mingle in a tourist destination, who all have a different relationship with the place, some of them rather loose, some of them close. Some people draw their identity concepts out of this relationship to place, such as a football fan. Others, maybe more temporary visitors, such as commuters or international students, imitate such codes to highlight their distinction from classic tourists, without in-depth identification of the place. Such people gather as 'we' and distinguish themselves from 'they' – to use Schütz's (2020) concept of in-group and out-group – also by visiting (or rather not visiting) certain places, such as restaurants, shops or tourism-specific locations at certain times and on certain days.

This temporal or spatial relationship with place is therefore important for people's senses of belonging and their individual conceptions of self, which are far more complex than simply considering oneself as host or guest. Boundaries between these two outdated concepts are increasingly blurring as a reduced stereotyping in one particular respect does not live up to the complexity of an interwoven, fluid and entangled reality. People inhabiting tourist places are of various cultural backgrounds, biographies, motives and intentions. Some of them stay for a short period only, while others regard a tourist destination as their new hometown, where they put down roots and from where they draw their self-understanding. Families may inhabit a place for generations, and so regard it as theirs. Such roles and concepts might overlap, depending on the situation or perspective as a commuter or a resident at the same time, an international student or a tourist, a migrant or a newcomer, and so forth. An individual can also switch roles and grow into different positions, losing former points of view and gaining new ones.

No clear line can be drawn, but a field with manifold characters and personalities is to be discovered. By cherishing this range of protagonists inhabiting the place, a diverse spectrum of 'live worlds' (Schütz, 2020) opens up and invites closer examination. These 'live worlds' are not hanging loose in space nor are they separate from each other – in contrast, people mutually interact and interrelate with other people, constantly exchanging views, experiences and standpoints, which influence and stimulate one another. The motives, background features, skills and knowledge of other people are therefore as important as their own portfolio of learned capabilities, their own inventory of competences and incorporated characteristics over time. People therefore change in the everyday through practice, constantly relating to each other.

Accepting this nuanced, dynamic and sometimes ambiguous notion of people inhabiting a place, the mere counting of visitor numbers becomes obsolete. It is, rather, a matter of the individual projects and fluid mobilities one ascribes to the place, not simply the numbers of overnight stays or the frequency of arrivals and departures. It is about the various forms of engagement, the diverse identity concepts one draws out in relation to the place, which make a difference. This is what I call the *quality of people*, which must not be misinterpreted as a normative or judgemental stigmatisation of human beings but as a nuanced understanding of the variety of attributes the different inhabitants of the place have.

The next section will show how these manifold people relate to each other, how they enact, perform and co-create place through their distinctive practices.

Practices: It Is the Practices That Count and Make a Difference

People are not all the same. They have different cultural backgrounds, travel experiences, interests and intentions. Consequently, people have different needs and requests in relation to a tourism destination, which result in different practices (Schatzki, 2006; Stock, 2015). Following Reckwitz (2002: 249), a practice is defined as:

> a routinized type of behaviour which consists of several elements that are connected to one another: forms of bodily activities, forms of mental activities, 'things' and their use, background knowledge in the form of understanding, know-how, states of emotion and motivational knowledge.

This section now discusses how these practices differ, where they stand in concurrence to each other and where they are mutually enriching. Practices never stand loose or isolated in space but are rooted in a collective cognitive and symbolic structure, 'in a "shared knowledge", which enables a socially shared way of ascribing meaning to the world' (Reckwitz, 2002: 246). This meaning is crucial to an assessment of the stage a tourism destination is in, like *involvement*, *exploration*, *development* and so forth. Through practices, such a meaning gets discussed, negotiated and mutually elaborated. It is through the maze of interconnected and entangled activities that a tourist place is co-constructed and made sense of.

Let us take the example of a train ride to illustrate this conceptual thinking. Taking the train is a very common practice for many inhabitants, such as commuters, local residents or regular guests. Train rides, or other means of public transport, can be a mundane everyday activity, which does not get any particular attention. People might use the same entrance to the railway station, stand in a similar position on the platform every day and even sit on their preferred seat when available. It can be a daily routine, where local knowledge is inscribed and made sense of. For example, one knows short-cuts, or hurdles to circumvent, which make the daily commute easier and more convenient.

This is very different for passengers taking the same train for the first time. Everything is new, everything is exciting. But instead of knowing the short-cuts, such passengers can feel disorientated or even lost at an unknown railway station. They must look up timetables and platforms and are manoeuvring, sometimes clumsily, with their luggage through the maze of people. By bumping into others, they might get in contact with regulars, but this is rarely a friendly encounter. The same applies to encounters while moving on these trains. Whereas some people are trying to work remotely while commuting and thus need to concentrate, others are fascinated by the outside view. Discovering and discussing the sights passing by and taking photos might be a common practice for newcomers, but not for people using the same train for their daily grind. It is therefore through practices that a train is connoted either as a vehicle of transportation or as a tourist attraction. This is in line with many other activities, like shopping, strolling on the sidewalk or sitting on a bench. These practices differ significantly depending on the person performing them.

The debate on overtourism and carrying capacity should include a close examination and critical discussion of such practices, and not be concerned with determining upper limits. Rather than the number of people, it is more about what these people do, how and why they do it and what is meant by doing it. This conceptualisation is important to better understand the stages or phases of tourism destinations, where different actors co-constitute their specific ways of interpreting, producing and sharing the actual purpose, role and characteristics of a place. According to Reckwitz, a practice is 'a routinized way in which bodies are moved, objects are handled, subjects are treated, things are described, and the world is understood' (Reckwitz, 2002: 250), whereas the above-mentioned examples have shown that not only routinised but many spontaneous, unique and non-repetitive practices mutually inform tourist places too.

Practices depend greatly on the people performing them. Often, it is the individual's cultural background which informs these practices. Collectivism or individualism are, for example, both concepts which are rooted in a cultural understanding and therefore get assessed differently in different parts of the world. How people react to the *density* of a place therefore depends very much on how it is conceptually understood. Also, how people feel standing close to each other is very much related to the concepts of closeness and distance, which results in different practices of queuing, boarding a train and spacing in a compartment.

Regardless of any cultural disposition, people act differently if they are part of a group or if they explore a tourism destination on their own. Crossing a street, for example, is a common practice for each and every person mingling in a tourist place. But the practice of jaywalking is far more prevalent in groups, as one must keep up with the others, even when a traffic light turns red. In general, people moving in groups focus very much on the dynamics within their group and relate less to the outside world than individuals, as the insights gathered in the walking interviews impressively showed.

This often is due to restricted time windows that groups may have. But it is not only groups who have tight schedules or many things to tick off when visiting a tourism destination. The amount of disposable time is a decisive factor for many practices performed in tourist places. It takes time to interact with people, to exchange world-views as well as tips and tricks of travelling. Moreover, it often needs a common language, or at least some shared cultural understanding, to enter into fruitful encounters.

Practices are performed by everyone inhabiting a tourism destination: hosts, guests and all the other actors mingling in a place, like commuters, international students, investors, asylum seekers and so on. It is therefore not only the traveller who shapes and connotes the place through practices, but all people play their respective parts. It is through this confusing mix of practices that people relate to each other and conflicts, power relations and fluid dependencies are unveiled and actively dealt with.

This continuing contested negotiating, this constant co-production of place through practice, is at the core of this conceptualisation of a tourist destination. Practices are performed in highly active, aware and rarely adventitious ways. It is through their practices that people shape the realms they live in and provide meaning to their respective life worlds.

All these practices are closely related to each other and compete for the meaning and purpose of a place. They are 'thrown together', to use Massey's idea (2012: 154), controversially disputed and constantly arranged and rearranged to form a tourist place. It is through practice, through the 'negotiation of intersecting trajectories' that a place unfolds as an 'arena' (Massey, 2012: 154), as a place where power struggles are held, where combats are fought, where meaning and interpretation are disputed at the personal level. It is a constant controversy, which is never finished and always starts anew. As a result, the spaces of tourists and the spaces of locals are continually merging, and what were formerly conceptualised as separate front- and back-stage areas (MacCannell, 1976) turn into an overall contested, mutually produced and jointly lived space.

Place: How Place Unfolds Out of the Practices of the People

Places are not static, but constantly evolving, adapting and changing in a sometimes fruitful, sometimes contested interplay of different actors. Places are like ships, as Sheller and Urry (2006: 14) have noted, 'moving around and not necessarily staying in one location'. Sheller and Urry (2006: 14) describe places as 'dynamic places of movement', which are travelling themselves, 'slow or fast, greater or shorter distances, within networks of human and nonhuman agents'. A place therefore does not stay as it is but develops according to trends and influences of the outside world, the needs and wants of the people dwelling in it, and the manifold practices going along with it. Places are shaped, moved, interpreted and reinterpreted by the practices of their inhabitants. Places are therefore 'about relationships, about the placing of peoples, materials, images, and the systems of difference that they perform' (Sheller & Urry, 2006: 14), drawing on a tourism destination's constant genesis and demise by means of the dynamic, encompassing and fluid production of place. Places thus are in constant play, as Sheller and Urry (2004) note.

A tourist destination is thus not a fixed and determined container filled with definite purpose and meaning, but a fluid, dynamic and ever-changing place, which is constantly negotiated, shaped, and produced by those living in it. Tourism in this process is not regarded as an alien entity, which emerges on top of a pre-existing cityscape or landscape, but is an interwoven, interrelated and mutually constitutive element, which is part and parcel of the nuanced, complex and vivid fabric of the place. A tourism destination is co-constituted 'by flows of people, objects, memories and images', which perform and stabilise 'material natures, social relations and cultural conception' (Bærenholdt *et al.*, 2004: 32).

To illustrate how a place unfolds out of the practices of the people, one can take a restaurant as an example. Depending on the restaurant guests, who can be locals, regulars, first-timers, gourmets or just hungry mouths, the fabric of the place is changing. It is not only the atmosphere of the restaurant that depends on the people visiting it, but also the characteristics of its offer. Menus differ in price and size, as well as in quality, as does the service, which very much depends on the needs and wants of the guests, from expecting detailed expertise and recommendations to wanting a fast and smooth provision of food and drink. Some clients lack understanding and knowledge of the products served, and so some restaurants put pictures and multilingual explanations on the menu. These signs and symbols can indicate whether a restaurant is considered to be tourist-focused or a local eating place. It is about how a place reacts and adapts to the people visiting it and how these people co-create the fabric of the restaurant by their mere presence (or absence).

Just as in the case of the restaurant, a destination as a whole unfolds out of the practice of the people who are constantly co-producing it by their engagement. As these people are mobile and fluid, distinct locations within a destination are changing purpose and meaning over time. People may be deliberately avoiding certain locations within a destination or, alternatively, fashionable places may be attracting manifold visitors from one moment to another. The fabric of a tourism destination is therefore neither static nor evenly structured. Some places are popping up while others are transforming or vanishing. A destination is therefore always on the move, always reinventing itself, but this does not happen in a linear way, as for example the TALC model suggests. It is not an entire destination which matures from one stage to the other. A tourism destination in a more dynamic understanding has no single, all-encompassing position, but many nuances, disparities and particularities. It would therefore not be appropriate to lump together the total variety of sights, locations and even districts as one entity. A tourism destination has, rather, to be regarded as an amalgam of different places, all constituting, together with its facets, the space in which people dwell.

These different facets of places are all linked to each other. While some parts of a tourist destination might become overcrowded at times, other places benefit as counterpoints and hide-aways. There is a fluid, dynamic process within a tourism destination, which rarely flows in a single direction. If a restaurant becomes 'touristy', possibly the other restaurants at the same street may be affected too and adapt equally to the increasing tourism needs. On the other hand, restaurants in another part of the destination, away from the main spotlight, may be developing as fresh alternatives. Such interdependencies and tourism-induced transformation processes are never without conflict. Many different views and interests are interrelated and sometimes opposed. Places are indeed on the move, as Sheller and Urry suggested, but who is at the steering wheel is a political question. Places are not stable but constantly evolving, changing identity, purpose and meaning. It is a process to which many people are actively contributing with their individual projects, practices and mobilities. People are trying to take possession of certain places and marking them as their own. Places are connoted through the practices of the people, indicating meaning and allocating them a dedicated use.

The purposes and meanings of such places are far from permanent. Indeed, places are in a constant process of elaboration, movement and development. Places can be conquered and reconquered. The conceptions, images and values of a place are in a state of constant flux and are continually being renegotiated. A tourism destination is never finished but is always becoming, as meaning and purpose are rarely attributed conclusively. Tourism contributes significantly to the interpretation and reinterpretation of such places. It is through their practices and mobilities that people make sense of place and arrange and rearrange its quality. A destination thus does not stagnate, rejuvenate or decline, but constantly learns and adapts and therefore accumulates what Stock *et al.* (2014) call the 'touristic capital' of a place. This is 'a place's set of characteristics accumulated over time and engaged advantages *vis-à-vis* the institutions, practices, markets of competing tourist places, which can be described as formed a *tourism field*'. A destination thus differentiates itself from other destinations by 'accumulating and engaging resources, governance, image, monetary income, urban qualities and knowledge' (Stock *et al.*, 2014: 13), all elements which constantly shape and reshape the characteristics of a place and thus its touristic capital.

Conclusion

Conceptualising a tourist place as co-constructed by the practices of the people rather than by the mere visitor numbers opens-up for more nuanced and differentiated measures to deal with tourism within a destination. Despite diverting tourism flows and imposing caps on visitor numbers, a more qualitative engagement with tourism is suggested. For a better 'living with tourism' (Eggli, 2021), several approaches are suggested, which go beyond the assessment of the carrying capacity of a place.

First, there is a need for more fruitful encounters with more possibilities to enter into relationships with one another, where individuals can meet at eye level and generate experiences which go beyond monetary benefit. This enables people to bridge intercultural misunderstandings and enhance mutual appraisal. Second, there is a need for meaningful tourism products and services, which enable people to stay longer and engage more intensively with a place, creating the resonance that is widely sought. Third, destinations need more suitable infrastructure, which meets the requirements of the many inhabitants, permanent and temporary. This infrastructure, though, must be carefully balanced, to avoid both monoculture and the alienation of certain actors. In the end, tourism can be used as a tool to progress and advance local life, as well as for the renewal of a destination's manifold infrastructure. Fourth, there is a need to establish clarity and greater transparency. The major tourism players need to build trust and create confidence for a better understanding of, and support for, their industry. By actively sponsoring sport, cultural and social life, the main beneficiaries could share their profit and divert the discourse on other valuable aspects of 'living with tourism' to more than solely the economic benefits. Also, rules and regulations must be clear, transparent and fair. Fifth, there is a need to open an all-embracing debate, which includes all relevant stakeholders from civil society, academia, arts and culture, interest groups and associations. This leads, sixth, to a different and more nuanced understanding of tourism, not regarding it as an intruder but as a constitutive and constructive element of a place. This more positive and productive conceptualisation allows us to exploit the regenerative force of tourism, to rebuild cultural life, social bonds and increase economic potential. Finally, we need to move forwards by accepting differences and using them for our own good. Tourism can be used as a productive learning field for much-needed competencies in an increasingly globalised world. In understanding a place as being entangled with tourism rather than as separate from it, it is necessary to stimulate a form of tourism which integrates well into local life. This results in a *living-with-tourism*, or a *not-possible-living-without tourism*, rather than accepting the overused and misleading notion of *over-* or *undertourism*, respectively.

Tourism in this context is only one of many aspects to manage. Tourism entangles life to a great extent, shedding light specifically on the many questions a place has to deal with anyway. It is through the perspective of tourism that many aspects of a place can be discussed. But tourism is not a separate issue. It cannot be discussed in isolation from its interrelated aspects but should be approached in a holistic manner. Simply counting tourists and surveying residents therefore does not lead to an encompassing way of dealing with current challenges. By overcoming the host/guest divide, and grasping a tourist place as being performed, inhabited and made sense of by all its people, is a promising way to look forward.

Author's note

This chapter reflects the main findings of a PhD thesis titled 'Living with tourism in Lucerne: How people inhabit a tourist place', supervised by Professor Mathis Stock and published at the University of Lausanne in 2021.

References

Bærenholdt, J.O., Haldrup, M., Larsen, J. and Urry, J. (2004) *Performing Tourist Places* (New Directions in Tourism Analysis). Milton Park: Routledge.

Büscher, M., Urry, J. and Witchger, K. (2011) *Mobile Methods*. London: Routledge.

Butler, R. (1980) The concept of a Tourist Area Life Cycle of evolution: Implications for management of resources. *Canadian Geographer* 24 (1), 5–12.

Eggli, F. (2021) Living with tourism in Lucerne: How people inhabit a tourist place. PhD thesis, University of Lausanne. Posted at the University of Lausanne Open Archive http://serval.unil.ch.

MacCannell, D. (1976) *The Tourist: A New Theory of the Leisure Class*. New York: Schocken Books.

Massey, D.B. (2012) *For Space*. Los Angeles: Sage.

Reckwitz, A. (2002) Toward a theory of social practices: A development in culturalist theorizing. *European Journal of Social Theory* 5 (2), 243–263.

Schatzki, T.R. (ed.) (2006) *The Practice Turn in Contemporary Theory*. Conference 'Practices and Social Order'. Transferred to digital print. London: Routledge.

Schütz, A. (2020) *Strukturen der Lebenswelt*. Alfred Schütz Werkausgabe, IX. Edited by Martin Endress and Sebastian Klimasch. Cologne: Halem.

Sheller, M. and Urry, J. (eds) (2004) *Tourism Mobilities: Places to Play, Places in Play*. London: Routledge.

Sheller, M. and Urry, J. (2006) The new mobilities paradigm. *Environment and Planning A* 38 (2), 207–226.

Stock, M. (2015) Spatial practices, theoretical implications. EspacesTemps.net, Works, https://www.espacestemps.net/en/articles/spatial-practices-theoretical-implications.

Stock, M., Clivaz, C., Crevoisier, O., Kebir, L. and Nahrath, S. (2014) *The Circulation of Wealth: Resort Development and Touristic Capital of Place*, Working Paper 5 – 2014/E. Neuchâtel: MAPS (Maison d'analyse des processus sociaux).

UNWTO (2018) *'Overtourism'? Understanding and Managing Urban Tourism Growth beyond Perceptions*. Madrid: UNWTO.

UNWTO (2019) *'Overtourism'? Understanding and Managing Urban Tourism Growth beyond Perceptions, Volume 2: Case Studies*. Madrid: UNWTO.

Urry, J. (2007) *Mobilities*. Cambridge: Polity Press.

World Travel & Tourism Council (WTTC) and McKinsey & Company (2017) *Coping With Success: Managing Overcrowding in Tourism Destinations*. Chicago: McKinsey & Company.

19 Spare the Child, Spoil the Long-Term Sustainability of the Tourism Industry: What Does That Mean for the TALC?

Hugues Séraphin, Maximiliano E. Korstanje and Shem Wambugu Maingi

A life span framework (or perspective) which divides the life of individuals into different stages is used to study the development of individuals, through the analysis of the connection between age (presented as a variable which impacts on an individual's knowledge, skills, abilities, motives and so on) and individual development (growth, decline, maintenance). This includes experience, functioning, personality adjustment and growth, social goals, emotional experience, strategies, vocational behaviour (work and career) within different contexts (the life course framework), shaping various aspects of an individual's life, such as family, school, social background, organisation structures, government or organisation policies/practices, social context, labour laws, culture, norms, gender and job demands (Zacher & Froidevaux, 2021). However, theories on life span and life course frameworks and perspectives have largely overlooked the childhood stage (age 0–12 years) and adolescence (13–19 years), while giving priority to the stages included between youth (20–24 years) and very old age (85+ years).

Like research on life course/span frameworks, tourism and related studies have also overlooked the role and importance of children (Cullingford, 1995; Koščak *et al.*, 2021). Taking the example of overtourism, the latest internal issue related to sustainability in the tourism industry (Séraphin *et al.*, 2018), academic research has not considered children, either as victims of the phenomenon or in relation to some of the solutions to overcome the issue, such as smart technologies (Pasquinelli & Trunfio, 2020). Anti-tourism movements, such as protests enabling locals to voice their concerns regarding the negative, perverse impacts of continuously growing number of tourists in their hometown (Séraphin *et al.*, 2020a), and related research (Hughes, 2018; Milano *et al.*, 2019; Séraphin *et al.*, 2020a) also tend to overlook children.

Academic research on social movements does not attach much importance to children either. For instance, the academic journal *Social Movement Studies* had, at the time of writing, published only one article focusing on children. In that article, Moor *et al.* (2020) point out the growing involvement of children as activists in climate change movements (such as Fridays for Future and Extinction Rebellion). The journals putting children on a pedestal are those on childhood studies or childism (Wall, 2019), such as *Children's Geographies*, which has, for instance, published some articles on children and activism (Bosco, 2010; Nissen *et al.*, 2020; Trott, 2021), or education-related journals such as *Education, Citizenship and Social Justice* (Torres-Harding *et al.*, 2017). Tourism and related sectors, particularly hospitality, are in limbo with regard to their positioning of the importance of children, as tourism is simultaneously creating products and services for children and their families (Backer & Schänzel, 2013; Khoo-Lattimore *et al.*, 2017), while developing 'adult only' products and services, including hotels and camp sites (see for instance the website of the International Hotel Consulting Services, https://www.ihcshotelconsulting.com/blog/adult-only-hotels).

Despite the limited interest in children shown in some areas of research directly related to this study (Josefsson & Wall, 2020), this study posits that anti-tourism movements have the potential to educate children on tourism issues and, equally important, to empower them to become tourism sustainability thinkers, actioners and transformers, and to achieve Sustainable Development Goal 4 (SDG4; https://www.un.org/sustainabledevelopment/education), namely, 'Quality education', the only SDG to focus exclusively on children and young adults (Unterhalter, 2019). Objective 4.7 reads:

> By 2030, ensure that all learners acquire the *knowledge and skills needed to promote sustainable development*, including, among others, *through education* for sustainable development and sustainable lifestyles, human rights, gender equality, promotion of a culture of peace and non-violence, global citizenship and appreciation of cultural diversity and of culture's contribution to sustainable development. (Emphasis added)

This position is also supported by academics such as Bosco (2010: 381), who claims that 'Young people often mobilize and become agents of change in their communities and beyond', and Torres-Harding *et al.* (2017: 3), who argue that 'School-based social activism projects have much potential to foster civic engagement, self-efficacy, and positive youth development'. This perspective is realistic; Séraphin *et al.* (2020b) explain that when children are educated about sustainability in tourism, they move from different stages, namely sustainability thinker to transformer. Schill *et al.* (2020) evidenced that the personal determinant (knowledge; concern), environmental determinant (spatial organisation;

communication style; encouragement) and behavioural determinant (past experience) regarding recycling and sustainability more broadly impact on the environmental sensitivity of children. From an adult perspective, Séraphin *et al.* (2020b) provided evidence that activists (adults) involved in anti-tourism movements went through different stages in their attitude, namely from victims, peaceful activists, vandals, to resilience. As a result, this study is at the intersection of research on social movement outcomes, life span/course studies and tourism studies, and could be said to be a radical innovation in academic research, as it is proactive and disrupts current conventions (Brooker & Joppe, 2014; Zacher & Froidevaux, 2021). Social justice is a major topic of research in tourism (Jamal & Higham, 2021) and underlies this study too.

This chapter is placed in a continuity with Weber *et al.* (2019), as suggesting how to turn overtourism (a negative context) into something positive by an educational tool, and how to educate people (visitors and locals) on the negative impacts of overtourism on the local community. Additionally, the study relates to those by Torres-Harding *et al.* (2017), who investigated how activism projects can contribute to the empowerment of children, and Nissen *et al.* (2020), who investigated the long-term potential impacts of climate activism on children and young people. However, this chapter is different in that it focuses on children (a marginalised group) and on anti-tourism movements (an industry-specific type of activism). More importantly, this chapter discusses how the growth of the role and importance of children in the tourism industry could impact on the current structure of the Tourism Area Life Cycle (TALC).

This research is of importance because sustainability is an urgent objective for the tourism industry and related sectors (Higham *et al.*, 2021). So far, these sectors have mainly focused on short-term and reactive strategies, as opposed to long-term and proactive strategies (Broker & Joppe, 2014; Visser, 2015), and have considered some stakeholders such as children as unimportant for the sustainability of the industry, although they can massively contribute to that goal (Koščak *et al.*, 2021; Séraphin *et al.*, 2020b). A prerequisite for the sustainability of the industry is the involvement of all stakeholders (Sun *et al.*, 2013).

In summary, this chapter provides an innovative strategy to achieve the sustainability of the tourism industry, while also making a theoretical contribution to academic research in tourism. To do so, it is based on the Critical Environment Determinant Framework (CEDF), which explains that children's knowledge, attitudes and consumption varies according to the level of the sustainability context in which they are involved (Schill *et al.*, 2020). The CEDF is derived from social cognitive theory (SCT), a concept stating that people's behaviour is based on both their interaction with other people (social structure) and the environment they are in (personal agency). This connects to the life span/course framework as well as social movements (in tourism). The CEDF is a framework which centres on individuals' sustainable consumption and attitudes (Phipps *et al.*, 2013).

Theoretical Framework

From social cognitive theory to the Critical Environment Determinant Framework

Social cognitive theory is a framework used to investigate how personal behaviour in terms of consumption and interactions with others is influenced by the social environment (Wang *et al.*, 2019). In other words, SCT argues that individuals are the results of their social environment (Schill *et al.*, 2020), which is why individuals tend to reproduce behaviour they have observed. While learning by observing is central to SCT (Schill *et al.*, 2020), the environment is not the only determinant of human behaviour, as personal determinants such as motivation, goals, morals and standards have an equal impact (Wang *et al.*, 2019).

SCT explains that social and personal behaviour and norms (Wang *et al.*, 2019) influence sustainability preferences, actions and competencies (Font *et al.*, 2016). As a framework, SCT is used in a wide range of research related to sustainability and was used by Schill *et al.* (2020) to understand factors which can influence children's sensibility to sustainability. Those authors went on to develop their own framework, known as the CEDF, which reveals that children's recycling knowledge and concern (personal determinants) vary according to environmental and behavioural determinants. The higher the different determinants (environment and behavioural) are, the more sustainability concerned and knowledgeable the children are (Schill *et al.*, 2020). CEDF also presents personal determinants as dependent variables, which are factors that are influenced by other experimental factors (Hammond & Wellington, 2013), in this case environmental and behavioural determinants.

From CEDF to the life span/course framework

Life-course research, which is used in many disciplines (sociology, psychology, history, economics, etc.), postulates that individual development depends on its environment or context (at the macro-, micro- or meso-level), even though the life course is individualised as opposed to standardised (Levy & Buhlmann, 2016). Braungart and Braungart (1986) explain that age is also related to the role the individual can play in the community, and the power and prestige granted to the individual. 'Experience' and 'behaviour' are also closely connected with age (Braungart & Braungart, 1986). As age group (therefore experience and behaviour) are constructs which are changing according to the evolution of society (Braungart & Braungart, 1986), it could be argued that, based on the current poor state of tourism sustainability, and the urgency of reaching sustainability (Higham *et al.*, 2021), the current segmentation of stakeholders involved in making things change should alter. They do seem to have changed with the growing emergence of young activists coming forward for many causes, such as race equality, climate change and gender rights (Pickard, 2019).

Equally important, Rudolph and Zacher (2016) explain that to understand age group, it is important to explore the context and the contemporary issues (such as terrorism, national politics, earthquakes, hurricanes, war) a group has faced, as this influences their attitudes, values, beliefs, motives and behaviour. Based on CEDF, pro-environment behaviour should be high in children, as sustainability is the most pressing issue (Pickard, 2019).

Social movements within the life span/course framework

Activists are individuals who are highly involved in the affairs of their local community. Such affairs may concern politics, the well-being of the community, the mode of consumption of members of the community, protection of the environment, and the raising of awareness and education, quite often through protests or expert lobbying (Brochado *et al.*, 2017; Hysing, 2011; Pancer *et al.*, 2007; Tranter, 2010). Séraphin (2022) provided key traits of sustainability tourism activists, and argued that most of these activists: (1) are female, (2) are empowered to be sustainability activists, (3) have a higher-education qualification in tourism or related topics, (4) work in the tourism industry or related sectors and (5) are self-employed/entrepreneurs. In terms of their personalities they are (1) conscientiousness, (2) emotionally stable, (3) extrovert, (4) agreeable and (5) open to experience.

Children have a major role to play in the sustainability of the tourism industry, despite the fact they are not often really involved (Ernst & Burcak, 2019; Koščak *et al.*, 2021). At the moment, most of the strategies put in place in the tourism industry aim to encourage children to be sustainability thinkers, in other words, individuals with critical thinking and a questioning attitude (Séraphin *et al.*, 2020b). The industry presently does not have tourism sustainability activists, or sustainability actioners, and/or transformers, who are willing to effect changes in their community (Séraphin *et al.*, 2020b).

If in tourism sustainability there are no children activists, there are many child activists in other areas (Mkono *et al.*, 2020; Séraphin, 2022). According to the Complex website (https://www.complex.com/life/young-activists-who-are-changing-the-world/indya-moore) the 32 leading child activists changing the world are in the fields of: race equality and civil rights, mental health, climate change, weapons and violence, water usage and quality, women's conditions, immigrants' rights, sustainability in general, child rights, education, health, and culture promotion. These child activists, who are mostly girls, are involved in and/or are founders of movements such as Black Lives Matter, Teens4Equality, We Cycle, A Heart of Hope, Fridays for Future, Climate Generation, Surfers against Sewage (Séraphin, 2022) and School Strikes for Climate (https://childrenvsclimatecrisis.org).

Nissen *et al.* (2020) explain that the social movements led by or at least involving children, adolescents and young adults have a strong legacy potential, which includes:

- *Biographical legacies.* Involvement in these movements can have a long-term positive effect on those involved and their surroundings but also negative effects potentially following the experience of surveillance or repression. Involvement in movements can also influence future career.
- *Movement legacies.* Movements can eventually leave a lifetime collective memory for all those involved, and an *intergenerational legacy* in the form of knowledge transfer and experience.
- *Political legacies.* There is the potential to influence not only policies but, equally important, young activists themselves.

Social movements led by young people can have a legacy only if they are perceived positively by others; otherwise, the public will resist change. As a result, it is important for these activists and social movements to have a clear understanding of how they are perceived (Bashir *et al.*, 2013).

Despite the fact that tourism is directly connected to topics such climate change (Higham *et al.*, 2021) and sustainability (Mkono *et al.*, 2020), no young activist has come forward specifically to shed light on tourism's specific impacts and/or issues, and yet tourism has impacted the lives of all stakeholders within the communities (Diaz-Parra & Jover, 2020; Milano *et al.*, 2019). While no direct reference has been made to children, they have been impacted as much as anyone else within a community (Séraphin & Korstanje, 2022), but they have not been associated with any of the anti-tourism movements or protests or organisations aimed at sending tourists home (Associació de Veins de la Barceloneta, Arran, Assemblea de Barris per un Turisme Sostenible, etc.) (Hughes, 2018). Based on the literature covered so far, not only could children, adolescents and young adults have been involved, but the communities would have benefited in the long term, due to the educational dimension that such protest could have if used as an educational tool. In some destinations it has been used to turn protests into educational tools for visitors, so that they have a clear understanding of the impacts of overtourism on destinations and residents (Weber *et al.*, 2019). Huneault and Otomo (2022) have clearly highlighted the fact that the well-being of children is still not a priority of the tourism industry.

Pro-environmental behaviour

Schill *et al.* (2020) explain that the education of children (at home) plays a significant role in their behaviour with regard to the environment. Han (2021) and Higham *et al.* (2021) argue the same when it comes to stakeholders of the tourism industry. The other drivers identified by Han (2021) are outcomes of this cognitive dimension, and as a result offer more specific information: image (what is considered 'green'); pro-environmental behaviour in everyday life (contributing to protecting the environment, and impacting on consumption); green product attachment (tending to remain loyal to a product); descriptive social norm (pressure from the external environment to behave in a pro-environment manner); anticipated pride and guilt (evaluating behaviour or consumption with regard to its values); environmental corporate social responsibility (CSR) (ethical organisations are getting competitive); perceived effectiveness (individuals with pro-environment behaviour are likely to reinforce their efforts/initiatives with regard to the environment); connectedness to nature (which has a significant role in sustainability beliefs and behaviour); and green value (the efficiency of a product and/or service, when the value received is greater than that sacrificed). All these drivers are prerequisites for unlocking changes towards sustainability (Visser, 2015).

The education strategy seems to be paying off as a growing number of children, adolescents and young adults (Moor *et al.*, 2020: 619), also known as 'do-it-ourselves protesters' (Pickard, 2019), are involved in social movements, such as sustainability activism. Indeed, 'young people have been at the vanguard of a global wave of environmental activism' (Pickard, 2019: 4), as, more than anybody else, they have been impacted by environmental issues; as a result, 'they seek to defend their rights to a sustainable future' (Jourdan & Wertin, 2020: 1245). They are considered as effective environmental agents of change (Malone, 2013).

Children sustainability (tourism) activism model

This chapter is promoting 'childism' (Wall, 2019), in other words, a more child centred research/approach, and less 'adultism', and supporting the wellbeing and safety of children, adolescents and young adults (Josefsson & Wall, 2020). The study has so far evidenced that children, adolescents and young adults are fully fledged stakeholders for sustainability (Bosco, 2010) and that the tourism industry, and particularly anti-tourism movements, have failed to consider in their strategy. Figure 19.1 provides a summary of the literature covered in this chapter and a model of sustainability in tourism, taking overtourism and children as examples.

OVERTOURISM / ANTI-TOURISM MOVEMENTS
(context/contemporary issue)

Childhood (0-12)	Adolescence / Youth (13-24)
	(For efficiency, the focus should be on this age group)

EDUCATION OF STAKEHOLDERS
(Cognitive dimension of sustainability)

STAKEHOLDERS' ENGAGEMENT / ACTIVISM
(Do-It-Ourselves Protesters /sustainability thinkers, actioners, and transformers)

Independent variables	Dependent variables
Gender	Personal behaviour (consumption)
Chronologisation	Interaction with others
Sequentialisation	Consciousness
Biographisation	Emotional stability
Knowledge	Extraversion
Materials available for their education & their properties/features	Agreeable
Experiences	Openness to experience
Encouragement	
Communication	
Place of birth (pro-environment context or not)	
Motivations, goals	
Moral, standards & norms	
Perception by others	

LEGACIES
▪ Biographical ▪ Movement ▪ Political

Figure 19.1 A model of sustainability in tourism, taking overtourism and children as examples (Source: Authors)

Tourism Area Life Cycle (TALC) and Children, Adolescents and Young Adults

An overview

The Tourist Area Life Cycle model as developed by Butler (1980) traces the six stages of evolution of a tourist area over its life course. In its nature of paedomorphosis, a tourism area goes through the rapid transformation of a place as a result of tourism growth and development (Christou, 2019). Butler's widely adopted TALC model (Figure 19.2) examines the evolutionary nature of destinations, and conceptualises tourism development as a continuous process that involves stages of exploration, involvement, development, consolidation and stagnation, which can lead to decline, rejuvenation or prolonged stagnation of tourist numbers. It argues that a continuous increase in tourism activity has a significant impact on communities, the environment as well as the local economy. Several studies have used the TALC framework to examine the evolutionary effects of tourism activities in destinations using tourist arrivals, changes in accommodation patterns and government expenditures in tourism (Albaladeyo & Martínez-García, 2017; Foster & Murphy, 1991; Weaver, 2006).

Children represent a large community that often has been adversely affected by the nature of tourism in destinations. At the *exploration* stage, the tourism area is in the initial stage of development, which is marked by a small number of visitors. This stage involves a high level of contact between tourist and host (including children) (Loebach & Cox, 2020). As the number of visitors increases, the second stage, *involvement*, kicks in. In this stage, the private sector provides facilities for visitors. Locals start accommodating visitors. At this stage children come into direct contact with them and become not only active agents of the family experience, as

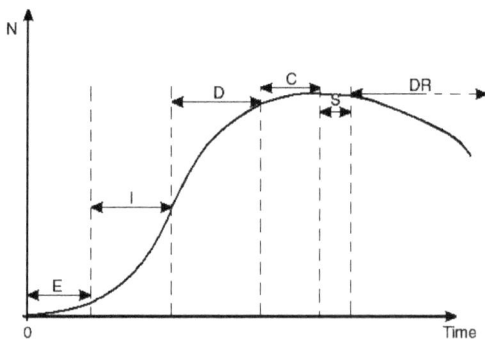

Figure 19.2 The evolution phases based on TALC theory. E = Exploration; I = Involvement; D = Development; C = Consolidation; S = Stagnation; DR = Decline or Rejuvenation

noted by Carr (2011), but also passive participants in leisure, recreation and tourism experiences. They are indirectly but positively affected by tourism developments in the tourist area. However, at this stage community protection mechanisms are needed to guarantee children's health, status and well-being (Martin & Buyi, 2011). As the number of visitors continues to increase, with private sector investments in tourism, the third stage emerges, that is, the *development* stage. This involves a rapid growth and transformation of the sector towards providing many different products and services. Even though tourism growth provides significant advantage to local communities in terms of economic well-being and employment, there are significant negative impacts, for instance on children's well-being and in the form of cultural disruption (Tirasattayapitak *et al.*, 2015).

The TALC model needs to be broadened to include some of the behavioural and health impacts of tourism on host children, adolescents and young adults. Family influences have been well documented as tourism consumption factors (Horner & Swarbrooke, 2021; Mathieson & Wall, 1982) but tourism studies have not addressed the influences of tourism consumption on children (Maingi & Gowreesunkar, 2023). Uncontrolled tourism growth can have adverse impacts on host children (Yang *et al.*, 2020). Overtourism and its associated effects may have negative effects on children. These impacts are mental, social, emotional and, to some extent, physical in nature. In addition to the health risks faced by children due to the recent COVID-19 pandemic, there are increasingly social effects such as overcrowding in tourism facilities and a strain on social relations. The behavioural effects on children follow William McDougall's (1912) theory of emotions in terms of the intensification of impulsive emotions with the rising number of crowds in an area. As per McDougall's theory, emotional experiences are shared and the effects of these emotions on children are rapidly felt with the increasing crowding (Izard, 1977). Children are also eco-socialised and in a way are influenced by their immediate environments and changes in their environments affect children's experiences, well-being and quality of life (Maingi & Gowreesunkar, 2023; Liu & Draper, 2022).

Why TALC needs to be reviewed

The absence of a focus on children in the debates on the impacts of tourism on destinations is an issue that has gained considerable attention in the scholarly world (Canosa *et al.*, 2016; Canosa & Graham, 2016; Small, 2008). Children play a significant role in tourism communities and therefore the impact of tourism on children should not be ignored. The Butler model of tourism destination areas has been widely taught and cited in the sector, but it has also undergone wide argumentative discussion in the academic world (Numpty Nerd, 2014; Piuchan, 2018). Globally, some tourism areas have undergone a metamorphosis with a greater emphasis on degrowing tourism, promoting environmental justice, children and native rights in tourism (Higgins-Desbiolles *et al.*, 2019; Maingi & Gowreesunkar, 2022). However, despite this, the impacts of tourism numbers on children have not been sufficiently addressed. Studies have shown that tourism has physical, social and moral impacts on children, particularly with the rising impacts of such elements as sex tourism (Freeman, 1997; King *et al.*, 1993; Yang *et al.*, 2020).

New TALC model taking into account children, adolescents and young adults

In moments of great transition in the world, tourism areas need to take account of children, adolescents and young adults. The effects of tourism on this niche domain within their life course has not been documented, especially with regard to the extent that children, adolescents and young adults have become more vulnerable to the adverse environmental, economic and social impacts of tourism (Maingi, 2019). Such vulnerabilities tend to heighten the thresholds (or limits) to acceptable change and are subject to and caused by exogenous influences. Children represent a very significant portion of this domain and a very important stakeholder group in the wider tourism discourse that has largely been ignored in research and practice. Rising tourism numbers have more adverse impacts on younger children than on young adults. Children's development is not homogeneous and varies with the stage of childhood: infancy (aged 2 years and below), early childhood (aged 3–6 years), middle childhood (aged 7–10) and adolescence (11–18) (Poria & Timothy, 2014). The harmful social impacts of tourism numbers on children and young adults are common (Huberman, 2005). Studies have shown some of these harmful social effects include children dropping out of school, alteration of socio-cultural values and adoption of negative tourism behaviours (Haddad *et al.*, 2019; Milman & Pizam, 1988). These impacts are more pronounced in popular tourism areas that have accommodated mass tourism and are facing overtourism. The establishment of child-sensitive standards and codes of conduct are critical to addressing the social impacts of tourism on children. However, it is important to note that most tourism areas have not prepared such standards and therefore the negative impacts of tourism are more pronounced than they need be.

Coming back to the TALC, it is important to note that impacts of tourism on communities are not homogeneous and children are affected the most, qualitatively as well as quantitatively. It is therefore paramount that the model is reviewed to address the child-specific impacts of tourism from an ecological, social and economic context.

References

Albaladeyo, I.P. and Martínez-García, M.P. (2017) The post-stagnation stage for mature tourism areas: A mathematical modelling process. *Tourism Economics* 23 (2), 387–402.

Backer, E. and Schänzel, H.A. (2013) Family holidays – vacation or obli-cation? *Tourism Recreation Research* 38 (2), 159–173.

Bashir, N.Y., Lockwood, P., Chasteen, A.L., Nadolny, D. and Noyes, I. (2013) The ironic impact of activists: Negative stereotypes reduce social change influence. *European Journal of Social Psychology* 43, 614–626.

Bosco, F.J. (2010) Play, work or activism? Broadening the connections between political and children's geographies. *Children's Geographies* 8 (4), 381–390.

Braungart, R.G. and Braungart, M.M. (1986) Life-course and generation politics. *Annual Review of Sociology* 12, 205–231.

Brochado, A., Teiga, N. and Oliveira-Brochado, F. (2017) The ecological conscious consumer behaviour: Are the activists different? *International Journal of Consumer Studies* 41, 138–146.

Brooker, E. and Joppe, M. (2014) Developing a tourism innovation typology: Leveraging liminal insights. *Journal of Travel Research* 53 (4), 500–508.

Butler, R. (1980) The concept of a tourist area cycle of evolution: Implications for management of resources. *Canadian Geographer* 24 (1), 5–12.

Canosa, A. and Graham, A. (2016) Ethical tourism research involving children. *Annals of Tourism Research* 61, 219–221.

Canosa, A., Moyle, B. and Wray, M. (2016) Can anybody hear me? A critical analysis of young residents' voices in tourism studies. *Tourism Analysis* 20 (2–3), 325–337. doi:10.3727/108354216X14559233985097.

Carr, N. (2011) *Children's and Families' Holiday Experiences*. Abington: Routledge.

Christou, P.A. (2019) Neoteny: The paedomorphosis of destinations. *Annals of Tourism Research* 81 (1), 102698.

Cullingford, C. (1995) Children's attitudes to holidays overseas. *Tourism Management* 16 (2), 121–127.

Diaz-Parra, I. and Jover, J. (2020) Overtourism, place alienation and the right to the city: insights from the historic centre of Seville, Spain. *Journal of Sustainable Tourism* 29 (2–3), 158–175.

Ernst, J. and Burcak, F. (2019) Young children's contributions to sustainability: The influence of nature play on curiosity, executive function skills, creative thinking, and resilience. *Sustainability* 11 (15), 4212. https://doi.org/10.3390/su11154212.

Freeman, M.D. (1997) *The Moral Status of Children: Essays on the Rights of the Children*. New York: Martinus Nijhoff.

Font, X., Garay, L. and Jones, S. (2016) A social cognitive theory of sustainability empathy. *Annals of Tourism Research* 58, 65–80.

Foster, D.M. and Murphy, P. (1991) Resort cycle revisited: The retirement connection. *Annals of Tourism Research* 18 (4), 553–567.

Haddad, R., Harahsheh, S. and Boluk, K. (2019) The negative sociocultural impacts of tourism on Bedouin communities of Petra, Jordan. *E-review of Tourism Research* 16 (5).

Hammond, M. and Wellington, J. (2013) *Research Methods. The Key Concepts*. London: Routledge.

Han, H. (2021) Consumer behaviour and environmental sustainability in tourism and hospitality: A review of theories, concepts, and latest research. *Journal of Sustainable Tourism* 29 (7), 1021–1042. https://doi.org/10.1080/09669582.2021.1903019.

Higgins-Desbiolles, F., Carnicelli, S., Krolikowski, C., Wijesinghe, G. and Boluk, K. (2019) Degrowing tourism: Rethinking tourism. *Journal of Sustainable Tourism* 27 (12), 1926–1944.

Higham, J., Font, X. and Wu, J. (2021) Code red for sustainable tourism. *Journal of Sustainable Tourism* 30 (1), 1–13. https://doi.org/10.1080/09669582.2022.2008128.

Horner, S. and Swarbrooke, J. (2021) *Consumer Behaviour in Tourism* (4th edn). London: Routledge.

Huberman, J. (2005) 'Consuming children': Reading the impacts of tourism in the city of Banaras. *Childhood* 12 (2), 161–176.

Hughes, N. (2018) Tourists go home': Anti-tourism industry protest in Barcelona. *Social Movement Studies* 17 (4), 471–477.

Huneault, G. and Otomo, M. (2022) From unlikely to likely partnership for change – child welfare and indigenous tourism in Canada. *Journal of Sustainable Tourism* 30 (10), 2476–2493. https://doi.org/10.1080/09669582.2020.1817047.

Hysing, E. (2011) Who greens the northern light? Green inside activists in local environmental governing in Sweden. *Environment and Planning C: Government and Policy* 29, 693–708.

International Hotel Consulting Services (IHCS). Retrieved from https://www.ihcshotelconsulting.com/blog/adult-only-hotels.

Izard, C.E. (1977) Theories of emotion and emotion–behavior relationships. In C.E. Izard (ed.) *Human Emotions: Emotions, Personality, and Psychotherapy*. Boston: Springer. https://doi.org/10.1007/978-1-4899-2209-0_2.

Jamal, T. and Higham, J. (2021) Justice and ethics: Towards a new platform for tourism and sustainability. *Journal of Sustainable Tourism* 29 (2–3), 143–157. https://doi.org/10.1080/09669582.2020.1835933.

Josefsson, J. and Wall, J. (2020) Empowered inclusion: Theorizing global justice for children and youth. *Globalizations* 17 (6), 1043–1060.

Jourdan, D. and Wertin, J. (2020) Intergenerational rights to a sustainable future: Insights for climate justice and tourism. *Journal of Sustainable Tourism* 28 (8), 1245–1254.

Khoo-Lattimore, C., Del Chiappa, G. and Yang, M.J. (2017) A family for the holidays: Delineating the hospitality needs of European parents with young children. *Young Consumers* 19 (2), 159–171.

King, B., Pizam, A. and Milman, A. (1993) Social impacts of tourism: Host perceptions. *Annals of Tourism Research* 20 (4), 650–665.

Koščak, M., Knežević, M., Binder, D., Pelaez-Verde, A., Işik, C., Borisavljević, K. and Šegota, T. (2021) Exploring the neglected voices of children in sustainable development: A comparative study in six European tourist destinations. *Journal of Sustainable Tourism*, 1–20. https://doi.org/10.1080/09669582.2021.1898623.

Levy, R. and Buhlmann, F. (2016) Towards a socio-structural framework for life course analysis. *Advances in Life Course Research*, 30–42.

Liu, Y. and Draper, J. (2022) The influence of attending festivals with children of family quality of life, subjective well-being and event experience. *Event Management* 26, 25–40.

Loebach, J. and Cox, A. (2020) Tool for observing play outdoors (TOPO): A new typology for capturing children's play behaviours in outdoor environments. *International Journal of Environmental Research and Public Health* 17 (15), 5611. https://doi.org/10.3390/ijerph17155611.

Maingi, S.W. (2019) Sustainable tourism certification, local governance and management in dealing with overtourism in East Africa. *Worldwide Hospitality and Tourism Themes* 11 (5), 532–551.

Maingi, S.W. and Gowreesunkar, V.G.B. (2022) Child rights and inclusive sustainable tourism development in East Africa: Case of Kenya. In H. Séraphin (ed.) *Children in Sustainable and Responsible Tourism* (pp. 143–157). London: Emerald.

Maingi, S.W. and Gowreesunkar, V.G.B. (2023) Childhood memories, family events, nostalgia and Sustainable tourism: Conceptual and theoretical perspectives. In H. Séraphin (ed.) *Events Management for the Infant and Youth Market* (pp. 25–38). London: Emerald.

Malone, K. (2013) 'The future lies in our hands': Children as researchers and environmental change agents in designing a child-friendly neighbourhood. *International Journal of Justice and Sustainability* 18 (3), 375–395.

Martin, P. and Buyi, M. (2011) *An Exploratory Study on the Interplay Between African Customary Law and Practices and the Children's Protection Rights in South Africa*. Stockholm: Save the Children Sweden.

Mathieson, A. and Wall, G. (1982) *Tourism: Economic, Physical and Social Impacts*. London: Longman.

McDougall, W. (1912) *Psychology: The Study of Behavior*. New York: Routledge.

Milano, C., Novelli, M. and Cheer, J. (2019) Overtourism and degrowth: A social movements perspective. *Journal of Sustainable Tourism* 27 (12), 1857–1875.

Milman, A. and Pizam, A. (1988) Social impacts of tourism on central Florida. *Annals of Tourism Research* 15 (2), 191–204.

Mkono, M., Hughes, K. and Echentille, S. (2020) Hero or villain? Responses to Greta Thunberg's activism and the implications for travel and tourism, *Journal of Sustainable Tourism* 28 (12), 2081–2098.

Moor, J.D., Vydt, M.D., Uba, K. and Wahlstrom, M. (2020) New kids on the block: Taking stock of the recent cycle of climate activism. *Social Movement Studies* 20 (5), 619–625.

Nissen, S., Wong, J.H.K. and Carlton, S. (2020) Children and young people's climate crisis activism – a perspective on long-term effects. *Children's Geographies* 19 (3), 317–323.

Numpty Nerd (2014) The Butler model of tourism development. At http://www.numptynerd.net/tourism-the-butler-model.html.

Pancer, S.M., Pratt, M., Hunsberger, B. and Alisat, S. (2007) Community and political involvement in adolescence: what distinguishes the activists from the uninvolved? *Journal of Community Psychology* 35 (6), 741–759.

Pasquinelli, C. and Trunfio, M. (2020) Overtouristified cities: An online news media narrative analysis. *Journal of Sustainable Tourism* 28 (11), 1805–1824.

Phipps, M., Ozanne, L.K., Luchs, M.G., Subrahmanyan, S., Kapitan, S., Catlin, J.R. and Weather, T. (2013) Understanding the inherent complexity of sustainable consumption: A social cognitive framework. *Journal of Business Research* 66 (8), 1227–1234.

Pickard, S. (2019) Young environmental activists are doing it themselves. *Political Insight* 10 (4), 4–7.

Piuchan, M. (2018) Plog's and Butler's models: A critical review of Psychographic Tourist Typology and the Tourist Area Life Cycle. *Turizam* 22 (3), 95–106.

Poria, Y. and Timothy, D.J. (2014) Where are the children in tourism research? *Annals of Tourism Research* 47, 93–94.

Rudolph, C.W. and Zacher, H. (2016) Considering generations from a lifespan developmental perspective. *Work, Aging and Retirement* 3 (2), 113–129.

Schill, M., Godefroit-Winkel, D. and Hogg, M. (2020) Young children's consumer agency: The case of French children and recycling. *Journal of Business Research* 110, 292–305.

Séraphin, H. (2022) Understanding the traits of tourism sustainability activists through a life course framework. *Journal of Policy Research in Tourism, Leisure and Events*. https://doi.org/10.1080/19407963.2022.2029873.

Séraphin, H. and Korstanje, M. (2022) Overtourism and children's experiences: Analysis and perspective. In D.R. Agapito, M.A. Ribeiro and K.M. Woosman (eds) *Handbook of the Tourist Experience: Design, Marketing and Management* (pp. 210–225). London: Edward Elgar.

Séraphin, H., Sheeran, P. and Pilato, M. (2018) Overtourism and the fall of Venice as a destination, *Journal of Destination Marketing and Management* 9, 374–376.

Séraphin, H., Ivanov, S., Dosquet, F. and Bourliataux-Lajoinie, S. (2020a) Archetypes of locals in destinations victim of overtourism. *Journal of Hospitality and Tourism Management*. https://doi.org/10.1016/j.jhtm.2019.12.001.

Séraphin, H., Yallop, A., Seyfi, S. and Hall, M. (2020b) Responsible tourism: The 'why' and 'how' of empowering children. *Journal of Tourism Recreation*. https://doi.org/10.108 0/02508281.2020.1819109.

Small, J. (2008) The absence of childhood in tourism studies. *Annals of Tourism Research* 35 (3), 772–789.

Sun, Y.Y., Rodriguez, A., Wu., J.H. and Chuang, S.T. (2013) Why hotel rooms were not full during a hallmark sporting event: The 2009 World Games experience. *Tourism Management* 36, 469–479.

Tirasattayapitak, S., Chaiyasain, C. and Beeton, R.J.S. (2015) The impacts of nature-based adventure tourism on children in a Thai village. *Tourism Management Perspectives* 15, 122–127.

Torres-Harding, S., Baber, A., Hilvers, J., Hobbs, N. and Mally, M. (2017) Children as agents of social and community change: Enhancing youth empowerment through participation in a school-based social activism project. *Education, Citizenship and Social Justice* 13 (1), 3–18.

Tranter, B. (2010) Environmental activists and non-active environmentalists in Australia. *Environmental Politics* 19 (3), 413–429.

Trott, C.D. (2021) What difference does it make? Exploring the transformative potential of everyday climate crisis activism by children and youth. *Children's Geographies* 19 (3), 300–308.

Unterhalter, E. (2019) The many meanings of quality education: Politics of targets and indicators in SDG4. *Global Policy* 10 (1), 39–51.

Visser, W. (2015) *Sustainable Frontiers. Unlocking Change through Business. Leadership and Innovation*. Sheffield: Greenleaf Publishing.

Wall, J. (2019) From childhood studies to childism: Reconstructing the scholarly and social imaginations. *Children's Geographies* 20 (3). https://doi.org/10.1080/14733285.2019.1 668912.

Wang, S., Hung, K. and Huang, W.J. (2019) Motivations for entrepreneurship in the tourism and hospitality sector: A social cognitive theory perspective. *International Journal of Hospitality Management* 78, 78–88.

Weaver, D.B. (2006) The 'plantation' variant of the TALC in the small-island Caribbean. In R. Butler (ed.) *The Tourism Area Life Cycle, Volume 1: Applications and Modifications* (pp. 185–197). Clevedon: Channel View Publications.

Weber, F., Eggli, F., Ohnmacht, T. and Stettler, J. (2019) Lucerne and the impact of Asian group tours. In R. Dodds and R. Butler (eds) *Overtourism: Issues, Realities and Solutions* (pp. 169–184). Berlin: De Gruyter.

Yang, M.J.H., Yang, E.C.L. and Khoo-Lattimore, C. (2020) Host-children of tourism destinations: Systematic quantitative literature review. *Tourism Recreation Research* 45 (2), 231–246.

Zacher, H. and Froidevaux, A. (2021) Life stage, lifespan, and life course perspectives on vocational behaviour and development: A theoretical framework, review, and research agenda. *Journal of Vocational Behaviour* 126, 1–22.

20 The Role of Entrepreneurship in Tourism Destinations: Implications for TALC

Mike Peters and Sarah Schönherr

The importance of entrepreneurs in the development of tourist destinations is well established but has received limited attention in the context of their potential influence on the pattern of development portrayed by the TALC model. This chapter discusses the role of entrepreneurship in shaping patterns of development, particularly in the context of sustainable tourism. Destination development is strongly influenced by entrepreneurial action. Research on the corporate life cycle has shown that the demands on managers, entrepreneurs or employees change dynamically, and likewise the behaviour of various stakeholders in the development of destinations often changes. Sustainable tourism development needs innovation, which is usually attributed to entrepreneurship. Entrepreneurs are proactive and innovative, and take the risk for these innovations (Schumpeter, 2000). Tourism entrepreneurs such as hoteliers, cable car operators, restaurateurs or event organisations thus drive the economic development of tourism destinations. However, entrepreneurs who are not active in tourism can contribute just as significantly to destination development. Innovations developed essentially for residents also improve the tourism offer (e.g. public transport, trade and other services). In this context, entrepreneurial ecosystems are often referred to as the basis for entrepreneurial innovation in a region (Eichelberger *et al.*, 2020).

This chapter explores the relevance of entrepreneurship, looking at the different stages of the tourism area cycle of evolution. First, the concept of the business life cycle is analysed and discussed. Furthermore, it will be shown that sustainable development also affects the concept of entrepreneurship, as new constructs such as 'sustainable entrepreneurship', 'social entrepreneurship' or 'responsible entrepreneurship' play an increasingly important role in destination development. The chapter concludes with recommendations for tourism research and practice.

Entrepreneurship and Business Life Cycles

Entrepreneurs are founders who establish businesses. Major entrepreneurial activities happen before new ventures are founded. Theories of entrepreneurship and small business often use the enterprise life cycle to understand major activities before and after enterprise start-ups. In the literature (Parks, 1977) several typical hurdles in enterprise development are described.

Chronologically, the first is the *start-up hurdle,* in which ignorance of the industry and lack of preparation or of entrepreneurial qualifications in particular cause problems (Hering & Vincenti, 2005; Terpstra & Olson, 1993). The *cash flow hurdle* plays a role, especially in industries with few but well-paying customers (e.g. management consultancies or market research institutes) (Hutchinson *et al.*, 1986). Typical leadership problems accompany the first strong growth phase. *Delegation and leadership hurdles* are characterised by the problem of clearly assigning rights and duties within the founding team. The *idea hurdle* is often observed after a strong growth phase, namely when sales stagnate but the company has failed to create an innovative corporate structure (Parks, 1977). Another hurdle that can be observed in strong growth periods is the *financing hurdle:* large investments are due and new investors are needed when, for example, building structures must be renewed or improved (qualitative growth) or new operating facilities (e.g. hotels or restaurants) have to be built to expand capacity. Particularly during periods of long-term growth, complacency creeps into well-off industries; Parks (1977) calls this the *hurdle of complacency.* Entrepreneurs are self-satisfied and oversee trends and industry developments.

It is possible to see that some of these hurdles are also present in tourism destinations, even though destinations incorporate a large number of entrepreneurs from different industries. However, community-oriented or corporate-oriented destinations are very different (Flagestad & Hope, 2001) and, therefore, entrepreneurial requirements and challenges along the TALC are diverse. Furthermore, service industries are characterised by low entry barriers and relatively low levels of professionalisation. Also, in tourism two types of entrepreneurs are often distinguished. Burns and Dewhurst (1999) separate the 'lifestyle entrepreneur' from the 'growth-oriented entrepreneur'. Both types can be found in the development phase of European mass tourism from the 1960s to the 1980s. Many of those entrepreneurs who wanted to profit from the tourism boom were lateral entrants, and in doing so (at the beginning, mostly alongside their agricultural obligations) founded guest-houses or bed and breakfasts (see López-Chávez and Maldonado-Alcudia, this volume, Chapter 14). Those establishing bed and breakfasts fall into the category of lifestyle entrepreneurs (Pesonen *et al.*, 2011; Schuckert *et al.*, 2008; Shaw & Williams, 1998, 2004). But the Schumpeterian type of entrepreneur can also be identified in these development phases, albeit to a much lesser extent and in a weakened form. These entrepreneurs have clear visions in the development of the first lifts and cable cars and/or luxurious hotel palaces, for instance. Not surprisingly, these innovative entrepreneurs, or their successors, in particular, are more capable of managing entrepreneurial adaptation processes: they are the first to install new organisational forms, to recommend new technologies for use in tourism associations and to push the development of new products and services. These pioneer entrepreneurs develop the tourism infrastructure that is used by a broad mass of imitators, accompanied by low barriers to entry in terms of skills, technology or capital (Weiermair, 2001). These imitators are to a large extent lifestyle entrepreneurs who, for example, follow in the footsteps of their parents in their place of birth and use local personal networks (Peters & Kallmuenzer, 2018). The change from a seller's to a buyer's market in European tourism in the 1990s meant the end for a majority of lifestyle companies because they could no longer meet new demands. An urgently demanded strategic reorientation of the tourism offer can therefore come only from innovative entrepreneurs who are willing to take risks.

Nevertheless, in these years of stagnation in the growth of tourism arrivals, opportunities for innovation arise: tourism opens up to other sectors – cultural and event tourism, various sports tourism innovations – but also in health tourism many entrepreneurs find innovation opportunities. These entrepreneurs are not always tourism entrepreneurs but are lateral entrants from other industries. They bring new professional and technical know-how to the tourism and leisure industries.

Based on these two types of entrepreneur, Weiermair et al. (2007) describe the development for the Alpine regions in Europe and show how important entrepreneurial behaviour is in different phases of tourism development. Nevertheless, one can identify another mixed form of entrepreneurs in tourism: the 'constrained entrepreneurs' are mostly younger entrepreneurs who have clear growth motives and also previous experience in the tourism industry or related (service) industries. Even so, they also show many lifestyle motives when describing their entrepreneurial activities. Financing is mostly done with the help of the family and the focus is on socially sustainable business development (Peters et al., 2009; Weiermair, 2001). But constrained entrepreneurs are much more interested in developing new products and driving internal innovation processes. Moreover, they are less driven by their own actions or hobbies than by customers' wishes (Peters & Siller, 2014; Shaw & Williams, 1998, 2004).

Towards a New Concept of Responsible Entrepreneurship

Although entrepreneurs are often seen as part of the problem of environmental degradation, research has shown that they have the potential to transform negative environmental impacts (Cohen & Winn, 2007; Senge et al., 2001). In light of the development of considering not only economic impacts, entrepreneurship has increasingly been studied from the perspective of its contribution to sustainable development (Vallaster *et al.*, 2019). In this context, concepts such as sustainable entrepreneurship (Aquino *et al.*, 2018; Porter *et al.*, 2018), social entrepreneurship (Zahra *et al.*, 2009), eco- or green entrepreneurship (Allen & Malin, 2008; Wagner, 2009), as well as environmental entrepreneurship (York *et al.*, 2016) aim to understand sustainable development as part of entrepreneurial activities. In particular, social entrepreneurs are considered to emphasise social goals rather than economic objectives (Zahra *et al.*, 2009), as well as being seen as entrepreneurs who start a business that has primarily social purposes (Shaw & Carter, 2007). Sustainable entrepreneurship is a trade-off of entrepreneurial activities that contribute to environmental damage while also leveraging profitability (Cohen & Winn, 2007). While eco-entrepreneurs, green entrepreneurs and environmental entrepreneurs emphasise the environmental aspects of sustainable tourism development (Allen & Malin, 2008; Wagner, 2009; York *et al.*, 2016), by focusing on environmental progress as their core business (Schaltegger & Wagner, 2011) responsible entrepreneurs emphasise all three elements of sustainability: economic, environmental and social.

Besides the demonstrated relevance of sustainable tourism development in tourism research and practice (Liu, 2003), which is also visible in research focusing on sustainable or social entrepreneurship (Aquino *et al.*, 2018; Porter *et al.*, 2018), the concept of responsible tourism has gained prominence in the recent past (Saarinen, 2021). Responsible tourism refers to the ethical and moral responsibility for sustainable tourism development (Bramwell *et al.*, 2008). However, responsible tourism developed independently of the concept of sustainable tourism in the early 1980s, particularly in the context of studies on the impact of tourism on the environment and society (Bramwell *et al.*, 2008; Krippendorf, 1982; Mihalič, 2016). Responsible tourism aims to protect the natural environment with its resources, reduce pollution and also bring social and economic benefits to destination residents (Fang, 2020; Gong *et al.*, 2019). Thus, both concepts, sustainable and responsible tourism, aim to improve environmental, social, and economic sustainability (Bramwell *et al.*, 2008; Fang, 2020; Kuščer & Mihalič, 2019), which draws on the foundation of both concepts, namely ecological thinking (Dávid, 2011). While economic responsibility refers to supporting local products, services and businesses, reducing pollution and preserving the environment constitute environmental responsibility, and engaging with the local community and protecting human rights are part of social responsibility (Gong *et al.*, 2019; Mathew & Sreejesh, 2017).

In addition to the commonalities of sustainable and responsible tourism with the three pillars of sustainability, the concepts also have crucial differences in their contexts (Saarinen, 2021). In particular, responsible tourism is seen as the actual implementation of sustainable tourism development through responsible tourism behaviour and actions

(Medina, 2005; Mihalič *et al.*, 2021). Responsible tourism builds on sustainable tourism development strategies and policies that are reflected in the actual behaviour and actions of tourism stakeholders and contribute to the achievement of sustainability goals (Mathew & Sreejesh, 2017; Mihalič, 2016). In this context, it is assumed that all tourism stakeholders – tourists, residents, entrepreneurs, organisations, destination management organisations (DMOs) and governments – must contribute to sustainable tourism development through their responsible behaviour (Blackstock *et al.*, 2008; Mathew & Sreejesh, 2017; Mihalič *et al.*, 2021).

Saarinen (2021) in particular argued for the need for moral and ethical responsibility among tourism entrepreneurs throughout their involvement in tourism activities (Blackstock *et al.*, 2008). At the same time, responsibility for sustainable development is gaining importance in tourism businesses (Tiba *et al.*, 2019). Following Choi and Gray (2008), responsible entrepreneurs have emerged as a new type of entrepreneur that will soon be predominant. Responsible entrepreneurship thus focuses on entrepreneurs who manage to 'walk the line between profit creation and value creation for society' (Vallaster *et al.*, 2019: 538). Responsible entrepreneurs aim to contribute to sustainable development, in particular by taking responsibility for social and environmental aspects (Markman *et al.*, 2016; Roberts, 2001). However, entrepreneurship and sustainable development may not always coincide. On the one hand, entrepreneurs can increase environmental impacts, especially in tourism, while, on the other hand, sustainable development helps create market opportunities that enable new, innovative services (Vallaster *et al.*, 2019). In this regard, responsible entrepreneurship is also regarded as focusing on environmental activities that bring environmental innovation rather than management systems (Schaltegger & Wagner, 2011). Further, entrepreneurial opportunities arise for responsible entrepreneurs, which are enabled by innovations that reduce or reserve unsustainable conditions (Cohen & Winn, 2007). Following Dean and McMullen (2007), responsible entrepreneurship compromises the innovative process related to evaluating, exploring and discovering opportunities in market failures related to negative impacts.

Entrepreneurs who contribute to environmental sustainability and are thus considered responsible entrepreneurs are risk averse, as their businesses and innovations involve unpredictable outcomes. In addition to their intrinsic motivation to contribute to the natural environment, their entrepreneurial activities also have a positive impact on future sustainable development (Schaper, 2016).

Responsible Entrepreneurship in the Tourism Area Life Cycle

Following Weiermair *et al.* (2007), the Tourism Area Life Cycle (TALC) can be applied to understand changes in tourism entrepreneurship. In particular, the role of entrepreneurs and their responsibilities and interactions in relation to tourism development can be discussed. Against this background, it is argued that considering entrepreneurial activities from the perspective of responsible entrepreneurship can contribute to sustainable tourism development, approaching the following questions:

- What is the importance of entrepreneurship at each stage of the destination life cycle?
- What forms of entrepreneurship need to be provided in the future?
- How can the destination create an appropriate environment for the development of responsible entrepreneurship?

The following sections (see also Figure 20.1 for a summary) discuss these questions in light of the different phases of the TALC.

Exploration

During the initial phase of tourism development, where there are still few businesses and the number of tourists is very small (Butler, 1980), entrepreneurship, especially small-scale tourism entrepreneurship, can have beneficial impacts on a destination (Lordkipanidze et al., 2005). In this phase, a few local entrepreneurs anticipate the tourism trend early and react quickly to the increasing demand. These early adopters act from different motives, but mostly generate local leverage and manage largely sustainable available resources. Thus, already, some constrained entrepreneurs who establish start-ups and hire local employees can be found. For many residents, the emerging tourism industry offers new employment opportunities, while others migrate from other sectors (e.g. agriculture) to tourism. Therefore, the majority of suppliers become tourism and hospitality entrepreneurs through learning by doing.

In the context of responsible entrepreneurship, positive impacts on all three levels – economic, social and environmental – are in focus from the very beginning (Bramwell et al., 2008; Fang, 2020). In concrete terms, this relates to entrepreneurs who start businesses for social motives, as described above (Shaw & Carter, 2007; Zahra et al., 2009), or their primary aim is to make positive contributions to the natural environment based on their intrinsic motivation (Schaltegger & Wagner, 2011). Thus, responsible entrepreneurship requires the incorporation of not only economic goals (as usual in the early stages) but also economic and social objectives. However, the individual entrepreneur is often not aware that the main focus on profit-oriented behaviour, which might deliver short-term benefits, can lead to negative effects in the long term.

Involvement

As part of the second phase of tourism development, an increasing number of residents establish businesses and thus taking on the role of

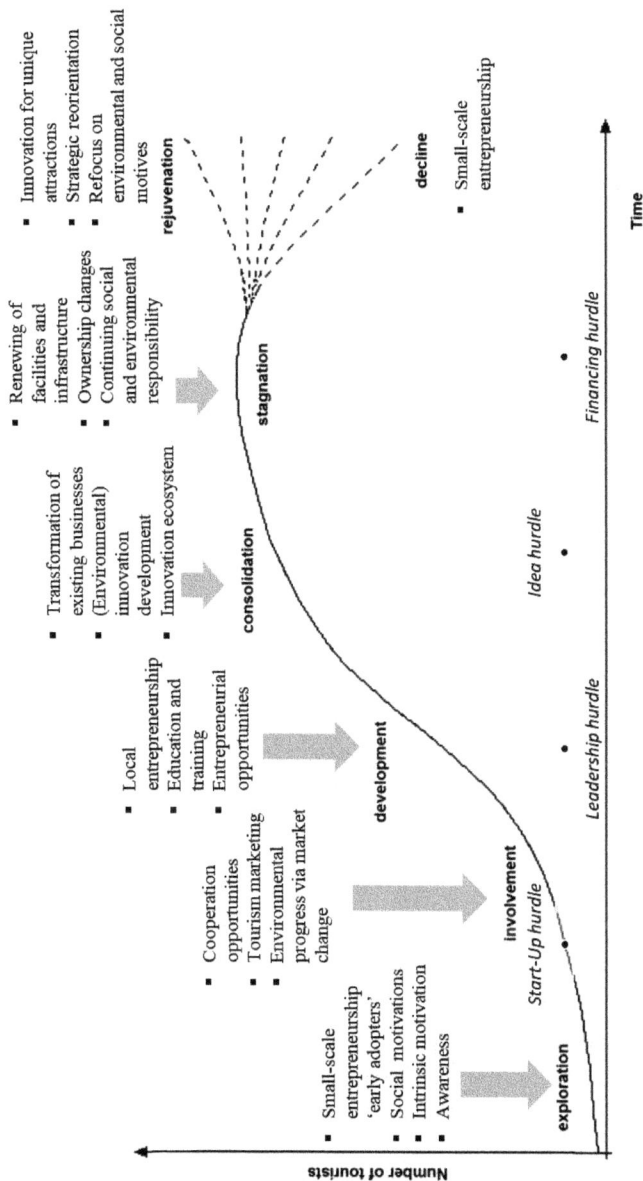

Figure 20.1 Responsible entrepreneurship in the TALC based on Butler (1980)

entrepreneurs (Butler, 1980). Destinations thus develop entrepreneurial qualifications in order to overcome start-up hurdles (Terpstra & Olson, 1993). As designated tourism districts emerge, outsiders and external investors show interest in the tourism area. Opportunities for cooperation lie in the promotion of sustainable development.

In terms of contributing to sustainable tourism development, entrepreneurs have the potential to influence the industry by affecting other actors, such as suppliers, competitors and customers (Fischer *et al.*, 2018). In this sense, entrepreneurs have the possibility of influencing demand, especially consumers' interest in sustainable offers. According to Schaltegger and Wagner (2011), 'eco-preneurs' even have the potential to shift the entire market towards making environmental progress. In this phase, it is necessary to formulate the corresponding target market segments. The challenges relate to the need to develop tourism marketing, which must optimise the fit between destination promise and demand. Correspondingly, and to overcome the above-mentioned leadership hurdle, the destination needs to delegate and assign respective tasks and roles (Parks, 1977).

Development

In the development phase of the TALC, more large companies are invest alongside small, local entrepreneurs due to the growing number of tourists (Butler, 1980). Although local entrepreneurs are becoming more professional, they are often overruled by experienced international investors, who cause tourism leakage: revenues from tourism development are 'leaked away' by foreign firms (Jönsson, 2015: 1). Local entrepreneurship needs to develop fast in order to meet tourism demand. Professional education and training, but also strong local cooperation and networks, are of utmost importance to avoid such leakage effects.

In the past, many destinations were overrun by high demand and reacted in a very short time perspective by expanding capacity and infrastructure. Today, destinations often formulate rules for this expansion, thus preventing the over-exploitation of resources and discouraging large investors. This corresponds to responsible entrepreneurship, which requires exploiting, acknowledging and evaluating entrepreneurial chances and opportunities following the three dimensions of sustainability during this phase of the TALC (Choi & Gray, 2008). Here, small-business entrepreneurs are asked to pursue opportunities to remain successful in the future: scanning market changes and trends in consumer behaviour. At the same time, monitoring the effects of this development phase on the destination's resources, as well as on residents' quality of life, is of utmost importance (Schönherr *et al.*, 2023; Weiermair & Peters, 2012).

Consolidation

In the phase of consolidation, total tourist numbers are still increasing, although growth rates in visitor number will decline (Butler, 1980). Entrepreneurs at this stage face increasing antagonism towards tourism development, but residents appreciate the responsible entrepreneur's focus on local resources and the preservation of the quality of life in the region.

Following Vallaster *et al.* (2019), responsible entrepreneurship consists of the capability to transform a business towards adapting sustainable processes and practices as responsible behaviour. Therefore, comprehensive transformations of existing tourism businesses are necessary. In light of the economic responsibility of responsible entrepreneurship, tourism destination stakeholders are asked to support remaining businesses with their local products and services (Gong *et al.*, 2019; Mathew & Sreejesh, 2017), in the sense of the circular economy (Manniche *et al.*, 2021).

The transformation can be enabled through the development of innovations, for responsible entrepreneurship, environmental innovations in particular (Schaltegger & Wagner, 2011). However, the entrepreneurial ability to act proactively must be created earlier, for example at the end of the development phase, as a basis for innovation. In this phase, the tourism destination could profit from a strong innovative ecosystem to tackle the idea hurdle (Galbraith, 1982).

Stagnation

After the peaks are reached, many facilities are no longer attractive to tourists. This is described in the stagnation phase of the TALC. In particular, destinations will have reached their maximum capacity, leading to social, environmental and economic problems (Butler, 1980). Thus, large investments are needed to renew operating facilities and destination infrastructure. This financing hurdle is often accompanied by the above-described lack of innovation management. Many destinations have reached this phase and failed to develop alternative means of growth. If the tourism industry is dominant and the region depends on tourism, it will be difficult to find political majorities to develop alternative industries. Nevertheless, this option is necessary, on the one hand to offer young residents different income options and on the other hand to create a balanced, healthy ecosystem.

Furthermore, although existing businesses are likely to change ownership during this phase of development, responsible entrepreneurs in particular are called upon to help offset the negative impacts of tourism. This should be done by continuing to emphasise the culture and traditions of the destination and developing entrepreneurial activities to reduce pollution (Gong *et al.*, 2019; Mathew & Sreejesh, 2017).

Rejuvenation/refocusing/reorientation and decline

After the stagnation phase in the TALC, tourism destinations may enter a decline or rejuvenation/refocusing/reorientation phase (Butler, 1980). After a decline in visitor numbers, destinations in a decline phase face difficulties in competing with others. Thus, tourist facilities may be replaced by other structures. On the one hand, entrepreneurs are likely to shift their businesses to other industries; on the other hand, local entrepreneurs are likely to take over tourist facilities as they become more affordable and appeal to the few remaining tourists. In this sense, day visitors can be served by small-scale entrepreneurship.

In the rejuvenation stage, unique attractions are required. Therefore, fundamental changes in the destination's core attractions are mandatory. This could be achieved, for example, by using resources that have not yet been exploited. However, with respect to responsible entrepreneurship, further exploitation of resources has to be carefully evaluated in order to avoid environmental damages and increasing residents' negative attitudes towards tourism development (Fang, 2020; Gong et al., 2019). In the European Alps, there are discussions about new ski area developments or mergers of ski areas. The expectation is to gain competitive advantages through larger ski areas and high-tech cable cars. However, this debate leads to clashes between tourism advocates and their opponents. Another potential avenue for rejuvenation is the development of attractions that are difficult to replicate in other areas. With this in mind, new attractions based on entrepreneurial innovation (Schaltegger & Wagner, 2011) are needed to prevent others from following this lead.

Alternatively, a reorientation of the destination can be undertaken. This means changing the positioning of the destination by changing its strategic orientation, for example by expanding low-season provision (e.g. in winter destinations) with new services and products. Alpine destinations, for instance, have changed from typical winter sports destinations to year-round destinations by developing new products and services. This reorientation has attracted new target groups: for example, they no longer address the traditional sport-oriented skiers, but new segments such as health-oriented connoisseurs (Zach et al., 2021). Here, the responsible entrepreneurs are particularly in demand by a year-round tourism, to distribute the tolerance for tourism by the creation of year-round offers, to provide all-year-round jobs and to optimise capacities.

Moreover, by refocusing, entrepreneurs can draw on previous paths in the success of development. As in the spirit of responsible entrepreneurship, social and environmental factors that were prominent at the beginning of development can be refocused (especially for entrepreneurs who have lost that emphasis). In Alpine destinations, a multitude of community-based strategies have been initiated in the past, which as a result demanded a return to the original destination values, traditions and responsible resource consumption (Bausch & Gartner, 2020; Heimerl & Peters, 2019).

Future Research and Recommendations for DMOs and Tourism Policy

Entrepreneurship can develop in many ways, and it is impossible to predict which forms and qualities of entrepreneurship will prevail in specific regions and tourism destinations. Nevertheless, the appropriate conditions can be created to lay the foundation for a corresponding entrepreneurial ecosystem (Eichelberger *et al.*, 2020). The discussion of responsible entrepreneurship in the different phases of the TALC enables the derivation of implications for tourism research and practice. In particular, it is well known that tourism development is supported by different parties, such as tourism policymakers and DMOs. As is the case for tourism development, these actors are asked to support entrepreneurship; in light of responsible tourism, this is regarded as responsible action (Blackstock *et al.*, 2008; Mathew & Sreejesh, 2017; Mihalič *et al.*, 2021).

Cooperation between tourism actors is particularly important in responsible entrepreneurship during the involvement phase (Fischer *et al.*, 2018). Here, DMOs are called upon to facilitate collaborations. Looking at destinations as a business network, DMOs can form communities of entrepreneurs who support and assist each other during the different phases of tourism development (Strobl & Peters, 2013).

Consumers can be influenced by entrepreneurs, especially with regard to the demand for sustainable offers (Fischer *et al.*, 2018; Schaltegger & Wagner, 2011). In terms of joining forces, the DMO's business networks can be used for joint actions, but destination marketing also needs to be developed to inform consumers accordingly. Instead of each individual business trying to convince customers of environmental contributions, the DMO can take on this role. The same applies to innovations, which are particularly required in the consolidation phase of the TALC. The promotion of environmental innovations in particular (Schaltegger & Wagner, 2011) requires joined forces. Here, too, the DMOs need to support cooperation and, in concrete terms, they should think about their own innovation labs and transformations in the destination services and products (Pikkemaat *et al.*, 2018). Many destinations in Alpine European tourism have managed to refocus on the strengths of the region with the help of community-based strategies in times of climate change and ongoing criticism of tourism by residents. What is needed, however, are facilitators such as DMOs that can efficiently bring the various stakeholders together.

Even though some businesses are founded in the first phase of tourism development, for social and environmental reasons (Schaltegger & Wagner, 2011; Shaw & Carter, 2007; Zahra *et al.*, 2009), many other individual entrepreneurs are not aware of the negative effects of an exclusive focus on economic profits. Therefore, it is necessary to create and follow an appropriate tourism development plan or strategy from the very first development of tourism. In such a tourism master plan, sustainability has to be considered as an integral part of strategic, tactical and operational action to avoid negative impacts.

According to Vallaster *et al.* (2019), responsible entrepreneurship and thus the contribution of entrepreneurs to sustainable development should be incentivised by governmental as well as non-governmental institutions. Incentives drive not only the development of responsible entrepreneurship but also responsible innovations. At the same time, the discussion about the TALC phases (especially in the development phase) demonstrates that regulations are necessary for responsible entrepreneurship. On the one hand, it is a matter of prohibiting the waste of resources as well as establishing concrete regulations for the expansion of visitor numbers (for example, by restricting the number of overnight stays or limiting the size of hotels and other forms of accommodation). In addition, even before the involvement phase in the TALC, training and educational facilities need to be created, not only for the entrepreneurs but also for their employees. The improvement of education increases the professionalisation of the destination and contributes to an improved offer.

Future research on responsible entrepreneurship is recommended to develop qualitative indicators for the development of tourism in addition to the quantitative indicators in the TALC (number of tourists). In this sense, it is necessary to monitor not only the number of overnight stays/ arrivals but also the quality of life in the destinations (of residents, entrepreneurs, employees). The increasing criticism of tourism by the residents, as described in the TALC, can be countered with responsible entrepreneurship, which should be the subject of future studies. In addition, it is relevant for further research to investigate the influence and cooperation of DMOs and responsible entrepreneurs. Here, studies can show how collaborative efforts can contribute to sustainable tourism. Furthermore, it is necessary to investigate the option to foster the concept of the circular economy during the different phases of the TALC.

References

Allen, J.C. and Malin, S. (2008) Green entrepreneurship: A method for managing natural resources? *Society and Natural Resources* 21 (9), 828–844. https://doi.org/10.1080/08941920701612917.

Aquino, R.S., Lück, M. and Schänzel, H.A. (2018) A conceptual framework of tourism social entrepreneurship for sustainable community development. *Journal of Hospitality and Tourism Management* 37, 23–32. https://doi.org/10.1016/j.jhtm.2018.09.001.

Bausch, T. and Gartner, W.C. (2020) Winter tourism in the European Alps: Is a new paradigm needed? *Journal of Outdoor Recreation and Tourism* 31, 100297. https://doi.org/10.1016/j.jort.2020.100297.

Blackstock, K.L., White, V., McCrum, G., Scott, A. and Hunter, C. (2008) Measuring responsibility: An appraisal of a Scottish national park's sustainable tourism indicators. *Journal of Sustainable Tourism* 16 (3), 276–297. https://doi.org/10.1080/09669580802154090.

Bramwell, B., Lane, B., McCabe, S., Mosedale, J. and Scarles, C. (2008) Research perspectives on responsible tourism. *Journal of Sustainable Tourism* 16 (3), 253–257. https://doi.org/10.1080/09669580802208201.

Burns, P. and Dewhurst, J. (eds) (1999) *Small Business and Entrepreneurship* (2nd edn). Macmillan Small Business Series. https://doi.org/10.1007/978-1-349-24911-4.

Butler, R. (1980) The concept of a tourist area cycle of evolution: Implications for management of resources. *Canadian Geographer* 24 (1), 5–12. https://doi.org/10.1111/j.1541-0064.1980.tb00970.x.

Choi, D.Y. and Gray, E.R. (2008) Socially responsible entrepreneurs: What do they do to create and build their companies? *Business Horizons* 51 (4), 341–352. https://doi.org/10.1016/j.bushor.2008.02.010.

Cohen, B. and Winn, M.I. (2007) Market imperfections, opportunity and sustainable entrepreneurship. *Journal of Business Venturing* 22 (1), 29–49. https://doi.org/10.1016/j.jbusvent.2004.12.001.

Dávid, L. (2011) Tourism ecology: Towards the responsible, sustainable tourism future. *Worldwide Hospitality and Tourism Themes*, 3(3), 210–216. https://doi.org/10.1108/17554211111142176

Dean, T.J. and McMullen, J.S. (2007) Toward a theory of sustainable entrepreneurship: Reducing environmental degradation through entrepreneurial action. *Journal of Business Venturing* 22 (1), 50–76. https://doi.org/10.1016/j.jbusvent.2005.09.003.

Eichelberger, S., Peters, M., Pikkemaat, B. and Chan, C.-S. (2020) Entrepreneurial ecosystems in smart cities for tourism development: From stakeholder perceptions to regional tourism policy implications. *Journal of Hospitality and Tourism Management* 45, 319–329. https://doi.org/10.1016/j.jhtm.2020.06.011.

Fang, W.-T. (2020) Responsible tourism. *Tourism in Emerging Economies* 50, 131–151. https://doi.org/10.1007/978-981-15-2463-9_6.

Fischer, D., Mauer, R. and Brettel, M. (2018) Regulatory focus theory and sustainable entrepreneurship. *International Journal of Entrepreneurial Behavior and Research* 24 (2), 408–428. https://doi.org/10.1108/IJEBR-12-2015-0269.

Flagestad, A. and Hope, C.A. (2001) Strategic success in winter sports destinations: A sustainable value creation perspective. *Tourism Management* 22 (5), 445–461. https://doi.org/10.1016/S0261-5177(01)00010-3.

Galbraith, J.R. (1982) Designing the innovating organization. *Organizational Dynamics* 10 (3), 5–25. https://doi.org/10.1016/0090-2616(82)90033-X.

Gong, J., Detchkhajornjaroensri, P. and Knight, D.W. (2019) Responsible tourism in Bangkok, Thailand: Resident perceptions of Chinese tourist behaviour. *International Journal of Tourism Research* 21 (2), 221–233. https://doi.org/10.1002/jtr.2256.

Heimerl, P. and Peters, M. (2019) Shaping the future of Alpine tourism destinations' next generation: An action research approach. *Tourism: An International Interdisciplinary Journal* 67 (3), 281–298.

Hering, T. and Vincenti, A.J. F. (2005) *Unternehmensgründung*. Munich: Oldenbourg Verlag.

Hutchinson, P.J., Piper, J.A. and Ray, G.H. (1986) Surviving the financial stress of small enterprise growth. In J. Curran, D. Stanworth and D. Watkins (eds) *The Survival of the Small Firm: The Economics of Survival and Entrepreneurship* (pp. 53–71). Farnham: Gower.

Jönsson, C. (2015) Leakage, economic tourism. In J. Jafari and H. Xiao (eds) *Encyclopedia of Tourism*. Cham: Springer. https://doi.org/10.1007/978-3-319-01669-6_527-1.

Krippendorf, J. (1982) Towards new tourism policies. *Tourism Management* 3 (3), 135–148. https://doi.org/10.1016/0261-5177(82)90063-2.

Kuščer, K. and Mihalič, T. (2019) Residents' attitudes towards overtourism from the perspective of tourism impacts and cooperation – The case of Ljubljana. *Sustainability* 11 (6), 1823. https://doi.org/10.3390/su11061823.

Liu, Z. (2003) Sustainable tourism development: A critique. *Journal of Sustainable Tourism* 11 (6), 459–475. https://doi.org/10.1080/09669580308667216.

Lordkipanidze, M., Brezet, H. and Backman, M. (2005) The entrepreneurship factor in sustainable tourism development. *Journal of Cleaner Production* 13 (8), 787–798. https://doi.org/10.1016/j.jclepro.2004.02.043.

Manniche, J., Larsen, K.T. and Broegaard, R.B. (2021) The circular economy in tourism: Transition perspectives for business and research. *Scandinavian Journal of Hospitality and Tourism* 21 (3), 247–264. https://doi.org/10.1080/15022250.2021.1921020.

Markman, G.D., Russo, M., Lumpkin, G.T., Jennings, P.D.D. and Mair, J. (2016) Entrepreneurship as a platform for pursuing multiple goals: A special issue on sustainability, ethics, and entrepreneurship. *Journal of Management Studies* 53 (5), 673–694. https://doi.org/10.1111/joms.12214.

Mathew, P.V. and Sreejesh, S. (2017) Impact of responsible tourism on destination sustainability and quality of life of community in tourism destinations. *Journal of Hospitality and Tourism Management* 31, 83–89. https://doi.org/10.1016/j.jhtm.2016.10.001.

Medina, L.K. (2005) Ecotourism and certification: Confronting the principles and pragmatics of socially responsible tourism. *Journal of Sustainable Tourism* 13 (3), 281–295. https://doi.org/10.1080/01434630508668557.

Mihalič, T. (2016) Sustainable-responsible tourism discourse – Towards 'responsustable' tourism. *Journal of Cleaner Production* 111, 461–470. https://doi.org/10.1016/j.jclepro.2014.12.062.

Mihalič, T., Mohamadi, S., Abbasi, A. and Dávid, L.D. (2021) Mapping a sustainable and responsible tourism paradigm: A bibliometric and citation network analysis. *Sustainability* 13 (2), 853. https://doi.org/10.3390/su13020853.

Parks, G.M. (1977) How to climb a growth curve: Eleven hurdles for the entrepreneur-manager. *Journal of Small Business Management* 15 (1), 25–29. https://search.proquest.com/openview/d3f4891e9b34cd0dab04998fa8a9557f/1?pq-origsite=gscholar&cbl=49243.

Pesonen, J., Komppula, R., Kronenberg, C. and Peters, M. (2011) Understanding the relationship between push and pull motivations in rural tourism. *Tourism Review* 66 (3), 32–49. https://doi.org/10.1108/16605371111175311.

Peters, M., Frehse, J. and Buhalis, D. (2009) The importance of lifestyle entrepreneurship: A conceptual study of the tourism industry. *PASOS Revista De Turismo Y Patrimonio Cultural* 7 (3), 393–405. https://doi.org/10.25145/j.pasos.2009.07.028.

Peters, M. and Kallmuenzer, A. (2018) Entrepreneurial orientation in family firms: The case of the hospitality industry. *Current Issues in Tourism* 21 (1), 21–40. https://doi.org/10.1080/13683500.2015.1053849.

Peters, M. and Siller, H. (2014) Tourismusentwicklung im alpinen Lebensraum: Zur Erforschung der Rolle der Einheimischen. In K. Matzler, H. Pechlaner and B. Renzl (eds) *Strategie und Leadership* (pp. 175–189). Wiesbaden: Springer. https://doi.org/10.1007/978-3-658-04057-4_11.

Pikkemaat, B., Peters, M. and Chan, C.-S. (2018) Needs, drivers and barriers of innovation: The case of an alpine community-model destination. *Tourism Management Perspectives* 25, 53–63. https://doi.org/10.1016/j.tmp.2017.11.004.

Porter, B.A., Orams, M.B. and Lück, M. (2018) Sustainable entrepreneurship tourism: An alternative development approach for remote coastal communities where awareness of tourism is low. *Tourism Planning and Development* 15 (2), 149–165. https://doi.org/10.1080/21568316.2017.1312507.

Roberts, L. (2001) *Rural Tourism and Recreation: Principles to Practice*. Wallingford: CABI.

Saarinen, J. (2021) Is being responsible sustainable in tourism? Connections and critical differences. *Sustainability* 13 (12), 6599. https://doi.org/10.3390/su13126599.

Schaltegger, S. and Wagner, M. (2011). Sustainable entrepreneurship and sustainability innovation: Categories and interactions. *Business Strategy and the Environment* 20 (4), 222–237. https://doi.org/10.1002/bse.682.

Schaper, M.A. (2016) Understanding the green entrepreneur. In M.A. Schaper (ed.) *Making Ecopreneurs: Developing Sustainable Entrepreneurship* (pp. 7–20). Corporate Social Responsibility Series. London: Routledge.

Schuckert, M., Peters, M. and Fessler, B. (2008) An empirical assessment of owner-manager motives in the B&B and vacation home sector. *Tourism Review* 63 (4), 27–39. https://doi.org/10.1108/16605370810912191.

Schönherr, S., Eller, R., Kallmuenzer, A. and Peters, M. (2023) Organisational learning and sustainable tourism: The enabling role of digital transformation. *Journal of Knowledge Management* 27 (11), 82–100.

Schumpeter, J.A. (2000) *Entrepreneurship as Innovation*. University of Illinois at Urbana-Champaign's Academy for Entrepreneurial Leadership, Historical Research Reference in Entrepreneurship. Available at https://ssrn.com/abstract=1512266.

Senge, P.M., Carstedt, G. and Porter, P.L. (2001) Innovating our way to the next industrial revolution. *MIT Sloan Management Review* 42 (2), 24–38.

Shaw, E. and Carter, S. (2007) Social entrepreneurship. *Journal of Small Business and Enterprise Development* 14 (3), 418–434. https://doi.org/10.1108/14626000710773529.

Shaw, G. and Williams, A.M. (1998) Entrepreneurship and tourism development. In D. Ioannides and K.G. Debbage (eds) *The Economic Geography of the Tourist Industry: A Supply-Side Analysis* (pp. 235–255). London: Routledge.

Shaw, G. and Williams, A.M. (2004) From lifestyle consumption to lifestyle production: Changing patterns of tourism entrepreneurship. In R. Thomas (ed.) *Small Firms in Tourism* (pp. 99–113). New York: Elsevier.

Strobl, A. and Peters, M. (2013) Entrepreneurial reputation in destination networks. *Annals of Tourism Research* 40, 59–82. https://doi.org/10.1016/j.annals.2012.08.005.

Terpstra, D.E. and Olson, P.D. (1993) Entrepreneurial start-up and growth: A classification of problems. *Entrepreneurship Theory and Practice* 17 (3), 5–20. https://doi.org/10.1177/104225879301700301.

Tiba, S., van Rijnsoever, F.J. and Hekkert, M.P. (2019) Firms with benefits: A systematic review of responsible entrepreneurship and corporate social responsibility literature. *Corporate Social Responsibility and Environmental Management* 26 (2), 265–284. https://doi.org/10.1002/csr.1682.

Vallaster, C., Kraus, S., Kailer, N. and Baldwin, B. (2019) Responsible entrepreneurship: Outlining the contingencies. *International Journal of Entrepreneurial Behavior and Research* 25 (3), 538–553. https://doi.org/10.1108/IJEBR-04-2018-0206.

Wagner, M. (2009) Eco-entrepreneurship: An empirical perspective based on survey data. In G.D. Libecap (ed.) *Advances in the Study of Entrepreneurship, Innovation and Economic Growth. Frontiers in Eco-Entrepreneurship Research* (Vol. 20, pp. 127–152). Leeds: Emerald. https://doi.org/10.1108/S1048-4736(2009)0000020009.

Weiermair, K. (2001) Theoretical foundations or considerations regarding the growth of tourism enterprises. *Tourism Review* 56 (3/4), 17–25. https://doi.org/10.1108/eb058363.

Weiermair, K. and Peters M. (2012) Quality-of-life values among stakeholders in tourism destinations: A tale of converging and diverging interests and conflicts. In M. Uysal, R. Perdue and M.J. Sirgy (eds) *Handbook of Tourism and Quality-of-Life Research* (pp. 463–473). Dordrecht: Springer.

Weiermair, K., Peters, M. and Schuckert, M. (2007) Destination development and the tourist life-cycle: Implications for entrepreneurship in Alpine tourism. *Tourism Recreation Research* 32 (1), 83–93. https://doi.org/10.1080/02508281.2007.11081526.

York, J.G., O'Neil, I. and Sarasvathy, S.D. (2016) Exploring environmental entrepreneurship: Identity coupling, venture goals, and stakeholder incentives. *Journal of Management Studies* 53 (5), 695–737. https://doi.org/10.1111/joms.12198.

Zach, F.J., Schnitzer, M. and Falk, M. (2021) Product diversification and isomorphism: The case of ski resorts and 'me-too' innovation. *Annals of Tourism Research* 90, 103267. https://doi.org/10.1016/j.annals.2021.103267.

Zahra, S.A., Gedajlovic, E., Neubaum, D.O. and Shulman, J.M. (2009) A typology of social entrepreneurs: Motives, search processes and ethical challenges. *Journal of Business Venturing* 24 (5), 519–532. https://doi.org/10.1016/j.jbusvent.2008.04.007.

21 Applying the TALC Model to Northern Ireland: A Destination Facing Recovery from Multiple Crises

Stephen Boyd and Peter Bolan

In the original publication, Butler (1980) acknowledged that the life cycle model for a destination experiencing a period of protracted conflict would be dramatically different from the TALC – its development path would be suddenly interrupted and the hypothetical S-shaped growth trajectory would not be followed. Northern Ireland was cited in that seminal publication as an example of such a scenario. It is therefore fitting in this volume, where many case examples illustrate varying scenarios of normalcy linked to the S-shaped evolutionary pattern, to present the case of Northern Ireland, as its tourism journey has indeed been anything but normalised. The journey that Northern Ireland has been on is even more complicated by the fact that the early stages of the cycle took place in an era before Northern Ireland was constitutionally formed. While it would enjoy a period free of conflict, when early tourism development could take place, much of its history has been linked to crises – political (conflict), economic (Brexit) and, recently, health-related (COVID-19).

This chapter, therefore, sets out a chronology across three distinct time periods. First, tourism pre-conflict, where it is argued that the North of Ireland and then Northern Ireland had 'explored' and was 'involved' with tourism, creating the context for its embarking on a 'development' path. Second, tourism during conflict, when Northern Ireland experienced 'development interrupted', during which it reverted to being perceived as just a place as opposed to a destination, with a reduced tourism presence and infrastructure as a the basis for future recovery. Third, tourism post-conflict, when Northern Ireland returned to being a destination but one shaped, first, by a 'Phoenix' era, with the promotion of dark and political tourism, and, second, by destination revisioning around a wider cultural and heritage tourism opportunity. Both provided the basis for reaching 'destination normalcy', where Northern Ireland started to resemble those destinations that had never experienced conflict in living memory, only to be faced with the potential impact of two new challenges, one that was region-specific (Brexit) followed by a second that was global in its impact (COVID-19).

The chapter concludes by proposing a revised TALC model where multiple crises are taken into consideration. Instead of the S-shaped pattern, development is best reflected as a series of waves, where wave depth is a measure of destination resilience and adaptive capacity towards recovery. This thinking around waves will be discussed in more depth in the conclusion, but it is necessary first to return to the context which created the antecedents of early tourism.

Early Cycle: Exploration and Involvement with Tourism

At many destinations, tourism takes place around the appeal of visiting unique spaces and attractions, and in the case of the North of Ireland this attraction was to see the Giant's Causeway and to enjoy cold-water bathing associated with the emergence of seaside resorts across the north coast region. The market was the English elite travellers who viewed this geographic space as something akin to what Ireland offered as its 'Grand Tour'. The Giant's Causeway attracted visitors as early as the 1750s and was depicted in many lithographs and paintings. Visitors were drawn to see this natural wonder of the world, with its unique columns protruding upward, and it ushered in what could be termed the 'exploration stage' for tourism in the region, with the first lodging house opening in the coastal community of Portrush in 1822, followed by the first hotel, the Antrim Arms, in 1838 (Bolan, 1995). In 1837 Portrush saw one of the first man-made harbours completed in Ireland, and the railway arrived there in 1855 (Mullin, 1982).

With such developments, it could be argued that the north coast of Ireland as a region had entered the 'involvement' tourism stage. Across the Victorian era (1837–1901), tourism to the north coast was clearly at the early 'development' stage, with coastal communities across the region transformed into well recognised destinations famed for their expanse of beaches, the appeal of cold-water bathing, enjoying golf in the newly created links course in Portrush (see Bolan & Boyd, this volume, Chapter 15) and visiting the Giant's Causeway. The last was facilitated when a roadside track was completed in 1883 that saw tourists travel out and back from Portrush, taking in en route the sites of the remains of Dunluce Castle (Bolan, 1995). At the outbreak of the First World War and still ahead of Ireland being partitioned into north and south (which took place in 1922), it would be fair to say tourism was clearly 'developed' across the north coast of Ireland. This pattern of development is important as this region would become a pleasure area for Northern Ireland when it was formed from the northern six counties of Ireland. Given the extent to which tourism had developed across the north coast, it was not surprising that a tourism agency was quickly established after partition, and in 1923 the Ulster Tourist Development Association was founded with a remit of promoting tourism for the newly created Northern Ireland (Boyd, 2017).

The Giant's Causeway remained popular for British and European travellers, as did the Victorian and Edwardian resorts situated along the north coast. Open-air museums had grown in popularity since the first, Skansen, had opened in Stockholm in 1873, and Northern Ireland was keen to showcase its culture and heritage. By the end of the 1960s, Northern Ireland offered visitors a strong heritage (and cultural) product, including sandy beaches with 'bucket and spade' Victorian and Edwardian seaside resorts.

Northern Ireland as a Province (of the United Kingdom) moved quickly after the Second World War to establish an official tourism body. The 1948 Tourist Act saw a national tourism body established, the Northern Ireland Tourist Board (NITB), with a remit to provide leadership to a fledgling industry as well as to promote the region, primarily to the British market. What is significant about the establishment of this body is that it was the first in any region of the UK (Boyd, 2013a). Early statistics recorded by the NITB demonstrated that over the decade 1959–1969, expenditure by overnight visitors doubled from £7.1 million to £14.5 million, enabled by a visitor accommodation stock of 210 locally owned hotels (4368 rooms) and 226 guest-houses (2281 rooms) (Boyd, 2000, 2013a). Table 21.1 reveals that over the same period, spending by excursionist travellers quadrupled, from £2.6 million to £10.7 million. When both staying and day-trip visitors are combined, the tourism industry in Northern Ireland between 1959 and 1969 would see tourism receipts more than double, from £9.7 million to £25 million. Figures on the purpose of visits for 1967 reflect a region that was perceived as a 'holiday destination': 35% holiday, 25% business-related, 38% visiting friends or relatives (VFR). By 1968 tourism in Northern Ireland was showing characteristics consistent with what Butler had argued reflected a destination well within its 'development' stage of growth: over 1.1 million staying visitors, a clearly defined coastal,

Table 21.1 Visitor numbers and expenditure (spend, in £millions), 1959–1969

Year	Staying visitors (tourists)			Day visitors (excursionists)		All visitors
	Trips	Nights	Spend	Trips	Spend	Spend
1959	633,000	5,892,400	£7.1	2,019,000	£2.6	£9.7
1963	704,600	7,670,900	£10.1	4,526,000	£7.5	£17.6
1967	1,080,000	8,697,400	£16.9	8,387,000	£10.1	£27.0
1968	1,139,000	9,164,500	£17.6	8,565,000	£11.5	£29.2
1969	1,066,000	8,592,000	£14.5	7,479,000	£10.7	£25.2

Source: Boyd (2013a).

heritage and a cultural tourism product base supported by a locally owned accommodation industry. This would, however, quickly change with the onset of political instability in 1969, as shown in Table 21.1 with the start of reduced visitor numbers and expenditure.

Mid-Cycle: 'Development Interrupted'

At the end of the 1960s, with the outbreak of overt violence in the form of terrorist activity, and against the backdrop of civic unrest, Northern Ireland moved from being a destination that had developed a clearly defined tourism product, with a focus on an established pleasure periphery along the north coast, to becoming a 'difficult environment'. According to Mansfeld (1999), that is any context in which the maintenance of positive images aligned with multiple experiences becomes problematic. Northern Ireland quickly reverted from being a destination to just a physical space. In the early years (especially the 1970s) of what would be termed by the British media 'the Troubles', Northern Ireland's image was anything but a destination desirable to visit. The British army became a constant presence on the streets, border crossings with the Irish Republic were either closed or heavily patrolled, people were searched when entering shops and town centres were deserted places in the evening. Two aspects best sum up the 'development interrupted' era: loss and resilience. In terms of loss, while the pleasure periphery was less affected by overt terrorist activity, the destination lost almost 60% of its visitors between 1968 and 1974, and 35% of its accommodation stock between 1969 and 1972. While visitor numbers would slowly recover, they would not return to pre-conflict levels until 1991, and accommodation stock, especially hotels, would continue to witness decline (see Table 21.2).

Resilience was first evidenced by the actions of key industry stakeholders. Many locally run hotels kept their doors open, and the Europa Hotel in Belfast became renowned for being the most bombed hotel in Europe, becoming a symbol of wider industry resilience. Second, Northern

Table 21.2 Visitor numbers and accommodation stock (hotels) for selected years, 1972–1991

Year	Visitor numbers	Accommodation stock (no. of hotels)
1972	435,000	137
1974	628,100	144
1981	588,000	143
1983	865,300	139
1987	942,800	128
1991	1,186,000	121

Source: Northern Ireland Tourist Board (NITB) (1980, 1990, 1992).

Ireland had always benefited from a large 'holiday' and 'VFR' market. The early years of the Troubles saw the former decline from 36% in 1967 to 8% in 1977, and so the NITB focused its attention on appealing to the VFR market. Over the same period (1967–1977), this market segment increased from 38% to 61%; while overall numbers halved over the same period, the VFR market prevented the complete collapse of tourism and offered the basis for recovery. By 1982, the VFR segment still accounted for 59%, but the pure 'holiday' market had witnessed only a modest recovery, accounting for 16% of all visits. It would not be until 1988 that the VFR market dropped below 50%, whereas the holiday market would recover but to account for only 18% of overall visitor numbers. Business-related travel accounted for the second largest market segment (ranging between 20% and 25% between 1977 and 1989).

Baum (1995) referred to the period between 1969 and 1991 as the 'lost years', where Northern Ireland lost out year on year in investment in tourism infrastructure compared with its competitors. Others were critical of the lack of initiative taken by the Northern Ireland tourism authorities (Leslie, 1999). But is such criticism warranted, given that much of the accommodation stock had been damaged or was closed down due to lack of market demand? With political decision-making having moved to Westminster during the Troubles, there was a lack of local political governance to promote the development of the tourist industry beyond what already existed from pre-conflict times. Tourism, despite years of conflict, was always viewed as offering employment potential but the administrative arrangements around tourism remained disjointed between responsibilities for tourism marketing and policymaking (Buckley & Klemm, 1993). It would not be until 1989 that a more professional approach to marketing the region was adopted. Under the 'Indicative Plan for Tourism', clearer market targets were set, and new administrative arrangements saw greater powers and responsibilities devolved to the leading tourism authority body, the NITB, including the setting of targets (Boyd, 2013a).

As shown in Table 21.2, visitor numbers continued to increase, resulting in visitor spend increasing tenfold, from £13 million in 1974 to £136 million in 1989 (NITB, 1990). The Indicative Plan published in 1990 set an ambitious target of reaching 1.6 million visitors by 1994, an increase of 400,000 beyond what was enjoyed pre-conflict. This Plan was, however, set against a wider context of an ongoing protracted conflict. By the early 1990s, lines of communication had been opened between the UK government and Sinn Fein, the political wing of the Irish Republican Army (IRA). Eventually, a negotiated peace commenced with a cessation of violence by the IRA on 31 August 1994. Peace held until 9 February 1996, a period of 18 months; this showed what could be achieved in a period of peace. It also set the context for ongoing negotiations, which culminated in a formal peace agreement called the Good Friday Agreement (GFA), signed on 10 April 1998.

With the first full year free of conflict since 1968, tourism records for 1995 showed that, for the first time, the pure holiday market accounted for 30% of all visits, compared with 21% the previous year, although VFR remained the largest market segment (36%). When key market regions are considered, 1995 compared with 1994 witnessed double-digit growth from visitors from Britain (+14%), the Irish Republic (+21%), Continental Europe (+25%), North America (+53%) and 'other overseas' (+56%). These tourism statistics demonstrate clearly how quickly people respond to positive change, as overall visitor numbers exceeded the 1.5 million mark for the first time, although still below the target in the 1990 Indicative Plan (Boyd, 2013a). The return to a conflict situation in 1996 with the end of the ceasefire saw many of those gains lost. 'Holiday' as main purpose of visiting fell back to 21% and VFR accounted for 41% (as it had been throughout 1991–1994). In terms of key market regions, visitors declined from all regions – Irish Republic (–21%), Europe (–11%), North America (–15%), other overseas (–12%) – with the exception of Britain (+2%). The tourism statistics recorded for 1996 demonstrate how quickly gains achieved can be easily lost.

Research by Boyd (2000) shows that the majority of the Northern Ireland visitor attraction base before the GFA was predominantly heritage-centric, subdivided to include historical, cultural, industrial, educational and natural categories. Visitor numbers to attractions that received over 5000 visitors demonstrated double-digit growth in 1995, the year free of overt violence, only to be lost in 1996, with limited recovery the following year (see Table 21.3).

These statistics illustrate that before the official peace agreement was signed in 1998, the base on which to build on a previous 'development' stage was in place. Overall visitor numbers had recovered to well beyond those experienced pre-conflict (remaining around 1.4 million in 1996 and 1997) and the tourism industry was poised to benefit from the forthcoming potential peace dividend. Early problems existed, however, as new product development had been lacking and much existing stock

Table 21.3 Visits to heritage attractions receiving over 5000 visitors between 1994 and 1997

Type	1994	1995	% change	1996	% change	1997	% change
Historical	276,896	326,820	+15	304,744	–7	293,578	–4
Cultural	549,586	599,325	+8	506,861	–18	525,595	+4
Industrial	236,979	384,879	+38	351,353	–9	383,564	+8
Educational	210,651	273,747	+23	215,047	–27	219,000	+2
Natural	1,598,047	1,984,564	+19	1,854,678	–7	1,853,017	0
Total	2,872,159	3,569,335	+20	3,232,683	–10	3,274,754	+1

Source: Boyd (2000).

needed considerable quality enhancement (O'Neill & Fitz, 1996). Further-more, while industry reports called for a substantial programme of hotel development, with an additional 18,000 beds by the year 2000 (Howarth, 1996), occupancy levels had increased to only 62% in 1995 and then fell back to 56% the following year, suggesting that the requirement for new accommodation might be questioned. Despite this, the industry called for a programme of new investment, improved service standards, and training and retraining to provide a more professional workforce. Over the period 1992–1998, governance in the form of Corporate Plans by the NITB facilitated, first, a restructuring of the tourism industry, offering grants and improving standards across the serviced accommodation sector and, second, a refocus on promoting Northern Ireland as a quality, competitive destination aimed at attracting first-time holiday visitors and not focused on further development of its VFR base (Boyd, 2013a). What was unexpected was the nature of the new opportunity offered by the private sector, in the form of dark tourism. Promotion by the media during the Troubles of how different communities across Northern Ireland used murals (street art) not only to showcase their culture but also to demarcate and demonstrate both territoriality and dissonance of their heritage helped create a unique attraction connected to the Troubles. This attracted new visitors in the years leading up to the formal signing of the GFA peace accord and acted as a major element in the 'development recovered' stage.

Mid-Cycle: 'Development Recovered'

An argument could be made that this stage of 'development recovered' commenced in 1991, when visitor numbers exceeded those pre-conflict, but that would hold true only if the measurement of recovery was based on visitor numbers alone. While overall numbers stayed above those recorded pre-conflict across the first part of the 1990s, the return of violence in 1996 demonstrated that any lasting recovery would be possible only if a lasting peace agreement was reached. The various Corporate Plans (1992–1998) mentioned above were just that – plans – and even though they set in place better governance and industry preparedness, visitor numbers never exceeded the 1.5 million enjoyed in 1995. The game changer was the signing of a formal peace settlement on 10 April 1998. That agreement set in place a unique opportunity to rebuild tourism in a positive climate free of concern around safety and security.

This 'development recovered' stage had three distinct characteristics. First, new product development emerged around dark and political tourism, shaping a distinct but short period of tourism development, which we term 'phoenix development'. This involved new products linked to the past conflict, driven by economic development goals, and also opportunities for social benefits, where storytelling would act as a form of catharsis and social healing, with tourists sharing stories of how other conflicts affected them, offering opportunities around reconciliation tourism. Second, the existing heritage and cultural base was revisioned by government and public sector tourism bodies, to develop new world-class tourism attractions. And third, a more diverse, multi-niched tourism development base was achieved through opportunities around screen/film, events, sports and food, to move Northern Ireland towards what we term 'destination normalisation', characteristic of a destination entering the latter stages of the 'development' phase. Each of these is discussed briefly below; for a more extensive discussion, see Boyd (2013a, 2017, 2019a, 2019b).

An extensive literature has developed around the discussion of dark tourism (Lennon & Foley, 2000; Sharpley & Stone, 2009). The connection of dark tourism with Northern Ireland is a complex one, as it was focused on both dark heritage and spaces that offered opportunities to present distinct political narratives (Boyd, 2016). What quickly became famous were the open-air galleries of murals with their storytelling of community heritage that Simon Calder (a well-known UK travel writer) urged people to see before they vanished; they are still an integral part of the street art of major cities across Northern Ireland, but some specific changes have taken place. Added to viewing murals linked to the past and other conflicts were opportunities to sell dark heritage through black taxi tours of 'Trouble' sites, walking tours of political spaces operated by former prisoners (both Protestant and Catholic) telling 'their stories', as well as community-based museums showcasing heritage memorabilia of both communities and also offering the opportunity for storytelling as a form of catharsis. Causevic and Lynch (2013) found the same situation had played out in Bosnia-Herzegovina; they argued that such 'phoenix tourism' had more of a social benefit value than an economic one. Similarly in the case of Northern Ireland, private sector initiatives helped to facilitate a complex phoenix stage, comprising economic development of new tourism opportunity and also community-driven initiatives that focused on social aspects of community healing, showcasing heritage and being part of a wider reconciliation tourism. Boyd (2000) had cautioned against emphasising a tourism opportunity that had a dark tourism focus, but issues of territoriality, contested identity, dissonance and commodification of conflict heritage, noted by other authors (Graham, 1996; McDowell, 2008; Tunbridge & Ashworth, 1996), did become key elements of the narrative that tourists experienced and were sold first-hand. This new dark tourism opportunity was not wholly responsible for improved visitor numbers and spend – in 2007 overall visitor numbers exceeded 2 million (2,107,000) and tourism contributed half a billion pounds (compared with £280 million in 1998) to the local economy (Boyd, 2013a) – undoubtedly a more peaceful destination and positive perception of levels of safety and security contributed significantly.

Accompanying this private sector initiative around dark tourism, government and tourism bodies embarked on a revisioning of the heritage and cultural tourism base that had survived the conflict era. Northern Ireland in the early 1990s lacked 'stand-out' visitor attractions that would draw more international visitors and an ambitious programme to fill this gap had its genesis prior to the GFA. Called the Strategic Framework for Action (2004–2008), it identified a number of signature projects linked to Northern Ireland's heritage. These included a visitor attraction for RMS *Titanic* (maritime heritage), rebuilding a visitor centre at the Giant's Causeway and marking out a coastal route with highlight stops (natural and cultural heritage), improving the public realm around Derry's walls (built and historical heritage), making a religious route around St Patrick (religious heritage) and developing the country's first national park (natural heritage). An ambitious, perhaps more aspirational programme of infrastructure development, with no central-government capital funding, saw only one element, the marked out coastal route (Causeway Coastal Route), completed by 2007, and that was through the cooperation of the local county councils that the route traversed (Boyd, 2013b). With peace still in place (albeit imperfect), out-of-state (OOS) visitor numbers exceeded the 2 million mark for the first time (2.1 million in 2007) and generated almost £400 million in spend. With funding (£75 million) from the Northern Ireland Assembly Programme for Government (PfG) (2008–2011), National Lottery monies and private sector commitments, all but one of the signature projects were completed by 2012, the exception being the national park; that proposal was replaced by one for another coastal route (the Mournes) as no community support could be reached for the park.

The Corporate Plan 2008–2011 had set ambitious targets for OOS visitors to increase by 25% to 2.5 million and for spend to grow by 40% to £520 million. With the signature projects completed, the Titanic Belfast opened in April 2012, just ahead of the centenary of the ship's sinking, and the new visitor centre at the Giant's Causeway opened later that summer, tourism authorities saw 2012 as a tipping point. Northern Ireland had successfully hosted the Irish Open that year (see Bolan & Boyd, this volume, Chapter 15) and had won the bid for Derry~Londonderry to be the UK's first recipient City of Culture (2013). However, visitor numbers failed to grow beyond the 2 million mark (1.98 million in 2012), though they were double what they were pre-conflict, and while spend increased to £488 million, it did not reach the £520 as set out in the Plan. Revisioning around cultural and heritage capital had focused on a boosterism approach at the expense of a community-driven focus. The focus on 'big builds' and the hosting of mega-events would receive considerable criticism outside corporate and commercial circles. As well, city councils (in cooperation with Arts Council and Community Cohesion Units) embarked on a strategy to remove the most politically emotive murals to take the politics out of what was on view to visitors, replacing some of the street art with a narrative around sporting heroes (George Best), Belfast's maritime past (RMS *Titanic*) and literary figures (C.S. Lewis) (Boyd, 2019b). However, the majority of the political street art that drew early visitors in the 1990s remained and was showcased through walking and bus tours.

The period 2013–2019 represents a situation where Northern Ireland had reached the state of 'destination normalisation', reflecting characteristics normally found in destinations that had never experienced any sort of conflict or long-term interruption in living memory. Table 21.4 lists key tourism statistics across that period. For domestic visitors, the trend was one of relative stability, with similar numbers being recorded near the start (2014) and with growth being demonstrated at the end (+7%). As for the OOS visitor, numbers were on an upward trajectory across the entire time period, reaching 3 million in 2019, a trebling of what was recorded pre-conflict. Spend across both markets combined was also on an upward path, culminating in a £1 billion spend, meeting the target set in the 2010–2020 tourism strategy. Across this period there were notable accolades that evidenced a mature destination: hosting the start of the Giro de Italia cycle race in 2014, a whole year (2016) of celebration of food and drink, the return of the Irish Open in 2017 and the hosting of the Open in 2019 (see Bolan & Boyd, this volume, Chapter 15). Northern Ireland had also become the home of *Game of Thrones* tourism (as the site of much of the filming of the television series); it is estimated that since 2014 this generated £251 million for the economy, with as many as one in six OOS visitors citing it as their main reason to visit in 2018.

While a multi-niche offer developed across this period, a cursory glance at the 2018 Visitor Attitude Survey shows that alongside Northern Ireland hosting mega-events, attractions across the heritage and cultural base (some surviving the conflict, others built post-conflict) shaped demand and places visitors actually experienced. While the order of preference varies across the three destination regions shown in Table 21.5, what

Table 21.4 Number of overnight trips and expenditure, 2013–2019

Year	2013	2014	2015	2016	2017	2018	2019	Change, 2018–2019
Overnight trips (1000s)								
Domestic	1980	2335	2230	1984	2193	2188	2332	+7%
External	2089	2179	2301	2587	2658	2809	3001	+7%
Overall	*4069*	*4513*	*4531*	*4571*	*4851*	*4997*	*5333*	+7%
Expenditure (£million)								
Domestic	192	238	219	237	270	299	313	+5%
External	524	507	545	613	656	669	731	+9%
Overall	*715*	*745*	*764*	*850*	*926*	*968*	*1044*	+8%

Source: Tourism statistics NISRA annual publication 2019 (2020).

Table 21.5 Visitor Attitude Survey, 2018

Rank	Greater Belfast		CC and Glens		Derry and Strabane	
	Attraction	OOS (%)	Attraction	OOS (%)	Attraction	OOS (%)
Influenced visit						
1	Belfast City	65	Giant's Causeway	80	Derry~Londonderry	66
2	Titanic Belfast	56	CC Route	61	Giant's Causeway	64
3	Giant's Causeway	50	Belfast City	50	CC Route	52
4	CC Route	39	Game of Thrones	33	Belfast City	48
5	Game of Thrones	15	Titanic Belfast	32	Titanic Belfast	31
Top attractions visited						
1	Titanic Belfast	69	Giant's Causeway	86	Derry Walls	87
2	Belfast City Hall	57	Dark Hedges (GoT)	61	Peace Bridge	76
3	Botanic Gardens	44	Carrick-a-rede (rope bridge)	58	Guildhall	60
4	The murals	37	Dunluce castle	48	Bogside murals/Free Derry corner	46
5	Ulster museum	36	Bushmills distillery	32	Derry walking tours	34

Source: Tourism Northern Ireland (2019).

comes across as a constant was the appeal of natural, built and cultural attractions over more niche experiences (e.g. visiting places associated with *Game of Thrones*), and that a strong interest in political and contested spaces and heritage (i.e. murals) also remained.

By the end of 2019, Northern Ireland, at a macro-level (the entire province), could be seen to have positioned itself at the top end of the 'development' phase of the TALC; it was still growing, adding over a million visitors since 2013. Indeed, 2018 would witness the first year when visitor numbers exceeded a million at the Giant's Causeway, and approximately half a million at the nearby Carrick-a-rede rope bridge. The latter attraction had to initiate an online timed ticket to manage such numbers; its appeal had been boosted by its appearance in the sixth series of *Game of Thrones*. When considered at a micro-level, some of Northern Ireland's top attractions were experiencing issues around sustainability, congestion in particular, in sections of the north coast region, placing them within the 'critical zone of capacity'. In light of this, discussion began on how Northern Ireland was marketed and whether places such as the Giant's Causeway and nearby attractions need to be marketed at all.

Mid-Cycle: 'Development Challenged'

A unique political/economic event (Brexit) occurred across the later part of the 2013–2019 period, which had major potential to impact on tourism in Northern Ireland. The British people voted on 23 June 2016 (52% in favour of leave) to exit the European Union (EU) having first joined the then EC (European Communities) on 1 January 1973. A transition period was put in place that would run to the end of 2020, and the completion of an agreement with the EU was reached whereby the UK left on 31 January 2020. From a tourism point of view, there were potential issues around (1) border controls with the Republic of Ireland (RoI), (2) transport and (3) competitiveness. A common travel market had existed between Northern Ireland and the RoI since 1923 and was maintained as agreement was reached, with the border being moved to the Irish Sea and not between Northern Ireland and the RoI. Transport concerns existed over liberalisation of air travel but as the UK was a signatory of the European Common Aviation Area (ECAA), this provided UK airlines with access to the single aviation market. Decisions over route access, whether some routes would be lost, or new ones opened up became an internal airline matter.

As for competitiveness, the Brexit outcome had the potential to cause a 20% reduction in bilateral trade between the UK and Ireland and a weaker UK economy, which might see Ireland and Irish tourism suffer (Irish Tourist Industry Confederation, 2016). Tourism Ireland (an all-island body responsible for marketing all of Ireland, an outcome of the GFA) expressed concern over the impact of Brexit on visits to Ireland from the

British market. However, there is very little evidence that the visitor flow to Northern Ireland from the RoI was affected by Brexit, as border arrangements remained unchanged. Tourists appear more often concerned about factors such as safety and security and the strength of their own currency than political matters that do not directly affect them. The strength of the external (OOS) market (Table 21.4) would suggest that Brexit did not have any significant impact on tourism in Northern Ireland. The only realistic concern that the industry expressed was the potential loss of access to an EU-wide (cheaper) employment market, meaning wages might have to rise to attract a homegrown market. Again, with the border eventually set in the Irish Sea, Northern Ireland found itself in a unique trading position, with free access to both the British and the EU market, so that potential impact also did not materialise.

What was a game-changer that interrupted the ongoing development phase was the impact of the COVID-19 pandemic on tourism. Tourism was severely affected from early 2020 up to 2022; for most of this period tourism was not permitted. A complex pattern of regulatory control was imposed on the sector: a number of lockdown periods were enforced then lifted, social distancing rules were in constant flux and quarantine periods were imposed on travellers in a complicated coding where countries were given red–amber–green (in the end five different variations) categories of restrictions. As a result, only domestic tourism within Northern Ireland was possible, with limited OOS visiting toward the latter part of 2021, opening up further across 2022. International overseas travel remained negligible until the start of 2022. Over this time frame (2020–2022), no meaningful tourism statistics were collected that were comparable to those pre-COVID-19. The 2020 statistics were called 'alternative tourism statistics', with the focus on the impact of COVID-19. Overall visitor numbers and spend were not calculated, although the Visitor Attraction Survey was undertaken and recorded considerable declines to top attractions, with, for example, the Giant's Causeway down to 138,000 visits (a 93% drop), Titanic Belfast 150,000 (82% drop) and Carrick-a-rede 34,000 (93% drop). At the time of writing there are still no officially published tourism statistics, but Visitor Attraction Surveys have been carried out. In 2022 the numbers to the Giant's Causeway were recorded at 422,000 (less than half the pre-COVID-19 figure of 1 million). The Irish Central Statistics Office (2023) stated that in January–September 2022 more than 800,000 trips were made by residents of the RoI to Northern Ireland; this is positive news as these overall numbers exceed those recorded in 2019 and suggest that this local market has remained resilient despite not being able to travel in significant numbers across the COVID-19 years.

In light of the foregoing, where can one realistically in 2022 position Northern Ireland on the TALC? Northern Ireland has always drawn most of its visitors from the British market and with normal movement reinstated in 2022, alongside a vibrant RoI market, despite uncertainty over whether the international overseas market would return, it would be reasonable to suggest that overall numbers could have declined to those experienced across the early 2000s (1.5–2 million), with a potential decline of a third in OOS visitors. What this would mean is that Northern Ireland post-COVID-19 would start from a base earlier in the development stage of the TALC, but from which it could recover if the international overseas market returns.

Concluding Comments

The tourism journey that Northern Ireland has embarked on over the years is one of post-conflict tourism development and is similar to other destinations that have sought to recover from long-term disruption (Buultjens *et al.*, 2016; Castillo-Palacio *et al.*, 2017). Research into post-conflict tourism is still in its infancy; few destinations have faced long and multiple periods of instability (Séraphin *et al.*, 2020; Skoko *et al.*, 2018). The Post-Conflict Tourism Opportunity Spectrum (POCTOS) framework (Boyd *et al.*, 2023) offers a road map for destinations moving out of conflict where a set of opportunity factors are measured under different conflict contexts (before, during and after conflict) with implications for management identified. The 'development recovered' stage discussed in this chapter is illustrative of the post-conflict phoenix stage within POCTOS (see Figure 21.1). The era that saw a re-envisioning of heritage and culture, the mega attractions, with international appeal but where some of the phoenix dark tourism product (murals) was partly rebranded, reflects the post-conflict hybrid stage of POCTOS. The latter stage of Northern Ireland's tourism opportunity with the focus on capitalising on its culture and heritage along with niche opportunities (e.g. hosting sporting mega-events, location of major screen productions) symbolises the post-conflict normalised stage of POCTOS. Of all the opportunity factors outlined in the POCTOS framework, four in particular stand out in the Northern Ireland context: reducing risk associated with safety and security; developing and maintaining a positive destination perception; building strong resilience; and demonstrating a willingness to adapt and change.

Given the crises that have impacted tourism development in Northern Ireland, the authors propose a revised TALC model (see Figure 21.2). The conflict era prevents the adoption of the synoptic S-shaped curve. Instead, the pathway that best reflects the Northern Ireland situation is one of a series of waves. The first wave charts tourism across the early cycle to the start of the conflict (up to 1968). The curve follows a wave that crests in the year prior to conflict, dips dramatically as conflict escalates (1969–1972), creates a long trough that starts to level off with some degree of minor fluctuation (1978–1983) before starting a new second wave that slowly builds, eventually cresting in 1995 with the first year of peace, only

Opportunity Factors	PRE-CONFLICT	DURING CONFLICT	POST CONFLICT		
			Phoenix	Hybrid	Normalised
Safety & Security	Limited to none	Real & extensive	Reduced	Reducing	Limited to none
Perception of Destination	Safe to visit, no risk	Dangerous & need to heed government advice	Fluid & changing to more positive	Positive over negative image established	Greater feeling of being safe
Attraction Mix	Established & small (heritage focused)	Natural & cultural heritage, loss of built and artificial	Dark & political tourism dominant	Cultural heritage base (inc. dark tourism)	Diversified base (events, festivals, novelty, specific projects)
Access	Establishing routes (numbers small)	Loss of route development	New routes established (national & inter-regional; some international)		Established pattern of route development
Market	Local & national	Return to local (national, visiting friends and relatives)	Local, national (holiday) growing. Inter-regional & international base		Local, national & international markets established
Investment	Low but expanding	Little to non-existent	Narrow focus	Expanding base	Extensive portfolio
Industry Size	Small and stable	Decling but some resilience. Slow growth toward peace	Elective growth around selective products & services (dark & non-dark)		Extensive growth – new businesses, partnerships, bodes, service providers
Resilience	Developing	Sector highly vulnerable with loss	Re-establishing around small base		Strong & wider based
Capacity	Limited & evolving	Capacity loss	New opportunities for adaptive change; new capacity created		Established capacity (maintained & developing new)

Figure 21.1 Post conflict tourism opportunity spectrum (POCTOS) (Source: Boyd, 2023)

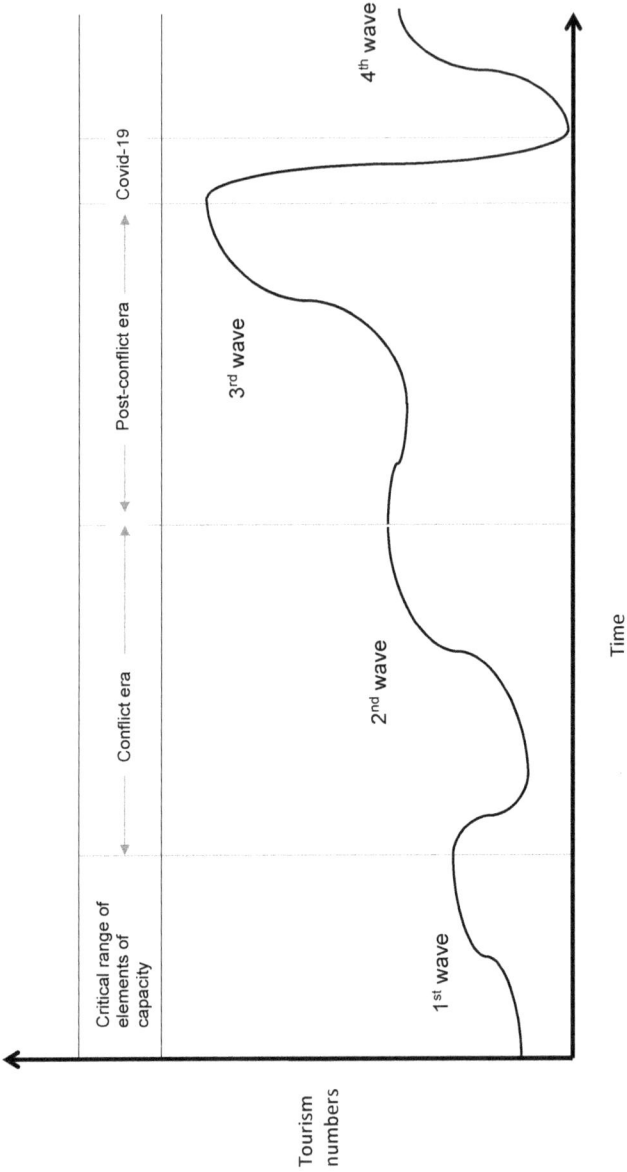

Figure 21.2 Application of a revised TALC model to Northern Ireland: A series of waves over the S-shaped curve

again to dip with minor fluctuations before rising consistently again in a third wave (2012–2019).

The anticipated crisis of Brexit had no impact on the third wave. The COVID-19 pandemic crisis, however, resulted in immediate wave collapse with no movement until the crisis abated. Anecdotal evidence would suggest a new wave is building but at present it remains well below the crest of the previous wave, with a possible scenario that the peak of the last wave will not be reached for some years to come, as Northern Ireland faces a global marketplace in which established destinations free of conflict are also looking to recover. Whether destinations such as Northern Ireland, which have survived multiple crises of long duration, through their built-in resilience and adaptive capacity are better positioned to recover in a post COVID-19 world, only time will tell.

References

Baum, T. (1995) Ireland – peace dividend. *Insights*, July, A9–A14.

Bolan, P. (1995) The lifecycle concept in tourism: a study of the coastal resort of Portrush. MSc dissertation, Ulster University.

Boyd, S.W. (2000) 'Heritage' tourism in Northern Ireland: Opportunity under peace. *Current Issues in Tourism* 3 (2), 150–174.

Boyd, S.W. (2013a) Tourism in Northern Ireland: Before violence, during and post violence. In, R. Butler and W. Suntikul (eds) *Tourism and War* (pp. 176–192). London: Routledge.

Boyd, S.W. (2013b) The Causeway coastal route and Saint Patrick's trail: Tourism route development in Northern Ireland. In B. Garrod and A. Fyall (eds) *Contemporary Cases in Heritage* (pp. 204–228). Oxford: Goodfellow Publishers.

Boyd, S.W. (2016) Heritage as the USP for tourism in Northern Ireland: Attraction mix, effective storytelling and selling of a dark past. In G. Hooper (ed.) *Heritage and Tourism in Britain and Ireland* (pp. 245–262). London: Palgrave Macmillan.

Boyd, S.W. (2017) Tourism and political change in Ireland: North and South. In R. Butler and W. Suntikul (eds) *Tourism and Political Change* (2nd edn) (pp. 153–168). Oxford: Goodfellow Publishers.

Boyd, S.W. (2019a) Tourism policy and planning in post-conflict destinations: Comparative cases of Northern Ireland and Sri Lanka. In K. Andriotis, D. Stylidis and A. Weidenfeld (eds) *Tourism Policy and Planning Challenges: Issues and Challenges* (pp. 53–77). Oxford: Routledge.

Boyd, S.W. (2019b) Post-conflict tourism development in Northern Ireland: Moving beyond murals and darks sites associated with its past. In R. Isaac, E. Cakmak and R. Butler (eds) *Tourism and Hospitality in Conflict-Ridden Destinations* (pp. 226–239). Oxford: Routledge.

Boyd, S.W., Reddy, M.V., Kulshreshtha, S. and Nica, M. (2023) Post-conflict tourism opportunity spectrum (POCTOS): A framework for destinations recovering from conflict. *Journal of Sustainable Tourism* 31 (1), 131–148.

Buckley, P.J. and Klemm, M. (1993) The decline of tourism in Northern Ireland. *Tourism Management* 14 (3), 184–194.

Butler, R. (1980) The concept of the tourist area cycle of evolution: Implications for management of resources. *Canadian Geographer* 24 (1), 5–12.

Buultjens, J.W., Ratnayake, I. and Athula Chammika Gnanapala, W.K. (2016) Post-conflict tourism in Sri Lanka: Implications for building resilience. *Current Issues in Tourism* 19 (4), 355–372.

Castillo-Palacio, M., Harrill, R. and Zuniga-Collazos, A. (2017) Back from the brink: Social transformation and developing tourism in post-conflict Medellin, Colombia. *Worldwide Hospitality and Tourism Themes* 9 (3), 300–315.

Causevic, S. and Lynch, P. (2013) Phoenix tourism: Post-conflict tourism role. *Annals of Tourism Research* 38 (3), 780–800.

Graham, B.J. (1996) The contested interpretation of contested landscapes in Northern Ireland. *International Journal of Heritage Studies* 2 (1), 10–22.

Howarth, A.S.M. (1996) *Review of Accommodation Needs in Northern Ireland – 1996*. London: New Street.

Irish Central Statistics Office (2023) *Statistical Releases: Tourism and Travel*. Cork: CSO.

Irish Tourist Industry Confederation (ITIC) (2016) Brexit and implications for Irish tourism. Briefing paper accessed online at https://www.itic.ie (accessed 7 May 2023).

Lennon, J. and Foley, M. (2000) *Dark Tourism: The Attraction of Death and Disaster*. London: Continuum.

Leslie, D. (1999) Terrorism and tourism: The Northern Ireland situation – a look behind the veil of uncertainty. *Journal of Travel Research* 38, 37–40.

Mansfeld, Y. (1999) Cycle of war, terror, and peace: determinants and management of crises and recovery of the Israeli tourism industry. *Journal of Travel Research* 38 (1), 30–36.

McDowell, S. (2008) Selling conflict heritage through tourism in peacetime Northern Ireland: Transforming conflict or exacerbating difference? *International Journal of Heritage Studies* 14 (5), 405–421.

Mullin, J. E. (1982) *The Causeway Coast*. Belfast: University Press.

Northern Ireland Statistics and Research Agency (NISRA) (2020) *Tourism Statistics 2019*. Online publication, 7 October.

Northern Ireland Tourist Board (NITB) (1980) *Tourism Facts 1979*. Belfast: NITB.

Northern Ireland Tourist Board (NITB) (1990) *Tourism Facts 1989*. Belfast: NITB.

Northern Ireland Tourist Board (NITB) (1992) *Tourism Facts 1991*. Belfast: NITB.

O'Neill, M.A. and Fitz, F. (1996) Northern Ireland tourism: What chance now? *Tourism Management* 17 (3), 161–163.

Séraphin, H., Korstanje, M., and Gowreesunkar, V. (2020) Diaspora and ambidextrous management of tourism in post-colonial, post-conflict, and post-disaster destinations. *Journal of Tourism and Cultural Change* 18 (2), 113–132,

Sharpley, R. and Stone, P.R. (eds) (2009) *The Darker Side of Travel: The Theory and Practice of Dark Tourism*. Bristol: Channel View Publications.

Skoko, B., Jakopovic, H. and Gluvacevic, D. (2018) Challenges of branding in post-conflict countries: The case of Bosnia and Herzegovina. *Tourism* 66 (4), 411–427.

Tourism Northern Ireland (2019) *Visitor Attitude Survey 2018*. Belfast: Tourism Northern Ireland, Department for the Economy.

Tunbridge, J.E. and Ashworth, G.J. (1996) *Dissonant Heritage: The Management of the Past as a Resource in Conflict*. London: Wiley.

22 Can Destinations Have Multiple Life Cycles?

Bob McKercher and IpKin Anthony Wong

This chapter explores the idea that destinations can have multiple life cycles. By extension, it argues that Butler's original model captures only one phase of a destination's evolutionary path and that the whole picture of a destination's life cycle can be discerned only by combining multiple phases over time. The chapter begins with a discussion of the dynamic forces that may prompt a shift from maturity or the consolidation/ stagnation phase to one of three post-stagnation stages, of growth, stability or decline. It then reports on a study conducted by McKercher and Wong (2021) that tested this idea empirically, based on statistics from the United Nations World Tourism Organization (UNWTO) on international overnight visitor arrival. The chapter concludes with a discussion of the implications of multiple life cycles on the Butler model.

Butler's (1980) life cycle is brilliant in its simplicity. But it also has a layer of subtlety and complexity that has gone largely unrecognised, for the model is open ended. Both the x (time) and y (volume of visitors) axes have arrows at their ends, while the post-stagnation phase presents the reader with five future options: two growth scenarios, a stability scenario and two possible decline scenarios. Further hints of this complexity come from both the title of the original paper 'The concept of a tourist area cycle of evolution' and its opening gambit, which reads: 'there can be little doubt that tourist areas are dynamic, that they evolve and change over time' (Butler, 1980: 5). These observations raise the intriguing question of whether the TALC model captures the entire life cycle of a destination or simply describes one phase of an area's total evolutionary path.

Proponents of complexity theory (Baggio, 2008; Faulkner & Russell, 1997; McKercher, 1999; Scott et al., 2008) argue for the multiple life cycle model using the concept of a phase shift that can prompt large, interactive dynamic systems (Lewin, 1992) to shift rapidly from an apparently stable state into new phases. Faulkner and Russell (1997) were the first to argue that tourism systems may be upended from time to time and be completely reorganised, resulting in a new, stronger and more resilient system. Cochrane (2010) adds that how quickly this rearrangement occurs

depends on how well the system can adapt to and/or absorb the distur-
bance and reorganise itself. Some systems may be able to absorb shocks
with no change, while others may change dramatically.

The Dynamism of Destinations

Butler's life cycle represents a variation on the theme of the product
life cycle, which has been applied in marketing for over 60 years (Osland,
1991). Its origins can be traced to the biological sciences. However, as
Crawford (1984) argues, business took the wrong life cycle model from
biology. Two forms of biological life cycle model have been developed.
The most common one adopts the analogy of an individual's life, which
is both finite and fixed. It begins with birth, then follows an inevitable
pattern of growth, maturity and death (Tellis & Crawford, 1981). Not
all entities will follow the full cycle as some may not survive birth, while
others may expire before maturity. But, as Crawford (1984) illustrates, the
fixed and predictable life cycle can be applied only to individual specimens
and not to groups of things, including complex systems.

Instead, a biological evolutionary life cycle approach may better
explain the growth, change and proliferation of species and ecosystems
over time (Tellis & Crawford, 1981). Tellis and Crawford (1981: 127) write:

> while the life-death cycle is rigid, highly predictable and one telling the
> story of each biological specimen (the individual horse, dog, etc.), the
> evolutionary cycle is dynamic, open ended and one telling an even more
> exciting story of the origin, growth and proliferation of entire species.

Crawford (1984) added later that this model depicts gradual but continuous change that is cumulative, directional and motivated. Cumulative
change means that the evolution of an entity builds on previous stages,
while directional changes move the object in question to greater complexity and diversity. The motivation element refers to both internal factors,
which encourage cohesiveness and repetition, and externalities, which
favour certain mutations over time, giving some species an advantage.
The net result can be one of five outcomes, ranging from divergence
(the creation of new species) through development and differentiation
(whereby systems may become more complex through the emergence
of subspecies), stabilisation (where no change occurs) or demise (where
extinction occurs).

This model applies equally to species and ecosystems. Over time,
ecosystems evolve to form increasingly complex relationships between
and among their constituent elements. From time to time, though, the
ecosystem may be subjected to a great shock that fundamentally alters
its state and propels it on a new, modified evolutionary path. Examples
from the natural world include fire or flood. Murphy (1985) was the

first to use the analogy with the living ecosystem to describe the many interrelationships among tourism's diverse component parts. McKercher (1999: 428) developed this idea further when he wrote:

> just as one cannot understand how a wetlands ecosystem functions by identifying all the living species within that wetland and understanding their biological processes, one cannot understand how a tourism system functions by reducing it to its component parts and trying to understand how each works.

As a 'living' ecosystem, the tourism system should also evolve over time from a simple to a complex form and may also be subjected to shocks that transform its very fabric.

The traditional product life cycle model cannot reflect this inherent complexity found in tourism systems, nor can it account for the diverse range of actors that constitute dynamic destination areas. However, this dynamism has been recognised in various portfolio models that highlight how the product–market mix can be managed to ensure ongoing development and likely change in the mix. The Ansoff growth strategy matrix (as cited in Morrison, 2013), for example, identifies four strategies in a two-by-two matrix that considers both products and markets. On the one hand, existing markets can be encouraged to consume more of the same product or can be enticed by new products. On the other hand, new markets can be attracted to consume the existing product array or may be enticed to consume through the development of new products. By extension, then, Ansoff is arguing for the type of directional change that is found in the biological evolutionary model.

In a similar manner, Evans (2015) and Hsu *et al.* (2008) have applied the Boston Consulting Group's Growth–Share Matrix model to argue that a healthy destination needs to offer products in all four of the components of the growth–share matrix, by constantly developing new products, fostering the growth of products in the expansion phase of their life cycle, defending products in the maturity phase and using so-called dog products either as complementary activities or as defensive products to stop competing destinations from launching similar products. McKercher (1995) offered a modification of the Boston Matrix, only this time focusing exclusively on the need for destinations to manage their market portfolios. He argued that healthy destinations must appeal to all markets in the different NEST (new, emerging, stable and tired) life cycle stages.

The recognition of an evolutionary biological model reminds us that the only constant in tourism is change. As destinations mature and evolve, by definition, they will diversify their product offerings and broaden their market bases. In doing so, the character of a destination will change. But that does not mean that ongoing growth is inevitable. Instead, using a biological analogy, and in accordance with complexity theory, destinations, like other ecosystems, may experience a prolonged period of stability before being subjected to shocks that change their trajectory (Ibanez *et al.*, 2017). Some shocks will be radical enough to induce major change, while other shocks may be less intense, but still cause real though more gradual change. How a system reacts, the extent of the change and the length of time involved to respond fully to that change depends on the inherent resilience of a place (Holladay, 2018). In some cases destinations may emerge unscathed, while in other cases they may be shaken to their core and be forced to embark on a new path. In extreme cases decline may occur that could ultimately lead to the virtual abandonment of a destination (Baum, 1998).

Two types of shock can alter the evolutionary path of a destination and send it to one of Butler's five post-stagnation trajectories, including internal and external shocks. Internal shocks will be discussed first.

Both Plog (1974) and Butler's (1980) original model suggest that the revitalisation of a destination after the stagnation stage is challenging. Indeed, Plog (2001) suggests change can only occur in places that are subjected to 'earthquakes'. Butler (1980) was more circumspect, but again felt that revitalisation involved targeting a specialist interest group of tourists who may provide a short-term period of growth before the place loses its competitiveness once more.

Both arguments ignore the proactive role governments can play through policy initiatives and the introduction of structural changes that can change the fortunes of destinations almost overnight (Ibanez *et al.*, 2017). The most stunning example is the case of the Macau Special Administrative Region of China (see Chapter 16 of this volume). Prior to reverting back to Chinese sovereignty in 1999, the former Portuguese colony was a sleepy backwater that was popular with day trippers from Hong Kong. Visitor numbers had stagnated. However, the Chinese central government liberalised the gaming sector by creating new casino licences, resulting in the number of casinos increasing from 11 to 32 between 2002 and 2007. The hotel room stock increased fourfold in the same period as major hotel companies built integrated resort hotels (Wan & Pinheiro, 2014). Until COVID-19 emerged, Macau generated more than seven times the annual gaming revenue of Las Vegas, making it the gambling capital of the world (Greenwood & Dwyer, 2017). In fact, overnight visitor arrivals more than tripled between 2001 and 2010, to almost 19 million, while another 20 million same-day visitors came. While this growth engendered a range of adverse social impacts (Greenwood & Dwyer, 2017), it does show that the destination entered a radical new phase of its life cycle.

In addition, visa liberalisation policies can stimulate the development of the next life cycle phase. The link between visa liberalisation and increased tourism flows is axiomatic (European Migrant Network, 2018; Lawson & Roychourdry, 2013). As an example, visa-free travel for South Koreans visiting Japan produced a 12% increase in arrivals in the first year and a 25% increase in the second (Lee *et al.*, 2010).

Changes in markets targeted by destinations also can induce phase shift. Plog (1974, 2001) adopts a rather pessimistic view of destination evolution in his classic papers. The main reason is that he feels newer, less robust markets will displace existing markets, leading to a destination being able to draw only from a smaller pool of potential visitors. As he argues, 'when the appeal of the resort passes the magic mid-point in the population curve of travellers ... from now on it begins to draw on a smaller number of travellers ... [as the] destination moves toward the psychocentric end of the continuum' (Plog, 1974: 58). He then goes on to write about the inevitability of a destination moving through its life cycle 'however gradually or slowly but far too often inexorably towards the potential of its own demise' (Plog, 1974: 58).

Prideaux (2000a, 2000b, 2004) challenges this argument both conceptually and empirically by demonstrating that markets aggregate rather than displace. His Resort Development Spectrum model argues that the evolution of resort areas occurs through the progressive attraction of different geographic markets, often beginning with the local market, then moving to regional, national and international markets, or vice versa in the case of island resort destinations. The ability to draw different markets induces phase shift, with each new market propelling a destination into new growth, maturation and stability phases, as shown in Figure 22.1. Growth may be supply driven through the development of new infrastructure and superstructure or may be demand-driven, with the destination playing catch-up to build facilities to cater for tourists. He then illustrates that each new development phase will attract new tourist sectors that are prepared to pay a different price than the previous sector, including transport costs, accommodation costs and attractions and activities. Each new phase, therefore, induces change in the character

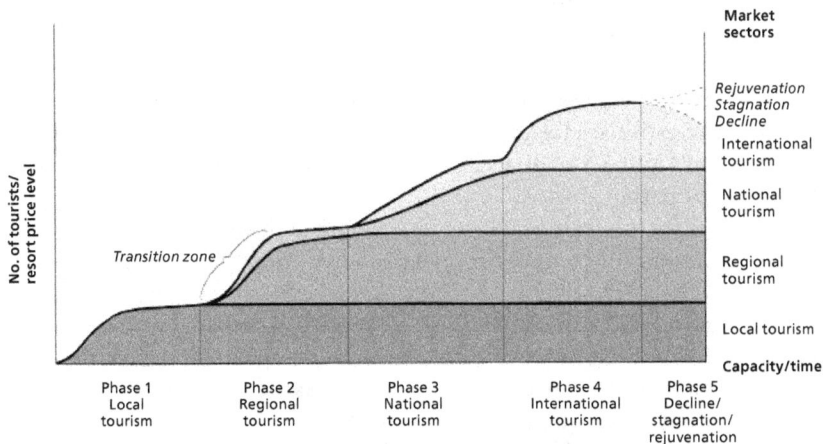

Figure 22.1 Prideaux's Resort Development Spectrum (Source: Prideaux, 2000a)

of a destination [and, as Keller suggests (1987; and in Chapter 10 of this volume), it may also induce instability – editor's note].

Russell and Faulkner (2004) introduced the idea of entrepreneurial activity as another dimension that can lead a destination to a new development phase. They argued that entrepreneurial activity essentially destroys the existing equilibrium, for the shift to different stages of the destination life cycle brings with it a period of instability driven by fundamental alteration in the relationship between stakeholders and tourists. Here the work of a forward-thinking entrepreneur can alter the tourism landscape forever.

Butler's model talks about carrying capacity as a critical factor that may limit development, affect tourist satisfaction or, when exceeded, lead to a deterioration of the very features of a destination that make it appealing. But, as Weaver (2001) argues, carrying capacity is not fixed and can be raised through a variety of management actions, including infrastructure development, improved transport systems, sewage treatment and a range of actions designed to 'harden' sites. He gives by way of example how the simple act of placing patio-type stones on a dirt trail could increase the trail's carrying capacity 10-fold. In much the same way, the carrying capacity of destinations can be increased dramatically through infrastructure development. The capacity of a resort can be expanded by the actions of individual organisations providing goods and services to tourists (Prideaux, 2000a) or through concerted efforts to expand the terrestrial and air transport linkages (Prideaux, 2000b), which in turn will stimulate other measures to harden sites.

This points leads to the next option available to destinations, and that is the development of new and different attractions that both enlarge the existing market and broaden the market base (Pritchard & Lee, 2011). Changing the product base is explicit in both Plog's (1974) and Butler's (1980) models. Plog adopts a demand-side perspective in arguing that a less sophisticated tourist demands attractions that are easier to consume as destinations move through their life cycles, while Butler adopts a supply-side perspective and suggests the character of places change as the product mix evolves. However, neither notes explicitly how new product development can be a revitalisation tool that sets a destination on a new development path.

External factors can also send shocks through tourism systems. The aggressive actions of competitors can push once popular destinations into decline (McKercher, 1999). The geographic concept of market access, first introduced by Pearce (1988), is also a critical factor. The concept of market access is used to argue that, all things being equal, the tourist will prefer the most proximate destination if it can satisfy their needs. Destinations may derive their competitive advantage based solely on good market access. But, if another destination area develops better market access, then the former basis for advantage becomes one for disadvantage, pushing the destination into decline. Spain's policy of encouraging low-cost carriers dramatically improved its market access, rendering air travel from the UK cheaper and faster than ground transport to Belgium, France and the Netherlands. This policy has transformed Spain's tourism sector, as the volume of tourists has increased, accompanied by changes in accommodation choices and visitor profile (Rebello & Baidal, 2009).

It would be remiss not to mention briefly the impact of COVID-19 on tourism, for both domestic and international tourism ground to a halt during the pandemic. How fast destinations will recover is dependent on their in-built resilience (Holladay, 2018), how quickly consumer confidence in certain destinations can return and whether or not 'revenge travel' (Tiwari & Chowdary, 2021) is a fad or a beacon of future behaviours. One feature of COVID-19 that has not been discussed in detail is the total dismantling of much of the tourism distribution system, as both inbound and outbound tour operators, intermediaries and travel agents have either gone out of business or lost key staff. Rebuilding those relationships will be a key to how fast destinations recover.

Evidence of Multiple Life Cycles

Intuitively, Butler's model is compelling. Moreover, the recognition that the life cycle model is open ended, coupled with complexity theory's ideas of the edge of criticality leading to phase shift, causing the resultant entry into a new life cycle phase that is distinct from the previous one, is also intuitively appealing. The preceding discussion of both internal and external factors that may lead to the emergence of different phases adds further credence to the argument. The premise of this chapter, then, is that Butler's life cycle model best captures different phases of a destination's 'biological' evolution, rather than the more constrained fixed-cycle birth, maturity, death cycle. It is predicated on the belief that destinations are evolving ecosystems where change over time induces fundamental changes to their character, the products on offer and markets they appeal to. Tourism changes tourism, which suggests that destinations are not independent but co-evolve into a networked eco-system. Over time, the evolved destination may look nothing like its earlier incarnations, even though it may be able to trace its genetic roots to its origins. Metaphorically, some dinosaurs may evolve into birds.

Each individual phase can be aggregated to display the total evolutionary path destinations follow, as depicted in Figure 22.2. In doing so, the end of one phase leads to the commencement of the next phase, as hypothesised in the original open-ended model. Figure 22.2 illustrates the aggregate evolution of a destination by combining individual life cycle phases into a holistic whole; it plots a consistent growth scenario, but it must be recognised that this model is only one of a number of paths available. In some cases, the destination may have only one prolonged

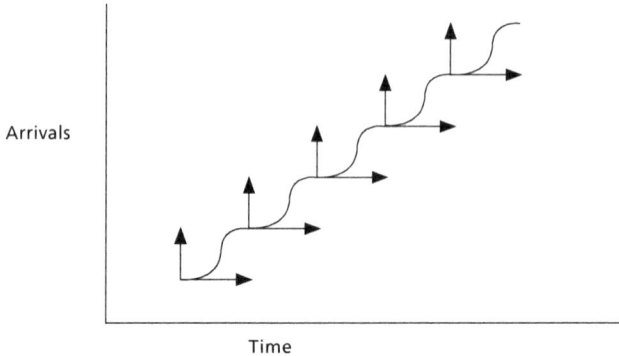

Figure 22.2 Cumulative life cycle phases (Source: McKercher & Prideaux, 2020)

life cycle. In other instances, a series of declining phases may be observed over time, while in other cases still a more volatile pattern of decline and growth cycles may be evident.

While conceptually the idea has merits, the challenge is how to demonstrate it empirically. Butler had to rely on visitor arrival data to frame the *y* axis of his model, although problems with reliable statistics for many destinations render this simple measure difficult to obtain with any confidence (Butler, 2009: 348). The study by McKercher and Wong (2021) used international overnight visitor arrival figures provided by the UNWTO covering the period 1984–2017. As a result, their unit of analysis is the economy in question. In an ideal world, finer data focusing on overnight arrivals to individual destinations within economies would be used, but such information simply is unavailable. The information presented below reflects arrivals to 202 countries and territories. A total of 178 economies displayed some form of multiple life cycle pattern, while another 24 were still in the preliminary stages of their evolutionary path. Table 22.1 presents a summary of the six patterns that could be discerned, along with information on the number of discrete life cycles typically observed, the typical number of life cycle stages observed and how long on average it took each destination to evolve through both its entire life cycle and individual stages.

The two most common patterns involved multiple life cycle phases, typified by either unbridled growth (85 cases) or by destinations where arrivals evolved through a full life cycle of growth, maturity and decline, before rebounding to a new growth stage (77 cases). Cases showing un-fettered growth typically registered two to four discrete life cycle phases, followed by a period of stability before embarking on the next growth spurt. By contrast, only three destinations registered what could be described as long-term decline, challenging Plog's (1974) assumption that

Table 22.1 Six different life cycle patterns

	Single exploration	Single growth	Multiple long-term decline	Multiple scalloped growth	Multiple full life cycles	Volatile with no discernible life cycle pattern
Number of economies displaying this pattern	4	20	3	85	77	13
Median number of life cycles	1	1	4	3	2	4
Range of life cycles	1	1	3 to 4	2 to 5	1 to 5	3 to 5
Median number of life cycle stages	1	4	8	6	6	8
Range of life cycle stages	1	1	8	3 to 13	2 to 12	6 to 14
Median years per discrete life cycle	34	34	8.5	8.7	12.0	8.5
Median years per life cycle phase	34	7.5	4.3	5.0	4.9	4.2
Range of years per life cycle phase	32–34	4–17	4	3–11	3–17	2–6
Mean number of phases per discrete life cycle	1.0	4.3	2.0	2.2	2.8	2.2

Source: McKercher and Wong (2021).

tourism destroys tourism. A total of 13 had such volatile arrival numbers that no discernible pattern could be observed, while another 24 were still in their exploration or rapid growth stages.

No consistent pattern was observable in the duration of either a single life cycle phase or individual stages within a phase, suggesting that each destination was evolving through its own path independently. The total life cycle phase could be as short as five years or as long as 34 years. Likewise, the duration of each stage was variable, passing relatively quickly in a matter of a few years, or in the case of emerging destinations lasting almost two decades. Little evidence was available to discern all full six steps in Butler's model. Instead, evolution tended to occur in such a short time frame that it was more common for stages to be amalgamated. It is challenging to identify discrete involvement and exploration stages, as well as distinct consolidation and stagnation stages.

The following text and figures highlight the findings of the McKercher and Wong (2021) study by briefly introducing each of the six evolutionary styles observed and using examples from destinations to illustrate the patterns.

The two least common life cycle patterns were those depicting destinations still in the exploration phase (Figure 22.3) and long-term decline (Figure 22.4). Each of the four places still in the exploration stage were small, remote, Pacific island micro-states. The example of Tuvalu is shown in Figure 22.3. Data were available from 1984 through to 2017, and during that time it never attracted more than 3000 overnight visitors a year.

Another three destinations appeared to be in long-term decline, as illustrated by the change in visitor arrivals to Bermuda (Figure 22.4). Two of these destinations are located in the Atlantic Ocean, while one, Liechtenstein, is in Europe. As with destinations still in the exploration stage, all are small, relatively remote micro-states. As can be seen, the moderate expansion stage of each life cycle phase is met with a longer-term decline in arrivals. The pattern tends to be scallop-shaped downward. In the case of Bermuda, arrivals peaked in 1987 and since then the destination has displayed four distinct downward life cycle phases.

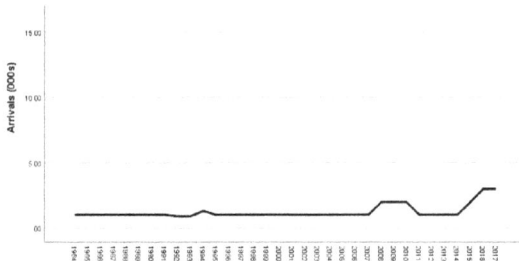

Figure 22.3 Exploration stage – Tuvalu

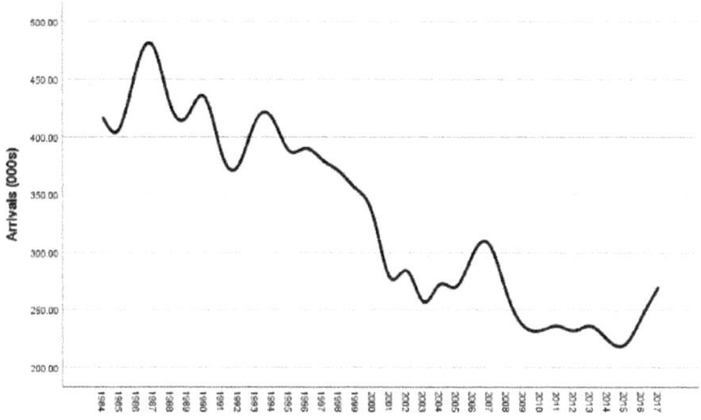

Figure 22.4 Long-term decline – Bermuda

About 20 destinations have enjoyed a single, unbridled period of growth, as typified by Bhutan (Figure 22.5). Destinations in this cohort recorded the longest duration of individual stages. Their life cycles involve a long exploration and discovery phase before visitor numbers begin to rise rapidly. Growth tends to slow after that, but still shows an upward trajectory as they are still in the development phase of their life cycle. Most of these places are developing economies in Asia and Africa. Most are relative newcomers to tourism, yet it has become a significant government priority in recent years.

Most of the economies under consideration, though, have experienced multiple life cycle phases over the preceding 34 years, with 77 destinations displaying multiple full life cycle phases including decline, as typified by

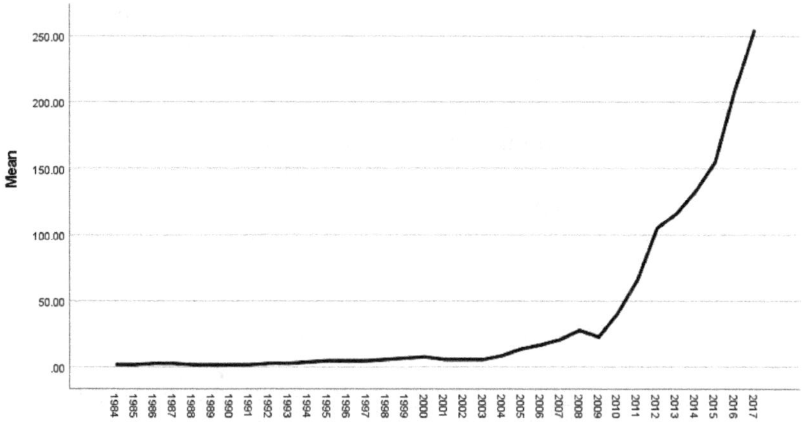

Figure 22.5 Growth – Bhutan

Figure 22.6 Multiple full life cycle phases – Monaco

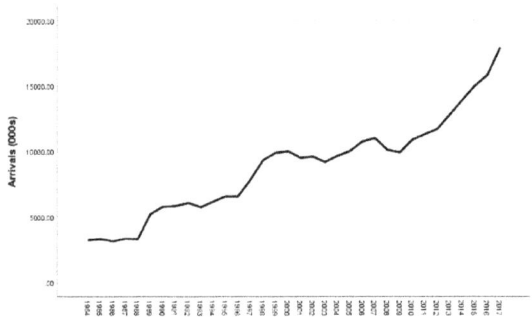

Figure 22.7 Multiple growth phases – Netherlands

Monaco (Figure 22.6), and another 85 showing an upward growth pattern, as shown here for the Netherlands in Figure 22.7. Those economies displaying the full life cycle pattern had periods of strong growth, coupled with a period of decline in arrivals, before rebounding sharply into their next growth phase. This type of pattern is most likely to been seen in Europe (17 cases), Africa (16 cases) and the Caribbean (13).

Destinations displaying continuous growth patterns, on the other hand, are typified by a period of growth followed by consolidation before embarking on another growth phase. None of these places has encountered a prolonged decline in visitors. Each of these destinations has moved through between two and five discrete life cycles, lasting up to 12 years. This pattern is most common among European (25), Caribbean or Pacific island (20), South American (13) and Asian (12) countries. It is less common in Africa. Mature destinations with a long history of tourism development and where tourism represents a significant aspect of the local economy are typical.

Finally, 13 economies have highly volatile arrival patterns [cf. Figure 21.2 in Chapter 21 by Boyd & Bolan, this volume – editor's note] that defy simple classification into any life cycle stage or prolonged phase.

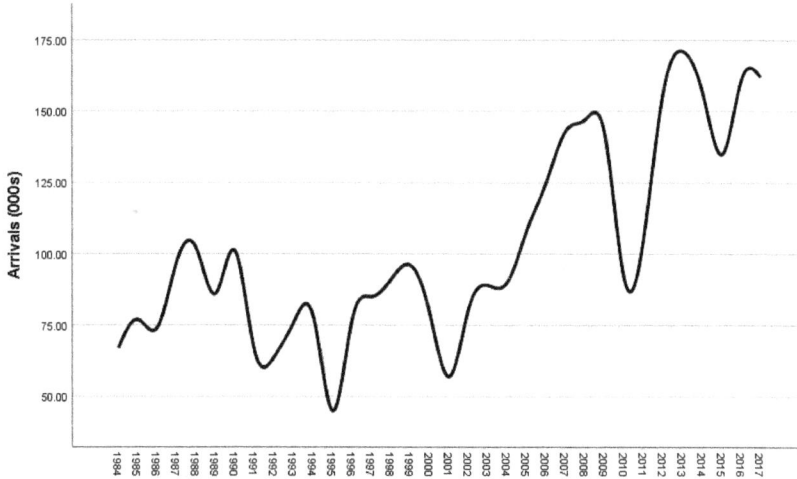

Figure 22.8 Volatile pattern – Gambia

Instead, arrivals fluctuated wildly year to year, as shown in the case of Gambia (Figure 22.8). None of these destinations has ever entered a cycle of prolonged growth or decline and none has demonstrated stability in arrival figures. Seven of the 13 economies are located in Africa, with the rest scattered around the globe.

Discussion

Analysis of 34 years of UNWTO international overnight visitor arrival data suggests most destinations have experienced multiple life cycle phases. For the most part, these phases have resulted in a cumulative positive growth in visitor numbers, characterised by either a short period of stability or a period of decline before growth recurs. By contrast, new and emerging destinations have shown one of two patterns. Most have had long gestation periods typified by extensive exploration and involvement stages, before embarking on a prolonged growth stage as markets discover the destinations and national tourism organisations begin to pursue tourism in earnest. Alternatively, a smaller number of economies have experienced great volatility in their arrival figures over time, with no discernible pattern evident. These places tend to place relatively low importance on tourism as an engine of economic growth.

Butler's model may adequately explain the first life cycle phase destinations encounter but may not be particularly relevant in the subsequent phases as destinations mature over time. Clearly, any destination can experience the exploration and involvement life cycle stages only once, at least from a product development perspective. Thus, while one market segment may be at the post-mature phase of its life cycle, another may still be in the early stage of discovering a destination. This cycle of existing international markets maturing and new markets exploring places may explain the appearance of multiple life cycle phases, especially in an Asian context where Japan fist and now China (pre-COVID 19) were the engines of growth of global tourism.

While the evidence indicates that the gestation period for new and emerging destinations is quite long, once a destination reaches a level of maturity, it tends to cycle through different phases rapidly. The appearance of an upward curve further suggests national and state tourism organisations play a proactive role in market intervention, adopting strategies to revitalise the destination at the first sign of consolidation. By contrast, destinations that evolve through the full life cycle of growth, maturity and decline, before growing again, imply a reactive policy and marketing approach by waiting until the destination has stagnated before acting. Of course, such a comment is speculative, at this point in time, but is worthy of further study.

The inability to digest the more qualitative aspects of Butler's model is one of the challenges faced by an empirical study such as this one. As such, one cannot explore whether the patterns of declining local involvement and deteriorating community attitudes to tourism noted during the rapid development phase may occur, nor whether local involvement in industry increases in the stagnation and decline stages. Here, evidence from elsewhere must be considered. A meta-analysis of community attitudes to tourism related to life cycle stage revealed that attitudes to tourism actually stabilised and improved during the maturity phases of the life cycle as tourism became accepted as a social and economic norm of the community that provided a range of benefits to local residents (McKercher et al., 2015). In a similar manner, it is unlikely that the local community will re-enter the market in a meaningful manner once properties of an international calibre have been developed. Instead, a change in management contract or property ownership may occur as destinations evolve upward or downward through different phases. The local community may play a relatively minor complementary role as destinations evolve to cater to more and more tourists by providing alternative forms of accommodation, such as Airbnb lodging.

The McKercher and Wong (2021) study, on which this chapter is based, acknowledges that the destination life cycle model is a visual metaphor that vividly delineates fluctuations in tourist demand over time. However, empirical evidence suggests that, based on arrival figures alone, life cycles deviate sharply from those described in the original model. Instead of displaying a single pattern, by and large, most destinations have multiple cycles. This empirical observation confirms the open-ended nature of the original model that few people have appreciated. Moreover, it also highlights the need to consider destination evolution as involving a series of phases that aggregate to reflect the evolution of a destination area from its rather simple origins to a series of increasingly complex dynamic 'eco-systems' that change significantly over time.

This conclusion indicates that evaluation of a destination depends not merely on its own seed (i.e. internal forces such as tourism infrastructure and strategy), as Butler (1980) suggests, but it also depends on environmental forces, such as the growth/decline of major economies, technological innovations and the outbreak of a highly pathogenic influenza. This view provides a fuller understanding of the destination evolution process, which resonates closely with the evolution of each biological specimen. Moving beyond a single destination, evidence collated in this chapter points to a seldom discussed concept, namely destination co-evolution. As evident from Table 22.1, life cycle patterns of destinations fall into six different categories, within a typology of networked life cycles, as evidenced by the geographic concentration of pattern types. In other words, the evolution of a destination is not isolated but can be shaped by other destinations. Similar to the biological form of co-evolution, interactions among destinations could result in reciprocal evolutionary change.

Do destinations have multiple life cycles? The short answer is yes. Butler's open-ended model implies such a situation can occur but it does not state this explicitly. The study on which this chapter is based suggests that multiple life cycle phases that accumulate to reflect the total destination evolution are the norm and not the exception. As a result, a rethink of Butler's model may be needed to recognise that the simple S-shaped curve captures one of many possible phases that a destination evolves through and not the full cycle on its own.

References

Baggio, R. (2008) Symptoms of complexity in a tourism system. *Tourism Analysis* 13 (1), 1–20.

Baum, T. (1998) Taking the exit route: Extending the Tourism Area Life Cycle model. *Current Issues in Tourism* 1 (2), 167–175. https://doi.org/10.1080/13683509808667837.

Butler R. (1980) The concept of tourism area cycle of evolution: The implications for management of resources. *Canadian Geographer* 24, 5–12.

Butler, R. (2009) Tourism in the future: Cycles, waves or wheels? *Futures* 41, 346–352.

Cochrane, J. (2010) The sphere of tourism resilience. *Tourism Recreation Research* 35 (2), 173–185. https://doi.org/10.1080/02508281.2010.11081632.

Crawford, M. (1984) Business took the wrong life cycle from biology. *Journal of Consumer Marketing* 1 (3), 5–11.

European Migrant Network (2018) *Impact of Visa Liberalisation on Countries of Destination*. Luxembourg: EMN. https://orbilu.uni.lu/bitstream/10993/36673/1/LU%20EMN%20NCP_VISA%20LIBERALISATION%20FINAL.pdf.

Evans, N.G. (2015) *Strategic Management for Tourism, Hospitality and Events*. London: Routledge.

Faulkner, B. and Russell, R. (1997) Chaos and complexity in tourism: In search of a new perspective. *Pacific Tourism Review* 1, 93–102.

Greenwood, V. and Dwyer, L. (2017) Reinventing Macau tourism: Gambling on creativity? *Current Issues in Tourism* 20 (6), 580–602. https://doi.org/10.1080/13683500.2016.118 7585.

Holladay, T. (2018) Destination resilience and sustainable tourism development. *Tourism Review International* 22, 251–261.

Hsu, C., Killion, L., Brown, G., Gross, M. and Huang, S. (2008) *Tourism Marketing: An Asia-Pacific Perspective*. Milton: Wiley.

Ibanez, C., Wilson, J. and Clavé, S.A. (2017) Moments as catalysts for change in the evolutionary paths of destinations. In, P. Brouder, S.A. Clavé, A. Gill and D. Ioannides (eds) *Tourism Destination Evolution* (pp. 81–102). London: Taylor and Francis.

Keller, C.P. (1987) Stages of peripheral tourism development: Canada's Northwest Territories. *Tourism Management* 8 (1), 20–32.

Lawson, R. and Roychoudhury, S. (2013) *Do Travel Visa Requirements Impede Tourist Travel?* O'Neil Center for Global Markets and Freedom – Working Paper Series 2013–06. http://oneil.cox.smu.edu/system/media/838/original/Visa_and_Travel_Paper. pdf (accessed 24 June 2014).

Lee, C., Song, H. and Bendel, L. (2010) The impact of visa-free entry on outbound tourism: A case study of South Korean travellers visiting Japan. *Tourism Geographies* 12 (2), 302–323.

Lewin, R. (1992) *Complexity: Life at the Edge of Chaos*. New York: Macmillan.

McKercher B. (1995) The destination–market matrix. *Journal of Tourism and Travel Marketing* 4 (2), 23–40.

McKercher, B. (1999) A chaos approach to tourism. *Tourism Management* 20 (4), 425–434.

McKercher, B., Wang, D. and Park, E. (2015) Social impacts as a function of place change. *Annals of Tourism Research* 50, 52–66. http://dx.doi.org/10.1016/j.annals.2014.11. 002.

McKercher, B. and Prideaux, B. (2020) *Tourism Theories, Concepts and Models*. Oxford: Goodfellow Publishers.

McKercher, B. and Wong, A. (2021) Do destinations have multiple lifecycles? *Tourism Management* 83. https://doi.org/10.1016/j.tourman.2020.104232.

Morrison, A. (2013) *Marketing and Managing Tourism Destinations*. Oxon: Routledge.

Murphy, P. (1985) *Tourism: A Community Approach*. London: Routledge.

Osland, G. (1991) Origins and development of the product life cycle concept. *Scholarship and Professional Work – Business* 237. http://digitalcommons.butler.edu/cob_papers/237.

Pearce, D. (1989) *Tourist Development* (2nd edn). Harlow: Longman Scientific.

Plog, S. (1974) Why destination areas rise and fall in popularity. *Cornell HRA Quarterly* 14 (4), 55–58.

Plog, S. (2001) Why destination areas rise and fall in popularity: An update of a *Cornell Quarterly* classic. *Cornell Hotel and Restaurant Quarterly* 42 (3), 13–24.

Pritchard, A. and Lee, Y. (2011) Evaluating tourist attractions: The case of Luang Prabang, Laos. *Tourism Analysis* 16, 305–314.

Prideaux, B. (2000a) The resort development spectrum – A new approach to modeling resort development. *Tourism Management* 21 (3), 225–240.

Prideaux, B. (2000b) The role of transport systems in destination development. *Tourism Management* 21 (1), 53–63.

Prideaux, B. (2004) The resort development spectrum: The case of the Gold Coast, Australia. *Tourism Geographies* 6 (1), 26–58. https://doi.org/10.1080/14616680320001722328.

Rebello, J. and Baidal, J. (2009) Spread of low-cost carriers: Tourism and regional policy effects in Spain. *Regional Studies* 43 (4), 559–570.

Russell, R. and Faulkner, B. (2004) Entrepreneurship, chaos and the tourism area lifecycle. *Annals of Tourism Research* 31 (3), 556–579.

Scott, N., Baggio, R. and Cooper, C. (2008) *Network Analysis and Tourism: From Theory to Practice*. Clevedon: Channel View Publications.

Tellis, G. and Crawford, C. (1981) An evolutionary approach to product growth theory. *Journal of Marketing* 45 (4), 125–132.

Tiwari, P. and Chowdhary, N. (2021) Has COVID-19 brought a temporary halt to over-tourism? *Tourism/Turyzm* 31 (1), 89–93. https://doi.org/10.18778/0867-5856.31.1.20.

Wan, P. and Pinheiro, F. (2014) Macau's Tourism planning approach and its shortcomings: A case study. *International Journal of Hospitality and Tourism Administration* 15 (1), 78–102. https://doi.org/10.1080/15256480.2014.872901.

Weaver, D. (2001) Ecotourism as mass tourism: Contradiction or reality? *Cornell Hotel and Restaurant Administrative Quarterly* 42 (2), 104–112.

23 Final Thoughts: Revisions and Modifications to the TALC Model

Richard Butler

In reviewing the many criticisms of and suggested changes to the TALC model, one could summarise the discussions on revisions to its form and content as falling into two main categories. One group consists of those concerns relating to the written text, mostly involving the elaboration of existing elements or adding features; and the other group has issues relating to the shape of the curve in the diagram setting out the model (Butler, 1980), as summarised a long time ago by Prosser (1995). This final chapter addresses those concerns and begins by briefly discussing new issues raised by recent literature on evolutionary studies and development pathways. It concludes by proposing a modified model reflecting some of the criticisms and also the suggestions and alternatives proposed by contributors to this volume and others.

New Developments

A number of trends and concepts have appeared in recent years in the literature that are relevant to the TALC model. These include continued discussion on sustainable tourism management, the application of path dependency concepts, and the linkage of development and growth with evolutionary economic geography (EEG), as noted by Saarinen *et al.* (2017). Some of these developments have been discussed in earlier chapters (particularly Chapter 13, by Romão), and Brouder's highly relevant paper (2017) links these concepts and arguments together and proves highly relevant to the ongoing application of the TALC model and related arguments.

'Sustainable tourism' is a term which has gained massive support in theory and principle, although one can argue strongly that it has had little overall effect on tourism and its environmental impacts at the global scale. Both Butler and Dodds (this volume, Chapters 2 and 4) have noted the similarity in arguments about development within limits between the TALC model and the principles of sustainable development. A great number of individual tourism enterprises in destinations have moved significantly towards sustainable operations by such actions as reducing energy consumption, carbon emissions, food miles, imported labour and the use of non-renewable resources. However, an apparently insatiable demand for tourism of most kinds and especially the continued growth of long-haul tourist travel and cruise tourism has left the tourism footprint larger than ever. The rapid recovery of many areas from the economic effects of the COVID-19 pandemic suggests that both the tourist market and the tourism industry, along with many governments at all levels, do not yet accept the need to curtail and possibly redirect tourism development. It has fallen to individual destinations to take steps to avoid what has become known as overtourism (Dodds & Butler, 2019; Milano *et al.*, 2019) and the failure to deal with the problem (Butler & Dodds, 2022) has mirrored the failure to implement sustainable tourism policies, despite their widespread approval, at least in principle.

Saarinen (2004) argued two decades ago that the competing viewpoints in destination development failed to work together to define and reach common goals. Little has changed in the intervening period, with continued growth remaining the dominant approach in most locations, sometimes despite local opposition, but often with local support in an absence of perceived viable alternatives. As Hall (2011) has argued, there is little evidence of widespread support for a massive change in policy with regard to development, and although others (e.g. Fletcher, 2011) regard sustainable development as sustaining capitalism when they wish for an alternative ideological approach, there have been few developments along a sustainable pathway in any ideological context in terms of practical implementation. Thus, despite continued academic and political support for sustainable development, commitment in practice to the principles involved such as carrying capacity (as argued in the TALC) tends to be left to individuals for implementation rather than by destinations as united entities with a common goal, reflecting the range of opinions about continued growth experienced in many destinations at different scales.

The concept of path dependency in tourism can be linked directly to the TALC in the sense that the original model illustrates a common development path or projection, albeit based on probable continued growth unless external forces cause decline. The volume by Brouder *et al.* (2017), *Tourism Destination Evolution*, makes a significant contribution to the literature in this area by explaining how tourism development evolves and the development options involved. There is considerable scope in the context of the TALC for further examination of how specific pathways develop in individual cases to identify common traits and forces, under whose control these are formulated and directed, and how pathways can be modified and refocused if and when appropriate. Ma and Hassink (2014) demonstrated how path dependency can affect specific tourism destination development, and in a similar vein Halkier *et al.* (2019)

explored the relationships between governance, development and evolutionary economic geography (EEG). While the TALC model suggests a common pathway for most destinations, clearly not all follow such a trajectory and the reasons why such deviation occurs is of considerable importance. How and why a specific destination may choose to leave, or be forced to leave, an agreed path of development was illustrated by Gill and Williams (2014) in their work on Whistler (Canada). Deviation from the traditional model of continuous growth to a more sustainable option can be supported or opposed by both internal and external forces. Such a situation makes for vulnerability, a position illustrated clearly, for example, by the often limited development alternatives in remoter or insular locations (Carson & Carson, 2017). In the original TALC article (Butler, 1980) too little attention was paid to emphasising the benefits of stability and sustainability as a desirable or even preferable pathway over continued growth. The result has been that over the intervening decades most attention has been paid to avoiding not only a no-growth scenario, but more particularly any decline in the number of visitors, as such an outcome could be taken to signify the first step towards ultimate decline and even exit from tourism. Such an interpretation was not the intention of the model but the expectation of long continual growth meant such an outcome was perceived as inevitable.

The emergence of EEG was the focus of a special issue of *Tourism Geographies* (16 (4) 2014) and the editors (Ionnides *et al.*, 2014: 536) noted that it had the ability to 'better understand how tourism evolves through time', which is, of course, the primary focus of the TALC model in the context of tourist destinations. Despite the limited reference to tourism in Boschma and Martin's (2010) handbook, which described this new approach in economic geography and its relevance to fields outside geography, its relevance to tourism was quickly realised. The links and examples of how that approach could be adopted in the tourism context were discussed by Sanz-Ibáñez and Clavé (2014), and the relevance of EEG to the concept of destination development is particularly strong because the TALC is based partly on the argument that destinations can be treated as products. Research in tourism on aspects of the agglomeration and clustering of attractions and services (Weidenfeld *et al.*, 2010, 2013) supports this approach and is relevant with respect to incorporating the contribution of entrepreneurs (Peters & Schönherr, this volume, Chapter 20) with the efforts of public bodies and local operators in shaping the development pathway of destinations. Brouder's (2017: 444) conclusion that it should be possible to use 'the concept of sustainable development as a critical lens on EEG in tourism studies and vice versa' fits well in the context of viewing the TALC as essentially a model of sustainable development (Dodds, this volume, Chapter 4).

In the context of the TALC, most of the initial studies followed a descriptive application of the model, focusing on one or a small group of destinations. Sanz-Ibáñez and Clavé's paper (2014) has gone some way in this direction in linking evolutionary studies with economic and destination development, as did Brouder (2017) in drawing attention to the difficulties in challenging the pro-growth model. This highlights the vulnerability of attempts by local destination stakeholders to move towards a more sustainable future on a permanent basis, particularly when facing the legacy of institutional inertia maintaining the status quo in favour of growth. Such a situation deserves closer examination, and a relevant research field in this regard is the political ecology of tourist destinations, including, in particular, the themes of communities and power, conservation and control, and development and conflict, as discussed by Mostafanezhad *et al.* (2016). The ways destination communities are managed and controlled, and the decision-making processes at work within them, are of key importance and build on the research of Gale (2005) and Saarinen and Kask (2008). Also relevant to these issues is the development of the concept of regenerative tourism (Bellato *et al.*, 2023), which may represent an alternative way of moving towards a more positive and less problematic form of development of tourist destinations (similar to the approach suggested by Eggli in Chapter 18 of this volume).

One problem in pursuing a non-growth or 'degrowth' (Andriotis, 2018) agenda is that many local stakeholders and tourists at large may not support it, and neither may 'the industry' or many public sector agencies. While some residents may oppose further growth in some locations, such as Barcelona, Venice and other cities (Dodds & Butler, 2019; Milano *et al.*, 2019), others, particularly those engaged in tourism operations, are often not willing to accept the negative costs perceived to result from reduced visitor numbers, and the tourist population in general appears to be in favour of more, rather than less, development of opportunities. Since the original TALC article appeared over four decades ago, new lines of research and alternative concepts relating to growth, degrowth and the more meaningful definitions of success (Dwyer, 2022) have inevitably developed. Combined with the global impact of COVID-19, this means that a further examination of key features of the model and a revision of the shape of the model itself are equally relevant and appropriate.

Elements and Features of the TALC

There has already been some discussion of modification of the key elements of the TALC model in earlier chapters of this volume and this chapter responds to comments on other elements of the model.

Tourist area

Clarification of what is meant by 'tourist area' is clearly needed in any revision of the TALC (Haywood, 2006: 52; and this volume, Chapter 8).

Cooper (2015: 216), in a glossary added to Butler's (2015) chapter on the Tourism Area Life Cycle, defines a tourist destination as 'A place where tourists plan to spend time away from home'. He goes on to note: 'This geographical area could be as small as a self-contained centre, such as a village, town or city, or be as broad as a region, island or country'. While accurate, this is perhaps not very helpful as a definition. Tourist resorts he describes as 'Small geographic areas with attractions and services for the tourist' (Cooper, 2015: 217). Clearly, the suggestion is that resorts are different from tourist destinations, although in fact resorts, especially those on the scale of the Disney theme parks, were designed as or have grown into destinations with accommodation and other services as well as amusements and rides.

It could be argued that while there may be a need for a clearer distinction between tourist destinations, tourist centres, tourist resorts and tourist communities and many other locations that are given the prefix of 'tourist', in the context of the TALC, such a distinction is not a major issue. What is more important is the scale or size of the location involved, as the original model was clearly meant to be applied to a place, not an amorphous region. The discussion in the model of earlier works (e.g. Christaller, 1963; Plog, 1974) that described changes in single communities makes this unavoidable, as does the mention of local residents. Created amusement or theme parks such as the Magic Kingdom, wherein there is no resident population, were implicitly not included, although the model has been discussed in the context of the life cycle of such developments (e.g. Lu, 1997) and there can be no doubt they are tourism 'products'.

So, if 'tourist area' is to be defined in the context of the TALC, it should be taken to refer to 'a settlement or community which attracts staying tourists'. Such a definition has the advantages of being short and of including the key elements of both a resident population and staying tourists (rather than being limited to day visitors). If the model is then applied to a region, island or group of communities or islands, so be it; the fitness of the concept may not be as good as when applied to a single community. Based on the number of applications of the model, it is obvious that such a definition is what the majority of researchers consider a 'tourist area' in this context to be, as most cases studies have been of single communities, or a small number of neighbouring similar communities in close proximity and offering the same types of attractions. When applied to islands, such examples have normally been small, in many cases with a single significant settlement, normally the main or only point of entry (e.g. Wilkinson, 1996). Thus, it can be concluded that the term 'tourist areas' as used in the context of the TALC refers to small, clearly identifiable (i.e. specific rather than amorphous) locations and involves both a permanent population and a (probably seasonal) visiting population, with a range of facilities and services catering to both.

Stages of development

The model depicted five common stages of development through which, it was argued, a destination proceeded: *exploration, involvement, development, consolidation* and *stagnation*. These are followed by alternative pathways of *rejuvenation* and *decline,* and three other unnamed paths of operation within the limits of the latter two. The original article did *not* propose that *stagnation* was inevitably followed by *decline* (although the name of that phase is somewhat negative in implication and three of the five pathways following that stage showed declines in numbers of visitors compared with two showing increased numbers); indeed, the whole point of the article was to argue that appropriate management of resources was necessary to avoid decline and should be an essential part of a destination's life cycle. A final reference in the paper to Plog's (1974) comment about destinations carrying with them the seeds of their own destruction may unintentionally have given the wrong impression. The names given to the stages were purely indicative of what each stage was meant to portray and as such are self-explanatory. The original paper did briefly describe the characteristics of each stage, but it was recognised that, given the unique characteristics of every destination, not all such characteristics may be relevant or present for each stage in each destination.

It could be suggested that there it is not a great need to add additional stages of development; indeed, there is an argument for reducing the number of stages because of the perceived difficulty of identifying the ones that were listed. However, if one were to contemplate additional or alternative stages for the cycle, the strongest case would probably be to incorporate a *reorientation* (or something similar such as *refocusing*) stage, as proposed by Agarwal (1994, 2006), and this point is returned to later in this chapter. The stages were never intended to be hard and fast clearly defined periods of growth or change, but to act as generalised markers depicting progress through the cycle, and to serve as a comparative tool when examining a specific destination. With hindsight, it might have been more positive to title the *stagnation* stage instead as *stability*, as the former term, as noted above, carried a somewhat negative implication in an era in which growth was the uniform goal. In an era supposedly aiming for sustainable development, *stability* might be a more appropriate and positive-sounding title and is applied in the modified model set out below (see Figure 23.1).

Beginning with Berry (2001), attempts have been made to identify suitable measures against which progress through a life cycle could be demonstrated and if the stages are to be meaningful they deserve to be more clearly identified. To do so requires not only appropriate characteristics to be confirmed but data to allow those characteristics to be clearly drawn and delimited. In many cases, such data are not available and, as noted in the original article, 'not all areas experience the stages of the cycle as clearly as others' (Butler, 1980: 9). In some cases the identification of specific stages may be determined by the absence of specific characteristics as well as the early appearance of others. A feature normally anticipated late in development, for example resident concern over perceived excessive numbers of visitors, might appear in one of the earlier stages if small numbers in absolute terms increase rapidly, or the type and behaviour of visitors change suddenly. It is interesting that most researchers, when discussing the stages through which specific destinations have passed, rarely include empirical evidence of how those stages were defined and measured; most refer to the brief general descriptions from the original paper. More detailed examination and discussion of the stages based on empirical work needs to be undertaken to address more specifically how stages could be measured with assurance.

One might propose that fewer stages would make the TALC more realistic and involve less time and effort in trying to define individual stages, which, after all, were meant to be simply indicators of 'progress' through the cycle. In discussing the impact of COVID-19 on destinations at different stages of development (Butler, 2021) the TALC was compressed into *early, mid-* and *late cycle* to simplify matters and avoid detailed discussion of stage identification. Other researchers have used other terms to describe the development of tourist destinations. Miossec (1977) was one of the earliest, with four phases – pre-tourist, pioneer, development and saturation – with a possible fifth phase relating to environmental recovery and maintenance of tourism dynamics. Another example is Chadefaud (1987), who used three phases, creation, maturity and obsolescence (decline). In most cases, even where has been the use of fewer stages, there has been a general agreement on the overall shape of the curve of development.

The shape of the curve

The shape of the curve is a key issue in contemplating any modification of the original model. A model is a picture of simplified reality and, thus, in drawing the curve, it was inevitable that it would be portrayed as a smooth single line. To suggest that if a life cycle curve were carefully plotted for any specific destination it would be a smooth single line is unrealistic, but that is what happens when aggregating and simplifying the real-world situation. To emphasise that reality, the 'future' line of the original curve was shown as open to a number of variations, from continued growth to absolute decline, with alternatives between these two extremes. It was assumed that the past was capable of documentation and therefore the curve up to the present could be generalised, as shown. No destination has an uninterrupted or unmodified process of development. The influence of regular mundane forces such as fluctuations in weather (now, in 2023, being far from mundane as the effects of global warming change weather, the nature and length of seasons and probably climate), accidents and local disasters (such as fires, floods, disease outbreaks, violence, temporary loss of access and services, short-term pollution) to major impacts such as COVID-19, economic recession, radical political change, terrorism and war (Aldao *et al.*, 2021), mean that an accurate curve of growth for any specific destination will be marked by accelerations and decreases in growth of numbers of visitors (see Figure 23.1). Acceptance of the inability to illustrate every minor diversion from the average means that 'smoothing' of the curve is an unavoidable reality.

It is, however, more important to identify major deviations from the 'norm' (partly to go on to explain the reasons for such deviations) in order to compare and contrast such responses to stimuli to determine what is a 'normal' response and what is unique to a specific destination (and why). Many disruptions to the normal pattern are unique to each destination, but some are shared more widely, up to and including global disruptions to travel like COVID-19 (Duro *et al.*, 2021) or widespread conflict. The latter has been explored by several researchers (for example Jordan, 2000; O'Hare & Barrett, 1993; Weaver, 2002) and illustrated by Zimmermann (1997: Fig. 1.1). It is easy to impose a break in the curve to portray a halt or severe decline in tourism. What is difficult is to determine how the curve should continue after the time allocated for a break or massive decline in tourism. A very short break or a series of short breaks, for example caused by one or more acts of terrorism, as experienced in Egypt (12 incidents between 1995 and 2015), is reflected in corresponding declines in visitor numbers to the country, as portrayed by Tomazos (2017: 220), but skilful management of media and adjusted security arrangements there have resulted in much less disruption to the overall life cycle pattern than might have been expected.

COVID-19

One major change in the life cycle curve for virtually all destinations is now unavoidable and that is a reflection of COVID-19 and its influence on tourism patterns. Many destinations would most likely have proceeded through their life cycle without major disruption had the COVID-19 pandemic not radically altered global patterns and levels of tourism. Almost all destinations whose life cycles include the period 2019–2023 will now have to show this major disruption/break in their curves. How this break and, more importantly, the subsequent continuation of their curves will be portrayed is too early to tell and, indeed, it may be impossible in most cases to be certain that any portrayal is accurate (Butler, 2021). It is extremely difficult, especially in tourism, where so many economic activities are involved and interacting, to obtain accurate statistics on most measures of development apart from visitor numbers, as already noted. Irrespective of accuracy, the fact remains that, from this point in time onwards, almost all portrayals of destination life cycles will have to include the effect of COVID-19 on visitor arrivals, and where alternative measures of development arc used, on those measures also.

Agents of change

While COVID-19 fits the category of an unintentional–external agent of change in Weaver and Oppermann's (2000) matrix, other major disruptions that would feature in life cycles include intentional–internal and intentional–external forces. In most cases these relate to development or redevelopment (*rejuvenation?*) of a destination, either by private sector entrepreneurs or by public (government) agencies. Russell and Faulkner (1999) pioneered some of the work on this topic over two decades ago, and it is clear that entrepreneurs can change the life cycle of destinations not only by kick-starting development but also by intervening in later stages of a cycle to redirect growth, and change the image and nature of tourism in a destination (see also Peters & Schönherr in this volume, Chapter 20). Such interventions can be by local (internal) entrepreneurs or by agents in other areas or other countries (external). Interventions such as those by low-cost airlines have radically changed the development pathway of a considerable number of destinations, in Europe especially, although affected destinations remain vulnerable to the withdrawal of such services as quickly as they began.

In recent years there has been increasing interest in two relevant and related areas of research. One is the study of development pathways, which one might view as akin to the suggested life cycle approach to destination development. The second area is what has been termed evolutionary economic geography, and although originally conceived in the context of production, has been linked to both destination development and sustainable development (Brouder, 2017).

Such inputs may be the result of Agarwal's (1994) restructuring, where the destination has deliberately brought about change in its form and pattern of tourism, fitting the intentional–internal agent of change model. In terms of the portrayal of the life cycle, the amended form may resemble that of Agarwal (2006: 215). It also may be an entirely different series of curves, as illustrated by Russell (2006: 177), or a spectrum, as proposed by Prideaux (2000), but it has been chosen to continue with a life cycle approach in this instance. Whether the upturn in a cycle will be a result of re-orientation, as Agarwal suggested, or from some action such as a simple large expansion of existing capacity and promotion, will depend on the nature and purpose of the intervention, which may be to refocus the destination on a new market, or simply to enlarge the existing offerings to increase visitor numbers and/or visitor spend.

Refocusing

Refocusing or reorienting efforts are generally brought about because of the fear or reality of a destination entering a decline phase. Older Mediterranean resorts received a boost in visitor numbers when the Soviet Union dissolved and eastern Europeans were able to visit western resorts. In more recent years there have been increasing numbers of destinations, including some of those facing overtourism, attempting to refocus on alternative markets to what were their traditional ones. Often this has been accompanied by claims to represent a move towards a more sustainable form of tourism, mostly a green smokescreen to justify attempting to attract a higher-spending and less negative form of tourist, so that a destination can experience fewer visitor numbers while receiving the same or more income. In some cases it is a fairly blatant attempt to attract 'travellers' rather than continuing to attract 'tourists', especially when the latter are of the 'mass' variety. New Zealand is one country that announced it is following this path and, at the more local level, Amsterdam, too, is aiming to change its tourist visitors to a more 'appropriate' form. The leader of the governing party in Amsterdam described cruise-ship passengers as 'Like a locust plague', following on from initiatives in March 2023 which used the slogan 'Stay Away' to deter undesirable market segments from visiting the city (Waterfield, 2023). Whether such efforts will reduce overall numbers sufficiently to require an adjustment to the life cycle of tourism in Amsterdam remains to be seen, but it may well be that such a reorientation or refocusing could result in a permanent dip in the graph in terms of volume of tourism and not be followed by a rise in volume as Agarwal portrayed.

Along with calls for 'degrowth' (Andriotis, 2018; Fletcher *et al.*, 2019) in tourism generally at destinations and globally, there have been calls for more radical changes in tourism overall. The temporary pause in tourism caused by COVID-19 was portrayed as an opportunity to achieve such a goal, and a special issue of *Tourism Geographies* (2020, 22 (3)) focused on such expressions. Apart from the rather inappropriate timing of such calls, when destinations and all elements of the tourism industry were suffering from catastrophic losses of employment and income and unlikely to focus on anything except restoring tourism to pre-COVID-19 levels, the nature of some of the calls went far beyond a simple refocusing of tourism to a more sustainable form. Some called for a less harmful tourism and included the demise of the capitalist system and various other well-intentioned but unlikely scenarios at that time, including greater equality, justice and fairness in the industry. Despite the unlikely scenario of such a total refocusing of tourism and its many interacting partners, particularly immediately after COVID-19, such calls draw attention to a much wider concern about how success is understood in terms of tourist destinations. Whereas, in the past, success was almost automatically defined in terms of growing visitor numbers, there have been increasing calls for alternative measure of success (see for example Dwyer, 2022). As noted earlier, the TALC was never intended nor claimed to be a portrayal of success, but rather a common development pathway experienced by the majority of tourist destinations.

Sustainability

As Dodds notes (this volume, Chapter 4), the TALC model has much in common with the concept of sustainability, although it appeared almost a decade before that term was coined (World Commission on Environment and Development, 1987). It was created to argue the case that without appropriate management, including a regard to limits (then expressed primarily in terms of numbers), destinations would suffer a decline in appeal. It is true that following such a decline in appeal, there might be a decline in visitor numbers, which gave the impression that such a decline would be a 'bad thing' for any specific destination, tacitly implying that at least stability in numbers was a desirable outcome. Implicitly, the idea of a destination continuing on its development pathway on a stable basis within its capacity limits was a desirable route. It could be argued that such a scenario is still an appropriate one and in line with current general thoughts on sustainable development (i.e. growth within limits). To support such a situation, it was felt appropriate to add the title *sustainability* to one of the possible future phases, to suggest that the main focus of destinations should be to demonstrate growth only in line with sustainable principles, which is what many destinations and governments claim to be aiming at.

Boyd and Bolan (this volume, Chapter 21) in their Figure 21.2 show a hypothetical TALC as a series of waves and this is perhaps a realistic way to portray the reality of the curve for many destinations. The ups and downs may not be as dramatic as in their figure, but most destinations do experience short declines and rises in visitor numbers, as noted above. If one goes back to the original TALC figure, and continues the curve on the right-hand side, then a decline in visitor numbers followed by a rejuvenation, or an intervention creating a sudden upswing in visitor numbers would produce an image reminiscent of that of Agarwal (2006: 215) and Boyd and Bolan. It was an omission in the original figure to fail to portray the possibility of declines and upswings in the pathway of most destinations. COVID-19 has dramatically revealed what can happen to destinations and caused all graphs to be redrawn to recognise that fact. As argued above, no life cycle or pathway of destinations can be drawn now without including the dramatic impact of COVID-19 on the volume of tourism and the variance in possible post-COVID-19 directions is greater than before 2019, especially when considering the added possibility of destinations exiting tourism in short order during or shortly after the pandemic, as suggested in Figure 23.1.

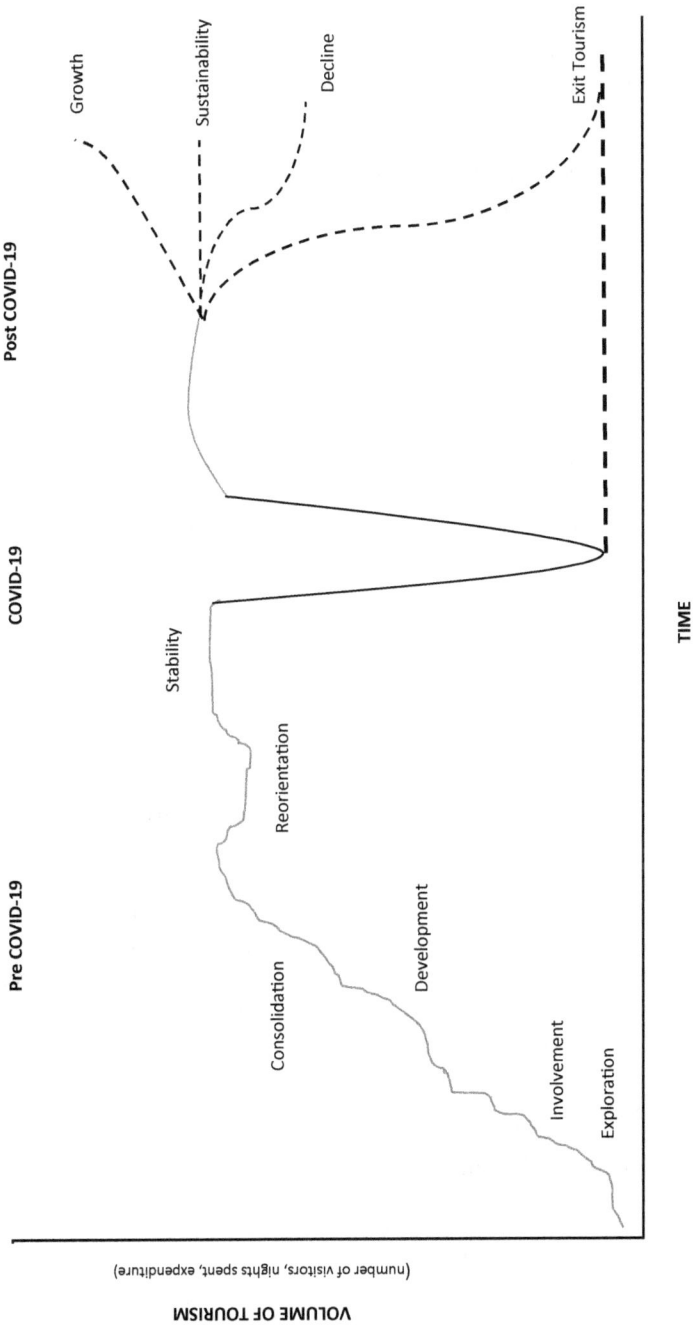

Figure 23.1 A modified TALC

One curve or several?

Of more significance is the likelihood, if not certainty, that for each destination there is always more than one life cycle curve and that the single curve shown in the original model is simply the aggregate of these. McKercher and Wong (2021) raised this question (Chapter 22). Their argument is that destinations evolve through multiple life cycles and they suggest six forms that these cycles can take. In illustrating the cumulative life cycle stages in Chapter 22 of this volume, their Figure 22.2 is extremely similar to the one produced by Brougham and Butler (1972) to demonstrate how destinations expanded spatially in a region (shown as Figure 2.2 in Butler, 2006: 19). McKercher and Wong depict a *variety of forms* of life cycles for destinations but it can be argued that these are all forms of one life cycle of each destination. Some are rather smooth curves with minor growth or decline periods (*scalloped* forms) while others have a high degree of variability (*volatile and full cycles*), but essentially these are variations on a theme, and in some cases, Bermuda in particular (McKercher & Wong, 2021), the cycle begins only in the early 1950s, representing the last stages to date in what is clearly a much longer life cycle.

It is argued that there are multiple life cycles present in all destinations for the many different elements or factors in each destination. It makes sense to accept that, just as Zimmermann (1997) portrayed different life cycles for individual forms of recreation/tourism (see Figure 1.1), so there are life cycles for each form of accommodation within a destination, for each type of attraction and for each type of service or facility. One example is Margate, one of the oldest of the classic tourist destinations in the UK (Rickey & Houghton, 2009), which has had a life cycle of rise and fall and attempted rejuvenation (Weidenfeld *et al.*, 2016). One of the main attractions in Margate, an amusement park (the Hall of the Sea), was established in 1860 and was later renamed Dreamland. Over the course of its life cycle, it 'illustrates the pattern of the TALC and closely mirrors the pattern of tourism in the host town of Margate' (Weidenfeld *et al.*, 2016: 54). One could note other life cycles in Margate, including the short life cycle of the Turner Contemporary art gallery (established in 2001), the life cycles of various lengths of the individual hotels in Margate, and even of its original attraction, its beach. One could aggregate the life cycles of all forms of accommodation (hotels, guest houses, bed and breakfasts and Airbnb properties) and even of all individual accommodation establishments in Margate, as each would have a slightly, sometimes greatly, different and distinctive life cycle compared with the aggregated cycle of the destination as a whole. Some of the forms of accommodation, such as hotels, will have cycles lasting almost two centuries, while other forms, Airbnb in particular, will go back for only a decade or two. Again, we have to return to the fact that the TALC is a model used to illustrate the life cycle of all elements of a destination combined into a single form.

Baum (2006: 226) illustrated what the result might look like if the life cycle of all attractions at a destination were graphed. He used the example of sigmoid curves from Handy's (1994) variation of the product life cycle whereby new products or new forms of products are introduced at critical or appropriate stages in the development and marketing of a product (a tourist destination in this case). As one product or model begins to decline, or a new market is seen and pursued, a new model or new product is added, to be represented by another life cycle curve. So, in short, there are multiple life cycles in any one destination, as many as there are elements which could be studied, including, of course, resident attitudes towards tourism and tourists, although the latter aspect is much more complicated and dynamic than, for example, in Doxey's (1975) early model which suggested a simple linear change in attitude of residents from positive to negative towards tourists. Such a process can be seen currently in complaints about overtourism, which seem to be mostly based on perceptions of excessive numbers of tourists, as well as their behaviour (Mihalič, 2022). It is important to note that alternative forms showing changing attitudes of residents towards tourists exist, one illustrated in Figure 23.2, which was created originally in the context of intercultural relations but has been easily adapted to the context of tourism to show the possible changing relations between visitors and visited, and which illustrates the multiple directions in which attitudes can change with varying circumstances. In that sense it responds to Eggli's concerns (this volume, Chapter 18) about the nuances in different and differing relationships and interactions between all people present in tourist destinations.

A Modified TALC?

In this volume it has been argued that there is continued relevance, indeed value, of the TALC model, particularly in a comparative and historical context, in examining the generalised pathway of development of tourist destinations. It was not intended to be a quantitative model for predicting future levels of tourism at a specific destination, nor for forecasting where new tourism development might take place. It was envisaged as a tool to assist in placing a destination in an overall context which could then be compared with other destinations, suggesting and portraying what might be expected to be an overall scenario of development. Changing priorities and circumstances, as discussed in many of the chapters in this volume, make clear that what fitted the situation in the latter half of the 20th century is likely to be less accurate or appropriate for the first half of the 21st century. Appreciation of the need to conserve the world's overall environment, the problems associated with global warming, overpopulation and natural resource reduction, as well as ongoing conflicts and other disasters such as COVID-19, all mean attitudes and eventually actions change. One such change affecting tourist destinations is the move to

Attitudes/Behaviour

Active ◄- - - - - - - -┊- - - - - - - -► Passive

Positive	Aggressive promotion of something favoured ◄- - - ► Silent acceptance of something favoured
Negative	Aggressive opposition of something disliked ◄- - - ► Resigned acceptance of something disliked

Attitude/Behaviour

(Arrows indicate possibility of change)

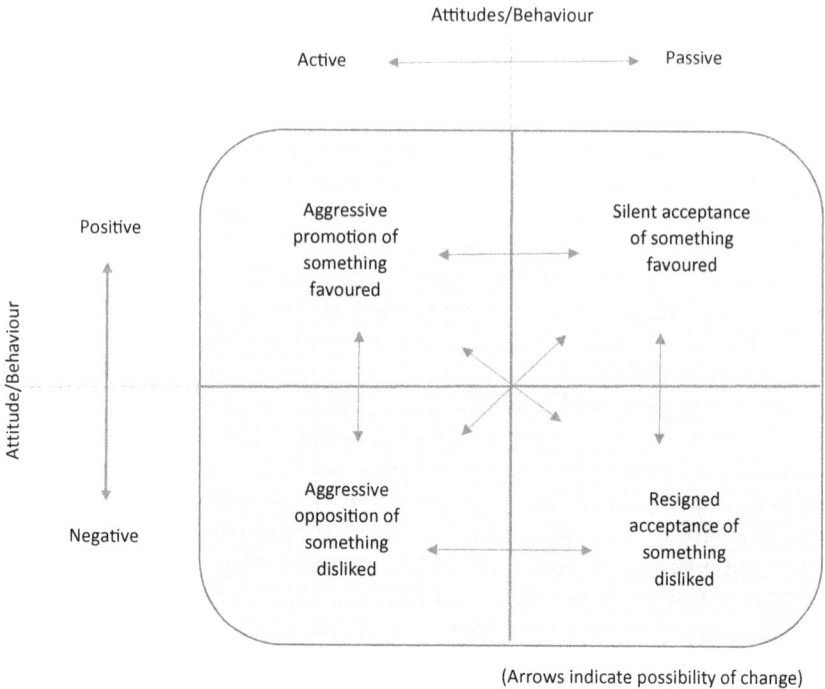

Figure 23.2 Alternative and changing attitudes and behaviour of destination residents. (Source: Based on Bjorklund & Philbrick, 1972)

see success in terms other than simple numbers, to encompass not just economic elements like income, jobs and tax returns, but quality of life, for residents and visitors alike. A nice place to visit can and should be a nice place in which to live, and perhaps vice versa. At the heart of the TALC model was such an aspiration, although not as clearly expressed, namely that those responsible for managing and controlling tourist destinations (and by implication, those affecting such destinations, which includes transport agencies, accommodation suppliers, marketers and promoters and any other agencies benefiting from tourism, including higher levels of government) should be aiming to establish and maintain a destination catering to tourists over the long term within the environmental, social-cultural and economic limits of the community.

Figure 23.1 presented a revised TALC curve, reflecting the effects of COVID-19 and a range of other, much less serious rises and falls in whatever factor is used to portray volume of tourism, and continuing into a future which is not predictable with accuracy, but which could be symbolised by a tourism development pathway that is truly sustainable within the current meaning of the term. The smooth curve of the original figure has been replaced by one reflecting the fact that such a pathway is not without minor disruptions, although the resulting curve loses much of its simplicity and elegance. It now includes a *reorientation* phase and shows the stage formerly titled *stagnation* renamed as *stability*, representing a more optimistic situation, rather than perhaps implying impending *decline*. Such a graph cannot incorporate the impacts on destinations of future actions or factors such as energy use restrictions, conflicts, pandemics and other disasters, major political changes, or radical changes in tourism preferences and behaviour in any realistic sense. Figure 23.1 makes one massive assumption which certainly will be demonstrated to be inaccurate in a number of cases, namely, that the impact of COVID-19 will be short term and temporary, because, as shown at the bottom of the figure, it is possible that some destinations will not recover from COVID-19 and will exit tourism relatively quickly, if not immediately, as many individual enterprises have already done. The majority of destinations will recover, with tourism continuing at many destinations in much the same manner and scale that they had been operating before 2020. Such an outcome will both please and disappoint tourists, residents and many other players and observers of tourism, but that is what tourism has been doing for several centuries and will most likely continue to do so in the future, regardless of its scale and nature. The TALC has always been more about portraying the effect of tourism on destinations over time past rather than predicting patterns for time future.

References

Agarwal, S. (1994) The resort cycle revisited: Implications for resorts. In C. Cooper and A. Lockwood (eds) *Progress in Tourism, Recreation and Hospitality Management* (vol. 5, pp. 191–208). London: Belhaven.

Agarwal, S. (2006) Coastal resort restructuring and the TALC. In R. Butler (ed.) *The Tourism Area Life Cycle, Volume 2: Conceptual and Theoretical Issues* (pp. 201–218). Clevedon: Channel View Publications.

Aldao, C., Blasco, D., Espallargas, M.P. and Rubio, S.P. (2021) Modelling the crisis management and impacts of 21st century disruptive events in tourism: The case of the COVID-19 pandemic. *Tourism Review* 76 (4), 929–941.

Andriotis, K. (2018) *Degrowth in Tourism: Conceptual, Theoretical and Philosophical Issues*. Wallingford: CABI.

Baum, T. (2006) Revisiting the TALC: Is there an off ramp? In R. Butler (ed.) *The Tourism Area Life Cycle, Volume 2: Conceptual and Theoretical Issues* (pp. 219–230). Clevedon: Channel View Publications.

Bellato, L., Frantzeskaki, N. and Nygaard, C.A. (2023) Regenerative tourism: A conceptual framework leveraging theory and practice. *Tourism Geographies* 25 (4). https://doi.org/10.1080/14616688.2022.2044376.

Berry, E.N. (2001) An application of Butler's (1980) Tourist Area Life Cycle theory to the Cairns region, Australia, 1876–1998. PhD thesis, Tropical Environment and Geography, James Cook University, Cairns Campus. www.geocities.com/tedberry_aus/tourismarealifecycle.html.

Bjorklund, E. and Philbrick, A. (1972) Spatial configurations of mental processes. Unpublished paper, Department of Geography, University of Western Ontario.

Boschma, R. and Martin, R. (2010) *The Handbook of Evolutionary Economic Geography*. Cheltenham: Edward Elgar.

Brouder, P. (2017) Evolutionary economic geography: Reflections from a sustainable tourism perspective. *Tourism Geographies* 19 (3), 438–447.

Brouder, P., Clavé, S.A., Gill, A.M. and Ioannides, D. (2017) *Tourism Destination Evolution*. London: Routledge.

Brougham, J.E. and Butler, R. (1972) The applicability of the asymptotic curve to the forecasting of tourism development. Paper presented to the Research Workshop, Travel Research Association 4th Annual Conference, Quebec, July.

Butler R. (1980) The concept of tourism area cycle of evolution: The implications for management of resources. *Canadian Geographer* 24, 5–12.

Butler, R. (2006) The origins of the Tourism Area Life Cycle. In R. Butler (ed.) *The Tourism Area Life Cycle, Volume 1: Applications and Modifications* (pp. 13–26). Clevedon: Channel View Publications.

Butler, R. (2015) Tourism Area Life Cycle. In C. Cooper (ed.) *Contemporary Tourism Reviews* (vol. 1, pp. 183–226). Oxford: Goodfellow Publications.

Butler, R. (2021) COVID-19 and its potential impact on stages of tourist destination development. *Current Issues in Tourism* 77 (1), 35–53.

Butler, R. and Dodds, R. (2022) Overcoming overtourism: A review of failure. *Tourism Review* 77 (1), 35–53.

Carson, D.A. and Carson, D.B. (2017) Path dependence in remote area tourism development. Why institutional legacies matter. In P. Brouder, S.A. Clavé, A.M. Gill and D. Ioannides (eds) *Tourism Destination Evolution* (pp. 103–122). London: Routledge.

Chadefaud, M. (1987) Aux origines du tourisme dans les pays de l'Adour, du mythe à l'espace: Un essai de géographie historique. Dép. de géographie et d'aménagement de l'Université de Pau et des pays de l'Adour, Centre de recherche sur l'impact socio-spatial de l'aménagement, Pau, UPPA.

Christaller, W. (1963) Some considerations of tourism location in Europe: The peripheral regions – underdeveloped countries – recreation areas. *Regional Science Association Papers*, Lund Congress (vol. 12, pp. 95–105).

Cooper, C. (2015) Glossary. In C. Cooper (ed.) *Contemporary Tourism Reviews* (vol. 1, pp. 217–218). Oxford: Goodfellow Publications.

Dodds, R. and Butler, R. (2019) *Overtourism Issues: Realities and Solutions*. Berlin: De Gruyter.

Doxey, G.V. (1975) A causation theory of visitor–resident irritants: Methodology and research inferences. In *Proceedings of the Travel Research Association 6th Annual Conference* (pp. 195–198). San Diego: Travel Research Association.

Duro, J.A., Perez-Laborda, A. and Turrion-Prats, A. (2021) Covid-19 and tourism vulnerability. *Tourism Management* 38 (2), 100819.

Dwyer, L. (2022) Tourism development and sustainable well-being: A beyond GDP perspective. *Journal of Sustainable Tourism* 20, 1–18.

Fletcher, R. (2011) Sustaining tourism, sustaining capitalism? The tourism industry's role in global capitalist expansion. *Tourism Geographies* 13 (3), 443–461.

Fletcher, R., Murray Mas, I., Blanco-Romero, A. and Blázquez-Salom, M. (2019) Tourism and degrowth: An emerging agenda for research and praxis. *Journal of Sustainable Tourism* 17 (12), 1745–1767.

Gale, T. (2005) Modernism, post-modernism and the decline of British seaside resorts as long holiday destinations: A case study of Rhyl, North Wales. *Tourism Geographies* 7, 86–112.

Gill, A.M. and Williams, P. (2014) Mindful deviation in creating a governance path towards sustainability in resort destinations. *Tourism Geographies* 16 (4), 546–562.

Halkier, H., Müller, D.K., Goncharova, N.A., Kiriyanova, L., Kolupanova, I.A., Yumatov, K.V. and Yakimova, N.S. (2019) Destination development in Western Siberia: Tourism governance and evolutionary economic geography. *Tourism Geographies* 21 (2), 261–283.

Hall, C.M. (2011) Policy learning and policy failure in sustainable tourism governance: From first- and second-order to third-order change? *Journal of Sustainable Tourism* 19 (4–5), 649–671.

Handy, C. (1994) *The Age of Paradox*. Boston: Harvard Business School Press.

Haywood, K.M. (2006) Evolution of tourism areas and the tourism industry. In R. Butler (ed.) *The Tourism Area Life Cycle, Volume 1: Applications and Modifications* (pp. 51–69). Clevedon: Channel View Publications.

Ionnides, D., Halkier, H. and Lew, A.A. (2014) Special issue introduction: Evolutionary economic geography and the economies of tourism destinations. *Tourism Geographies* 16 (4), 535–539

Jordan, P. (2000) Restructuring Croatia's coastal resorts: Change, sustainable development and the incorporation of rural hinterlands. *Journal of Sustainable Tourism* 8 (6), 525–539.

Lu, L. (1997) A study on the life cycle of mountain resorts: a case study of Huangshan Mountain and Jiuhanshan Mountain. *Scinta Geographic Sinica* 17 (1), 63–69.

Ma, M. and Hassink, R. (2014) Path dependence and tourism area development: The case of Guilin, China. *Tourism Geographies* 4, 580–597.

McKercher, B. and Wong, I.A. (2021) Do destinations have multiple lifecycles? *Tourism Management* 83, 104232.

Mihalič, T. (2022) Conceptualising overtourism: A sustainability approach. *Annals of Tourism Research* 84, 103025.

Milano, C., Cheer, J.M. and Novelli, M. (2019) *Overtourism Excesses, Discontents, and Measures in Travel and Tourism*. Wallingford: CABI.

Miossec, J.M. (1977) Un model de l'espace touristique. *L'Espace Geographie* 6 (1), 41–48.

Mostafanezhad, M., Norum, R., Shelton, E.J. and Thompson-Carr, A. (2016) *Political Ecology of Tourism Community: Power and the Environment*. London: Routledge.

O'Hare, G. and Barrett, H. (1993) The destination life cycle – international tourism in Peru. *Scottish Geographical Magazine* 113 (2), 66–73.

Plog, S.C. (1974) Why destinations areas rise and fall in popularity. *Cornell Hotel and Restaurant Association Quarterly* 13, 6–13.

Prideaux, B. (2000) The resort development spectrum – A new approach to modelling resort development. *Tourism Management* 21 (3), 225–240.

Prosser, G. (1995) Tourism destination life cycles: Progress, problems and prospects. Paper presented to National Tourism Research Conference, Melbourne.

Rickey, B. and Houghton, J. (2009) Solving the riddle of the sands: Regenerating England's seaside towns. *Journal of Urban Regeneration and Renewal* 3 (1), 46–55.

Russell, R. (2006) Chaos theory and its application to the TALC model. In R. Butler (ed.) *The Tourism Area Life Cycle, Volume 2: Conceptual and Theoretical Issues* (pp. 164–179). Clevedon: Channel View Publications.

Russell, R. and Faulkner, B. (1999) Movers and shakers: Chaos makers in tourism development. *Tourism Management* 20, 411–423.

Saarinen, J. (2004) 'Destinations in change': The transformation process of tourist destinations. *Tourist Studies* 4 (2), 161–179.

Saarinen, J. and Kask, T. (2008) Transforming tourism spaces in changing socio-political contexts: The case of Parnu, Estonia as a tourist destination. *Tourism Geographies* 10 (4), 452–473.

Saarinen, J., Rogerson, C.M. and Hall, C.M. (2017) Geographies of tourism development and planning. *Tourism Geographies* 19 (3), 307–317.

Sanz-Ibáñez, C. and Clavé, S.A. (2014) The evolution of destinations: Towards an evolutionary and relational economic geography approach. *Tourism Geographies* 16 (4), 563–579.

Tomazos, K. (2017) Egypt's tourism industry and the Arab Spring. In R. Butler and W. Suntikul (eds) *Tourism and Political Change* (2nd edn) (pp. 214–229). Oxford: Goodfellow Publishers.

Waterfield, B. (2023) The Netherlands. *The Times*, 22 July, p. 41.

Weaver, D.B. (2002) The exploratory war-distorted destination life-cycle. *International Journal of Tourism Research* 2 (3), 151–162.

Weaver, D.B. and Oppermann, M. (2000) *Tourism Management*. Wallingford: CABI.

Weidenfeld A., Butler, R. and Williams, A. (2010) The role of clustering, cooperation and complementarities in the visitor attraction sector. *Current Issues in Tourism* 14 (7), 595–629.

Weidenfeld, A., Williams, A.M and Butler, R. (2013) Spatial competition and agglomeration in the visitor attraction sector. *Service Industries Journal* 34 (3), 175–195.

Weidenfeld, A., Butler, R. and Williams, A. (2016) The visitor attraction life cycle. In A. Weidenfeld, R. Butler and W. Williams (eds) *Visitor Attractions and Events: Locations and Linkages* (pp. 49–67). London: Routledge.

Wilkinson, P.F. (1996) Graphical images of the commonwealth Caribbean: The tourist area cycle of evolution. In L.C. Harrison and W. Husbands (eds) *Practicing Responsible Tourism: International Case Studies in Tourism Planning, Policy and Development* (pp. 16–40). Toronto: Wiley.

World Commission on Environment and Development (1987) *Our Common Future*. Oxford: Oxford University Press.

Zimmermann, F. (1997) Future perspectives of tourism: Traditional versus new destinations. In M. Oppermann (ed.) *Pacific Rim Tourism* (pp. 231–239). Wallingford: CABI.

Index

For Product Safety Concerns and Information please contact our EU Authorised Representative:

Easy Access System Europe

Mustamäe tee 50

10621 Tallinn

Estonia

gpsr.requests@easproject.com

www.ingramcontent.com/pod-product-compliance
Lightning Source LLC
Chambersburg PA
CBHW062339300326
41947CB00012B/362